Library of
Davidson College

Romania in the 1980s

Also of Interest

Romania: A Profile, Lawrence S. Graham

An Economic Geography of Romania, David Turnock

**Eastern Europe in the 1980s*, edited by Stephen Fischer-Galati

Social Deviance in Eastern Europe, edited by Ivan Volgyes

Agricultural Policies in the USSR and Eastern Europe, edited by Ronald A. Francisco, Betty A. Laird, and Roy D. Laird

Eastern Europe: An Industrial Geography, David Turnock

The German Democratic Republic: Politics, Economics, Society, Bradley C. Scharf

The German Democratic Republic: A Profile, Henry Krisch

Czechoslovakia: Profile of a Socialist Republic at the Crossroads of Europe, David W. Paul

Czechoslovakia, William V. Wallace

Background to Crisis: Policy and Politics in Gierek's Poland, edited by Maurice D. Simon and Roger E. Kanet

Hungary: Profile of a Nation of Contradictions, Ivan Volgyes

Innovation in Communist Systems, edited by Andrew Gyorgy and James A. Kuhlman

**The Domestic Context of Soviet Foreign Policy*, edited by Seweryn Bialer

**The Soviet Union in World Politics*, edited by Kurt London

**The Soviet Union in the Third World: Successes and Failures*, edited by Robert H. Donaldson

*Available in hardcover and paperback.

Westview Special Studies on the Soviet Union and Eastern Europe

Romania in the 1980s
edited by Daniel N. Nelson

In several respects, Romania is unique among communist states. It has been the only Warsaw Pact member to deviate consistently from Soviet foreign policy norms, and it remains the sole Eastern European country to avoid oil imports from the USSR. At the same time, the Romanian government is committed to orthodox socioeconomic centralization and control, and intellectual freedom, artistic liberty, and workers' rights remain minimal.

This configuration of international and domestic policies, along with Romania's impressive record of industrial growth, calls for an effort to understand the dynamics of the country's socioeconomic and political life. The authors of this book delineate and assess the political, economic, and social trends likely to be influential in Romania during this and ensuing decades.

Dr. Daniel N. Nelson is currently associate professor of political science at the University of Kentucky. He has done field research in both Romania and Poland and has written extensively on Romania and communist politics.

Romania in the 1980s

edited by Daniel N. Nelson

Westview Press / Boulder, Colorado

Westview Special Studies on the Soviet Union and Eastern Europe

Chapter 6, by Daniel N. Nelson, first appeared in *Soviet Studies* 32 (1980): 542-560. It is reprinted here by permission.

All rights reserved. No part of this publication may be reproduced or transmitted in any form or by any means, electronic or mechanical, including photocopy, recording, or any information storage and retrieval system, without permission in writing from the publisher.

Copyright © 1981 by Westview Press, Inc.

Published in 1981 in the United States of America by
    Westview Press, Inc.
    5500 Central Avenue
    Boulder, Colorado 80301
    Frederick A. Praeger, Publisher

Library of Congress Cataloging in Publication Data
Main entry under title:
Romania in the 1980s.
    (Westview special studies on the Soviet Union and Eastern Europe)
    1. Romania--Politics and government--1944-   . 2. Romania--Economic conditions--1945-   . 3. Romania--Social conditions--1945-   .
I. Nelson, Daniel N., 1948-   . II. Series.
DR267.R65   949.8'03   81-3412
ISBN 0-86531-027-0   AACR2

Composition for this book was provided by the editor.
Printed and bound in the United States of America.

Contents

List of Tables ix
Preface xi

PART 1: THE SETTING OF ROMANIAN COMMUNISM

Introductory Remarks 2
1 Romania's Development as a Communist State
    Stephen Fischer-Galati 4
2 Romania's Past as Challenge for the Future:
    A Developmental Approach to Interwar Politics
    Paul A. Shapiro 17

PART 2: LEADERS AND CITIZENS IN ROMANIAN POLITICS

Introductory Remarks 69
3 Family, Farm, and Factory: Rural Workers in
    Contemporary Romania
    John W. Cole 71
4 Idol or Leader? The Origins and Future of
    the Ceausescu Cult
    Mary Ellen Fischer 117
5 Political Socialization in Romania:
    Prospects and Performance
    Trond Gilberg 142
6 Workers in a Workers' State
    Daniel N. Nelson 174

PART 3: FOREIGN AND ECONOMIC POLICIES

Introductory Remarks 199
7 Romanian Military Policy in the 1980s
    Walter M. Bacon, Jr. 202
8 Romanian Foreign Policy in the 1980s
    Ronald H. Linden 219
9 Perspectives on Romania's Economic Development
    in the 1980s
    Marvin R. Jackson 254

Conclusion: Development, Communism, and
  Balkan Tradition
    Daniel N. Nelson 306

Tables

2.1 Percent of Total Number of Votes Cast Received by Each Party, 1919-1922 44
2.2 Percent of Total Number of Votes Cast Received by Each Party, 1926-1937 46
2.3 Percent of Total Votes Cast Received by the Major Parties, by Province, 1919-1922 . . . 49
2.4 Percent of Total Votes Cast Received by the Major Parties and the "Governmental Dowry," by Province, 1922-1937 50
2.5 Percent of Total Votes Cast Received by the Major Right-Wing Extremist Parties, by Province, 1926-1937. 53
2.6 Percent of Total National Liberal Party Vote Received in the Regat, 1919-1937 55
2.7 The "Governmental Dowry" in Romanian Elections, 1926-1937. 55
2.8 Eligible Voters and Participation Levels in Romanian Elections, by Province, 1919-1937 . 56
3.1 Agricultural and Industrial Contribution to Total Social Product Compared to National Investment in Agriculture and Industry . . . 99
3.2 Investment in Agriculture, 1950-1975 100
3.3 Ownership of Productive Land (1976) 101
3.4 Production of Major Crops by Type of Farm for 1976 102
3.5 The Rural Population Since 1948 104
3.6 Growth of Total Population and Urban Population 105
3.7 Selected Vital Statistics, 1948-1976 106
3.8 Zonal Variation in Agricultural Investment . . 107
3.9 Net Migration per 1000 of Population by County 108
3.10 Urban and Rural Birth Rates, Death Rates and Rates of Natural Increase 109
3.11 Dependency Ratios, by County (1973) 110
3.12 Personal Agricultural Production. Expressed as a Percentage of Total National Production 111

6.1	Participation at General Assemblies of the Enterprise by Political Identity	192
6.2	Participation in Production Meetings by Young Workers	193
6.3	Sense of Efficacy Among Workers Who Make Proposals at Production Meetings	194
7.1	Military Budget of the RSR in (1) Billions of Lei; (2) As a Percent of Total Government Expenditure; (3) As a Percent of GNP	209
7.2	Relative Rank (of 7) for Romania on Nine Measures of Military Expenditures for European Warsaw Pact States	210
9.1	Population and Labor Resources 1950-1980	256
9.1b	Growth of Production, Labor and Capital, 1950-1980	258
9.2	Labor Migration Tendencies in the Iasi District (1972)	268
9.3	Comparative Romanian and Bulgarian Foreign Capital Dependence	271
9.4	Projected Growth of Production and Investments, 1975-1990	276
9.5	Projections of Population and Labor Resources, 1980-1990	281
9.6	Sources of Labor, 1971-1980 and 1981-1990	282
9.7	Level and Growth of Personal Consumption Indicators	290
9.8	Growth of Consumer Expenditures and Saving	294

Preface

Among communist states, Romania is, in several respects, a unique case. Romania has been the only Warsaw Pact member to deviate consistently from Soviet foreign policy norms and, alone within Eastern Europe, to avoid oil imports from the USSR. The leadership of Nicolae Ceausescu since 1965 has, meanwhile, governed through a studious commitment to socio-economic centralization and control often reminiscent of Stalinist orthodoxy. Intellectual freedom, artistic liberty and workers' rights have changed little relative to Poland, Hungary or the transient Prague Spring.

Such international and domestic policy distinctions, as well as a record of impressive industrial growth, necessitate an effort to understand the dynamics of Romania's socio-economic and political life. This volume is meant to delineate trends in political, social and economic life which will constitute dynamic elements for the Romanian system during the 1980s and beyond. Contributors, all scholars with lengthy research experience in Romania, the Balkans and communist states generally, have sought to identify factors likely to be influential during this and ensuing decades. In that sense, this is a "predictive" volume containing not "crystal-ball gazing" but the careful identification and assessment of trends influencing Romanian foreign and domestic policies, economic and political performance, and societal transformations. By suggesting elements crucial to socio-economic and political change in Romania, we hope to make observing this intriguing communist state somewhat less haphazard and more systematic.

Professor Stephen Fischer-Galati has written a challenging introductory chapter in relationship to which the reader should compare subsequent analyses in this collection. In Fischer-Galati's view, assessments regarding Romania's prospects "revolve on an appraisal of Ceausescu's motives for the pursuit of policies of rapid multilateral development at home and of an independent foreign policy...." Fischer-Galati's own judgment is that Ceausescu's own political survival demanded efforts to industrialize and to emphasize nationalism. Legitimacy of the Ceausescu regime, then, could only be maintained via linkage to the internal goal of modernization and development and the external identity of national communism. Any "liberal" phase one may wish to denote in Ceausescu's years, e.g., from 1965-1971, is seen by Fischer-Galati as merely characteristic of transition periods, with the autocratic nature of subsequent years merely "complet(ing) the traditional political cycle of Romanian rulers."

From such a background, Fischer-Galati expects that the rigidity of political life in Romania, notwithstanding a popular toleration of autocracy and Ceausescu's personality cult, will be subject to harsher criticism. Moreover, the inability of Romania to retain a semblance of importance on the international stage will diminish Ceausescu's position.

Fischer-Galati has, then, portrayed a "waning star" for Nicolae Ceausescu and a dubious future for Romania's development as a communist state. These are forthright and intriguing propositions which, for readers of this volume, should raise the important questions toward which chapters are addressed.

-Are Romanian political traditions as described by Fischer-Galati? Specifically, is there any evidence to suggest that general tendencies other than authoritarian and autocratic leadership have existed within the Romanian polity?
-As an essentially agrarian nation has been pushed towards an urban, industrial future, what problems are solved and what new ones are created? Specifically, have Romanian leaders, as Fischer-Galati argues, erred by the uncompromising drive towards self-sufficiency and industrialization insofar as the transformation of peasants into workers is incomplete and counterproductive?
-Does Ceausescu's own personal legitimacy, as Fischer-Galati suggests, rest on economic performance and identification with nationalism vis-à-vis the Soviet Union? What is the future of the Ceausescu "cult"?
-What are the mechanisms by which Romanians are told about the expectations of Party leaders and through which explanations of policy are conveyed? Does the performance of such socialization mechanisms compensate for any antagonism generated in the population by a denial of consumer items or political liberty?
-Are some critical segments of the Romanian population, such as blue-collar labor, likely to

become a greater problem for the regime in the 1980s and later? What evidence is available regarding workplace participation and attitudes about such involvement?

-How does Romania propose to defend itself? Is its military policy geared toward the potential of Soviet intervention? What political benefits accrue to Nicolae Ceausescu's regime as a result of specific military policy?

-To what extent has Romania been a foreign policy "maverick"? What are the factors that engender and/or limit Romanian foreign policies? Are the prognoses for Romanian international activity as limited by dependency on the Soviet Union as Fischer-Galati argues?

-Are Romania's economic achievements significant under communism? Is the regime's economic plan, through 1990, one which can be met? What are the positive and negative factors which have a role in Romanian economic planning?

Responses to these and related questions are sought by eight scholars following Fischer-Galati's introductory chapter. A concluding note will reassess such issues and offer a broadly integrative summary regarding the relationships among communism, development and Balkan traditions in Romania.

As with any edited volume, the individual whose name is on the book's cover owes a great deal to the authors, typists, and publishers. The experience of each scholar in this book is reflected in the care with which they have analyzed their respective subjects, providing a unique, predictive view of a communist state. I am indebted to each of these individuals for their cooperation and patience. Ms. Kim Hayden prepared the manuscript for publication, and her labor, accuracy and diligence are very much appreciated.

Daniel N. Nelson

Part 1
The Setting of Romanian Communism

Romania's development as a communist state, argues Professor Stephen Fischer-Galati, has resulted in little more than the completion of a cycle, returning the country to rule by an autocratic cult. In Fischer-Galati's view, Romanian communism is set firmly in the personalistic and familial political heritage of Romania, with both internal and foreign policies explained in large part by the requirements of political survival for one man and his immediate entourage.

The position taken by Fishcer-Galati is one which directs attention to other chapters in this volume, but particularly those by Paul Shapiro and John Cole. Shapiro utilizes electoral data from inter-war Romania to assess critically assumptions he finds too common in existing literature; namely, that Romania lacked any open or competitive political experience, which suggests that no alternative to communist rule was available, and the corollary that Romanian fascism triumphed because the inter-war party system failed to develop. These data corroborate Shapiro's argument that Romania did exhibit an institutionalized, competitive party system by the late 1920s. Implicit to such a finding, of course, is a challenge to the view that Romanian political traditions are solely autocratic and non-competitive. At the least, one is led to view the political setting of Romanian communism in a different light, not only the successors to a long line of one-man regimes, but the product of a much more complex political tradition. The problem for the Romanian Communist Party has been, as with regimes before it, to "bridge the gap between state and society..." A competitive party system had made, between the wars, progress in that regard. Now, however, Romania's rulers are confronted by a need to legitimize their rule with the aid of nationalism, vis-à-vis the USSR, while retaining Soviet-inspired governmental forms. The record of inter-war parties, then, is one with which the Party has had to "contend" since the RCP cannot accept the view that it does not have the ability to link leaders and masses, or that a party system, as between the wars, was a viable alternative.

John Cole has focused his attention on the transitional setting of Romanian communism, ruling a society in which peasant labor has been surging towards the jobs of urban industry. Romanian communism cannot, of course, be understood outside the context of the societal transformations it has encouraged. Faced with the contradiction of ruling in the proletariat's interests where there were few proletarians, Romanian communists recognized the link between their political survival and their country's independence, and pushed for modernization and development. But the reservoir of wealth in Romania was the peasantry--or, more specifically, their labor. Cole's analysis concerns the adaptation of peasants to the industrialization of agriculture and, for many, their migration or daily commute to cities. In Cole's view, the rural worker has been crucial to Romania's developmental strategy. Thus far, Cole concludes, Romania is "on the way to solving the problems it faces as an agrarian state". But, he points out, some of the means by which rural workers and their families have adapted to the social transformations encouraged by the regime's policies are, themselves, at odds with Party aims. The "second shift" phenomenon is described at length, for example, as simultaneously an integral part of the socialist system but "incompatible with a quality labor force."

Romanian communism must, then, exist in the milieu of both historical and social factors. Fischer-Galati posits an interpretation of Romanian politics in the context of personal political survival motivating internal and external policies, both conforming to traditional Romanian norms. Shapiro suggests that the institutions for a quite different Romanian political system once existed--institutions which offered greater potential for a resolution of the state-society gap long evident in Romania. Cole adds the context of an agrarian state in the transitional stage where rural workers play major socio-economic and political roles.

The setting of Romanian communism in the 1980s and after is not, then, a matter of unanimous interpretation. Fischer-Galati's positions are, implicitly, challenged by the views of Shapiro and Cole. While Shapiro acknowledges a recurring theme in Romanian politics, i.e., the gap between state and society, he has not adopted a cyclical view by which autocracy is the political "baseline" for Romania. Cole, although citing problems inherent to the migration of labor and related phenomena such as the "second shift", nevertheless emphasizes the Romanian Communist Party's ability to effect socio-economic change, and to manage the problems of modernizing an agrarian state. Clearly, Cole's paper implies that the policies taken by a communist party government have the aim of long-term social transformation as well as any immediate purpose related to the survival of Ceausescu's regime.

1
Romania's Development as a Communist State

Stephen Fischer-Galati

Perspectives for Romania's development in the 1980s are uncertain. They are less a function of factors related to the announced goals of the regime than of interpretations of successes or failures by Romanian and foreign political leaders, scholars, and propagandists. The ambiguity of this statement is reflective of the entire course of Romania's development as a communist state.

It is a continuing matter of dispute among actual or self-styled connoisseurs of Romanian affairs as to whether Romania has benefitted from communist rule and planning, and whether or not a multilaterally-developed Romanian economy and society is emerging after nearly forty years since the liberation of the country by the Soviet Union in 1944. There is also doubt as to whether communist Romania has actually achieved meaningful independence in the pursuit of a foreign policy of its own, or whether the rule of Nicolae Ceausescu has been beneficial to Romanian modernization and to world peace. And, finally, there are questions regarding Romania's future in the 1980s even among supporters and defenders of Ceausescu's independent course who, like skeptics and detractors, foresee a rough road ahead in a decade of economic stagnation, political conflict, and aggravated energy crises.

It is difficult to find the "juste milieu" because of Romania's peculiar position in the communist and non-communist worlds. This is to say that the foreign policies pursued by Nicolae Ceausescu and by his immediate predecessor, Gheorghe Gheorghiu-Dej, have both conditioned and obscured internal realities so as to render objective assessment of the nature and development of communist Romania extremely difficult. Thus, any such

---

Stephen Fischer-Galati is Professor of History at the University of Colorado and Editor of the East European Quarterly. His doctorate is from Harvard.

assessment of the true character of Romania's development as a communist state and any prognoses for development in the 1980s revolve on an appraisal of Ceausescu's motives for the pursuit of policies of rapid multilateral development at home and of an independent foreign policy during the last fifteen years.

It has been said often that the ultimate purpose of Ceausescu's rule is the transformation of Romania, before the end of the twentieth century, into a multilaterally-developed, modern, independent, "national" communist state. There can be little doubt that rapid, altogether too rapid, industrialization has occurred in Romania since World War II. Statistical data are truly impressive per se and in terms of comparative achievements under pre-communist and communist rule. Yet, at the beginning of the 1980s the Romanian economy is in disarray, plagued by shortages of raw materials and hard currency, by enormous trade deficits, inadequate food supplies, and inflation. Although many of these symptoms can be attributed to global economic and political factors beyond Romania's control, not all of such ills can be explained by external conditions. The ultimate question is whether rapid, multilateral, industrialization was actually necessary in Romania, or whether it is justifiable in any rational economic terms. Expert opinion is divided in these respects. However, communist modernization in Romania has never been a function of economic considerations alone. In fact, it seems fair to say that the socialist transformation of Romania from a retarded agricultural society into an advanced industrial one, thoroughly documented by Marvin Jackson in this volume, was at all times predicated on rather basic political considerations.

The industrialization of Romania antedates the communist era. It is true that until World War II, Romania's economy was primarily agricultural and that extractive industries were more developed than others. It is also true that the Romanians' standard of living was among the lowest in Europe. Be this as it may, plans for industrial development were drawn and even implemented in the twenties, thirties, and early forties by political forces other than the communists. Paul Shapiro discusses in the following chapter, for example, the inter-war political development entirely outside a Marxist party. In fact, during those years, there was little communist commitment to anything but revolutionary activities at the behest of Moscow. Even in the later forties, after Romania's liberation, the communists were infinitely more concerned with consolidation of Soviet power and with their own political survival than with industrialization and modernization. If anything, industrialization was viewed as a political rather than as an economic necessity, as the means of achieving the anti-rural and anti-bourgeois revolution, as an expression of the class struggle directed against "bourgeois-landlord" and other counterrevolutionary forces. It would be hard to prove, for instance, that the construction of the Danube-Black Sea Canal, a would-be monument to communist modernization, was undertaken for economic reasons.

Industrialization, even as it gathered momentum following the adoption of economic planning in the late forties, remained a function of Soviet and Romanian communist politics at least until the late fifties when it became a function of Romanian politics alone. This is to say that the emphasis placed on industrialization by Georghe Gheorghiu-Dej at the celebrated Plenum of November 1958 was an essential instrumentality for securing Gheorghiu's position in the incipient power struggle between Bucharest and Moscow. To survive the challenge posed to his authority and legitimacy by Khrushchev, the Romanian leader became the exponent of the doctrine of a "Romanian road to socialism" which entailed revival of the political slogan of pre-communist Romanian leaders "<u>Prin noi insine</u>!" ("By ourselves!") Romania was to concentrate on modernization within the objective historic conditions of the fifties -- they, themselves, a function of the entire historic tradition of the Romanians -- that is within the confines of the Romanian national state, by Romanians, and for the ultimate benefit of Romanians.

In that manner, Gheorghiu-Dej and the Romanian communists hoped to emancipate themselves, as best they could, from total dependence on Moscow and the Soviet bloc and to reestablish economic, cultural, and even political ties with countries outside the Soviet orbit. Industrialization was chosen as a primary vehicle for attainment of political goals because communism presupposes industrialization and thus could not be regarded as a deviationist or politically subversive action by Gheorghiu's enemies in the Kremlin. And, as the rift between Bucharest and Moscow widened in the early sixties, as Moscow opposed Romania's industrialization beyond the prescriptions of COMECON, Gheorghiu-Dej increasingly became intent on emphasizing the need for multilateral industrialization as the ultimate guarantee of national security and the ultimate expression of national goals and resolve. It was not until Ceausescu succeeded Gheorghiu-Dej in 1965, however, that multilateral industrialization became the ultimate purpose of the Romanian leadership.

Ceausescu's commitment to industrialization was directly and intimately related to the elemental political motive of survival. To secure and legitimize his power in the face of internal challenges and, particularly, of the Kremlin's opposition to Romania's independent course, Ceausescu opted for a political platform based on nationalism, communism, and modernization. He donned the mantle of executor of Romania's historic tradition which, according to him, called for the establishment of a multilaterally-developed national Romanian communist state ruled by an historic figure akin to that of great Romanian national leaders of the past -- of men such as Stephen the Great or Michael the Brave -- that of Nicolae Ceausescu. When Mary Ellen Fischer discusses the "cult" of Ceausescu in Chapter 4, the effort by Romania's current leader to grasp legitimacy from images becomes all the more evident. Therefore, industrialization and the corollary creation of a communist society proceeded with a vengeance after 1965. However, because of the eminently political character of all of Ceausescu's actions, the grandiose schemes enunciated in successive plans for economic development have tended to ignore economic realities.

The rapid industrialization of Romania was unrelated to availability of capital, markets, or raw materials, to labor productivity, quality of production, or modern technology, with the result that by the beginning of the 1980s Ceausescu's grandiose plans are in jeopardy. Although industrialization proceeds apace the strains on the agricultural sector are mounting since agricultural exports have become the primary source of the foreign capital required for continuing industrialization with resultant food shortages and growing social discontent. Disassociation from COMECON, within the limits of the prudent, is becoming less and less realizable because of growing dependence on Soviet oil and, from an economic standpoint, the outlook for further industrialization may become a function of factors related to the economic development of the Third World and of the industrial West. From a non-economic standpoint, however, Ceausescu's plans for the achievement of a multilaterally-developed Romanian communist society have thus far been more successful.

If the purpose of his drive for rapid industrialization was to secure political survival and aggrandizement, or perhaps to establish a Ceausescu dynasty, headed by Nicolae Ceausescu and his wife Elena, then the problems mentioned above may be overcome, at least in the short run, by skillful political maneuvering. It seems evident that the invocation of the Russian threat has been used since 1965 as the rationale for transforming the rather obscure Nicolae Ceausescu into the defensor patriae and protector of the historic interests of the Romanian people. The Czechoslovak crisis of 1968, during which Ceausescu announced Romania's determination to resist a possible Soviet invasion by force of arms, provided the basis for reinforcing the image of Ceausescu as the ultimate defender of Romanian interests and historic goals. Whether the Soviet threat was as grave as depicted by Ceausescu or whether techniques identified with "Peter and the Wolf" were used primarily to consolidate and expand his personal power, Ceausescu's political philosophy and actions have been, nevertheless, based on the assumption that he alone could secure Romania's future and safeguard and complete his own definition of the national historic tradition. That the Kremlin would have preferred different leaders in Romania is certain. But it is evident that Ceausescu's plans for securing his place in history transcended the threat of Soviet intervention. To the credit of this politically ambitious and intelligent man, as well as to that of his perhaps even more ambitious and intelligent wife, he has been able to diagnose and exploit the objective conditions which would insure attainment of his goals.

Ceausescu's foremost skills were revealed in his understanding and exploitation of international problems. He has exploited skillfully conflicts and contradictions involving China, the USSR, and the United States with a view to avoiding Soviet "intervention in Romania's internal affairs." Particularly important has been the prevention of maneuvers by Warsaw Pact forces on Romanian soil which, Ceausescu feared, would have erased the advantages gained in 1958 by the withdrawal of Soviet troops stationed in Romania. This partial disassociation from the Warsaw Pact, to which Walter Bacon refers in relationship to Romania's military policy, became a cardinal component of Ceausescu's doctrine of dissolution of military blocs in Europe after the invasion of Czechoslovakia. Romanian forces had failed to participate in the military actions directed by Warsaw Pact forces against Czechoslovakia. But in Ceausescu's estimate, protection against Soviet pressures had to transcend exploitation of the Sino-Soviet, Sino-American, and Soviet-American conflicts.

Thus, after 1968, Romanian foreign policy became all-encompassing through the gradual expansion of diplomatic and economic ties with Western Europe, Africa, Asia, Latin America, Israel, the Arab World, and almost every nation in the world. Such activism, which Ron Linden discusses more fully in Chapter 8, was all undertaken ostensibly for the purposes of securing world peace and acceptance, on a global basis, of Romania's principles regarding the rights of individual nations to pursue their own policies, external and internal, freely and without interference from the outside. But in another view, Romanian foreign policy was designed to establish Ceausescu as the arbiter of international conflicts and disputes involving the communist and non-communist worlds, to secure economic advantages for the developing Romanian industry, and ultimately to secure Ceausescu's position vis-a-vis the Kremlin by making implementation of the Brezhnev Doctrine in Romania if not impossible, at least very risky for the Soviet Union. There can be little doubt that that policy proved to be successful until the latter 1970s. For instance, Romania was instrumental in facilitating contacts between China and the United States in the late sixties and early seventies and between Egypt and Israel in the seventies. Romania has also established extensive economic and political ties with the Third World and has often taken stands different from those of other members of the Warsaw Pact in such delicate issues as the Arab-Israeli conflict or the Soviet invasion of Afghanistan (positions discussed more thoroughly by Linden's chapter).

Nevertheless, following the end of the Vietnamese war and the subsequent Sino-American rapprochement, the reorientation of American and Soviet foreign policies during the years of the Carter presidency, and the general international turmoil caused by the energy crisis and corollary problems in the Near and Middle East, Romania's importance in international affairs has declined considerably by the beginning of the 1980s. Whatever advantages Ceausescu may have obtained vis-a-vis the Soviet Union and on behalf of his own plans for Romania's development and for securing his place in contemporary and historic Romania through the pursuit of an ingenious foreign policy are apparently dissipating. In fact, it is improbable that Romania will be able to disassociate herself from active participation in Warsaw Pact, or even COMECON, affairs in the 1980s. Consequently, Ceausescu's security is likely to become more-and-more a function of his ability to defend his position of undisputed historic descendant of great Romanian leaders of the past and exclusive and indispensable champion and executor of Romania's communist destiny.

In these respects, Ceausescu's position appears quite secure at the beginning of the 1980s if, for no other reason, than that he has consolidated all power in his own hands and in those of his immediate personal and political families. It has long been argued that there are marked inconsistencies between Romania's enlightened foreign and Stalinist internal policies. The standard explanation for this dichotomy has been the need for maintenance of a domestic order acceptable to Moscow as a <u>quid pro quo</u> for Russian tolerance of Romanian deviations in foreign affairs. Thus, it has been said that as long as Ceausescu appeared to be more Stalinist than Brezhnev, the dreaded Brezhnev doctrine could not be enforced against Romania. For supporters of that theory, the recent harsh attacks directed by Ceausescu against the independent Polish trade union movement merely reflect necessity and not conviction. Nothing could be further removed from the truth.

The history of internal political developments in Romania reveals that Ceausescu, as well as his immediate predecessor Gheorghiu-Dej, has always had authoritarian, Stalinist or neo-Stalinist, views on the conduct of Romanian affairs. The reasons are fairly elementary. Gheorghiu-Dej was indeed more Stalinist than Stalin and had to be so to secure his own position in Stalin's days and later in those of Khrushchev. The beginnings of the Romanian road to independence, via a Romanian road to socialism, may indeed be traced to Khrushchev's determination to replace Gheorghiu-Dej in the period immediately following Khrushchev's de-Stalinization campaign. When, in 1957, Romanian supporters of Khrushchev sought to remove Gheorghiu-Dej from power following the elimination of the "anti-Party group" in Moscow by Khrushchev's forces, Gheorghiu-Dej purged the Khrushchevites and reinforced his campaign to build a Romanian road to socialism on neo-Stalinist lines, opposed to Khrushchevite innovations. However, as Romania's development by the early sixties required the development of meaningful economic and political ties with the capitalist West, the dangers of potential Soviet intervention and the spreading of "bourgeois" Western ideas into Romania proper became apparent to the Romanian communist leadership. Thus, such gestures of "liberalization" as were made by Gheorghiu-Dej prior to his death were reflective of need to alleviate Western concerns rather than of fundamental changes in the character of his rule. And the limits of "liberalization" became more clearly defined during the early years of Ceausescu's rule.

Ceausescu's early "liberalism" was characteristic of transition periods. As Ceausescu succeeded to power at a time of rising, if cautious, expectations in Romania as well as one of transition from Khrushchev to Brezhnev in the USSR, he moved carefully. Nevertheless, certain characteristics of his future rule became evident from as early as 1965 when he assumed the roles of defender of Romania's national and historic interests in his relations with the USSR and of executor of the Romanian historic tradition, equated with the proximate establishment of a communist Romania. He was soon to become a communist <u>domnitor</u> (ruling prince) who would identify his rule with that of Michael the Brave, the Romanian hero of the late sixteenth century. Within a few short years, the self-styled defender and promoter of Romania's historic interests redefined the character of the rule of Michael the Brave from "patriotic" to "authoritarian." The transition occurred only at the beginning of the seventies chiefly because of the opportunities afforded by the Czechoslovak, and corollary Romanian crises of 1968. In 1968, Ceausescu acted like Michael the Brave in asserting his determination to lead the Romanian people in defense of the national patrimony and honor against foreign enemies. If Ceausescu the Saviour did not become Ceausescu the Prince until 1971, it was because of continuing apprehension over Soviet intentions in the aftermath of the Czechoslovak crisis and the corollary need of securing Western support at a time of global reaction to the Soviet invasion of Czechoslovakia. President Nixon's visit to Romania, in the summer of 1969, coupled with Ceausescu's intense diplomatic activity in the name of international peace and of the rights of small nations greatly facilitated the consolidation of his power as a Romanian national hero. By 1971, the national hero was to become an absolute monarch. The genuine leadership of 1968, as Mary Ellen Fischer points out in her contribution, was not carried far into the 1970s, and now Ceausescu relies on images to preserve legitimacy.

It has been suggested that the turn to the left, directed against intellectuals, professional cadres, party leaders, and other individuals whose ideological purity and commitment to the rapid development of the multilaterally-developed national communist state was questioned in 1971, was adopted because of Ceausescu's admiration for the Chinese cultural revolution and continued fears over Soviet hostility toward his rule. It seems doubtful, however, that the Romanian cultural revolution of the seventies was an offspring of the Chinese and it is also questionable whether continuing Soviet hostility was a determining factor in the termination of the "liberal" phase of Ceausescu's rule. It is possible that internal Romanian forces, anxious to maintain a foothold in the communist power structure on more legitimate bases than historic continuity and mission, may have been encouraged by the Kremlin in their opposition to Ceausescu's rule. It is also possible that Ceausescu's plans for multilateral development could not have been achieved without the establishment of rigid party discipline and centralized control. It may also be true that Soviet pressure, exercised through military maneuvers, disputes over the legitimacy of the acquisition of Bessarabia in 1940, and encouragement of the aspirations of the dissatisfied Hungarian minority in Transylvania, may have contributed to Ceausescu's actions. However, in the last analysis, the turn to the left must be attributed to Ceausescu's determination to secure total power at the first available opportunity. By invoking the need for national unity, discipline, defense of the national patrimony, and modernization at a time when the gradual consolidation of power in his own hands and in those of his family had run its course, Ceausescu merely completed the traditional political cycle of Romanian rulers, communist or not, whereby security and power are guaranteed only by absolute rule. And indeed, Ceausescu's quest for power and security assumed, by the late seventies, the most accomplished forms of personal rule characterized by the most elaborate manifestations of a cult of personality unrivaled since the days of Stalin and Mao Tse-tung.

As the absolute ruler of Romania, Ceausescu has appropriated the traditional slogan of previous monarchs "Orthodoxy, Autocracy, Nationality," albeit within the context and objective conditions of the contemporary Romanian state. "Orthodoxy" presupposes enforcement of a nationalist, neo-Marxist ideology, formulated by Ceausescu and his close associates. Its essence consists of identification of the historic tradition and goals of the Romanians with communism and corollary rejection of all other possible interpretation of the Romanians' manifest destiny. Orthodoxy is by definition dogmatic and anti-intellectual. It tolerates no deviations from Ceausescu's pronunciamentos on matters ideological and requires constant reiteration of the official dogma in all media of intellectual expression. (Trond Gilberg's chapter in this volume considers, at length, the regime's socialization efforts.) Adulation of the leader and of his thoughts is a prerequisite for any and all Romanians and any form of dissent has become impardonable.

"Autocracy" has the simple meaning of total acceptance of one-man rule and of recognition of the infallibility of that man's actions and decisions. All power belongs to Ceausescu who rules with the assistance of the traditionally supportive spouse and members of the "king's household."

"Nationality" means rule by the Romanian majority and imposition of the Romanians' historic tradition on national minorities with a view to creating a Romanian national communist state. Internationalism is acceptable only as an expression of Romanian national interests and cosmopolitanism is rejected altogether.

The rigid enforcement of these cardinal principles of Ceausescu's dogma has led to increased public resentment of the Ceausescu dynasty, as Dan Nelson suggests among the working class, but has not threatened the security of that dynasty. The enforcement of the principles identified with Orthodoxy has harmed the intellectual and professional community but has had apparently little effect on the masses in general. The incessant calls for ideological purity and imposition of Ceausescu's ideological positions have had their most negative effects on the educational system, on writers of Romanian history, on writers and artists in general, on technocrats and scientists, on physicians, and on all thinking individuals who are aware of the motivations of the leaders and the emptiness of the official dogma. However, despite disaffection and despair, the majority of those exposed to and affected by the imposition of dogmatic communist orthodoxy are paying at least lip service to Ceausescu's line mostly because the opportunities for defection abroad have declined considerably in recent years. On the other hand, Ceausescu's dogmatism has won him the support of opportunists and of those elements of the population who stand to benefit from his anti-intellectualism, anti-cosmopolitanism, and acerbic nationalism. Advancement in the professions has become easier for the faithful and the incompetent both because of the leader's lack of confidence in cosmopolitan, bourgeois or embourgeoise, intellectual or neo-intellectual professional cadres and of the vacancies created by the loss of such cadres through emigration or defection abroad. Moreover, Ceausescu's determination to consolidate his power as the executor of the Romanian masses' historic aspirations has resulted in the broadening of the nominal participation of the masses in political life through the enormous enlargement of the size of the Romanian Communist Party. Indeed, through the deliberate political socialization, discussed by Gilberg, the Party has become a mass organization and the privileges bestowed upon its members have tended to secure the power of the rulers and the interests of the privileged groups in the Romanian communist state.

For these reasons too there has been wider popular acceptance, or at least toleration, of autocracy and the corollary deification of Ceausescu than critics would like to have us believe. Since autocracy is ostensibly necessary to defend the historic interests of Romanians, primarily against the Soviet Union, the Romanian masses generally subscribe to the view that Ceausescu can best defend Romania's independence. And even his critics, mostly intellectuals, students, and national minorities, who rightly ridicule the identification of Ceausescu with historic figures of the distant past such as Burebista, Vlad the Impaler, Stephen the Great, Michael the Brave, and others who are aware of the fact that Ceausescu's autocracy is designed primarily to build "socialism within one family," still believe that Ceausescu is preferable to Brezhnev. That Ceausescu's internal policies are regarded as faulty, if not disastrous, from an economic point of view by the majority of the population, does not mean that the same public, desiring Hungarian-style reforms, has any evident alternatives to Ceausescu's rule at this time. The most notable exception to this attitude is found among the immobile national minorities, specifically the Hungarians. Whereas Jews and Saxons have been able to leave Romania during the last fifteen years or so, the immobile Hungarians have been growing impatient with the Ceausescu regime in recent years. The alleged reason for the Hungarians' discontent is the adoption of Romanization policies detrimental to their constitutional and historic rights. The enforcement of the principle of "Nationality" has indeed affected the Hungarian minority more than any other. In theory, Ceausescu has abided by the letter of the constitution and implementing laws whereby the rights of national minorities are guaranteed. In practice, however, pressure has been intensified during the last decade for at least cultural assimilation through gradual reduction in the number of Hungarian-language schools and opportunities for professional advancement of unintegrated or unassimilated Hungarians. Moreover, the Hungarians have been resentful of the Romanization of urban centers inhabited primarily by Hungarians which has involved Romanization of street names, resettlement of Romanians from provinces other than Transylvania into enlarged industrial towns, and a general dismemberment of Hungarian urban values and traditions. And indeed, the rapid transformation of the historic character of Transylvania has been a deliberate policy of Ceausescu even though it is not necessarily directed against the Hungarians alone. In fact the Romanization of Transylvanian towns has been motivated primarily by the ruler's determination to destroy bourgeois or embourgeoise urban centers and traditions throughout Romania through transformation of commercial towns into industrial ones with corollary relocation of the masses. These policies have affected most directly the Transylvanian urban centers, the historic foci of Hungarian and Saxon culture and civilization.

Ultimately, however, the resentment of the Hungarians is based on their awareness of the differences between economic, cultural, and political conditions in Hungary and Romania and to their lack of allegiance to the doctrines of Romanian historic rights and manifest destiny enunciated by Ceausescu. In itself, the Hungarians' dissatisfaction is not too significant to the rulers of Romania. It assumes significance, however, in terms of its exploitation by the Kremlin and by Budapest as a means for potential interference in Romanian internal affairs. And it is this ultimate concern of Ceausescu for the security of his regime that brings us to the final assessment of Romania's status at the beginning of the 1980s and likely evolution of Ceausescu's

Romania during the rest of that decade.

As the possibility of direct Soviet military intervention in Romania appears increasingly more remote in view of Ceausescu's decreased opportunities for pursuing policies of genuine independence from Moscow, the gradual erosion of Ceausescu's legitimacy and power as leader of an independent national communist state appears inevitable. During the 1980s Romania is likely to become ever more dependent on the Soviet Union for attainment of her economic goals. In all likelihood, Ceausescu will continue to seek alternatives to greater reliance on the USSR and COMECON; yet the chances of securing continuing economic support from the West and the Third World at the levels required by the ambitious plans for multilateral development appear illusory. Increased dependence on Moscow is bound to devalue one of Ceausescu's main trump cards -- resistance to Soviet interference in Romanian affairs. It is also not likely to offer solutions to Romania's precarious economic conditions. As it is improbable that the Romanian leadership will abandon its grandiose plans for development, growing disenchantment with the Ceausescu regime by a discontented Romanian population will probably constitute the primary threat to Ceausescu's political survival in the eighties. Dan Nelson's contribution, for example, provides evidence of such a trend.

The 1980s are also likely to witness a further decline in Ceausescu's role as world leader. As Western Europe appears eager to seek long-range accommodation with Moscow, as the need for intermediaries between the Great Powers and the Third World diminishes, as America's relations with China stabilize and develop, the unique diplomatic opportunities grasped by Ceausescu during the sixties and seventies are not likely to recur. In all probability, Ceausescu will assume the position of just another leader of a communist country whose services may be used for tactical rather than for strategic purposes by interested parties, big or small.

The diminution of Ceausescu's importance in international affairs is also likely to contribute to exacerbation of Romania's internal problems. In the absence of any compelling need to overlook or justify the rigidity of Ceausescu's domestic policies by virtue of their being either required for the survival of his regime or excusable because of his great contributions to world peace, those policies are bound to be subject to harsher criticism by the West and by "dissidents" both at home and abroad. Thus, as the indispensable man will become increasingly less essential to more and more of his present supporters, it is probable that Ceausescu's star will dim in the near future. By the end of the 1980s he would be 73 years old; he may very well not be celebrating his seventieth birthday as President of the Socialist Republic of Romania or as General Secretary of the Romanian Communist Party.

Romania's development as a communist state is predictable only for the duration of Ceausescu's rule. The circumstances of the termination of that rule are a matter of conjecture. They will, however, determine the further evolution of Romania whenever they will occur. And the ensuing changes should be drastic.

2
Romania's Past as Challenge for the Future: A Developmental Approach to Interwar Politics

Paul A. Shapiro

INTRODUCTION

The principal dilemma of Romania's precommunist political heritage was conflict between dominant social interests and state interests, that is, between Romanian society and those who controlled the Romanian polity. This conflict, which remains central to Romanian life as the 1980s begin, had its origins in the seventeenth century. Then the principalities of Moldavia and Wallachia had to cope with the inroads and often contradictory influences of four neighboring power centers, each with a distinct sociopolitical and cultural orientation: the Ottoman Empire, to which the principalities owed fealty; the Habsburg Empire, Catholic and the strongest political and military force opposing the Ottomans; the Polish-Lithuanian Commonwealth, whose social order was attractive to the Romanian nobility but whose political disorder was slowly destroying the fabric of the state; and Muscovy, a rising autocratic power of Byzantine Orthodox heritage similar to that which predominated in the principalities themselves. With different elements of their societies attracted by the different cultural and organizational models offered by these states, the principalities moved toward autonomy, then independence, in fits and starts. The social and, increasingly, the economic interests of societal elites frequently worked

---

Paul A. Shapiro is an Associate Editor of the journal Problems of Communism, published by the International Communication Agency in Washington, D.C., and is completing his Ph.D. work at Columbia University. The author wishes to acknowledge the support of the International Research and Exchanges Board and the Institute for Sino-Soviet Studies of the George Washington University. The views expressed in this essay are those of the author and not necessarily those of the International Communication Agency or the government of the United States.

at cross-purposes to these political goals and pushed
the principalities in the direction of continued dependence on one or another of their great-power neighbors.[1]
Still, by the end of the nineteenth century, Romania was
independent, within borders established by the great
powers and given international recognition in the Treaty
of Berlin (1878).

Independence, however, by no means ended the conflict between state and society which had characterized
the two previous centuries. As central authority in the
state passed out of foreign hands into those of the
Romanian privileged and upper middle classes, thus
uniting the state and social forces active up to that
time, the body politic was extended down to lower societal levels. Public education policies in the principalities since the middle of the nineteenth century had
raised literacy levels dramatically. This made possible
"the entry of the masses into politics"[2] acknowledged
tentatively in the limited and indirect suffrage laws
passed before World War I, and conclusively in the
universal and direct suffrage laws of 1918-1919 and 1926
which regulated parliamentary elections between the two
world wars.[3]

Under these circumstances, the feudal conflict between state elites (the prince) and state interests and
societal elites (the boyars and, later, the bourgeoisie)
and their interests was transformed into a more modern
conflict between ruler and ruled.[4] For the societal
elites of Romanian history had now taken over the state,
and they proceeded to convert it into a manipulative
bureaucratic mechanism rather than a democratic one.[5]
The result was the reappearance, albeit lower on the
social scale, of a broad cleavage between the state and
Romanian society.

But if few among the masses felt they had reason to
identify with state elites before World War I, the geographical and sociopolitical transformations wrought by
the war forced the elites to engage the masses if they
hoped to prosper politically once the conflagration
ended. The degree to which the state elites were successful in this effort is the subject of the present
inquiry. How did independent Romania's principal
political movements, still in the making prior to 1916,
measure up when put to the practical test in the interwar period?

1918-1938: THE NEED FOR A SECOND LOOK

Conventional wisdom often proves no wisdom at all,
and nowhere has this been more the case than when Romanian interwar politics have come under scrutiny. For
years, nearly all works in the field have emphasized

negative judgments.6 It has been easy for non-Romanian historians to repeat harsh evaluations, since they have based final judgment on the fact that the interwar multiparty parliamentary regime failed to sustain itself and ceased to function in 1938.7 Communist historians, meanwhile, have frequently distorted history for ideological reasons.8 In the process, many interpretations have been consecrated by repetition rather than by scholarly demonstration.

Typically, studies of interwar Romanian politics have focused on the rise and fall of governments and on the crises of various political parties, and conclusions have contrasted the "debacle of parliamentarism" of 1938 with the hopeful future Romania seemed to have had in 1918.9 Political initiatives, intraparty factionalism, and interparty conflicts have all been cited as proof of the failures of leading politicians to develop viable political institutions for their country and have been evaluated separately in terms of their contribution to the presumably all but inevitable failure of the interwar regime. The regime has been judged a failure, in fact, without adequate consideration of analytical approaches which might allow a more positive view of Romania's political development in these years.

Judgments about the period might not be so harsh if trends rather than isolated events served as the basis of analysis. But the literature has paid relatively little attention to trends, and trends that have been discussed have served to divide the interwar years into segments rather than provide parameters for discussion of the whole period. Roberts' classic tripartite division of interwar years into periods of domination by the National Liberal Party (1918-1928), the National Peasant Party (1928-1930), and King Carol II (1930-1940) provides a case in point.10 Even here, political developments, while admittedly grouped together in a logical way, continue to be measured in terms of the systemic "collapse" of February 1938,11 and the "failure" of interwar Romania is attributed to the separate failures of the Liberals, the Peasantists, and the Carolists. Clearly, to say that each political force had a chance but failed to deal effectively with Romania's problems is to continue to base judgments on the examination of essentially isolated, if repetitive, phenomena. All such analyses ultimately depict the interwar years as a period of political stagnation.

In this chapter, we will attempt to modify this image by looking at the political system of Romania between the wars not in terms of party programs or governmental "successes" or "failures," but in terms of trends measurable over the entire period in national parliamentary election returns. Admittedly, the analysis of election results in a state where electoral corruption and manipulation were rife presents major problems, and there is no question that Romanian election returns do not offer the objective measure of public preferences that democratic elections ideally provide. Yet, analysis of the returns can be highly productive if one concentrates on trends rather than absolute figures. Even trends in the effects of voter coercion can usefully serve as the object of scrutiny.[12]

Since the end of World War I is our point of departure, we will begin by summarizing the political configuration of Romania in the immediate aftermath of the war. Election returns from the country's ten national parliamentary elections between 1918 and 1938 will then be used to determine major developmental trends of the interwar system. Finally, we will offer conclusions about the interwar system based on this analysis and discuss their relevance for Communist Romania in the 1980s and beyond.

TERRITORIAL UNITY AND THE LEGACY OF WORLD WAR I

Structural changes in Romanian political life during and immediately after World War I were so fundamental and far-reaching that to call Ion I. C. Bratianu's return to power in January 1922, after twenty-seven months in opposition, a "return to normal" of Romanian politics is very problematic.[13] For what was normal after 1922 bore little resemblance to what had existed before the war, when the National Liberal and Conservative parties, whose opposition to one another was more system-functional than ideological, took turns in the seat of power with little regard for preferences expressed by the public. And what set the tone for Romanian interwar politics was not the long and relatively stable Bratianu government of 1922-1926, but the turbulence of 1918-1921, when it seemed that no party was capable of governing for more than a few months at a time.[14] In fact, to understand the legacy of World War I in Romanian politics, it may be necessary to abandon the idea--sacrosanct to Romanian historians--of continuity in political structure between Old Kingdom Romania of before the war and the vastly enlarged state of the interwar years.

Many factors contributed to the discontinuity, which ironically occurred at the end of a long historical evolution toward the unification of all ethnic Romanians in a single state. Traditional analysis holds that the most notable shift in political patterns right after the war was caused by the disappearance of the old Conservative Party[15] and the concomitant rise of new political formations, some of which were very short-lived, to take its place. But the Conservative Party had been in considerable disarray even before the war, due to rivalries among its leaders and sharp disagreement over the entry of Romania into the war itself. The blows suffered by the Conservatives as a result of land reform and universal suffrage measures promised during the war to sustain the Romanian military effort and enacted at war's end, and the disastrous effect on party prestige caused by Conservative Alexandru Marghiloman's conclusion of a highly unfavorable separate peace treaty with Germany in May 1918, simply hastened a process already begun.[16] The final decline of this party, therefore, through the demise of Take Ionescu's "Democratic" wing in 1922 and of Marghiloman's "Progressive" wing in 1924, cannot itself have caused the structural discontinuity between the prewar and interwar Romanian regimes.

To discover real causes one must look not at the parties which passed away, but at those which took the old parties' places and the forces which shaped them. For, contrary to what Stefan Zeletin wrote at the time, it was not the social and democratic reform program precipitated by the war, i.e., the program which hastened the decline of the Conservative Party, but rather the successful creation of Greater Romania (<u>Romania Mare</u>) itself which "transformed the old mechanism of our political life, which had been so clear and so simple up to that time."[17] In this respect, what happened in Romania was comparable to what was happening in the other aggrandized or newly created successor states of East Central Europe. Many political problems of the region were rooted in the extraordinary difficulty of integrating into single administrative units territories which were formerly parts of two, three, or, in the Romanian case, even four different states.[18] To the extent that political parties vying for power in the successor states failed to adjust their behavior and outlook to drastically altered territorial situations, they were largely incapable of responding successfully to the challenges and demands of governing their states.

In Romania, each of the political parties claiming to be "national" after the war remained regional in outlook, organizational apparatus, and support base for some time. In the hope of coming to power without the benefit of nationwide constituencies, they resorted to electoral maneuvers and political tactics that stripped them of most ideological bearings and led to the disorientation and early crises of the interwar regime. In short, <u>the achievement of national territorial unity in the absence of national parties destabilized rather than stabilized Romania's political system</u>.

What did that system look like in the early postwar years? Four parties seemed to hold the future of

Romania in their hands.

The National Liberal Party

The National Liberal Party, which long before the war had come to be dominated by urban social and financial elites of the Old Kingdom (i.e., pre-1914 Romania, commonly referred to as the Regat), could no longer pose after the war as spokesman for the country's overwhelmingly peasant masses, in opposition to the land-owning gentry which had tended to concentrate in the Conservative Party. Newly enfranchised and anxious to make certain that the land reform promised by King Ferdinand and the Liberals in 1917 would actually serve peasant interests, the peasantry naturally sought its own representatives (see the discussion of the Peasant Party below). The Liberal Party survived the reaction against the prewar regime which swept through the Regat in the 1918-1921 period essentially because of the central role played by the party's long-time leader, Ion I. C. Bratianu, in gaining international recognition (or at least acceptance) of Romania's postwar borders. But the party's position was greatly weakened, as became clear in the first postwar elections, held in November 1919. Supervised by a specially appointed non-party government led by General Artur Vaitoianu and composed mainly of military men, these were the first elections held since Romanian idependence in 1878 in which the state bureaucracy did not step in to control the outcome.[19] The Liberals, who had been in power up to September 26, when Vaitoianu was appointed, got only 21 percent of the total number of votes cast nationwide (see Table 2.1). In the Regat including Dobrudja--that is, in their prewar bastions--the Liberals not only failed to win a majority but barely garnered one third of the votes cast (see Table 2.3). In the country's new provinces they did not even have candidates to run.

Rudely awakened to the electoral realities of universal suffrage and to the adverse consequences for their party of Bratianu's successes at the Paris Peace Conference, the Liberals immediately initiated a campaign designed to lay the groundwork for a return to power. Their strategy was simple. First, allow time for popular reaction against the old regime, of which they were the principal surviving element, to subside. The Liberals did not attempt a return to power until 1922. Second, stymie the consolidation of parties which could challenge their domination in the Regat. This policy explains the Liberal Party's support of the candidates of the People's Party in the elections of 1920 and 1926, as discussed below. Finally, overcome regional limitations on Liberal influence by expanding the party's organizational apparatus into Romania's new provinces. Since only a nationwide organizational network and electoral base could enable the Liberal Party to wield power as it had before 1919, the party solemnly declared in its program statement prior to the May 1920 elections:

> The Liberal Party believes it to be its duty after the elections to extend its political activity into the entire territory of the country, since the Liberal Party is the party with the greatest responsibility for the achievement and development of Greater Romania.[20]

In 1920-1921, even as the Liberals were attempting to extend their influence into Transylvania, the Banat, Bucovina, and Bessarabia by means of cooperative arrangements with parties already established there, they worked diligently to organize on their own in these provinces as well.[21] By March 1922, when the next national parliamentary elections were held, the results were already apparent. The Liberals received over 40 percent of the votes cast in Transylvania and the Banat and nearly 20 percent of the vote in Bessarabia (see Table 2.3). They failed to make inroads only in Bucovina, where the provincially based Democratic Unity Party of Bucovina continued its near monopoly among ethnic Romanians at the polls (see Table 2.1). The Liberals had made a giant step away from the regionalism they inherited from the war and toward the establishment of a national constituency.[22]

The People's Party

Unlike the National Liberal Party, which had managed to survive the postwar reaction against the old regime, the People's League--after April 1920, the People's Party--founded at Iasi in April 1918 grew out of the widespread popular resentment. Former Conservative Party members and a group of army officers joined forces around wartime hero General Alexandru Averescu in a cynical attempt to save the manipulative and authoritarian prewar order. They hoped that the high level of public disaffection from the country's old parties might lead the politically inexperienced, newly enfranchised masses to vote for any new one.[23] For a while it seemed they might be right. In 1918-1920 the People's League attracted members and supporters from all provinces of Greater Romania (see Table 2.3) and negotiated with a broad range of parties for electoral cartels or permanent mergers which might put the League in control of the country.[24] The negotiations produced no long-term alignments, but they did catapult Averescu to power in March 1920, at the head of the country's eighth government since the fall of Marghiloman's wartime cabinet eighteen months earlier.

Averescu became Prime Minister with the support of the National Liberals, who feared that the Parliamentary Bloc coalition of five parties governing Romania since the 1919 elections might solidify into a permanent and powerful competitor if not broken up quickly.[25] The Liberals hoped that Averescu would be able to run the country long enough for the Liberals to arrange their own return to power. Averescu reduced the size of the Chamber of Deputies from 568 to 369 seats, imposing the most drastic cuts on the provinces where neither his own party nor the National Liberal Party was strong,[26] and then announced new elections for the end of May. In the elections, the People's Party won 44 percent of all the votes cast in the Regat (including Dobrudja) and Bessarabia, 39 percent of the vote in Bucovina, and 69 out of 121 seats in Transylvania and the Banat (see Table 2.3). With 224 of the 369 seats in the Chamber--126 from the Old Kingdom and 98 more from the new provinces--the People's Party temporarily appeared to be developing into the second "government" party of Romania.

This status was more the result of Liberal design, however, than of People's Party efforts or merit, and it became clear even before the elections of May 1920 how fragile the "national" character of Averescu's movement was. The support which the People's Party had from leaders of Romania's new provinces began to dissipate as soon as Averescu moved to centralize the state administration. Only three weeks after assuming office, he issued two decree-laws on April 2-3, 1920, which ordered the abolition of the autonomous Ruling Council (Consiliu Dirigent) in Transylvania and the quasi-autonomous administrative directorates established for Bucovina and Bessarabia when they became parts of Romania. These institutions had been set up to preserve a degree of self-rule in the three provinces pending the adoption of a new constitution for Greater Romania to replace the prewar Regat constitution of 1866. When they were abolished prior to the calling of a constitutional convention, the leading political figures from the three provinces who had joined Averescu's government resigned in protest. Vasile Goldis of the Romanian National Party of Transylvania left the post of Minister of State for Transylvania; Ion Inculet, a leading member of the Bessarabian Peasant Party, resigned as Minister of State for Bessarabia; and Ion Nistor of the Democratic Unity Party of Bucovina left the post of Minister of State for Bucovina. Both Inculet and Nistor ultimately led their followers into the National Liberal fold.[27]

Averescu stayed in power for twenty-one months. During this time he succeeded in alienating not only initial supporters from Romania's new provinces, but also members of the Parliamentary Bloc parties who had supported him for the sake of maintaining order in the state and keeping the Liberals away from direct control of the government apparatus. It became clear that Averescu's government could not last, however, only when he began to quarrel openly with the Liberals as well.[28] On December 13, 1921, General Averescu forwarded his resignation to King Ferdinand, who accepted it. Slightly more than a month later, the Liberal Party was back in power.

In opposition, the People's Party rapidly lost any appeal it had left among the masses and gradually declined to little more than a coterie of devoted followers gathered around Averescu's person.[29] The party returned to power briefly, again with Liberal Party support, from March 1926 to June 1927, after the expiration of the four-year parliamentary mandate obtained by the Liberals in the elections of March 1922. But after this, the People's Party never again received more than 5 percent of the vote in the national parliamentary elections, and from 1933 onward could not even gather the 2 percent of the vote required under the electoral law of 1926 to gain representation in the Chamber of Deputies (see Table 2.4). What support there was for Averescu came predominantly from the Regat--from Averescu's native Oltenia and a few electoral districts around Bucharest. When the party reverted from national to regional status, it became an insignificant force in the interwar parliamentary regime.[30]

With the People's Party clearly on the decline as early as 1922, other parties quickly came to the fore as foci of public attention and possible challengers to the Liberals for dominance.

The Romanian National Party

In Transylvania and the Banat, the Romanian National Party, which had represented the Romanians of Habsburg Hungary at Budapest before the war, had a virtual monopoly on power after the Alba Iulia assembly of December 1918 voted in favor of unification of the provinces with the Regat. Ruling these provinces through the autonomous Ruling Council established at Alba Iulia, the party did all it could to preserve itself as the only organized political force among ethnic Romanians in the lands ceded to Romania by Hungary in the Treaty of Trianon (1920). The electoral law which it drafted for these lands (including Crisana and Maramures as well as Transylvania proper and the Banat) in August 1919 established a single-member-majority system of voting by electoral district. The law was intended to prevent smaller parties from obtaining proportional representation in the Chamber of Deputies, and thus to discourage the process of proliferation of parties already evident in the Regat. It also included a special stipulation that when only one candidate sought office in a district, no vote was required.[31]

When elections were held for the first parliament of Greater Romania in November 1919, 144 seats were awarded in Transylvania and the Banat to candidates unopposed in their districts, while actual voting was required in only 61 of 205 districts. The Romanian National Party secured for itself 199 of the 205 seats assigned to these provinces and thus became the strongest party in the Chamber of Deputies in Bucharest (see Tables 2.1 and 2.3).

But the National Party was a regional party par excellence, with no electoral support outside Transylvania and the Banat and with little desire to have such support if it meant sacrificing control in its home provinces. One of the leaders of the party, Alexandru Vaida-Voevod, presided over the Parliamentary Bloc government of November 1919-March 1920, but the president of the party, Iuliu Maniu, refused to occupy a position in the central government, preferring instead to remain head of the Ruling Council.[32] Despite defections from National Party ranks to Regat parties—especially to the People's Party at this early date—in protest over Maniu's parochial resistance to the dismantling of the Ruling Council,[33] it was not until after Averescu abolished the Council that Maniu acknowledged the need for greater communication and cooperation with Regat parties if the National Party were to remain a potential government party in Greater Romania.

In late 1921, Maniu entered into negotiations for cooperation with the National Liberal Party, but he made agreement conditional on a Liberal commitment not to organize independently on National Party turf. The Liberals refused this, and negotiations broke down.[34] The National Party did absorb the remains of Take Ionescu's Democratic Conservative Party in 1922 and temporarily merged with the electorally impotent National Democratic Party of Nicolae Iorga and Constantin Argetoianu in January 1925. But the inconclusive results of its intermittent negotiations with the Peasant Party from 1923 on reinforced the image of the National Party as willing to join forces only with parties unable to challenge its dominance in Transylvania and the Banat. Regional interests weighed far more heavily than ideological outlook or systemic considerations in determining National Party behavior.[35]

Only Averescu's reemergence as Prime Minister in March 1926 and the specter of the People's Party as the second government party in a Liberal-run state catalyzed the National Party into action.[36] Maniu agreed to an electoral cartel with the Peasant Party for the May 1926 elections, while groups within both parties declared themselves in favor of permanent fusion. Finally, in September 1926, Maniu and Peasant Party President Ion Mihalache reached a ten-point programmatic and organizational agreement, and on October 10 the two parties, meeting in joint congress, ratified their merger into the National Peasant Party.[37] Iorga and Argetoianu, as well as some former Democratic Conservatives, withdrew from the National Party rather than accept merger with the Peasantists. But in the final analysis the merger increased the power of the Transylvanian party. Maniu became president of the new party and its dominant personality. Two years after the merger he was called upon to be Prime Minister (November 28, 1928).

The Peasant Party

The Peasant Party, with which the Transylvanian Nationals had joined forces, had its origins in prewar Romania as a disparate and poorly coordinated movement among well-to-do peasants, rural educators, and village priests to obtain the right to vote and land for Romania's peasant masses.[38] Conditions for a peasantist political party, however, did not exist until both of these goals had been reached. Consequently, it was not until December 1918, a few weeks after the withdrawal of German troops from the Regat and following King Ferdinand's reaffirmation--on November 12--of his 1917 pledge of agrarian reform, that the Peasant Party formally came into existence.

The clear initial intent of the new party's founders was to make peasant social and economic interests of primary concern in the new state and, by preventing the peasantry from remaining the "governmental dowry" (zestre guvernamentala) of parties of other classes, to make the peasant voice dominant in Romanian politics as well.[39] The radical platform statements the party made prior to the November 1919 elections, stressing egalitarianism among peasants, peasant solidarity, and "class struggle," were inspired by the thinking of Bessarabian populist Constantin Stere.[40] Such ideas won the Peasantists of the Regat and Bessarabia 46 percent of the votes cast in those provinces, as the Peasant Party emerged as the strongest political force in the Old Kingdom (see Tables 2.1 and 2.3). Riding the wave of resentment against the old regime, the Peasant Party emerged with the second largest delegation in the Chamber of Deputies, after the Transylvanian National Party, and occupied an influential position in the Parliamentary Bloc government formed after the elections.

Nevertheless, after the Parliamentary Bloc was ousted from power in March 1920, in the wake of King Ferdinand's refusal to sign the progressive land reform bill proposed by the president of the Peasant Party, Minister of Agriculture and Domains Ion Mihalache, the Peasantists decided upon a process of ideological compromise as a means of returning to power. Under the guidance of Mihalache and chief Peasantist economist and theoretician Virgil Madgearu, the party gradually backed off from the "class struggle" verbiage which had colored many of its early ideological statements, and began to portray itself as a "defender of the peasantry" rather than as the sole representative of peasant interests and peasant interests alone. It sought to appear as the leader of a political, rather than class, struggle against Liberal Party domination of the country. Romania was not to become a peasant state, as party rhetoric once implied, but neither would the interests of the peasantry be disregarded.[41]

Even before the 1919 elections, the Peasant Party had sought to bolster its chances at the polls by cooperating with other parties. It discussed cooperation with Iorga's National Democrats and went so far as to offer the chairmanship of the Peasant Party to General Averescu. Neither plan bore fruit.[42] The Bessarabian Peasant Party, founded in 1917 and led by Constantin Stere, Pantelimon Halippa, and Ion Inculet, however, did begin to cooperate closely with the Peasant Party of the Regat in 1919, and those elements of the party truly peasantist in outlook merged with the Regat party in 1921. The peasantist splinter group led by Dr. Nicolae Lupu also entered the Peasant Party at this time.[43] Still, the Peasantists made little headway in Transylvania, the Banat, and Bucovina during the early 1920s (see Table 2.3), and despite being the strongest opposition party in the Regat and Bessarabia, lacked sufficient strength to come to power.[44]

This led, as we have seen, to drawn-out negotiations with the Romanian National Party and finally to a merger of the two parties in 1926. Along the way the Peasantists sacrificed much of their radical peasantism, though they continued to represent peasant interests far more than the Liberals did. Mihalache became a vice president of the National Peasant Party. Dr. Lupu, also initially a vice president of the new party, withdrew a few months after the merger to protest National Party domination of the new organization.[45] Mihail Manoilescu, a professor of economics and the leading advocate of corporatism in Romania, summed up the nature of the merger when he pointed out that it was a "union of social regionalism and geographic regionalism which attenuated the regional character of the National Party and the class character of the Peasant Party."[46] It was evident that the new party, which joined together the strongest political movements of the Old Kingdom and of the new provinces, would be a force to be reckoned with. King Ferdinand, who hoped that recreating the prewar two-party "rotational" system of government would bring stability to Romanian politics, readily acknowledged that the hybrid National Peasant Party might potentially serve on a regular basis as the second government party of Romania.[47] But he distrusted Maniu, who had refused to attend the King's coronation at Alba Iulia in October 1922, and refused to call the new party to power during the few months preceding the monarch's untimely death in July 1927.

Thus, the postwar Romanian party structure consisted of four major parties, each regional in its basis of support and outlook, each with an ill-defined or changing ideological orientation, and each looking for a formula which would enable it to come to power. How did the country fare under these four parties--which became three after the merger of the Romanian National and Peasant parties in 1926? More specifically, did the parties remain the limited, regional forces of the immediate postwar years, or did they succeed in making themselves authentic national parties? Did they attack the past and close the gap between ruler and ruled by engaging people in political processes and promoting greater political awareness among the masses? Finally, did they make progress toward the creation of a viable and defensible political system in the new Greater Romanian state? Affirmative answers to these questions would indicate that significant steps were made during the interwar period toward overcoming the historical dilemmas of Romanian politics, in the direction of political modernity.

STATISTICAL ANALYSIS OF INTERWAR POLITICS

Although they are not entirely reliable, returns from Greater Romania's ten national parliamentary elections, as published in the government's Monitorul Oficial (Official Monitor), can help determine whether such answers exist. These returns are compiled in Tables 2.1-2.8 to show: (1) the share of the total number of votes cast received by each party in each election; (2) the share of the vote received by parties which headed governments between 1919 and 1937, by province, and for 1922 through 1937, the increase in the share of the vote each party received when it organized the elections and controlled the electoral bureaucracy, also by province; (3) the share of the vote received by major right-wing extremist parties between 1926 and 1937, by province; (4) the share of total National Liberal Party vote which came from the Regat in each election; (5) trends from 1926 to 1937 in the size of the voting group which shifted its support according to who ran a particular election; and (6) the total number of voters and the percentage of eligible voters actually voting in each election, by province.[48] What do these data reveal?

Regional or National Parties?

First, they indicate that despite difficulties of national integration which Romania faced after World War I, the country's political parties did overcome the regional character they inherited from the war and the peace settlements.[49] From 1919 to 1928, a series of small regional parties, each closely identified with one or another of the provinces thrust together in Greater Romania, disappeared altogether. The two most important of these, the Bessarabian Peasant Party, which received nearly 80 percent of the vote in Bessarabia in 1919, and the Democratic Unity Party of Bucovina which received a similar proportion of the vote in Bucovina in both 1919 and 1922, had represented the desire for union with the Regat in their provinces during the war and had voted that union after the war. Both broke up in the early 1920s, as leaders of different factions led their followers into the National Liberal Party, People's Party, or Peasant Party, according to where each felt his interests could best be served.[50] The strength of some other parties, which were regionally based though not bound to any specific province's interests, also declined. Alexandru C. Cuza's anti-Semitic League of National Christian Defense, which drew its support from Moldavia in the Regat and from Bessarabia, received 4.7 percent of the national vote in 1926, but only 1.9 percent in 1927, and 1.1 percent in 1928. Similarly, support for Nicolae Iorga's National Democratic Party, based in the Regat, fell from over 5 percent in the Regat Dobrudja, and Bessarabia in 1919 to under 3 percent in 1922; in 1926 the party received less than 2 percent of the national vote and was excluded from the Chamber of Deputies altogether. The leaders of such parties moved in and out of the major parties, losing ideological bearings, followers, and rationale for their parties' independent existence.[51] The result was a general reduction in the number of parties which contested elections, from ten to twelve in 1919/1922 to seven to eight in 1926/28, as well as a reduction in the number of parties (or electoral coalitions) which actually won parliamentary seats, from eight to nine in 1919/1922 to only three to five in 1926/1928 (see Tables 2.1 and 2.2). The two-percent-minimum rule of the electoral law of 1926 in effect forced smaller, often regional, parties into electoral cartels or permanent mergers with larger, more national ones to obtain even token parliamentary representation and did much to reduce the fragmentation of Romania's political forces evident immediately after the war.

At the same time that small parties were declining in strength and numbers, the two "government parties" of interwar Romania--the National Liberal Party and the National Peasant Party--were steadily broadening their electoral strength in provinces outside their initial strongholds, and each eventually reached a position where it drew support more or less evenly in all regions of the country. To see this development, it is necessary to look at the electoral strength of each party not when it controlled the government at election time and could use the bureaucracy to cajole or coerce voters into supporting "the government slate" of candidates, but rather when it contested elections while "in opposition," when all odds were against it receiving votes from voters who did not have a permanent attachment to the party in question.[52] The share of the vote received by a party "in opposition" can be considered a fair measure of the party's firm base of support or real electoral strength.

The share of total votes cast received by the National Liberal Party when it was in opposition, for example--i.e., in the elections of 1919, 1920, 1926, 1928, and 1932--rose steadily in Transylvania, the Banat, and Bucovina from zero in all three provinces in 1919 and 1920 to 8 percent, 9 percent, and 12 percent respectively in 1932; and in Bessarabia, where the party got no votes in 1919 and only 1.25 percent of the vote in 1920, the Liberals got nearly 10 percent in 1932. These levels of real support in a country where the number of uncommitted voters was extremely high (see the discussion of the "governmental dowry" below) and in provinces where the Liberal Party had not even had candidates to run immediately after the war represented a significant achievement. They were not far below the party's real electoral strength in 1932 in provinces where the Liberals had done well from the start. In that year the party received 19 percent of the vote in the Regat and 15 percent in Dobrudja (see Tables 2.3 and 2.4).

That support for the Liberals became more evenly distributed throughout Romania as time went on is confirmed by the data in Table 2.6, which indicate that the proportion of the party's support which came from the Regat and Dobrudja showed a marked downward trend from 1919, when these provinces accounted for all of the party's votes, to 1937, when the party got only 55.7 percent of its votes here. Since just half of all votes cast nationwide originated in the Regat and Dobrudja, Liberal reliance on these provinces for voter support after 1928 cannot be said to have been disproportionate.[53] Clearly, then, between the 1920s and the 1930s the Liberal Party made great strides toward shedding its regional character and consolidating its position as a truly national party.

It is difficult to apply the same sort of analysis to the National Peasant Party, since its nationwide status was based on the merger of two regional parties rather than on the expansion of a single party from traditional base areas into new provinces. Nevertheless, it is clear from Table 2.4 that as the National Peasant Party's strength in opposition declined from almost 28 percent in 1926, when a nation tired of Liberal and Averescan rule gave it the largest share of the vote ever won by an opposition party, to a more realistic 22 percent in 1927, and finally to a low of 14 percent in 1933, when the country had tired in turn of National Peasant rule, the party lost proportionately more support in the National Party's traditional electoral strongholds than it did in the Peasant Party's base areas. Real support (i.e., support when the party was in opposition) for the party declined steadily between 1926-1927 and 1933 from its maximum of 35 to 40 percent of the vote in Transylvania to 14 percent and from 30 to 37 percent of the vote in the Banat to under 12 percent, reflecting an unabated erosion of the National Party's one-time monopoly status in these provinces. In contrast, while support for the National Peasantists in the Regat and Bessarabia did fall between the mid-1920s and early 1930s, most of the decline was over with quickly, by 1927-1928, after which support for the party held steady in these provinces overall and actually rose slightly in the Regat proper and Bessarabia during the 1930s. On the whole, losses for the party were smaller in these provinces, where the peasantist philosophy of the party, though diluted, continued to appeal to large numbers of voters.

One result of this was that by the early 1930s the party was receiving more or less equal support in all provinces. In 1927, voter support had varied markedly from province to province, ranging from a low of 11.5 percent in Bessarabia to a high of 39.8 percent in Transylvania (see Table 2.4). By 1933, the range was much narrower, with a low of 11.0 percent in Bucovina and a high of 15.4 percent in the Regat. To an even greater degree than National Liberals, the National Peasantists had developed a regionally balanced nationwide voter base.

Of course, the National Peasant Party continued to have regional forces at work inside it, and the interests of Regat-based elements frequently came into conflict with those of the country's new provinces. Such conflicts are normal in any moderate-sized country, however, and in Romania regional interests developed inside the once homogeneous National Liberal Party as well, especially after the economic crisis of 1929-1933 weakened the financial position of Regat-based Liberal banking institutions. That regional tensions continued to complicate National Peasant Party life was less significant than the fact that the party survived divisive years of decision-making during the economic crisis and emerged united in the 1930s to defend parliamentarism at home and the status quo abroad.[54] By this time, the hybrid party of 1926 had developed a national outlook and perspective suitable for its nationwide electoral base.

Thus, both National Liberals and National Peasantists overcame much of the regional parochialism acquired by Romanian political parties as a consequence of Romania's victories in war and peacemaking. By the mid-1930s, both parties reflected in outlook and support base the national territorial unity achieved in 1918-1920.

Ruler and Ruled in Interwar Politics

But what was the significance of the electoral support each of these parties received? Did elections make a difference in Romanian politics, or were elections really so corrupt--and the results so manipulated--as to be meaningless? Did voters merely cast ballots, or did they participate in political processes?

There can be little doubt that Romanian parliamentary elections did not provide an accurate measure of voter support for the party in power. Parties which organized elections generally won overwhelming victories, and crushing electoral majorities shifted rapidly from party to party according to which party was in control of the electoral bureaucracy.[55] In part, this was the result of coercion and corruption at the polls. But a factor at least as important was the existence of a large number of voters, newly enfranchised and with little political education or awareness, who voted "for the government" no matter which party was in power. Prewar Romania's feudal tradition had taught respect for--and fear of--authority. After the war, this translated for those who had benefited from the enactment of universal suffrage and land reform into the belief that "the government" was the only source of relief from the harshness of their lives. Large numbers of these citizens either always voted for the government chosen by the king or, at the very least, were highly susceptible to government pressure at the polls.

Automatic--or coerced--voting for the government by this element of the electorate and the manipulation of polling results accounted for the swing bloc of votes which parties running elections received in interwar Romania. Others who have looked at election returns from this period have called this swing bloc of votes, which was invariably much larger than the real strength of either major party, the "governmental dowry." The same term had been used in Romanian politics before World War I and in the early platform statements of the Peasant Party of the Regat to signify voters whose votes did not necessarily reflect their own interests. The approximate size of the dowry can be measured by subtracting from the vote a party received when running the governmental electoral machinery the vote it received in the last previous election when it was "in opposition."[56] Such calculations can only be approximate, of course, since citizens outside the "governmental dowry" undoubtedly shifted their votes from time to time. In addition, the support provided by small parties running in electoral cartel on common lists with major parties can only be estimated, and these estimates have to be subtracted from the vote tallies of the common lists before the dowry received by the major party can be determined.[57] Finally, it is difficult to say how much of the governmental dowry actually represented swing voters and how much resulted from the manipulation of electoral returns after the polls had closed. One can only assume that each party was fairly consistent over the years in the amount of manipulation it employed. On the whole the National Liberals were more prone, and the National Peasantists less prone, to falsify polling results.

Despite such difficulties, the notion of the governmental dowry is a useful tool for examining the evolution of Romania's parliamentary system. Table 2.4 shows the approximate size of the dowry received by the party in power in each election as a share of the total vote cast in each province and nationwide. The Liberal Party controlled the government during the elections of 1922, 1927, 1931, 1933, and 1937;[58] the National Peasant Party, in 1928 and 1932; and the People's Party, in 1926. What do these calculations of the dowry indicate?

First, they support the hypothesis that low levels of political education and awareness resulted in high levels of automatic--or coerced--voting for the government. The governmental dowry was highest in provinces which had lower than average living standards and cultural levels, while provinces with higher living standards and higher levels of mass culture produced lower dowries. The pattern of covariance was more or less the same in every election: smaller dowries in the relatively more advanced Banat and Transylvania--though the existence here of large national minority parties which consistently won many Magyar and German votes certainly made the dowries smaller than might have been expected on the basis of development level alone;[59] a somewhat larger dowry in Bucovina, where the existence of German and Jewish parties again made the dowries deceptively low, however; a considerably larger dowry in the Regat, where the level of mass culture was much lower than in any of the lands formerly part of Austria-Hungary and where minority parties had little effective support; and the largest dowry in Bessarabia, unquestionably Greater Romania's most backward province. The oversized dowry in Dobrudja was deceptive in terms of the level of development of the province, and may be attributed to automatic voting for the government by the Bulgar and Turkic ethnic minorities, which were not organized into their own political parties, and by the Romanian and Macedo-Vlach colonists settled in the region after World War I and dependent on the central government for their physical and economic security.[60] In terms of cultural development and living standards, Dobrudja probably fell somewhere between the Regat proper and Bessarabia.

Based on these data, it is possible to argue that in the more advanced regions of the country fewer voters supported the government list of candidates out of a lack of political conviction or awareness. In the Banat, Transylvania, and to some extent Bucovina--all once parts of the Habsburg domains--greater political maturity and greater socioeconomic differentiation appear to have produced in the electorate an awareness of differentiated interests and, as a result, lower dowries. In the Regat, Dobrudja, and Bessarabia--areas long under Ottoman and Tsarist domination--less political awareness had developed, and larger dowries resulted.

If one accepts this line of reasoning, what happened to the governmental dowry over time in Greater Romania takes on special significance. A shrinking dowry could indicate increasing levels of public awareness and greater engagement of voters in political processes--i.e., a narrowing of the gap between rulers and ruled in Romanian political life.

In fact, from 1927-1928 onward, the size of the governmental dowry declined, and drastically so, in nearly every part of the country.[61] In elections run by the Liberals, it fell from over 60 percent of the vote in the three more backward provinces in 1927 to between 38 and 48 percent in the same provinces in 1933, and further declined to 21 to 30 percent in 1937, when the Liberals were prevented from making full use of coercion at the polls.[62] Between 1928 and 1932, when the National Peasantists ran elections, the dowries they received in these provinces fell even more precipitously from over 60 percent to 20 to 37 percent in less than five years.

In the more advanced provinces, National Peasant Party dowries declined to a similar extent, as the monopolistic hold of the old National Party on Transylvania and the Banat broke up. The dowries of the National Liberals in these two provinces, by contrast, increased slightly between 1927 and 1933. This bucking of a trend can be attributed to four factors: (1) continued willingness of the Liberals to apply more pressure on uncommitted voters than the National Peasantists did;[63] (2) actual increased popularity of the Liberal Party as a result of the party reorganization carried out in the early 1930s by Ion G. Duca;[64] (3) improved Liberal Party apparatuses in these provinces; and (4) exaggerated hopes pinned to the Liberals' return to power, after a lengthy period of economic crisis and ineffectual National Peasantist government. The reversal was an occurrence of a specific historical moment in a specific region of the country and did not alter, as the results of the 1937 elections demonstrated, the overall downward trend in this region, as elsewhere, in the size of the governmental dowry. In the four elections run by the Liberals after 1926, the dowry fell from 54 percent of the national vote total in 1927 to only 37 percent in 1931, then to 35 percent in 1933, and finally reached a low of 22 percent in 1937. In elections run by the National Peasantists the decline in the size of the dowry was similar, from 52 percent of the electorate in 1928 to 24 percent in 1932.

At the national level, the governmental dowry of each major party fell from over 50 percent of the electorate early in the interwar period to just over 20 percent at the end of it (see Table 2.7). Part of this decline can be attributed to a slow but steady drop in the percentage of eligible voters who actually cast ballots, from a high of 77 percent in 1927 to 66 percent in 1937 (see Table 2.8). It is reasonable to assume that a majority of those who dropped out of the electoral process had been part of the uncommitted or easily swayed bloc of voters which made up the governmental dowry. A more substantial decline of voters actually voting in the less developed provinces where the dowry was greatest supports this view. Certainly disillusionment was not universal, however, for the absolute number of voters casting ballots increased somewhat in every election. Apparently, the inability of successive governments to resolve major problems, especially those linked to the economic crisis, led to the failure of some marginal voters to develop an attachment to any party and, ultimately, to disillusionment with the electoral process itself. Consequently, starting in 1931 and 1932, many of these people stopped voting, and government majorities began to shrink. In 1927 and 1928, the parties in power won over 60 percent of the total national vote. After that, the winning slate of candidates only once surpassed 50 percent of the vote (see Table 2.4).

But even if one assumed that all those who ceased voting had been in the ranks of the governmental dowry, the drop in voter participation (11 percent nationally) accounts for but one third of the decline in the size of the dowry itself (30 percent nationally). The remaining two thirds, as well as a majority of new voters, together representing some 20 to 30 percent of the total electorate, either escaped the dowry or, in the case of new voters, never entered it. This suggests that a process of political awakening was taking place among the masses in Romania during the interwar period. Organization by the political parties and greater sophistication in the electorate made the average voter less willing to accept the notion that only "the government" could help him, and more aware of the significance of policy positions assumed by contesting parties. As a result, he became less susceptible to government pressure and less fickle at election time. Between 20 and 30 percent more of the electorate cast meaningful ballots in the 1930s than had done so in the 1920s.

Political Profile of the 1930s

In Romania, greater political awareness and greater differentiation of views within the electorate fostered an increase in the number of political parties in the 1930s (see Table 2.2), and there can be no doubt that the reproliferation of parties, so shortly after the reduction of their number in the 1920s, destabilized the political system.[65] The extremism of the new parties, which was mostly right-wing extremism, was also a destabilizing factor. But from our perspective, what was most interesting was that as the six most significant new parties increased their combined share of the national vote dramatically, from under 5 percent in 1928 to over 20 percent in 1932 and 1933, and finally to 30 percent in 1937,[66] there was no decrease in the real electoral strength of the major moderate parties. Liberal Party voting strength while "in opposition" actually grew from 6.5 percent of the electorate in 1928 to 13.6 percent in 1932, while the National Peasant Party, after losing some support in the late 1920s, maintained a fairly stable strength "in opposition" of approximately 14 percent during the 1930s. Moreover, in provinces where the principal right-wing extremist parties increased their strength most spectacularly--in Bucovina in the case of the Iron Guard, and in Bessarabia and Northern Moldavia in the case of the combined League of National Christian Defense and National Agrarian Party--the moderate parties not only did not lose strength, but on a combined basis actually grew more powerful. The National Peasant Party gained supporters in these regions even as it lost them elsewhere (compare Tables 2.4 and 2.5).[67]

Not surprisingly, the governmental dowry declined most precipitously where both extremists and moderates were expanding their electoral bases. The votes received by the new extremist parties did not come from the permanent voter bases of the moderate parties, as has often been assumed, but from the ever-dwindling governmental dowry. New support for the moderates came from the dowry as well. In other words, during the 1930s marginal voters, previously politically indifferent or easily swayed by the pressures applied or enticements offered by the party in power, cast aside their passivity at election time and voted according to their interests as they understood them. Some voted their belief in new philosophies which promised comprehensive social and political change; some merely voted their disillusionment with old ways, as the better life the masses had expected in Greater Romania failed to materialize; and some voted continued faith in the moderate two-party structure, which they hoped could be reformed.[68] All showed new sophistication and awareness.

The decline in the size of the governmental dowry, therefore, reflected the engagement of masses of voters enfranchised after World War I in the workings of the Romanian political system. The proliferation of political parties did not signal disorientation, but rather the first step toward the transformation of the Romanian system from one of passive acceptance of the status quo by the voter to one of more conscious mass participation in the determination of the country's future course. To the extent that extremist parties benefited from the political polarization of the electorate, it was because people were looking for new solutions to Greater Romania's problems. The supporters of Mihail Manoilescu's corporatism, Alexandru Vaida-Voevod's Romanian Front movement, Gheorghe Bratianu's "Young Liberals," and the National Christian Party of Octavian Goga and Alexandru C. Cuza, wanted to sacrifice a measure of parliamentary democracy for the sake of "progress" and more efficient use of the country's resources. Advocates of King Carol's dictatorship had essentially the same goals. Only the Iron Guard sought more comprehensive, revolutionary change and an end to the bureaucratic machine that Liberals and National Peasantists alike had used to control democracy in Romania and that Carol tried to use to modernize the country.[69]

As polarization of the electorate proceeded, the real electoral strength of the moderate "government parties," the National Liberals and the National Peasantists, settled at about the same level--about 14 percent for each party in 1932-1933. Support for the Liberals had risen to this level from a much lower 6 to 7 percent in the 1920s despite the departure from the party of Gheorghe Bratianu and his followers in 1931. Throughout the 1930s, this Bratianu's "Young Liberals" attracted 4 to 6 percent of the national vote. The National Peasantists, on the other hand, saw their support decline from over 20 percent of the national vote before they first came to power in the late 1920s to the 14 percent level. These losses were related to the party's inability in office to keep promises made while in opposition and subsequent inability to regain power after 1933, as well as to the resignation from the party of four leading cadres and their followers. The parties of these four-- Nicolae Lupu, Grigore Iunian, Constantin Stere, and Alexandru Vaida-Voevod--controlled some 7 percent of the national vote in the mid-1930s (see Table 2.2).[70]

When it became clear that the interwar political system might be in danger, the two parties which stood at its heart began to reconsolidate lost strength, however. Nicolae Lupu reentered the National Peasant Party in March 1934; Stere and Iunian seriously considered reunification with the National Peasantists in January 1938; and Gheorghe Bratianu, preparing for elections scheduled for March, reentered the National Liberal Party on January 17, 1938.[71] Apparently King Carol II, whose role in Romanian politics has always been a matter of controversy, had not been as effective at destroying the moderate "government parties" as historians--and contemporaries of the events, for that matter--have tended to believe.[72] The factionalism that he promoted may have weakened the interwar parliamentary mechanism, but the interwar system broke down in 1938 because of foreign pressures to which the engagement of formerly uncommitted voters in extremist causes exposed the state, rather than as a consequence of King Carol's machinations against the moderate parties.[73] In 1938, there were still two moderate national parties of substantial and approximately equal strength preparing to defend the parliamentary regime against extremism. They were already the largest parties, and had they been given time to expand further, by reassimilating like-minded parties as they began to do in 1938 or by engaging additional uncommitted voters from the governmental dowry in the system's defense, they might have developed into the authentic party-bases of a genuinely democratic parliamentary regime described by sociologist Dimitrie Gusti in 1923:

> ...the political party is a free association of citizens, united permanently by common ideas and interests of a general nature; an association which strives in public view for the power to govern and realize a social, ethical ideal.[74]

Under pressure, Romania's parties had probably moved further toward this ideal than even the optimists of the turbulent 1918-1921 period had believed possible.

CONCLUSION: PAST, PRESENT, FUTURE

Thus, there are positive answers to all questions posed for investigation through statistical analysis. By the late 1920s, Romania's political parties had surmounted the regional character they acquired when Greater Romania was created. After this, they sought increasingly to engage in the parliamentary process the masses of new voters whose political, economic, and social expectations had to be considered, if not met, were the country to survive in a generally hostile international environment. Foreign antagonism was certain to increase unless Romania could avoid domestic upheavals of the sort that had rocked the Old Kingdom in 1907 and from which the new state had no immunity, as the 1924 uprising at Tatar Bunar in Bessarabia made clear.[75] The results were greater political awareness and more meaningful participation by voters in the electoral process, and a narrowing of the gap which had separated rulers from ruled in Romania for centuries. Especially after the Depression, voters identified more and more with specific parties, some extremist to be sure, but for the most part moderate parties favoring parliamentarism at home and a status quo policy based on friendship with Britain and France abroad. The two largest of these parties--the National Liberal Party and the National Peasant Party--could potentially have served as bases for a viable parliamentary democracy.

In terms of systemic development, the 1918-1938 period can be divided not into three parts, but neatly in half at 1928. Before 1928, emphasis was laid on consolidating the gains of World War I via land reform and universal suffrage for the masses, administrative integration of the new state, and the expansion of party apparatuses to reflect new territorial realities. After 1928, and especially after the onset of the economic crisis the following year, however, emphasis shifted to structural considerations as political parties began a search for processes and institutions which might bind state and society together in defense of the gains each had made.

Still subject to growing pains, the multiparty system succumbed in 1938 as right-wing extremists inside Romania and abroad increased their attacks on the system and the territorial integrity of the state. That the system disappeared was an indication of fragility, however, not of bankruptcy. For as long as the multiparty system survived, the interwar years were years of rapid political maturation in which modern values such as political participation and corresponding parliamentary institutions helped moderate the conflict between state and society which had been so much a part of Romania's political heritage.

This is the record with which the Romanian Communist Party has had to contend as it has tried to bridge the gap between state and society in contemporary Romania.[76] But the way in which the party came to power and the regime it imposed have made progress in this regard very difficult.

The party came to power, after all, in the wake of Romania's defeat in its 1941-1944 war effort against the Soviet Union. It then worked far more intimately with "foreign extremists"--for this is how most Romanians viewed the Soviets at the end of World War II--than the right-wing extremists of the interwar years had ever dared to do, in order to destroy all remnants of the surprisingly resilient interwar multiparty system which had revived in 1944. For a time, the party abandoned Romanian nationalism for "socialist internationalism," which in fact served Soviet interests in international affairs. And finally, it imposed the dictatorship of the proletariat, a system which by its very nature had to exacerbate rather than alleviate tensions between state elites and Romanian society.[77] In all these ways the communist regime seemed the opposite image of the interwar regime, strangely pre-modern rather than modernizing. The changes which have taken place since the late 1940s and early 1950s have not fundamentally altered this image.

The division of the Romanian population into two clearly differentiated groups, Communist Party members and non-members, is reminiscent of the situation in medieval Moldavia and Wallachia. Like the hospodars and boiars of the 17th century, communist state and societal elites are distinct from the rest of society "in character and prerogative, not simply in role."[78] Certainly parliament (the Grand National Assembly) is not the public forum for debate which it was between the wars. It therefore offers few opportunities for public sentiment to make itself heard. Since authentic participation in politics by the masses is kept to a minimum, there has been little chance for popular identification with the regime to develop. As before World War I, a bureaucratic elite of "party notables" runs the state with little regard for public opinion. Formalistic acclamation of the party's every move appears to mask underlying tension between an increasingly traditional elite class and the mass of the population.

Even more telling, from the perspective of the "party notables" themselves, state interests and societal interests conflict today more sharply than at any time since the Ottoman domination, when Romanian boiars were willing to sacrifice the sovereignty of the state in order to secure their own domination of Romanian domestic society. The Romanian Communist Party decries Soviet interference in its internal affairs and has declared its "independence" of Moscow in international affairs.[79] But the party cannot fully assert Romanian state interests vis-a-vis the Soviet Union because its own position of control in Romania depends, if not directly on Soviet military presence inside or on the borders of the state, then at least on the preservation of a sociopolitical system modelled after that of the Soviet Union. Simply put, the Communist Party's need to preserve the Soviet-style Marxist-Leninist sociopolitical system it has imposed on Romania, rather than international power considerations, is the principal limiting factor in Romanian national self-assertion.

Both rulers and ruled in Romania remain highly nationalistic as the 1980s begin. But the nationalism of the Communist Party does not coincide with that of the Romanian people. After a period in the 1960s and early 1970s when the public supported the party's foreign policy because it was accompanied by a modicum of domestic liberalization, relations between ruler and ruled reverted to what they had been in the early Communist period. The party now loses most of the support its independent stance vis-a-vis the Soviet Union might bring by continuing to impose an authoritarian, Eastern version of modernization on a population which has considered itself Western for generations and which has no stake in the preservation of Soviet forms on Romanian soil. By seeking independence from, but identity of system with, the Soviet Union, Romania's rulers are seeking independence only for themselves. Unless this changes, the conflict between ruler and ruled is likely to continue in

the Socialist Republic of Romania in the 1980s and
beyond.

TABLE 2.1

Percent of Total Number of Votes Cast Received by Each Party, 1919-1922

Party	1919	1920[g]	1922
Peasant	46.3[a]	13.5[a]	19.4[a,n]
National (of Transylvania)	--[b]	--[b]	(34.8)[o]
Liberal	21.4[a]	6.8[a]	53.9[a,p]
People's	1.2[a]	44.6[a,h]	7.7[a,q]
National Democratic (Iorga)	5.7[a]	1.3[a]	3.0[a,r]
Socialist	3.5[a]	4.8[a,i]	0.8[a,s]
Democratic	--	1.2[a,j]	--
Democratic Unity (Bucovina)	(79.0)[c]	--[k]	(83.7)[c]
Federation of National Social Democracy	--	7.4[a]	--
Progressive Conservative	3.9[a]	2.8[a]	--
National Peasantist	--	--	1.5[a]
Bessarabian Peasant	--[d]	--[d]	6.9[a]
Independents and minor parties	10.5[a,e]	7.6[a,l]	2.3[a,t]
Dissident fractions of major parties	7.5[f]	--	3.6[a,u]
Votes annulled	--	10.0[a,m]	--

Note: For elections of 1919, 1920, 1922, absolute figures are quite difficult to determine on a national basis since different voting systems were in effect in different provinces. Under the 1918 electoral law for the Regat (including Dobrudja) and Bessarabia, voters could cast ballots for more than one candidate, up to a number equal to the number of deputies to be elected from the respective electoral district. Thus figures for these provinces represent the percentage of the total number of votes cast which was received by each party, and not the percentage of voters who voted for each party. In Transylvania, the Banat, and Bucovina, on the other hand, each voter cast only one vote. In Transylvania and the Banat voting took place for only 61 of 205 seats in 1919; and for only 35 of 121 seats in 1920.

a Percentage of votes cast in the Regat (including Dobrudja) and Bessarabia only.
b The partial nature of voting in Transylvania and the Banat makes percentage figures impossible to determine. The National Party of Transylvania won 199 of 205 seats in these provinces in 1919, and 23 of 144 seats in 1920. It ran no candidates outside of these provinces.
c This was the regional party of Bucovina. Figure is the percentage of votes cast in this province won by this

   party.
d Contested the elections jointly with the Peasant Party.
e Independents and other individual candidates won 21.0 percent of the vote in Bucovina.
f Dissident major party candidates won six seats from Transylvania and the Banat. The percentage figure here reflects results only in the <u>Regat</u> and Bessarabia, however.
g Percentages for the 1920 elections, for which published results are incomplete, are calculated on the basis of the median number of votes received by each party's list of candidates in each electoral district (median number of votes=total number of votes received by all candidates on a list divided by the number of deputies to be elected from the district in question).
h Also received 39.3 percent of the vote in Bucovina.
i Also received 16.1 percent of the vote in Bucovina.
j Also received 15.8 percent of the vote in Bucovina.
k Contested the elections jointly with the People's Party.
l Also received 10.0 percent of the vote in Bucovina.
m 2.65 percent of the votes in Bucovina were annulled.
n Also received 2.7 percent of the vote in Transylvania and the Banat.
o The party ran no candidates outside of Transylvania and the Banat. The figure is the percentage of votes cast in these provinces won by this party.
p Also received 41.3 percent of the vote in Transylvania and the Banat.
q Also received 3.8 percent of the vote in Transylvania and the Banat and 4.6 percent of the vote in Bucovina.
r Also received 0.5 percent of the vote in Transylvania and the Banat.
s Also received 2.6 percent of the vote in Transylvania and the Banat and 9.8 percent of the vote in Bucovina.
t Also received 2.7 percent of the vote in Transylvania and the Banat and 1.9 percent of the vote in Bucovina.
u Also received 12.2 percent of the vote in Transylvania and the Banat.

TABLE 2.2

Percent of Total Number of Votes Cast Received by Each Party, 1926-1937

Party	1926	1927	1928	1931	1932	1933	1937
National Peasant	27.7a	22.1	77.8d	15.0	40.3h	13.9	20.4l
Liberal	7.3	61.7	6.6	47.5f	13.6	51.0j	35.9m
Magyar	--	6.3c	6.1	4.8	4.8	4.0	4.4
People's	52.1b	1.9	2.5e	4.8	2.2	1.6	0.8
Nationalist	1.4	--	--	--	--	--	--
National Democratic (Iorga)	--	1.0	--	--	2.3i	--	--
Peasantist (Lupu)	--	--	2.5	3.4	5.7	5.1	--
Social Democratic	1.6	1.8	--	3.3	3.4	1.3	0.9
League of National Christian Defense	--	--	--	--	--	--	--
Worker and Peasantist Bloc	4.8	1.9	1.1	3.9	5.3	4.5	--
Jewish	1.5	1.1	1.4	2.5	0.3	1.3	1.4
Iron Guard (All for the Fatherland)	--	--	--	2.2	2.3	--	--
"Young Liberal" (G. Bratianu)	--	0.4	--	1.1	2.4	--	15.6
National Agrarian	--	--	--	5.9	6.5	5.0	3.9
Conservative (Filipescu)	--	--	--	--	3.6	4.1	--
Agrarian League	--	--	--	--	0.6	--	--
Anti-usury League	--	--	--	2.8g	0.5	--	--
Merchant Council	0.1	0.01	--	--	1.5	0.04k	--

TABLE 2.2 (cont'd)

Party	1926	1927	1928	1931	1932	1933	1937
Democratic Peas- antist (Stere)	--	--	--	--	1.4	--	--
Independent Socialist	--	--	--	--	0.2	--	--
Citizen Bloc	--	--	--	--	0.1	0.5	--
Radical Peasant- ist (Iunian)	--	--	--	--	--	2.8	2.3
Agrarian Union	--	--	--	--	--	2.5	--
League of Work	--	--	--	--	--	0.1	--
Unitary Socialist	--	--	--	--	--	0.1	--
Ploughmen's Front	--	--	--	--	--	0.3	--
National Chris- tian	--	--	--	--	--	--	9.2^n
Agrarian	--	--	--	--	--	--	1.7
German People's	--	--	--	--	--	--	1.4
Front of Work	--	--	--	--	--	--	0.2
Others	1.1	0.1	0.3	0.1	0.1	0.2	0.4
Votes annulled	2.4	1.6	1.9	2.8	2.9	2.0	1.5

Note: Where no figure appears, party either did not exist, did not contest the elec- tions at all, or participated in an electoral cartel with another party (as indicated elsewhere in the table).

a Iorga's National Democratic Party ran in cartel with the National Peasant Party. The National Party and Peasant Party had joint lists in this election; the formal merger of the two parties actually followed the election.
b The German and Magyar parties ran in cartel with the People's Party.
c The German Party ran in cartel with the Magyar Party.
d The German and Social Democratic parties ran in cartel with the National Peasant Party.
e Iorga's National Democratic Party ran in cartel with the People's Party.

TABLE 2.2 (cont'd)

f   Iorga headed the government which organized these elections, but the Liberal Party provided the government's parliamentary base. The National Union slate of candidates which won this percentage of the vote was a cartel of the Liberal Party, Iorga's National Democratic Party, and the German Party.
g   The Democratic Peasantist Party (Stere) ran in cartel with the Anti-usury League.
h   The German Party ran in cartel with the National Peasant Party.
i   Iorga retained the National Union electoral label, but contested the elections alone, without Liberal or German party backing.
j   The German Party ran in cartel with the Liberal Party.
k   The Party of Work ran in cartel with the Merchant Council.
l   The National Peasant Party, Gheorghe Bratianu's "Young Liberal" Party, and the Iron Guard had an electoral "non-aggression pact" in this election, but each party presented its own list of candidates.
m   Iorga's National Democratic Party and Vaida-Voevod's Romanian Front ran in cartel with the Liberal Party.
n   The National Christian Party was the name adopted by the League of National Christian Defense and the National Agrarian Party when they merged in 1935.

TABLE 2.3

Percent of Total Votes Cast Received by the Major Parties, by Province, 1919-1922[a]

Party/Year	Oltenia	Muntenia	Moldavia	Dobrudja	Regat Proper	Total Regat	Transylvania and Banat	Bessarabia	Bucovina
National Liberal Party									
1919	40.1	32.1	32.7	58.0	34.1	35.4	--	--	--
1920	8.2	9.3	6.2	13.7	8.1	8.5	--b	1.3	--
1922	70.0	62.7	58.4	69.8	63.4	63.7	41.3	18.2	--
Peasant Party									
1919	27.6	28.9	15.8	1.6	26.1	24.7	--	--	--
1920	3.3	11.2	0.2	6.6	6.1	6.1	--b	35.6	--
1922	11.6	19.8	15.0	18.9	17.0	17.1	2.7	27.9	--
National Party (of Transylvania)									
1919	--	--	--	--	--	--	68.9	--	--
1920	--	--	--	--	--	--	--b	--	--
1922	--	--	--	--	--	--	34.8	--	--
People's Party									
1919	3.7	0.1	1.8	14.8	1.3	2.0	--	--	--
1920	56.7	45.4	51.3	45.7	49.9	49.0	--b	29.9	39.3
1922	9.0	8.5	12.3	1.7	9.4	9.0	3.8	2.8	4.6

Note: Where no figure appears, party did not contest elections. The Regat Proper includes Oltenia, Muntenia, Moldavia.
[a] On electoral statistics for these elections, see "Note" in Table 2.1.
[b] Electoral data for the 1920 elections in Transylvania are incomplete. In the province, the Liberals won 2 seats, the Peasantists 9, the Nationals 23, and the People's Party 69.

TABLE 2.4

Percent of Total Votes Cast Received by the Major Parties and the "Governmental Dowry," by Province, 1922-1937

Party/Year	Transylvania	Banat	Regat	Dobrudja	Bessarabia	Bucovina	Romania
National Liberal Party							
1920							6.0a
1922	38.7	45.2	63.4	69.8	18.2	--	52.0a-46
1926	3.0	4.2	10.4	12.4	7.1	6.4	7.3
1927	34.0-31	30.2-26	77.8-67	74.8-62	79.9-72	51.8-45	61.7-54
1928	1.8	2.1	11.1	8.3	3.9	6.4	6.6
1931b	33.1c-27	34.1d-24	57.0-43	62.5-54	52.8-48	33.7e-22	47.5f-37
1932	8.1	9.5	18.8	14.7	9.8	11.7	13.6
1933	44.6g-33	50.1h-33	56.4-44	62.5-48	48.4-38	35.9i-20	51.0j-35
1937	31.1k-22	26.7-17	39.9-21	45.6-30	36.5-26	26.0-14	35.9-22
National Peasant Party							
1926	35.2	30.1	22.7	32.7	27.8	23.9	27.7
1927	39.8	37.3	14.1	15.7	11.5	11.8	22.1
1928	70.3l-25	80.7m-31	78.4n-62	83.7-67	85.6o-70	78.5p-46	77.8q-52
1931	20.7	22.6	12.7	19.1	8.4	6.6	15.0
1932	42.6r-18	46.4s-16	41.4-28	56.3-37	28.5-20	26.7t-13	40.3u-24
1933	13.8	11.7	15.5	11.2	12.2	11.0	13.9
1937	18.9	15.8	21.4	24.3	18.7	26.0	20.4
People's Party							
1922	3.7	4.0	8.9	1.7	2.8	4.6	6.5a
1926	47.2v-25	41.3w-22	56.7-48	52.4-50	58.2-55	41.7x-30	52.1y-42
1927	1.7	1.7	1.4	5.8	3.3	1.3	1.9
1928	1.7	1.2	3.8	2.3	1.6	0.9	2.5
1931	4.2	3.0	7.0	2.9	2.3	2.0	4.8
1932	1.3	0.6	3.3	1.9	1.5	1.1	2.2

TABLE 2.4 (cont'd)

Party/Year	Transylvania	Banat	Regat	Dobrudja	Bessarabia	Bucovina	Romania
People's Party (cont'd)							
1933							1.6^z
1937							0.8^z

Note: All percentage figures include the percentage of the vote brought to the party list by minor parties with which electoral cartels were in force, as noted. Figures for the governmental dowry take the votes attributable to these minor parties into account by reducing the size of the dowry by the proper percentages. Figures for the Regat are for the Regat proper, without Dobrudja. Figures for the dowry appear underlined.

a Approximation of strength nationwide. Precise figures cannot be determined because of the different electoral procedures in effect in different provinces.

b In this year the National Liberal Party ran as part of the National Union electoral list headed by Nicolae Iorga.

c Of which 3.5 percent is attributable to the German Party and Iorga's National Democratic Party.

d Of which 7.0 percent is attributable to the German Party and Iorga's National Democratic Party.

e Of which 5.0 percent is attributable to the German Party and Iorga's National Democratic Party.

f Of which 3.5 percent is attributable to the German Party and Iorga's National Democratic Party.

g Of which 3.0 percent is attributable to the German Party.
h Of which 7.0 percent is attributable to the German Party.
i Of which 4.0 percent is attributable to the German Party.
j Of which 2.5 percent is attributable to the German Party.
k Of which 1.0 percent is attributable to Vaida-Voevod's Romanian Front.
l Of which 6.5 percent is attributable to the German and Social Democratic parties.
m Of which 12.0 percent is attributable to the German and Social Democratic parties.
n Of which 2.0 percent is attributable to the German and Social Democratic parties.

TABLE 2.4 (cont'd)

o Of which 3.0 percent is attributable to the German and Social Democratic parties.
p Of which 20.0 percent is attributable to the German and Social Democratic parties.
q Of which 3.0 percent is attributable to the German and Social Democratic parties.
r Of which 3.0 percent is attributable to the German Party.
s Of which 7.0 percent is attributable to the German Party.
t Of which 7.0 percent is attributable to the German Party.
u Of which 1.0 percent is attributable to the German Party.
v Of which 18.0 percent is attributable to the German and Magyar parties.
w Of which 15.0 percent is attributable to the German and Magyar parties.
x Of which 6.0 percent is attributable to the German and Magyar parties.
y Of which 3.0 percent is attributable to the German and Magyar parties.
z By 1933 and 1937, the People's Party and Averescu had lost all significance as parliamentary forces. Support was limited to a few districts around Averescu's home in Oltenia and in the vicinity of Bucharest.

TABLE 2.5

Percent of Total Votes Cast Received by the Major Right-Wing Extremist Parties, by Province, 1926-1937

Party/Year	Transylvania	Banat	Regat	Dobrudja	Bessarabia	Bucovina	Romania
League of National Christian Defense							
1926	3.1	10.0	4.9	0.4	2.0	12.9	4.8
1927	0.1	1.6	2.7	0.9	2.3	3.6	1.9
1928	0.1	1.2	1.5	0.3	1.4	3.5	1.1
1931	0.5	1.8	4.3	0.1	4.7	22.3	3.9
1932	0.8	2.5	4.9	0.0	14.8	14.2	5.3
1933	1.4	4.2	3.3	1.7	10.5	16.8	4.5
National Agrarian Party							
1932	3.6	4.1	3.9	4.6	2.7	2.6	3.6
1933	4.7	6.5	3.9	3.0	3.0	3.3	4.1
National Christian Party							
1937	3.9	5.5	9.9	5.5	21.3	9.3	9.2
Iron Guard (All for the Fatherland)							
1927	0.04	1.1	0.2	0.0	0.0	3.9	0.4
1928a	--	--	--	--	--	--	--
1931	1.2	0.0	0.5	0.0	2.9	2.4	1.1
1932	1.3	1.4	2.6	0.0	3.9	5.5	2.4
1933a	--	--	--	--	--	--	--
1937	16.5	20.0	16.4	14.1	5.0	22.8	15.6
League for National Christian Defense and National Agrarian Party							
1932	4.4	6.6	8.8	4.6	17.5	16.9	9.0
1933	6.1	10.6	7.2	4.7	13.5	20.1	8.6
1937	3.9	5.5	9.9	5.5	21.3	9.3	9.2

TABLE 2.5 (cont'd)

Party/Year	Transylvania	Banat	Regat	Dobrudja	Bessarabia	Bucovina	Romania
League for National Christian Defense, National Agrarian Party, and Iron Guard							
1926	3.1	10.0	4.9	0.4	2.0	12.9	4.8
1927	0.1	2.6	2.9	0.9	2.3	7.5	2.3
1928	0.1	1.2	1.5	0.3	1.4	3.5	1.1
1931	1.7	1.8	4.8	0.1	7.6	24.8	4.9
1932	5.7	8.0	11.4	4.6	21.4	22.4	11.3
1933	6.1	10.6	7.2	4.7	13.5	20.1	8.6
1937	20.5	25.5	26.2	19.6	26.3	32.1	24.7

Note: The Regat refers here to the Regat proper, without Dobrudja.
a The Iron Guard was illegal when the 1928 and 1933 elections were held.

TABLE 2.6

Percent of the Total National Liberal Party Vote Received in the Regat, 1919-1937[a]

Year	Percent
1919	100.0
1920	95.4
1922	92.7
1926	66.7
1927	59.9
1928	77.3
1931	56.1
1932	65.1
1933	53.9
1937	55.7

a The Regat here refers to all of pre-World War I Romania, including Dobrudja.

TABLE 2.7

The "Governmental Dowry" in Romanian Elections, 1926-1937 (in percent)

Party in Power	Year	Governmental Dowry
People's	1926	42
Liberal	1927	54
National Peasant	1928	52
Liberal[a]	1931	37
National Peasant	1932	24
Liberal	1933	35
Liberal	1937	22

a In this year the National Liberal Party ran as part of the National Union electoral list headed by Nicolae Iorga. The Liberal Party provided the Iorga government's parliamentary base, however.

TABLE 2.8

Eligible Voters and Participation Levels in Romanian Elections, by Province, 1919-1937 (in percent)

Year	Eligible Voters	Voters Voting	Participation						
			Transylvania	Banat	Regat	Dobrudja[a]	Bessarabia	Bucovina	Romania
1919[b]	1,916,225	1,324,563	--	--	66.7	73.5	72.2	76.7	69.1
1920[b]	1,977,644	1,549,226	--	--	82.9	84.7	72.2	57.0	78.3
1922	2,908,015	2,210,370	58.3	59.3	85.5	84.1	77.9	79.4	76.0
1926	3,496,814	2,622,565	71.5	73.6	79.5	77.4	70.4	71.0	74.9
1927	3,586,086	2,762,779	68.9	77.0	82.8	82.4	75.3	73.0	77.0
1928	3,671,352	2,840,680	74.1	81.5	80.3	82.0	71.8	74.0	77.3
1931	4,038,464	2,927,112	66.7	77.1	76.5	75.1	69.3	68.8	72.4
1932	4,220,731	2,987,129	64.3	77.4	75.1	75.4	66.2	65.9	70.7
1933	4,380,354	2,978,748	62.7	74.7	72.7	69.1	62.6	65.4	68.0
1937	4,649,163	3,071,695	62.2	75.0	72.3	64.5	51.6	70.5	66.0

a The Regat refers here to the Regat proper, without Dobrudja.
b Voter totals and the national participation figures for 1919 and 1920 do not include data on Transylvania and the Banat, where elections took place in only a limited number of electoral districts in these years.

NOTES

1. Witness the willingness of late 17th century Moldavian boiars to submit to Polish protection, against the will of the Moldavian hospodar (prince), on condition that the Polish king guarantee them the same rights and privileges as were enjoyed by the Polish szlachta. See E. Hurmuzaki, Documente privitoare la istoria Romanilor, vol. 3, supplement 2 (Bucharest: I. V. Socecu, 1900), Document no. 78, for the boiars' appeal to Polish King Ian Sobieski in July 1684; on the politics of the period, see I. Moga, Rivalitatea polono-austriaca si orientarea politica a tarilor romane la sfirsitul secolului al XVII (Cluj: Tipografia Cartea Romaneasca, 1936).
Nearly 150 years later an analogous situation developed when the nobilities of Moldavia and Wallachia increased their own economic and political power from 1828 to 1848 by accepting dependent status for the principalities and organizational codes (the Organic Regulations) imposed by Russia. See Jean C. Filitti, Les principautes roumains sous l'occupation russe, 1828-1834 (Bucharest: Imprimerie de l'Independence Roumaine, 1904) and idem, Domniile romane sub Regulamentul Organic, 1834-1848 (Bucharest: Librariile Socec & C. Sfetea, 1915).

2. For an excellent summary of the effects of public education in pre-World War I Romania, see Andrew C. Janos, "Modernization and Decay in Historical Perspective: The Case of Romania," in Kenneth Jowitt, Ed., Social Change in Romania, 1860-1940: A Debate on Development in a European Nation (Berkeley: Institute of International Studies, University of California, 1978), pp. 94-101.

3. On the prewar electoral laws, see T. Crisen Axente, Essai sur le regime representatif en Roumanie (Paris: Librairie du Receuil Sirey, 1937), pp. 235-436. On the electoral laws of November 14, 1918, for the Regat and Bessarabia, and of August 24, 1919, for Transylvania, the Banat, and Bucovina, see ibid., pp. 445-469. On the national electoral law of March 27, 1926, see ibid., pp. 525-555.

4. On the cleavage between state and society in the modern era, see Emanuel Turczynski, "The Background of Romanian Fascism," in Peter F. Sugar, Ed., Native Fascism in the Successor States, 1918-1945 (Santa Barbara: ABC-Clio, 1971).

5. Many authors have referred to the bureaucratic nature of Romanian politics before World War I. Those interested in controversial views of contemporaries on the workings of Romanian politics should consult Stefan Zeletin, Burghezia romana, origina si rolul ei istoric (Bucharest: Cultura nationala, 1925), Mihail Manoilescu, Rostul si destinul burgheziei romanesti (Bucharest:

Cugetarea-Georgescu Delafras, 1942), and in a different vein, Titu Maiorescu, Istoria contemporana a Romaniei, 1866-1900 (Bucharest: Editura Librariei Socec, 1925). In English, consult R. W. Seton-Watson, A History of the Roumanians (London: Cambridge University Press, 1934).

6. For a long time, scholarly treatment of the interwar period was confined to articles and early monographic efforts such as Henry L. Roberts, Rumania: Political Problems of an Agrarian State (New Haven: Yale University Press, 1951), and Lucretiu Patrascanu's very helpful, if biased, Problemele de baza ale Romaniei (Bucharest: Editura Socec, 1944) and Sub trei dictaturi, 4th ed. (Bucharest: Forum, 1946). Recent additions to the literature have been numerous and invite a reexamination of many issues, especially in domestic politics. Particularly useful are: Mircea Musat and Ion Ardeleanu, Viata politica in Romania, 1918-1921, 2nd ed. (Bucharest: Editura politica, 1976), Ioan Scurtu, Din viata politica a Romaniei, 1918-1926: Intemeierea si activitatea partidului taranesc (Bucharest: Editura litera, 1975), Mihail Rusenescu and Ioan Saizu, Viata politica in Romania, 1922-1928 (Bucharest: Editura politica, 1979), Emilia Sonea and Gavrila Sonea, Viata economica si politica a Romaniei, 1933-1938 (Bucharest: Editura stiintifica si enciclopedica, 1978), Florea Nedelcu, Viata politica din Romania in preajma instaurarii dictaturii regale (Cluj: Editura Dacia, 1970), Al. Gh. Savu, Dictatura regala (Bucharest: Editura politica, 1970), and idem, Sistemul partidelor politice din Romania, 1919-1940 (Bucharest: Editura stiintifica si enciclopedica, 1976).

7. On the establishment of Carol's royal dictatorship, see Savu, Dictatura regala, op. cit.; and Paul A. Shapiro, "Prelude to Dictatorship in Romania: The National Christian Party in Power, December 1937-February 1938," in Canadian-American Slavic Studies (Pittsburgh), 8, no. 1 (Spring 1974), pp. 45-88.

8. On the rewriting of history in Romania, see Michael J. Rura, Reinterpretation of History as a Method of Furthering Communism in Rumania (Washington, D.C.: Georgetown University Press, 1961), Vlad Georgescu, "Politica si istorie: Cazul comunistilor romani, 1944-1977," (manuscript, Bucharest, 1977), and Constantin Sporea, "Die sowjetische Umdeutung der rumanischen Geschichte," Saeculum (Freiburg), 11, no. 3, pp. 220-246.

9. See Joseph Rothschild's excellent survey of Romanian interwar politics in East Central Europe Between Two World Wars (Seattle: University of Washington Press, 1974), pp. 281-322.

10. Roberts, op. cit.

11. Or, for those who date the demise of the traditional parties later, in terms of the crises of September 1940, when King Carol abdicated and was replaced by a

military-fascist dictatorship; August 1944, when the military dictatorship was overthrown and Romania sought an armistice agreement with the Soviet Union; or December 1947, when King Michael was forced to abdicate by the communists and a people's republic was declared.

12. Roberts (op. cit., p. 91) says that the analysis of elections to explain the course of Romanian politics in this period would be "futile" and "misleading," and there is no doubt that the elections alone cannot give a complete picture of political life in interwar Romania. They can, however, help define trends in public attitudes and indicate the direction in which the parliamentary system was moving.

13. The quote is from Roberts (op. cit., p. 94), but the sentiment is that which the National Liberal Party itself hoped to promote. See Istoricul Partidului National Liberal dela 1848 si pana astazi (Bucharest: Imprimeriile Independenta, 1923). Ioan I. C. Bratianu was the longtime leader of the Liberals and had been Prime Minister in governments of 1909-1910, 1914-1918, and 1919. He served again as Prime Minister from 1922 to 1926, and for several months prior to his death in 1927.

14. On this period, see Musat and Ardeleanu, op. cit.

15. In a lecture entitled "Conceptia conservatoare si progresul," delivered on December 17, 1922, Conservative theoretician C. Radulescu-Motru admitted that the Conservative Party had lost its battle with the Liberals and was all but finished ("la pamant"). See the speech in D. Gusti et al., Doctrinele partidelor politice (Bucharest: Institutul Social Roman, n.d. 1923) p. 63.

16. On the Conservative Party before the war, see Anastasia Iordache, Viata politica in Romania, 1910-1914 (Bucharest: Editura stiintifica, 1972). Agrarian reform measures after the war are described in Roberts, op. cit., pp. 17-39, David Mitrany, The Land and the Peasant in Romania: The War and Agrarian Reform (New Haven: Yale University Press, 1930), and D. Sandru, Reforma agrara din 1921 in Romania (Bucharest: Editura Academiei Republicii Socialiste Romania, 1975). On the Marghiloman government and the Treaty of Bucharest (May 1918), see Sherman D. Spector, Rumania at the Paris Peace Conference: A Study of the Diplomacy of Ioan I. C. Bratianu (New York: Bookman Associates, 1962), pp. 53-55, and Alexandru Marghiloman, Note politice, 1897-1924, 5 vols. (Bucharest: Eminescu, 1927), vols. 3 and 4 on 1918.

17. Stefan Zeletin, op. cit., p. 165. On the diplomatic basis of the creation of Greater Romania, see Spector, op. cit.

18. On the difficulties of national integration in interwar East Central Europe, see C. A. Macartney and A. W. Palmer, Independent Eastern Europe (London: Macmillan, 1962), and Rothschild, op. cit. As both

studies indicate, the difficulties were magnified by the desire of dominant parties in Romania, Yugoslavia, Czechoslovakia, and Poland to create centralized rather than federal state administrations.

19. Musat and Ardeleanu, op. cit., p. 112.
20. Manifestul-Program al Partidului National Liberal (Bucharest: n.p., 1920), p. 2.
21. See Musat and Ardeleanu, op. cit., pp. 116-131.
22. Of course, because the Liberal Party's extensive banking and financial interests were most deeply embedded in the Regat, the Liberals remained regional in economic perspective even after they began to develop electoral strength in all regions of the country. It took five years of rule by rival parties and the economic crisis of 1929-1933 to break the Liberal Party's stranglehold on the national banking system based in the Regat. Finally, in the 1930s, as rival financial circles grew more powerful and as Bratianu family control over the Liberal Party waned, a substantial share of Liberal economic activity did shift out of the Old Kingdom, thus making the Liberal Party national economically as well as politically. See Patrascanu, Sub trei dictaturi, op. cit., pp. 10-19, and Virgil V. Madgearu, Evolutia economiei romanesti dupa razboiul mondial (Bucharest: Independenta economica, 1940), pp. 328-356.
23. This cynical but fairly accurate evaluation by one of interwar Romania's greatest cynics can be found in Arhiva Comitetului Central al Partidului Comunist Roman, fond 104, "Constantin Argetoianu, Pentru cei de miine--Amintiri din vremea celor de ieri," Part 4, f. 1174.
24. Musat and Ardeleanu, op. cit., pp. 241-261.
25. The Parliamentary Bloc formed on November 25, 1919, controlled 376 of the 568 seats in the Chamber of Deputies, as follows: National Party of Transylvania--199, Democratic Unity Party of Bucovina--20, Peasant Party of the Regat and Peasant Party of Bessarabia--130, National Democratic Party--27. The Liberals controlled only 103 seats.
26. Seats in the Chamber of Deputies were distributed among Romania's provinces in 1919 and 1920 as follows:

Year	Olt.	Munt.	Mold.	Dobr.	All Regat	Trans. Banat	Bess.	Buc.	Total
1919	47	108	69	23	247	205	90	26	568
1920	30	76	58	16	180	121	51	17	369
% Loss	36%	30%	16%	30%	27%	41%	43%	35%	35%

According to the most recent census information available on each province, the redistribution of seats did not bring representation more into line with respective provincial populations. The main effect of the redistribution was that stated in the text.

27. Autonomous administrative mechanisms of the new provinces were abolished by Decree-Law no. 1462 of April 2, 1920, and Decree-Law no. 1476 of April 3, 1920; see C. Hamangiu, Codul General al Romaniei, vol. 9-10 (Bucharest: Editura Librariei Viata Romaneasca, n.d.), pp. 293-294. On the reaction of adherents of the People's Party from these provinces, see Musat and Ardeleanu, op. cit., pp. 266-269.

28. By the May 1920 elections, an opposition coalition called the Federation of National Social Democracy had formed, made up of the five former member parties of the Parliamentary Bloc plus the radical peasantist splinter group led by Nicolae Lupu. In July 1921, the Federation withdrew all of its deputies from the Chamber, simultaneously with the Liberal Party, which by this time was ready to see Averescu fall and to return to direct control of the government. For more detail, see Musat and Ardeleanu, op. cit., pp. 217-228 and 295-299.

29. For an excellent early interwar discussion of what constitutes a party, a clique, a fraction, and a coterie ("a fraction...which represents a maximum of personalism and arrivism"), see Dimitrie Gusti's introductory essay entitled "Partidul Politic" in D. Gusti etal., op. cit.

30. The People's Party lost any semblance of being national in scope after the April 1932 resignation from its ranks of Transylvanian poet and later Prime Minister Octavian Goga. See Shapiro, loc. cit., pp. 46-48.

31. On Article 46 of the electoral law of August 24, 1919, for Transylvania and the Banat, see Axente, op. cit., pp. 467-469.

32. The National Party's role in the Parliamentary Bloc is discussed in Musat and Ardeleanu, op. cit., pp. 158-167.

33. The leading defector was poet-politician Octavian Goga, but he was followed by others. See Patria (Sibiu), April 1, 1920. By the time the Parliamentary Bloc government fell, there was widespread sentiment in the National Party in favor of the abolition of the Governing Council. See Musat and Ardeleanu, op. cit., pp. 165-166.

34. Ibid., pp. 175-176.

35. On the National Democratic Party, see Rusenescu and Saizu, op. cit., pp. 69-70 and 100-107. One National Party notable, Secretary General Sever Dan, reportedly stated outright in 1926 that to come to power "we are ready to reach an agreement with anyone who will give us a free hand in Transylvania." See Tara Noastra (Cluj), 7:27 (1926), p. 775. On the negotiations between the National Party and the Peasant Party, see Rusenescu and Saizu, op. cit., pp. 84-90.

36. For agreements to this effect as early as June 1924, see ibid., pp. 65-66 and 174.

37. The 10-point program included major concessions on both sides such as administrative decentralization and local autonomy, which the National Party wanted, and the protection and development of peasant properties and an end to tariff protection of industries with no resource bases in Romania, sought by the Peasantists. See Zece ani dela fuziunea partidelor national si taranesc (Bucharest: n.p., 1936), and Pamfil Seicaru, Istoria Partidelor National, Taranist, si National-Taranist, vol. 2 (Madrid: Editura Carpatii, 1963), pp. 51-85.

38. The prewar history of peasantism in Romania is discussed by Ioan Scurtu, "Miscarea taranista din Romania pina in 1907," Studii: Revista de istorie (Bucharest), 25, no. 3 (1972), and idem, "Contributii privind miscarea taranista din Romania in perioada 1907-1914," in ibid., 21, no. 3 (1968).

39. See "Actul de constituire a Partidului taranesc," Izbanda (Bucharest), December 11/24, 1918, and "Procesul-verbal de constituire a Partidului Taranesc," Tara noua (Bucharest), August 4/17, 1919. Point 2 of the latter document discussed the "governmental dowry."

40. See the 20-point program in "Ce vrea Partidul taranesc," Tara noua, September 15/28, 1919, calling for radical land reform; and "Declaratie de principii," in ibid., October 13/26, 1919, calling for even more radical land reform, the nationalization of Romania's natural resources, and abolition of the Senate as part of the legislature.

41. On the transformation of Peasant Party doctrine, see Roberts, op. cit., pp. 142-156. For Madgearu's definition of peasantism see his "Doctrina taranista," in D. Gusti et al., op. cit. On the land reform proposed by Mihalache, see Musat and Ardeleanu, op. cit., pp. 200-201, Mitrany, op. cit., and Sandru, op. cit. On the changed role of the party, contrast the organizational norms of October 1920, published in Tara noua, October 3, 1920, with those of November 1919, published in ibid., October 8, 1920.

42. Musat and Ardeleanu, op. cit., p. 211.

43. See ibid., pp. 223-232, on the consolidation of peasantist forces; also Scurtu, op. cit., pp. 53-89.

44. On the Peasant Party prior to its merger with the Transylvanian National Party, see ibid.

45. Dr. Lupu's political activity is discussed by Rusenescu and Saizu, op. cit., pp. 98-100, and Marcel Ivan, Evolutia partidelor noastre politice, 1919-1932 (Sibiu: Krafft & Drotleff, 1933), pp. 17-18.

46. Cited from Mihail Manoilescu, "O marturisire de credinta" (Bucharest: 1926), in Rusenescu and Saizu,

op. cit., p. 95.
    47. See the report on Maniu's audience with the king just prior to the merger, in Adevarul (Bucharest), September 4, 1926.
    48. Election returns for the ten elections under scrutiny here are published in Regatul Romaniei, Monitorul Oficial, Part I, as follows:
- 1919: No. 163 of November 7; No. 164 of November 8; No. 165 of November 11; No. 166 of November 12; No. 168 of November 14; No. 171 of November 18; No. 172 of November 19; No. 173 of November 20.
- 1920: No. 44 of May 30; No. 45 of May 31; No. 46 of June 1; No. 47 of June 2; No. 48 of June 3; No. 49 of June 5.
- 1922: No. 272 of March 4; No. 273 of March 5; No. 274 of March 7; No. 275 of March 8; No. 277 of March 10; No. 278 of March 11; No. 279 of March 12; No. 280 of March 14; No. 283 of March 17; No. 285 of March 19; No. 286 of March 21.
- 1926: No. 122 of June 4; No. 123 of June 5; No. 124 of June 6.
- 1927: No. 153 of July 14; No. 155 of July 16.
- 1928: No. 283 of December 19; No. 285 of December 21.
- 1931: No. 131 of June 10; No. 134 of June 13.
- 1932: No. 173 of July 26; No. 126 of July 29.
- 1933: No. 300 of December 29; No. 301 of December 30; No. 3 of January 3 (1934); No. 5 of January 5 (1934).
- 1937: No. 301 of December 31; No. 4 of January 4 (1938).

All percentages in the tables are rounded to the nearest one tenth of one percent.
    49. In this respect the Romanian experience compares favorably with that of interwar Yugoslavia or even Czechoslovakia, where parties retained their regional character. Of course, the ethnic factor played a more divisive role in party life in these countries.
    50. Musat and Ardeleanu, op. cit., pp. 223-228, 303-304, and passim.
    51. The parties led by Iorga and Cuza are considered in Rusenescu and Saizu, op. cit., pp. 100-113.
    52. Romanian practice was to have the king appoint a government to organize national elections. Only twice--in 1919 and 1937--did the government thus appointed fail to secure for itself an overwhelming parliamentary majority. See Shapiro, loc. cit., p. 56. Shifting majorities dependent upon which party oversaw the elections are evident in Table 2.4.
    53. The Liberals got 610,315 votes in these areas out of their total of 1,103,353 in 1937. In 1932, when the last elections not run by the Liberals were held, the share of the Liberal vote from these bastion areas

was 65 percent, but this was still far below the 77 percent of the 1928 elections, when the Liberals were also in opposition.

54. On the impact of the Depression on both parties, see Madgearu, Evolutia economiei romanesti, op. cit., pp. 328-356, Sonea and Sonea, op. cit., pp. 9-37, and Asociatia Generala a Economistilor din Romania, Aspectele crizei romanesti in cadrul crizei mondiale (Bucharest: Tip. Bucovina I. E. Toroutiu, 1937). On Romanian foreign policy and the attitudes of the major parties, see Institutul de studii istorice si social-politice al C. C. al P. C. R., Probleme de politica externa a Romaniei, 1919-1939 (Bucharest: Editura militara, 1971), and idem, Probleme de politica externa a Romaniei, 1919-1940 (Bucharest: Editura militara, 1977).

55. Conservative Party leader Petre P. Carp reportedly once summarized the electoral control of the governing party when he said, "Give me power and I will give you the parliament." Cited in Matei Dogan, Analiza statistica a "democratiei parlamentare" din Romania (Bucharest: Editura Partidului Social-Democrat, 1946), p. 1. The electoral law of 1926 made domination of the parliament even easier, since the party which won 40 percent of the vote was assured at least 70 percent of the seats in the Chamber of Deputies. See the discussion of this law in Axente, op. cit.

56. See, for instance, Ivan, op. cit., and Dogan, op. cit.

57. See Table 2.4 for these calculations.

58. The 1931 elections, run by the Liberals under Iorga's National Union electoral label, is considered a Liberal election.

59. It is difficult to estimate the share of voters in each province that voted for the German Volksgemeinschaft, the most influential German political organization. This party ran in cartel with the party in power every year after it was founded in 1922, with the exception of 1927, when it ran in cartel with the Magyar Party. Since the Magyar Party ran alone in every election except those of 1926 and 1927, its support base is easily determined. We have arrived at estimates of Volksgemeinschaft strength by subtracting the Magyar Party's estimated strength from the Magyar-German vote of 1927. The parties of the most important ethnic minorities drew votes (as a percentage of the total) more or less as follows:

Party	Trans.	Banat	Regat	Dobr.	Bess.	Buc.	Total
Magyar	16%	8%	--	--	--	--	5%
German	3%	7%	--	--	0.5%	7%	1.5%
Jewish	3%	1%	1%	--	5%	8%	2%

These votes were not available to fatten the governmental dowry.

60. According to the 1930 census of the Romanian population, there were 811,000 inhabitants of Dubrudja, of which 22.8 percent were Bulgarian and 21.2 percent were Turks and Tatars. See Dr. Sabin Manuila and D. C. Georgescu, Populatia Romaniei (Bucharest: Editura Institutului Central de Statistica, 1938), pp. 50-51. On the Macedo-Vlach colonists, see Mitrany, op. cit., p. 212.

61. The 1926 elections were a special case, since they were run by Averescu, but with the support of the Liberal Party. Prior to 1926, electoral procedures were not uniform throughout the country. As a result, no figure can be calculated for the governmental dowry.

62. See note 52.

63. The Liberals made much more use of the prerogatives of power during election campaigns and received dowries a few percentage points higher than the National Peasantists as a result. In the 1920s some of the difference in the sizes of the Liberal and National Peasantist dowries could be attributed to the stronger real support base of the National Peasantists (22 percent of the electorate in 1927, as opposed to 6.5 percent for the Liberals in 1928). But in the 1930s the difference was due essentially to greater Liberal Party coercion of voters.

64. On the Liberal Party under Ion G. Duca, see Sonea and Sonea, op. cit., pp. 40-68.

65. A similar trend toward a multiplication of parties has been evident in many developing countries freed from colonial rule after World War II. This may be a common stage in the political maturation of new states.

66. The six parties included here are the Peasantist Party of Nicolae Lupu, which broke away from the National Peasant Party in 1927; the Radical Peasant Party of Grigore Iunian, which split off from the National Peasantists in 1932; Alexandru C. Cuza's anti-Semitic League of National Christian Defense; the fascist Iron Guard (All for the Fatherland Party); Gheorghe Bratianu's right-leaning "Young Liberal" Party, which left the National Liberal Party in 1930; and Octavian Goga's xenophobic National Agrarian Party. In 1935 Goga and Cuza merged their parties into the National Christian Party. The People's Party and the Social Democratic Party are excluded since they were clearly on the decline; the Magyar and Jewish parties, because they were ethnic groupings.

67. For more detail, see the electoral returns themselves, as cited in note 48.

68. Those who voted for the Iron Guard sought compre-

hensive change, although it was never clear what that change would look like. Those who voted for most of the other new parties were voting either for change in the country's leadership or out of general disillusionment. The 56 percent of the electorate which chose to support the Liberal and National Peasant parties in 1937 apparently wanted the status quo at home and abroad defended.

69. On the bureaucratic Right and revolutionary Right in Romania, see Janos, loc. cit., pp. 102-113. For an interesting discussion of the "controlled democracy" of the National Peasant Party, the "directed democracy" of the National Liberal Party, and the "dynastic authoritarianism" of King Carol II, see Stephen Fischer-Galati, "Fascism in Romania," in Sugar, op. cit., pp. 112-113. Fischer-Galati argues that there are only limited differences among these three concepts. On the parallels between National Liberal and National Peasantist thinking, see Roberts, op. cit., p. 169.

70. Regarding Lupu and Iunian, see note 66. Vaida-Voevod, who left the National Peasant Party in 1935 to found the Romanian Front, is discussed by H Prost Destin, de la Roumanie (Paris: Editions Berger-Levrault, 1954), pp. 76-80. On Stere, who was forced out of the National Peasant Party in 1930, then formed the Democratic Peasantist Party, and finally united with Iunian in 1932, see Sonea and Sonea, op. cit., p. 20.

71. Shapiro, loc. cit., pp. 79-80, discusses the consolidation; also Prost, op. cit., p. 110, and Nedelcu, op. cit., pp. 42-43 and 242-243. The elections scheduled for March 2, 1938, never took place. King Carol promulgated a new constitution establishing a royal dictatorship on February 20. The circumstances which forced Carol to cancel the elections are considered by Shapiro, loc. cit., pp. 79-86.

72. On Carol's role in Romanian politics, compare Fischer-Galati, loc. cit., p. 112, Roberts, op. cit., pp. 170-222, M. I. Costian, Regele Carol II si partidele politice (Bucharest: Tipografia Lupta N. Stroila, 1933), and Sonea and Sonea, op. cit.

73. German influence on the new parties is analyzed in Paul A. Shapiro, "German Foreign Policy and the Romanian National Christian Party," mss., Columbia University, New York, 1972. For Nazi influence among the ethnic Germans of Romania, see Wolfgang Miege, Das Dritte Reich und die Deutsche Volksgruppe in Rumanien, 1933-1938 (Bern: Herbert Lang, 1972).

74. Gusti, loc. cit., p. 4.

75. Three neighboring states had revisionist claims against Greater Romania: the Soviet Union wanted Bessarabia; Hungary wanted Transylvania and the Banat; and Bulgaria wanted part of Dobrudja. Concerning 1907, see Philip G. Eidelberg, The Great Romanian Peasant Revolt

of 1907 (Leiden: E. J. Brill, 1974). On Tatar Bunar, see Roberts, op. cit., pp. 101, 251, and Charles Upson Clark, Bessarabia: Russia and Roumania on the Black Sea (New York: Dodd Mead, 1927), pp. 264-268.

76. On the desire of the party to engage the masses, see the speech by General Secretary Nicolae Ceausescu in Congresul al XI-lea al Partidului Comunist Roman, 25-28 noiembrie 1974 (Bucharest: Editura politica, 1975), pp. 67-68, and Ion Florea, Dialectica democratiei socialiste (Bucharest: Editura stiintifica, 1973).

77. Kenneth Jowitt considered the divisive effect of the dictatorship of the proletariat in "An Organizational Approach to the Study of Political Culture in Marxist-Leninist Systems," The American Political Science Review (Menasha), 68, no. 3 (September 1974), pp. 1175-1179.

78. Ibid., p. 1177.

79. See the April 1964 "Statement on the Stand of the Rumanian Workers' Party Concerning the Problems of the International Communist and Working Class Movement," in William E. Griffith, Sino-Soviet Relations, 1964-1965 (Cambridge: MIT Press, 1967), pp. 269-296. Romanian Communists themselves refer to this document as their "declaration of independence" from the Soviet Union.

Part 2
Leaders and Citizens in Romanian Politics

The political setting of Romania in the 1980s, albeit ruled by a communist party, must be seen in terms of non-communist political traditions and the country's agrarian character. Surely, the adaptation of Romania to communism has been equaled by the transformation of Marxism-Leninism in the Romanian context.

But in confronting the political and social setting of Romania, has the Party reached the people? Is there, or will there be, an identity of interests among the nationalities, socio-economic strata and communist leadership of Romania? The three chapters of Part Two, by Mary Ellen Fischer, Trond Gilberg and Daniel N. Nelson, address such linkages, and assess their impact for Romania's future.

Critical to Romania's immediate outlook, as Fischer-Galati's opening essay pointed out, is Nicolae Ceausescu's relationship to the populace. It is Fischer-Galati's contention that the ability of Ceausescu to seek, and to maintain, legitimacy via economic growth and anti-Soviet nationalism will fade. Confronted by increasing dependencies, and a diminishing international role, Ceausescu will likely fail to retain his hold on the Romanian people or Communist Party.

Mary Ellen Fischer, however, views Ceausescu's hold on the Party as "unchallengeable". While she sees obstacles to Ceausescu's authenticity as a leader, which necessitate efforts to assure obedience in lieu of genuine support by generating an image as an idol, the different emphasis in Fischer's analysis is important. For her, Ceausescu's leadership disabilities will mean that a cult is required when authentic leadership is absent; that the latter is missing, however, does not mean an imminent leadership problem.

In his chapter on political socialization, Trond Gilberg assesses the Romanian Communist Party's efforts to bond citizens to the regime; the long-term prospects for political stability are certain to be better where a populace is disposed positively towards existing institutions and procedures. But Gilberg, somewhat like Fischer-Galati, does not see trends that portend a quiescent political atmosphere in Romania. Although Gilberg is not inclined to expect Ceausescu's departure within the 1980s for any political reason, he does foresee a widening gap between "regime goals and popular expectations" which might generate a "real political crisis".

Focusing on the socio-economic stratum of industrial labor, support from which is crucial for any claim to legitimacy by a ruling communist party, Nelson finds considerable evidence that workers are not satisfied with their living standard, or the channels for workplace participation sanctioned by the R.C.P. Nelson suggests that the campaign begun in 1978 regarding "self-management" and "self-financing" was linked to regime fears of unrest in critical sectors of the economy. The path Ceausescu's policies have taken, however, is not likely to resolve worker-party differences, and the 1980s and beyond will not be devoid of such conflict in Nelson's view.

These chapters imply a growing distance between leaders and citizens in Romania. While overt obedience may be achieved through the use of a leadership cult and its image of an idol, and stringent socialization efforts combined with the rhetoric of self-management will blunt popular disenchantment, these analyses leave little doubt that the Romanian Communist Party cannot be sanguine about its legitimacy.

3
Family, Farm, and Factory: Rural Workers in Contemporary Romania

John W. Cole

PRELUDE TO SOCIALISM

Romania's creation as a nation-state in the nineteenth and early twentieth century was accompanied by the expansion into former Ottoman and Hapsburg lands of capitalist commerce and investment. While much of what Romania produced was consumed at home, exports of agricultural products to the industrializing countries of Northwestern Europe expanded markedly. The characteristics of the Romanian political economy were in large measure determined by its position in the expanding capitalist world system.[1] Romania became an agrarian state with a severe "peasant problem." The vast majority of its population lived and worked in the countryside. For most Romanians, life was filled with hardship and misery, conditions fostered by one of the lowest levels of productivity in Europe and a political economy that transferred much of what was produced into the hands of a numerically small elite.[2]

At the same time, the political forms which Romania adopted were based on Western models, political discourse was phrased in Western terms, and the upper classes attempted to emulate Western patterns of behavior.[3] In sum, Romania was in a position of nominal political independence accompanied by economic dependency and intensive cultural proselytization to Western norms. These are the classic characteristics of neocolonial peripheries in the capitalist world system, a structural position which Romania shared at the time with other countries in Eastern Europe, the circum-Mediterranean region and Latin America. It also has close parallels with the condition of many of the new countries created in recent decades out of former colonies in Africa, Asia and the Caribbean.

John W. Cole is a Professor of Anthropology at the University of Massachusetts, Amherst. He received his doctorate from the University of Michigan in 1969.

While different individuals and parties rose and fell in the turmoil of Romanian politics, none had much success in addressing the serious underlying political and economic problems of the country. Moreover, legitimate politics were dominated by the upper classes. The bulk of the population, the peasantry, was both economically disadvantaged and politically disenfranchised. While they at times pinned their hopes on one or another of the legitimate political parties or leaders, at other times they attempted to take matters into their own hands. There were frequent peasant revolts in the course of the nineteenth century, culminating in the uprising of 1907.[4] There was also a strong millenarian strain among the people which coalesced in dramatic fashion in the widespread movement of the League of the Archangel Michael in the 1920s and 30s.[5] Such attempts by Romanian peasants to enter the political arena had much in common with "pre-modern" political movements in other agrarian peripheries of the world system.[6]

Between world wars, Nazi Germany and the other industrial states of Northwestern Europe competed for economic control and political influence in Southeastern Europe. At the same time the advent of the Soviet Union introduced a new element into the situation. Under the banner of "socialism in one country", the Soviets severed relations with the capitalist world system and were in the process of industrial development and economic and social transformation to their vision of socialism. Recognition of similarities between the severe economic, political and social problems in Romania and in pre-revolutionary Russia induced a deep fear of Bolshevik inspired revolution among upper class Romanians. Under these conditions, models of the fascist corporate state proved more attractive to elites than democratic alternatives. This political trend coincided with the ascendancy of German influence and by the late 1930s Romania was firmly integrated into the German war economy and political schemes.[7] The war that resulted from Germany's ambitions brought the downfall of fascism in Romania, wrought havoc with Romanian political economy and social life and brought communism in its wake.

Romania's position in the world system was changed profoundly by communist rule and Soviet domination. As many commentators have noted, Marx expected communist parties to come to power in advanced industrial states, where the primary task would be to create socialist relations of production in countries with well developed forces of production. Instead, communist parties have faced the primary problem of carrying out economic, political and social development. Moreover, since Marx expected the advanced capitalist states to lead the way to socialism, he had not anticipated that one of the most severe problems facing communist parties would be how to build socialism in a world that continued to be dominated by hostile capitalist powers.

The Leninist strategy, then, has developed in response to the problems of undertaking modernization and at the same time resisting (if not subverting) a capitalist world system. Joining Marx in rejecting capitalism, Lenin also rejected the premise of Western economics that trade between industrial and agrarian societies was mutually beneficial. Instead, it favors the industrial states at the expense of the agrarian ones.[8] To successfully build socialism it would be necessary to withdraw from world trade. Moreover, modernizing primary commodity producers in the twentieth century do not have open to them the option of gradual economic growth under dispersed economic decision-making which characterized Britain and the United States in the late eighteenth and early nineteenth centuries. Nor are they able to accumulate overseas territories where wealth can be extracted to support economic growth at home. Instead, surpluses have to be created and mobilized from the country's own production in a process of primary socialist accumulation. Since the productive base inherited by the party is agrarian, this required a transfer of social product from the countryside to the cities in support of urban and industrial growth.

These considerations led, in the Soviet Union, to the attempt to build "socialism in one country" and to an emphasis on rapid industrialization as the best way to both socialism and fend off capitalism. This is carried out through plans developed by the Party and put into effect through an administrative organization which incorporates all essential economic, political and social functions. Its policies include the political repression of capitalist and feudal elites, the socialization of production, and the mobilization and deployment of social product in support of industrialization.

The Leninist program, including the process of primary socialist accumulation, was initiated in Romania, as in other countries in the "Soviet bloc" in the years following World War II. This resulted in a socialist system in large measure insulated from the capitalist world. The logic of the system demanded that the Soviet Union, as the first and most developed socialist society and with the military and economic power to shield the bloc from Western subversion, should retain primacy. This served to justify the transfer of social product from Eastern Europe to the Soviet Union. At the same time, the Soviet presence in Eastern Europe insured that these countries could adhere closely to Soviet models. Each country, including Romania, developed administrative hierarchies on the Soviet model and undertook to emulate Soviet industrialization. This combination of forced industrialization and outright Soviet exploitation amounted to, "colonialism of a new type."[9] By the late 1950s a measure of decolonization had taken place and a socialist system, COMECON (also referred to as CMEA), was created to promote the simultaneous development of all participating states through close economic cooperation. In this international division of labor, Romania was assigned its customary role as a producer of agricultural products and other primary goods. Romania adhered to this assignment for a time, but by the mid-sixties it had become clear that it rejected this role and was formulating ambitious plans to promote urban and industrial growth.[10] As a part of this independent development strategy, Romania expanded its trade relations outside of COMECON to include any nation that would buy its products and furnish it with the goods that it required.[11]

Throughout its socialist period, Romania has been firmly committed to a Leninist development program. Its long term planning presumes a continuation of its present pattern of international trade but also envisions the culmination of the period of primary socialist accumulation and the gradual change over to new policies befitting the status of developed socialist society which it expects to reach soon. In this paper I shall be examining the impact of this development process on the rural sector of the country and the prospects of rural people through the 1980s.

AGRICULTURE IN THE SCHEME OF THINGS

Some idea of the magnitude and direction of social change in Socialist Romania can be derived from a few statistics. Romanian government figures indicate that between 1950 and 1975 the total social product has increased ten times while the annual rate of growth has been just under ten percent. This is the highest rate of growth of any country in Eastern Europe and one of the highest in the world. Even allowing for problems in comparing the national statistics of different countries and for a certain degree of 'statistical inflation', it is clear that Romanian productivity has increased markedly.[12] As Romanian production has grown, the country's economic and demographic structure has been transformed. Industrialization and urbanization have proceeded apace so that the majority of the workforce is now employed in industry and nearly half of the population lives in cities. In 1950 over three-quarters (seventy-six percent) of the workforce was employed in agriculture; by 1977 this figure was reduced to thirty-five percent. Over the same period the industrial workforce increased from nineteen percent to fifty-two percent of the total. In 1948 there were only 23.4 percent of the people living in cities; by 1977 the number had increased to 47.8 percent. In 1950 there were only three cities with a population of over 100,000; today there are eighteen. Moreover, the rates of productivity, industrialization and urbanization either continue unabated or else are increasing. The picture that emerges from these data, and others as well, is that of a country well on its way to becoming an urban, industrial society.

This process has resulted from Romania's persistent adherence to the Leninist strategy of primary socialist accumulation. This strategy includes state control over agricultural production and distribution and the deployment of agricultural social product in support of industrial growth.[13] That is, state control has been used to effect a transfer of wealth from agriculture into industry. This is clearly indicated by a comparison of patterns of investment with relative contribution to social product (Table 3.1). Especially in the first two decades following World War II, agriculture produced a substantial percentage of social product, while receiving only a small portion of the total investment funds in return. In contrast, industry's share of the investment funds was larger, on a percentage basis, than its contribution to the social product. The preferential treatment of industry in investment policy was supported by wage differentials between industry and agriculture and by pricing policies which favored industrial over agricultural goods.

The interests of primary accumulation are also served by the Romanian policy of regulating the influx of people into cities. The state has attempted to limit migration to individuals who have already secured a job and a place to live. Until required in the city, workers remain in the countryside where they are employed in agriculture. One impact of this policy is that Romania has not experienced the large populations of unemployed or underemployed workers in its cities that characterize developing countries elsewhere in the world.[14] It also means that the state does not have to take on the expense of supporting workers out of urban funds until it requires them. In effect, urban workers are being produced in the countryside at the expense of the rural sector. Since over sixty percent of the urban workforce is made up of individuals born and raised in the countryside, this rural contribution to Romanian industrial development is indeed substantial.

In spite of the ongoing emphasis on industrial growth and the transfer of social product from agriculture to industry, Romanian development nevertheless depends upon agriculture in a number of crucial ways. One, discussed above, is to act as a labor reservoir for industry to tap as its manpower requirements expand. Another is to feed the population so that Romania will be self-sufficient in its production of food. Since the population has increased by 36.5 percent since 1948, this has meant that agricultural production has had to increase as well. In addition to satisfying these domestic needs, the agricultural sector is also required to produce commodities for export. While presently contributing only a little more than ten percent to the national social product, agricultural exports account for over one-quarter of Romanian exports and earn over thirty percent of its convertable currency.

These various considerations have meant that Romanian planning has had to attempt a delicate balancing act. As much as possible of the national investment fund should be earmarked for industry, yet agricultural production must be increased enough to meet the demand for industrial crops, food and export goods. It has also been necessary to mechanize agriculture to a certain extent, and to carry out other modernizing changes, in order to compensate for the loss of manpower as workers are drawn into the urban workforce. Yet, this should not be promoted too rapidly lest workers be pushed out of agriculture faster than they can be absorbed in the cities. The result of these varying and sometimes contradictory considerations is that, while Romania's development strategy has resulted in a net transfer of value from agriculture to industry, investment in agriculture has had to be increased. This has been done not so much by making agriculture's share of the investment pie bigger as by increasing the size of the pie itself. As overall Romanian productivity has grown, the amount of money available for investment has increased and so the amount represented by a given portion of the total has also increased (Table 3.2). Since 1950, agricultural production has tripled in Romania. While this has been more or less adequate for national needs, observers, including Romanians President Ceausescu, are aware that productivity has lagged well behind potential.[15]

As industrial capacity has expanded, the practice of transferring values earned in agriculture to industry has become less significant. In the 1950s, agriculture's contribution was essential to industrial growth, but by 1970 industry was capable of sustaining its own expansion. This is indicated by the changing contributions of the two sectors to the national social product. While agricultural production increased by a factor of three between 1948 and 1975, its share of the national social product fell from over forty percent to barely ten percent during the same period. Industrial production, meanwhile, increased eleven fold and its contribution to the social product grew from about one-third to over two-thirds.

The level of investment is, of course, an important factor in establishing the level of agricultural output. The character of the Romanian agrarian system, however, has undergone its most striking changes in organization and in relations of production. The pre-war system of financing agriculture, of accumulating and marketing agricultural produce, and the social relations through which this was all carried out have been destroyed and replaced by socialist forms. Immediately following the war the land of larger estates and the holdings of individuals who were deemed fascist collaboraters were redistributed. Between 1949 and 1962, a collectivization process left over ninety percent of all agricultural land in the hands of either state farms or producer's cooperatives (Table 3.3). After 1962 there was a consolidation of village-size cooperatives into multivillage farms, following which inter-cooperative councils were established to facilitate cooperation between these farms. Mechanization has been promoted through the establishment of Machine Stations, each of which is charged with assisting several farms. All farms are connected, through country agricultural boards, to the Ministry of Agriculture which is responsible for planning and managing all agricultural activities. While national agricultural planning began even before the cooperatives were formed, administrative means of articulating the farms vertically with county and national bureaus have continually been elaborated and strengthened.[16]

In place of the entrepreneurial middle men and marketing system of pre-socialist Romania, a system of collection and distribution has been established as a part of the Ministry of Agriculture and Food Processing. The state is now the purchaser, processor and distributor of most agricultural goods produced in the country. The products of individual production, as well, are included in state planning and local agricultural agents negotiate contracts with individual producers so as to stimulate production in directions desired by the plan.[17] Some produce is marketed by individuals, and even by state and cooperative farms, in town and city marketplaces. These are managed by the state and, while not interferring directly in the marketing process, limits are set on price fluctuation. In addition, there are goods which are transferred directly from producer to consumer without any state intervention, a phenomenon to which I shall return below. While some goods are thus produced and sold without recourse to the state, the vast bulk of agricultural produce is in state hands from producer to final consumer (Table 3.4).

Romanian economic planning has thus succeeded in establishing an agrarian sector which is overwhelmingly socialist in character. Over ninety percent of the productive land is held by either state or cooperative farms and production which is carried out by individuals outside of these institutions is in large measure incorporated into the socialist sector as well. Processing and distribution are largely in state hands and the state also attempts to regulate the circulation of goods which takes place outside of formal socialist institutions. Control of agricultural institutions has enabled the state to direct agricultural production so as to support its overall economic goals. Throughout most of its socialist history, Romania has effected a net transfer of social product to industry as a part of its overall effort to promote urban-industrial development.

URBANIZATION OF THE COUNTRYSIDE

In 1948 there were fewer than four million people living in cities in Romania and today there are well over ten million, representing over forty-seven percent of the total population. While the cities have experienced some natural increases in population, urban growth has been largely a product of migration from rural areas. Nearly sixty percent of the population of even Romania's seven largest cities are migrants and the majority of these come from rural areas. This rural-urban migration is reflected in the decreasing percentage of the population which lives in rural areas. However, the actual number of people living in the countryside has decreased only slightly. As recently as 1975 the number of rural people was over ninety-nine percent as great as it was in 1948 and even today there are over ninety-three percent as many people in villages as in 1948 (Table 3.5). In fact, the growth of Romanian cities has been fed primarily by a growth in the total population. Between 1948 and 1970 the increase in the urban population was 101.8 percent of the country's total population growth (Table 3.6). Migration from the countryside has not depleted the rural population, it has simply absorbed its expansion.

This phenomenon is less an indication of the persistence of agrarian life than it is an aspect of the nature of Romanian urban-industrial growth. What Romania is experiencing is the urbanization of rural life. One element in this process is that the pace of industrialization is greater than the pace of urban growth. While over fifty-two percent of the population and nearly fifty-seven percent of the workforce lives in the countryside, only thirty-two percent of the workforce is engaged in agriculture. This means that, on a national basis, a full quarter of the urban workforce lives in rural villages. Some of these are employed locally in service and retail activities, others are employed in industrial enterprises located in the countryside, but most are commuting workers.

The pattern of rural-based workers who commute to cities to work is a well established aspect of Romanian modernization and is an outgrowth of the logic of primary socialist accumulation. Workers who migrate to cities require an outlay in non-productive services that detracts from the state's investment fund for industry. Apartment complexes must be constructed as well as new facilities to care for their shopping, educational and medical needs. Workers who commute, however, receive most of their social support from their villages. Commuting does require the development of an effective transportation system, but the costs of this are relatively low and, besides, are largely born by the commuters through their purchase of tickets. Continued expansion of industrial capacity in existing large cities will require more migration, but long range Romanian planning includes an ongoing reliance on rural-based workers. Romanian plans promoting rural industrialization and industrial growth in regions that are still predominantly rural rely heavily on the assumption that much of the workforce of these new industries will continue to live in villages.

However, the presence of urban workers in rural areas is not the only indication of the modernization of the countryside. As Kenneth Jowitt has argued, the collectivization of agriculture is one of the most distinctive features of the Leninist strategy.[18] This has meant that the relations of production in the countryside, dominated by familistic and patron-client ties in the past, come to be formally established on an impersonal bureaucratic basis. Although family and networks of kith and kin are being reproduced under Romanian socialism, the formal social framework in which they operate is of paramount significance.[19] All but a small percentage of Romanians who work in agriculture are employed on state or cooperative farms where the norms of organization and the remuneration are established in terms of impersonal rules. Workers are organized into work teams, and these are clustered into brigades. Some are assigned work with crops and others are assigned to animal husbandry. Administration of the farm is in the hands of the president of the cooperative and his staff, which includes trained agronomists and zoo-technicians.

Accounting procedures are applied to all activities which are regarded as legitimate aspects of the farm's operation. Wages are paid to workers on the basis of some combination of hours worked and tasks accomplished, the method of calculation differing for different tasks, and being altered from time to time in response to changing circumstances. Pay is also partially dependent on the farms' productivity and income, a factor which recognizes the formal ownership of the farm by its workers. So, whether the villager is a commuting worker or a cooperativist, he or she is engaged in a corporate structure where relationships between individuals are defined in impersonal hierarchical terms.

THE PEOPLES' SHARE OF THE PIE

Romania's adherence to the Leninist strategy of primary socialist accumulation has not only called upon agriculture to contribute more to national growth than it receives in return, but has also kept remuneration of the workforce to a minimum. The rationale for this is along the following lines: Under the mixture of capitalism and feudalism which existed in Romania before World War II, workers and peasants were exploited as the wealth they produced was extracted and consumed by the upper classes. Because of Romania's agrarian status, much of this wealth flowed out of the country to the wealthy industrial states. In part this happened as returns on the investment of foreign capital and in part because of the consumption patterns of the elites. These were met through imports rather than by developing the indiginous forces of production. The Communist Party has terminated the consumption of wealth by an exploiting class and the uncontrolled export of social product and has diverted it toward the development of the Romanian economy. However, because the level of Romanian productive capacity was initially low, workers and peasants could not expect much immediate improvement in their standard of living. An attempt to direct production toward consumption would have had disappointing results because the total social product was so small. Moreover, this would divert funds away from investment, slow the rate of economic growth and perpetuate poverty. It is therefore in the interest of workers and peasants to postpone consumption in the present in favor of investment. This will result in a higher average standard of living over the long run.

Throughout its socialist period, then, policies have favored a low level of worker remuneration and an emphasis on the production of producer goods at the expense of consumer goods. At the same time, the state has an interest in maintaining a healthy and productive workforce and operates in the ideological framework of a worker's state where in the final analysis all policies must be justified on the basis of their contribution to the welfare of the worker. There has, therefore, been a steady increase in wages and in the production of consumer goods which has had the effect of gradually raising the standard of living of the population.[20] Moreover, in addition to direct wages, the state has also created and expanded a bundle of social services and welfare measures without sacrificing investment in production. Improvements in worker remuneration have, as in the case of agricultural investment, been tied to increasing productivity. The percentage share of national income distributed to workers remains approximately constant, but the actual amount grows as the national income grows.

In spite of the low rate of remuneration for workers, the level of material existence in Romania today has surpassed anything known in the past. In examining Romania's performance in social welfare, Trond Gilberg concluded that:

> . . . the Romanian leadership has succeeded in providing the population with a comprehensive system of social and medical benefits, pensions, child and old age care centers and other features of the welfare state. No one risks the previously common fate of periodic starvation in socialist Romania, and a minimum of material existence has been established. Within the historical context and experience of the Balkans this is a major achievement indeed.[21]

The results of these policies are apparent in a constant improvement in Romanian statistics on life expectancy, death rate, infant mortality rates, and other demographic data which serve as measures of the health of a population (Table 3.7).[22]

Workers appreciate the expansion in the productive pie and they also absorb the constant explanations from the state about the necessity to postpone consumption in the present in order to insure greater consumption in the future and over the long run. Certainly there is a measure of identification between the Party and the workers they claim to represent, even though the extent of worker participation in decision-making is problematic, as Professor Nelson points out in Chapter VI. Workers feel a degree of material security unknown in the past (and rare in developing countries in general). They also appreciate the opportunities which will be available to their children as they grow up. At the same time, they are also concerned about their present consumption needs and those of their family.

As a result of the state's guarantee of a 'minimum of material existence', workers have learned to take adequate food, clothing and shelter for granted. They have also come to expect the medical, educational and other social benefits provided by the state. There are few thoughtful individuals who doubt that the present is more materially secure than the past. The political and economic options of the presocialist era have become a dead issue. Socialism is here to stay. People's actions, economic and otherwise, are based on their

understanding of the realities of the socialist present
and their ideas about what it will be like in the future.
   An important factor in the formation of people's
ideas about what the future will be like are the proclamations which call attention to the advancement of the
Romanian economy and promise even greater feats in the
future. While there is a level of skepticism about the
state's more exuberant predictions, people have learned
to expect that the future will surpass the present in
material comforts, and find in this a measure of confir-
mation of the state's promises. This all contributes to
an atmosphere of rising expectations.
   The shaping of the consumption expectations of the
people is in large measure determined by inevitable comparisons of socialist and capitalist performance. In
proclaiming their superiority to capitalism, the socialist states promise both to surpass capitalist production
and to return more benefits to the worker since socialism
is unencumbered by a capitalist class. In so doing, the
state uses the performance of Western industrial capitalism as a standard of measure. While socialism may not
yet have overtaken the capitalist states, they claim that
it will do so in the not too distant future. Without
really intending to, the state thus sets the consumption
standards of the West as a goal to which people can
aspire. This they are perfectly willing to do, and in
their search for consumption norms Romanian workers have
become avid consumers of information about Western life-
styles. Various Western agencies, and individuals as
well, do their best to make this information available.
There are also examples available in films, TV programs,
in tourists traveling in socialist states, and, notably
in the Saxon areas of Transylvania, visits from relatives who have migrated to the West. It does not take a
public opinion poll to discover that Romanian workers
have a well developed case of rampant consumerism.[23]
   Since the state controls the means of production in
Romania, few workers can earn a living outside of the
socialist sector. While socialist ideology promises all
who will work a job, it does not promise that all jobs
will bring equal remuneration. Indeed, while the state
is wary of tendencies in wage differentials to expand,
it nevertheless rewards certain kinds of jobs better
than others in an effort to attract individuals into
those activities required for economic growth. We
have noted, for instance, that urban workers earn more
on the average than do agricultural workers, and within
each sector there are differences as well. As in other
countries, these wage differences, together with other
job characteristics, make some jobs more appealing than
others. Since not everyone can have the "better" jobs,
workers find themselves in competition, and a means is

required to allocate workers among the different positions. This is accomplished by the state which makes these decisions through an impersonal bureaucracy in accordance with the rationale of state planning. The state decision-making apparatus evaluates applications and petitions and allocates such things as advanced education, trade schools, jobs and urban apartments, all of which have a direct bearing on people's ability to earn a living.

Moreover, employment even at a substantial salary and with a bundle of benefits and a few perks does not necessarily guarantee a worker access to all of the goods and services that he or she requires. While goods and services for a minimum material existence are more or less readily available, if not in village consumer cooperatives, then in town shops, other goods are available only from time to time, in limited quantity and at unpredictable locations. These are generally goods produced especially for the domestic market, but goods manufactured for export are sometimes also marketed within the country. Since these are made to compete with Western goods, it is assumed that they are of superior quality and style to those for the home market. Even foreign goods appear from time to time in Romanian stores. Moreover, there are also goods and services produced privately, outside of the socialist sector, or which the social sector rarely or never produces. The pursuit of goods and services, then, is not simply a matter of earning the money and buying the commodity. Success as a consumer requires being in the know and of being able to be at the right place at the right time.

A worker in socialist Romania, then, is faced with a series of dilemmas. His rising expectations and the range of goods available in Romania tax his earning ability; his search for a satisfying job with lucrative pay is threatened by competition from his fellows; his search for goods and services beyond the minimum level of material existence is complicated by their irregular and limited distribution. Facing these dilemmas is the essence of domestic economics in modern Romania.

A DIGRESSION ON HOW THE BUREAUCRACY REALLY WORKS

Every facet of life in modern Romania, including the pursuit of domestic economic goals, requires interaction with the national bureaucracy.[24] As a highly centralized socialist state, Romania has an administrative system charged with organizing political, economic and social life. The state attempts to identify every significant aspect of society and to create administrative organizations which will control it. Through implementation of the state's plans, the administrative structure is expected to organize the economic development of the country, stimulate the population into active participation in the construction of a modern socialist state, and promote a strong socialist consciousness in the population.

Each individual with a position in this corporate state structure has control over some of the resources which are to be used to accomplish these goals. Their function is to distribute these in accordance with a rationale developed by the state. Both in relations among office holders within the bureaucracy, and in relations between office holders and individuals in the population at large, a rational-impersonal or <u>corporate</u> mode of social interaction is the norm.

But no corporate structure realistically can expect to take into account every eventuality that its members will encounter. Were the system to do so, the resulting rules and procedures would be so unwieldly and voluminous that no one would be able to fathom them, let alone put them into operation. To avoid such involuted complexity, every administrative system must necessarily allow a certain amount of "slippage". Office holders must have some discretion in the exercise of their duties. They must be able to make decisions where there are no clear-cut guidelines, and even deviate from the rules when extenuating circumstances make their application inadvisable. While every bureaucratic system holds a Weberian ideal of rational operation as its norm, all must tolerate a degree of "sloppiness" in order to function.[25]

While there are always numbers of routine tasks which can be performed in the corporate mode of rational-impersonal social relations, there are also many matters which are more problematic. When ad hoc decisions require negotiation between office holders, the corporate mode of behavior may be awkward. This is the case whenever the rationale of the system does not clearly apply, or where the application of a clearly defined directive is thought to be inadvisable. Such actions can be undertaken with a greater degree of assurance and less personal risk if the corporate relations between individuals involved in the decision are fortified by personal ties. That is, bureaucrats can operate with less risk if they can count on support from other office holders based on personal commitments rather than solely on impersonal corporate relationships. As a result of such considerations, every administrative system is permeated by networks of personal, non-corporate social relations among its members. An understanding of the way in which a bureaucracy functions requires an examination of the structure of these non-corporate networks as well as of the formal, corporate structure.

The nature of the social organization of an administrative system, the particular mix of corporate and non-corporate social relations and the way in which these function, depends upon the nature of the institutional system, its goals, and the setting in which it is established. The mix will be of one sort in a powerful capitalist industrial state, and of another in an agrarian periphery of the capitalist world system.[26] In Romania there is a three-tiered bureaucracy functioning under the conditions of primary socialist accumulation. Individuals within the system are charged with allocating resources in accordance with the rationale of primary socialist accumulation. However, there are different priorities for deployment of these resources. Some of these occur because of the differing perspectives of people at the national, regional and local levels. There is also competition between regions and between communities or enterprises within different regions. Different sectors of the economy also have their own priorities, which do not always mesh perfectly. Such differences should, in the logic of the system, be resolved in accordance with rational criteria, that is, in terms of what will most effectively promote primary socialist accumulation, and hence the common good. Yet, reasonable patriotic men and women can honestly differ in their interpretations of what will best promote the common good, and in seeking to promote their perspectives, personal non-corporate ties can be brought into play in order to achieve the best socialist outcome. Indeed, the actual planning process in Romania can be seen as an outcome of the interplay of corporate and non-corporate relations employed in the promotion of diverse perspectives.[27]

While the system does function much, if not most, of the time so as to promote the development of socialist Romania, it is also possible for individuals to use their positions to personal advantage. Indeed, temptations abound, growing out of the fact that office holders control resources which many want but which only some can have. At times they no doubt bend rules for altruistic reasons -- to aid an individual or organization which is deserving in their eyes but which would be excluded under a strict application of the rules. But it is also possible to perform their function as a personal favor, or what amounts to the same thing, to give the appearance of doing so. In either case, they will be in a position to collect a favor or favors in return. Mutual obligations established in this fashion are one of the principal ways in which non-corporate relations are built among bureaucrats.

The consumer of services, the worker or citizen, faces a system which claims to make its decisions on rational impersonal grounds. Yet, the individual knows that an edge can be gained in the competition for resources if he or she can approach the office holder on a personal basis. Such relations may already exist for the consumer, on the basis of such non-corporate relations as kinship, friendships built in school, ritual relations, and so on. Or, it may be necessary to establish a new relationship: a simple gift or favor may suffice as a starting mechanism, or, if a long term relationship seems desirable, one may attempt to build a friendship, or to involve the individual in a ritual relationship. Even marriage for economic advantage is not unknown. In any case, office holders come under considerable pressure from consumers to succumb to the temptation to use their office for personal advantage. At the same time, individuals who must approach the administrative system on an impersonal basis are inevitably at a disadvantage.

Non-corporate relations are an aspect of the everyday operation of Romanian administrative structures, as Sampson has demonstrated for <u>sistematizare</u> planning and Kideckel has shown in the operation of a cooperative farm.[28] Moreover, there is ample evidence for their operation at all levels of the Romanian bureaucracy. Romania watchers, both inside Romania and out, delight in tracing personal relationships between high ranking party and state officials and the ways in which these have influenced particular appointments. Scandals, such as those over the officials who were exposed for accepting bribes from failed applicants as a basis for admission to law school, are a regular feature of the Romanian press. At a lower level, enterprise or farm managers who divert labor or material to their own private use come to light from time to time. It is a truism of rural life that no country doctor need ever spend even one <u>leu</u> on food because of the in-kind gifts of his patients, and "everyone" relates experiences such as the case where a new shipment of stylish shoes was sold out even before the store opened because all of them had been purchased by the store's employees on behalf of friends, relatives, neighbors and important individuals whom they wished to influence. The most cynical observation on this phenomena comes from the Brasov worker who observes that PCR stands not for <u>Partidul Comunist Roman</u> -- The Romanian Communist Party -- but for <u>Pile, Cunostinte, si Relatie</u> -- influence, information and connections.[29]

REGIONAL VARIATION

While socialist institutions affect the lives of people in all parts of the country, all areas have not been integrated into the socialist political economy in the same way. In the interest of rapid industrialization and the most efficient use of investment funds, industrialization was pushed in areas which already had an industrial base rather than in more rural areas. As a result, the urban character of some areas was strengthened while other areas remained solidly agricultural. Today there are ten counties with over half of their population living in cities, but there are also ten counties where over seventy percent of the population lives in rural villages.[30] Other counties range in-between.

There are also significant differences between rural areas in different parts of the country. Agricultural cooperatives have not been established in mountain areas or in the most rugged hill country.[31] Although production in uncooperativized areas is included in socialist planning, with state policies and agents influencing production and distribution, agrarian life remains household-centered.[32] Production in all other areas is organized into state or cooperative farms, but there are important differences in these areas, too. The state has responded to ecologically based contrasts in agricultural potential with different levels of investment (Table 3.8). As a general rule, investment has been greatest on the fertile plains, where extensive grain cultivation lends itself well to mechanization, and in areas where irrigation is feasible. In areas with low levels of capitalization, the farms, even though socialist in organization, depend on large numbers of laborers often employed at tasks requiring minimum training. On highly capitalized farms, however, less labor is required and much of the agricultural work is more technical.

As a result of these contrasts in economic conditions, workers in different parts of the country have somewhat different living standards, lifestyles and economic opportunities. Life as a farmworker is considerably different in uncooperativized hill villages than it is for villagers who work on modern highly capitalized state or cooperative farms. The kind of life villagers experience is also influenced by how remote their villages are from cities. Villagers in urban zones inevitably have greater access to amenities of city life than do villagers in remote rural regions. Moreover, villages near cities will have many urban workers living in them while workers from remote areas who choose urban employment have no choice but to migrate, leaving agricultural villages behind.

The contrast in material returns between industry and agriculture, coupled with less tangible advantages of urban life, draw workers to industry from all parts of the country. This tendency is strengthened by an educational system which stresses preparation for life in a modern industrial state. Moreover, a constant media barrage of government proclamations stresses that Romania's future lies in industrial urban development. These factors all contribute to the migration of labor from agriculture to industry. As one would expect, remote rural areas experience a high rate of outmigration and little inmigration so that they constantly lose population to more industrial counties (Table 3.9).[33] High outmigration rates are especially characteristic of agricultural areas with high levels of investment and production where fewer farm workers are required. There is also less outmigration from rural areas in the vicinity of cities where many workers, even though they leave agricultural for industrial employment, continue to live in the village.

These contrasts in economic conditions have had an impact on the demographic and social characteristics of the different regions. Birth rates in the countryside continue to be higher than those in the city which partly compensates for the high rates of outmigration. However, the crude death rate and both fetal and infant mortality rates are higher in the rural areas, too, and life expectancy is lower. Because of the higher death rate, the natural population increase has recently dropped below urban areas first time (Table 3.10).

Natural population growth has contributed to the expansion of the urban population, but the main contributing factor has been a high positive net migration rate: a lot more people move to urban areas than leave them. Rural areas on the other hand, experience negative net migration rates, and, in spite of their higher birth rates (and until recently, rates of natural population increase) they have very low rates of population growth. One county, Botosani, has even experienced a population decline. Moreover, higher birth rates and increasing longevity of rural populations coupled with the outmigration of young workers leaves the rural areas with a higher proportion of non-workers to workers than in urban areas. Since urban areas both retain their own young workers, and more move in from other parts of the country, their dependency ratios are lower than in rural areas (Table 3.11). On the average, rural workers must support more dependents than do urban workers, and they do su with lower incomes.

When examined in total, these data indicate that people in rural areas experience a harder life than their urban counterparts. They also show that life is harder in rural areas remote from cities than it is in rural areas in the vicinity of cities.

THE SECOND SHIFT

Workers, then, have different degrees and kinds of

involvement with the socialist sector depending on a
number of social, economic and geographical factors. As
a consequence, there is also variety in the strategies
that workers have developed in their efforts to achieve
satisfactory lifestyles. Long term urban residents have,
generally speaking, the strongest claims on the socialist
sector. For one thing, they have better access to the
urban job of their choice: people who already live in
cities are always preferred over potential migrants,[34]
and their schooling is more likely to have better prepared them for urban jobs or for the training necessary
for many of the best jobs.[35] At least as important,
however, is that they will already have social networks
established in the city which will give them access to
crucial information about employment. Ties, both with
other workers and with people in the bureaucracy, help
to provide information and assistance in crucial matters
such as education, employment and finding an apartment.
These ties are also crucial on a day-to-day basis, as in
learning when and where desirable commodities will become
available, or in making sure that one is able to obtain a
commodity in short supply. Moreover, living in the city,
both the worker and his/her spouse will be able to hold
urban jobs so that urban households are best able to
"maximize" income and benefits from the socialist sector.

Workers from villages located near cities are also
in a good position to gain access to the socialist sector
and at the same time have certain benefits derived from
their rural origins. Living near the city, they can
count on contacts made over the years with urban relatives and friends for information and assistance.
Another advantage is that they have the option of either
commuting or moving to a nearby city. If they move, they
will have many of the same advantages as the long time
urban dweller: they know the turf, have contacts in
place, and both husband and wife can have a salary and
benefits. Moreover, they will still have social ties
with individuals in the village. If they elect to commute, they will have an urban income and can also tap
resources which are available in villages.

It is true that urban jobs offer more benefits than
those in agriculture. Agricultural workers earn less
money and for years lacked the social benefits which
urban workers received. There are, of course, certain
attractions to an agricultural job, not the least of
which is that many people simply like farm work. It also
has the advantage of providing direct access to food.
Farm workers are paid not only in cash, but in kind as
well, with an opportunity to produce food privately.
They will almost certainly have a kitchen garden attached
to their house, and all employees of a cooperative farm
are entitled to a small personal plot (currently .15
hectare). They can also raise a certain number of

animals, such as cattle, water buffalo, sheep or pigs, and flocks of chickens or geese are ubiquitous in Romanian villages. Moreover, rural houses are large, urban apartments are small, and rural life has advantages such as "good air" and sunshine. Nevertheless, in spite of these attractions, a one-on-one comparison of an urban job with a rural one leaves few doubts in a worker's mind about where the advantage lies. Large numbers of both men and women thus opt for urban employment and, as we have seen, migrate or commute to the city. However, even when urban jobs are available, not everyone leaves the village. For most individuals, career decisions are not simply a matter of selecting what is personally best for them. The choices that people make are influenced by the choices made by other individuals to whom they are closely related.

By commuting, a villager who lives near a city can have a salary from factory or office and reasonably effective urban networks. It will also be possible for both husband and wife to commute, their household thus enjoying the same sort of double income as an urban household. Moreover, by living in the village, the couple can, at the same time, partake of the advantages of rural life. They can even care for a few animals and crops after work. However, they can much more effectively tap the village's agricultural resources if they deploy some member of the household to full time agricultural work. Since men and women draw about the same salaries in agriculture, and since men still dominate the best paying urban jobs, it will probably be the husband who commutes and the wife who stays in the village. This combination of urban and agricultural incomes works best when there are more than two adults involved. In most cases, this would be a married couple and the parent(s) of one of them. It will then be possible for one (or two) adults to commute to the city, for another to devote full time to the household's private resources, and still another to work for the cooperative farm. By deploying its workforce in this way, a household, or pair of closely related cooperating households, is able to provide for its subsistence needs from the agricultural products they raise themselves and receive from the cooperative farm as in-kind income.[36] This means that much of the money earned by the urban worker can be devoted to consumer goods, which all can enjoy.

Workers who move to the city from nearby villages are not automatically excluded from the benefits of rural income. There are quantities of goods and services which flow between urban and rural households. Agricultural and craft goods produced in rural households are channeled to relatives who live in nearby towns, while consumer goods purchased with the higher salaries earned by

urban workers are presented to rural relatives. Urban
dwellers assist with labor in the countryside and keep
their rural brethern informed about urban matters of
interest. Villagers will care for urban relatives'
children during emergencies and, in some cases, the
children of urban couples will actually live in the village with grandparents and even go to school there, while
their parents continue to live and work in the city.
Indeed, cooperation between related households is often
as close as that among individuals who live in the same
household. For all intents and purposes, these households constitute a single socioeconomic unit, a domestic
group. While there are variations in the degree and
intensity of relations between urban and rural households, these ties are of considerable economic significance to the parties involved. This integration results
in a higher standard of living than could be achieved by
independent worker households whether employed in
industry or agriculture.[37]

Domestic groups, made up of either single households
or two-household units, constitute the elements of these
social networks. While individuals build ties with other
individuals, the obligations and benefits of these relationships extend to the domestic group as a whole. The
networks link together domestic groups both within villages and between village and town. Their strength is in
fact determined by the frequency of interaction between
their members so that rural-urban connections are most
effective when distances are not great. Sundays and
holidays find urban relatives visiting the village, or
rural folk traveling to the city to visit urban kin or
friends. Funerals, baptisms, and especially weddings,
bring together network members for anywhere from a day
to more than a week to help with preparations or simply
to attend the occasion. These ritual relationships,
centering on Orthodox ceremony, have their origins in the
pre-socialist past, but this does not explain their viability today, nor the kinds of prestige that accrues to
individuals, including priests, who facilitate them.
Rather, they are viable because of their significance in
promoting and validating social networks which serve
important household economic functions.[38]

Rural workers from villages located outside of commuting distance of cities are the most disadvantaged in
gaining access to the socialist sector. They are
typically less well trained for urban employment than
workers who live near town and they are much less likely
to have social networks established in distant cities,
although they may know a few other recent migrants from
their village or county. This means that they have less
familiarity with the workings of the bureaucracy in the
city and, lacking effective contacts, they are also less

likely to be able to use influence. Once they do succeed in locating a job and an apartment in the city, they are at a disadvantage in gaining access to consumer information, or of taking advantage of information once they do get it (there is no grandparent to send out to stand in line when both husband and wife must be at work). Moreover, migrants from distant villages have more difficulties in making use of rural-urban ties. Contacts limited to a few times a year do not have the same effectiveness as those which are operationalized weekly or even every few days.

The situation is also quite different for those who remain behind in the more remote rural areas.[39] For one thing, commuting is out of the question. In its place is the possibility of temporary employment in the city, but this means living in a dormitory away from one's family and having to work at the least desirable, lowest paying jobs. Young people are those most often employed in this way. Moreover, given the difficulty of maintaining urban-village ties over long distances, rural families cannot count on the same level of social, ritual and economic support from their urban kinsmen as can villagers living near cities. While strong social networks continue to exist within these villages, they more often serve the purpose of organizing rural life than of providing bridges between town and country. Finally, familial obligations serve in remote areas to help maintain a younger agricultural workforce than is found in villages around cities. While older siblings establish new households when they marry, the youngest is expected to stay at home, inheriting both his parents' house and the obligation to care for them. If he lives near a city, he will no doubt decide to work in town, but he will still be able to live at home and fulfill his obligation to his parents. On the other hand, the youngest son in a remote village must either stay in agriculture or desert his parents and move to the city.

Explanations for three-generation households, strong social networks between households and the persistence of Orthodox religious ceremonies in Romania, focus on links to the pre-socialist past and assume that their prevalence is inversely proportional to the strength of corporate socialist institutions.[40] A different explanation is offered here. While they lie outside of the organized socialist _sector_, they are nevertheless an integral part of the socialist _system_. These non-corporate relationships are constantly being reproduced under the conditions of primary socialist accumulation in Romania. Whether living in rural areas remote from urban centers and engaged as workers on cooperative farms, or living in rural areas located near cities and drawing incomes from both urban centers and the cooperative or state farm, worker households are engaged in private production. This production is carried out by working-age adults who also work in the socialist sector, together with their children and, in some households, adults who work only at home. From the perspective of the household, this production is a response to a combination of the low level of remuneration in comparison to the rising consumer expectations.[41] The social networks which link households within villages and between town and country serve as distribution networks both for private produce and services and for goods which originate in the socialist sector. Orthodox ritual serves to validate and strengthen the networks.

Romanian workers call the work that they do in agriculture after they come home to their village after a day of work in the factory their "<u>second shift</u>." Sometimes, they work on their own agricultural resources, sometimes they help a family member with her (less often, his) work on the cooperative farm, and sometimes they will help out a relative or neighbor. By extension of the way in which workers use the term, I will use second shift to refer to the entire process of production and distribution which is carried on through non-corporate social relations.

There is no direct measure of the magnitude of the second shift. Census counts of households do not record the extent of three generational strategies because they only count who lives in particular houses and have no way of recording the quality of relationships within or between houses. They sometimes count as separate households two structures within the same courtyard even though these may function as a single household. They will always count two physically separate structures as distinct households no matter how close their economic and social cooperation. Research conducted in villages in Brasov county showed that over one third of the households contained at least three adults, and that over one half of all adults lived in these extended family households. In many of the remaining households, moreover, nuclear families and single individuals were closely involved with other households in the village or town, and were parts of two residence domestic groups. Notwithstanding minimal statistical data, it is clear that most individuals in these villages participate in domestic groups practicing a three generational strategy and made up of either a single three-generational household, or of two households which between them contain three generations. Virtually all domestic groups are, in fact, enmeshed in extensive social networks. It is also clear from published research and discussions with Romanian and American colleagues, that Brasov county is not exceptional in this regard. The functions of domestic groups and social networks do differ by region, but in form they are ubiquitous.

There is also no direct measure of the total production of the second shift or of the magnitude of the distribution of goods and services through non-corporate social networks. However, some indication of its magnitude nationally can be derived from certain economic data available in published Romanian statistics. One of the figures included in agricultural production tables is for the personal production of members of the cooperative farms (Table 3.12). These data indicate what members of the cooperative farms produce using "free time" labor and their own land (i.e., their garden plots and the personal plots alloted for their use by the cooperative farm). This will include the second shift production of most village domestic groups since each will inevitably have a member who works for the cooperative farm. Since all members of the domestic group work together on the same resources, the tables are actually reporting the second shift output of domestic groups of which cooperative farm workers are members. As an estimate of second shift production, these figures are no doubt somewhat low, but they do provide a reasonable approximation. They make it clear that second shift production is indeed significant.

The second shift, then, is important not only for individual domestic groups which participate in it, but for the state and entire socialist system as well. It is accomplished without any direct cost to the socialist sector; labor inputs are during workers' free time and the means of production are personal. Although second shift production and distribution are outside the socialist sector, it is nevertheless essential to the socialist system. A strategy of primary socialist accumulation emphasizes rapid industrial growth supported by low levels of remuneration for workers, especially for agricultural workers, and promises to increase productivity and worker benefits, which results in rising material expectations. Low production of consumer goods, coupled with a distribution system which is uncertain, provide additional stimuli. In abstract terms, the cost of reproducing the workforce required by the socialist sector is not borne by the socialist sector alone, but is shared with the workers themselves. Workers produce goods on their own time with their own means of production, thus compensating for their low wages. This produce is distributed to other households, including urban ones, in return for other goods and services, thus serving to support households not engaged directly in agriculture. Goods produced in the socialist sector enter the non-corporate system and are distributed through it, thus compensating for the uneven availability of socialist produced goods through the socialist distribution system. Once set in motion, the second shift becomes one of the factors necessary for the reproduction of the process of primary socialist accumulation.

At one level of analysis, then, the second shift benefits the socialist system as a whole. A closer examination, however, reveals that there are associated costs as well. It functions to compensate for deficiencies in socialist sector production and distribution, masking problems which might otherwise be confronted and solved. It thus contributes to the reproduction of inefficiency and ineffectiveness. Second shift production also infringes in some measure on socialist sector agricultural production as farm cadres and workers sometimes transfer a measure of farm labor and materials to their own personal operations. The personal use of machinery, the private appropriation of material and the deployment of paid farm labor on personal resources all infringe on socialist agricultural production. Anecdotal material and newspaper reports of scandals suggest that such activities, while individually of small scale, are widespread. The total direct impact and the indirect effect of cynicism and poor morale that they engender are difficult to assess. More serious problems, however, are associated with the impact of the second shift on labor quality in the socialist sector.

Since the labor power workers bring to bear on second shift production is in addition to their work in the socialist sector, it apparently has no cost to the socialist sector but represents an increase in the socialist system's productivity. However, severe indirect costs to the system are evident. Second shift production is directly proportional to the amount of work invested in it. This leads second shift producers who are employed in the socialist sector to expand their second shift efforts even if it means that these efforts interfere with their socialist sector jobs. While there are general problems with labor productivity in the socialist sector, commuting workers (that is, those most likely to be engaged in second shift production) are singled out in Romanian studies as a special problem. Their rates of absenteeism and tardiness are higher than other workers, they report in sick more often, habitually exchange shifts among themselves, have higher accident rates than other workers and are seen as generally less effective when on the job.[43] Thus, while the socialist sector benefits from the second shift to the extent that it supports policies of low remuneration and high investment, it also suffers from the second shift as a cause of poor quality labor.

THE TRANSITION TO MATURE SOCIALISM

Romanian planners anticipate that the process of

primary socialist accumulation will be phased out during the 1980s. They have already set to work developing plans appropriate to a mature developed socialist society. The transition to mature socialism will be marked by levels of productivity and personal consumption which approximate those of other developed socialist societies in Eastern Europe. The economy will have achieved a predominantly industrial character and the agricultural workforce will be reduced to under fifteen percent of the total.[44] The society will be decidedly urban, but in the distinctive Romanian system of urban growth coupled with the urbanization of the countryside.

The transformation to mature socialism will not be sudden. As early as 1970, the Romanian Communist Party began to formulate concrete plans which express the economic, social and cultural goals of mature socialism. Under the strategy of primary socialist accumulation, the principal goal was the development of the forces of production and all other goals were subordinated to high levels of investment and to the employment of investment funds so as to achieve the greatest increase in productivity. Under mature socialism, the primary goals are to overcome certain economic and cultural inequalities. The rate of investment is to be reduced in favor of an increase in the level of consumption and social services. At the same time, while productivity is to continue to rise, the goal of investment will be to promote urban and industrial growth in backward agricultural regions, even though rates of return may well be less than if these funds were invested in more economically advanced counties. There will also be a drive to expand cultural and economic services in the countryside until they approximate those of urban areas.

The plans which have been developed to achieve these goals are encompassed in three concepts, multilateral development (<u>dezvoltarea multilateral</u>), systematization (<u>sistematizare</u>) and social homogenization (<u>omogenizarea sociala</u>). Multilateral development is a development strategy wherein all sectors of the economy will be simultaneously developed as an integrated whole. Discussions of this concept are widespread in Romanian planning literature.[45] It can be interpreted as an announcement of the transition from primary socialist accumulation, with its emphasis on industrialization, to a new more balanced development plan more appropriate to mature socialism. Systematization is a concept of territorial planning in which different land use patterns, economic enterprises and residential elements are distributed in accordance with a rational plan. This includes plans for the nation as a whole and for each county and community within the country.[46] Social homogenization, in spite of its rather Orwellian ring in English, simply means a process in which invidious distinctions and inequalities between different social categories are gradually eliminated.⁴⁷

While these plans are concerned with the development of many aspects of Romanian economy and society, I will touch here only on a few of their implications for people who live in the countryside. One of the most significant aspects of the plans for rural areas is the attention that they pay to agriculture. As Table 1 shows, agriculture's contribution to the Romanian social products has dropped to about ten percent. This means that feeding the population and providing marketable exports now far outshadows agriculture's importance in generating funds for investment. Investment in agriculture is being increased and at the same time new organizational measures are being taken to strengthen administrative control over cooperative farms and individual production. Total agricultural production is to be increased even if it is necessary to increase the cost per unit of production. This all occurs as the reduction in the size of the agricultural workforce is being accelerated and remuneration for agricultural workers is being increased. These policies bring to an end the process of transfering social product from agriculture to underwrite industrial development. Indeed, industry may come to be called upon to support agriculture.

The new plans also recognize and address problems associated with regional inequalities and are designed to reverse the flow of social product and labor from backward to advanced regions. Rates of investment, and hence of economic growth, will be slowed in the advanced regions in order to focus on the economic and social development of poorer agricultural ones where urban growth and industrialization are being promoted. As a result, the same range of employment opportunities will exist in all regions of the country. This will mean that all workers will be able to find urban employment within commuting range of their villages and will have the same options of either commuting or moving to a nearby city that workers in developed counties now enjoy. Each county should have sufficient economic growth, and attractive enough economic positions, to absorb the natural increase in its population. Migration between counties will then be reduced to a minimum and balanced in direction, with each county receiving about as many in-migrants as it loses outmigrants.

At the same time that regional differences are being erased, economic and cultural differences between town and country are to be reduced. Plans to transform several thousand villages into new towns are now underway throughout the country. Eventually, all villagers within the country will be within easy reach of one of these towns (or an existing town) where they will find a range of consumer cooperatives, cultural centers and social services that will fulfill most of their needs.

These plans clearly foresee the continuation of village life in Romania. Some villages will be transformed into small towns and some, in remote locations, will be allowed to "wither away." Most villages, however, will be transformed into communities of commuting urban workers, and most people who leave the village will move into a nearby town. What will the implications of the strategy of mature socialism be for the social life of village workers? The plans have, in fact, conflicting implications which make this a most intriguing question. On the one hand, the aspects of the plan which encourage people to remain in their home villages and counties perpetuate the conditions for three-generational strategies and the formation of non-corporate networks. At the same time, however, the expansion of remuneration and other benefits and the creation of cultural and consumer services will make the second shift phenomena less significant, and this, in turn, will remove some of the economic incentives to maintain these social forms. I expect that the forms will remain viable for some time, but that they will be transformed in form and function in response to changing economic and social circumstances. The nature of these changes and their interplay with national planning will make fascinating future research.

Finally, there is the question of how successful Romania will be in the transformation from the strategy of primary socialist accumulation to mature socialism. There can be little question, I think, that Romania is well on the way to solving the problems it faced as an agrarian state. In the process, however, it has created new problems, some of which have been discussed in this paper. Progress toward mature socialism, and the solution of these problems, will depend, in large measure, on Romania's foreign economic and political relations, discussed in this volume by Professors Jackson and Linden. Romania will face difficult internal problems if it cannot find markets for its products or obtain the petroleum and other imports it must have at prices which can be balanced by its export earnings. However, its success in selling its wares depends in large measure on their quality. While many different factors influence the quality of goods, one of central importance is the quality of labor. As we have seen, the second shift phenomena, created as a by product of primary socialist accumulation, and an integral part of its process of social reproduction, is yet incompatable with a quality labor force. Romania's success in transforming, managing or eliminating the second shift will be a significant factor influencing future economic and social trends.

TABLE 3.1: Agricultural and Industrial Contribution to Total Social Product Compared to National Investment in Agriculture and Industry (Percent)

	1950	1955	1960	1965	1970	1975
Industry's contribution to total social product	33.6	36.5	43.4	52.7	58.7	68.0
Investment in industry as a percentage of total national investment	42.9	53.1	42.8	48.9	47.5	49.2
Agriculture's contribution to total social product	42.7	34.0	25.4	18.2	13.1	10.9
Investment in Agriculture as a percentage of total national investment	11.1	13.8	18.8	16.4	16.0	13.0

Source: calculated from various issues of *Anuarul Statistic*.

TABLE 3.2: Investment in Agriculture, 1950-1975

A. In selected years:

	1950	1955	1960	1965	1970	1975
Investment in agriculture as a % of total national investment	11.1	13.8	18.8	16.4	16.0	13.0
Investment in agriculture in millions of lei (at 1963 prices)	524	1,644	4,402	7,450	12,454	17,587

B. At five year intervals:

	1951-55	1956-60	1961-65	1966-70	1971-75
Investment in agriculture as a % of total national investment	10.39	16.41	18.75	15.59	14.02
Investment in agriculture in millions of lei (at 1963 prices)	5,207	13,163	32,771	51,555	76,966

Source: calculated from various issues of Anuarul Statistic.

TABLE 3.3: Ownership of Productive Land (1976)

A. In hectares:

	Arable	Pasture	Meadow	Vineyards	Orchards
State Farms	1,658,890	217,255	64,155	54,842	65,168
Other State Owned	400,947	1,960,815	50,555	6,981	14,212
Cooperative Farms	7,239,036	633,858	667,656	254,079	260,530
Individual	461,288	220,424	621,959	10,986	91,218
Total	9,760,161	3,032,352	1,404,325	326,888	431,128

B. In Percent:

	Arable	Pasture	Meadow	Vineyards	Orchards
State Farms	17	7	5	17	15
Other State Owned	4	65	4	2	3
Cooperative Farms	74	21	48	78	61
Individual	5	7	44	3	21
Total	100	100	100	100	100

Source: 1978 Anuarul Statistic

TABLE 3.4: Production of Major Crops by Type of Farm for 1976 (in millions of tons)

Grain	Wheat & Rye	Barley	Oats	Corn	Legumes (seed plants)
State Farms	1,199.9	438.6	0.8	2,070.8	120.7
Other State Owned	54.1	42.0	11.6	147.5	15.8
Cooperative Farms	5,428.5	742.4	25.2	7,123.0	143.9
Individual Production by Cooperative Farm Members	6.4	1.7	1.8	1,703.6	15.4
Individual Farms	84.3	5.8	15.3	583.3	6.0

Industrial Crops	Sunflowers	Sugar Beets	Hay Annuals	Perennials	Green Fodder
State Farms	152.0	35.9	33.8	1,111.6	1,826.5
Other State Owned	1.2	8.3	17.3	136.1	196.1
Cooperative Farms	645.0	6,842.1	118.8	1,971.2	2,978.0
Individual Production by Cooperative Farm Members	0.7	20.6	43.0	142.6	209.9
Individual Farms	0.4	3.7	18.7	124.8	30.3

Vegetables	Potatoes	Legumes	Onions	Cabbage	Tomatoes	Garlic
State Farms	234.8	165.6	18.0	38.7	44.4	19.8
Other State Owned	35.6	409.7	2.4	34.5	39.8	19.9
Cooperative Farms	1,907.9	1,545.5	139.3	374.8	590.4	112.9
Individual Production by Cooperative Farm Members	1,617.5	1,158.3	128.2	334.8	427.8	17.4
Individual Farms	992.6	313.8	33.1	122.5	70.4	2.7

Livestock*	Beef	Pigs	Sheep	Fowl
State Farms	807.1	3,379.6	1,731.7	30,973.1
Other State Owned	89.8	235.1	200.8	647.5
Cooperative Farms	2,582.4	2,795.1	5,569.9	10,026.8

(*in millions of head)

TABLE 3.4 (cont'd)

Livestock	Beef	Pigs	Sheep	Fowl
Individual Production by Cooperative Farm Members	1,703.0	1,832.3	4,478.5	28,597.4
Individual Farms	943.8	571.2	1,884.2	8,381.1

Source: 1978 Anuarul Statistic

TABLE 3.5: The Rural Population Since 1948

	Rural Population	As % of the total Population	As % of 1948
1948	12,159,485	76.6	100.0
1956	12,015,186	68.7	98.8
1965	12,609,768	66.3	103.7
1970	11,994,403	59.2	98.6
1975	12,062,640	56.8	99.2
1977	11,332,570	52.5	93.2

Source: <u>Anuarul Statistic</u>, various issues.

TABLE 3.6: Growth of Total Population and Urban Population

	Total	Urban	Increase in Total Pop.	Increase in Urban Pop.	Urban Increase as % of Tot. Increase
1948	15,872,624	3,713,139	----	----	----
1956	17,489,450	5,474,264	1,616,826	1,761,125	108.9
1966	19,103,163	7,305,714	1,613,713	1,831,450	113.5
1970	20,252,541	8,258,138	1,149,378	952,424	82.9
1975	21,245,103	9,182,463	992,562	924,325	93.1
1977	21,559,416	10,236,846	314,313	1,054,383	335.5
		1948–1975	5,372,479	5,469,324	101.8
		1948–1977	5,686,792	6,523,702	114.7

Source: <u>Anuarul Statistic</u>, various issues.

TABLE 3.7: Selected Vital Statistics, 1948-1976

	1948	1956	1966	1967	1976	
Crude Birth Rate	23.9	24.2	14.3	27.4	19.5	(per 1,000 individuals)
Crude Death Rate	15.6	9.9	8.2	9.3	9.6	(per 1,000 individuals)
Natural Increase	8.3	14.3	6.1	18.1	9.9	(per 1,000 individuals)
Still Births	2.7	1.8	1.5	1.8	1.0	(per 100 births)
Infant Mortality*	142.7	81.5	46.6	46.6	31.4	(per 1,000 live births)

* Less than one year old at death.

While there is a long term reduction in each of these categories of data, there is a "bump" in the curve in 1967 when Romania introduced a pro-natalist policy.

	1956	1964-67	1977
Life Expectancy at birth			
Females	64.99	70.51	71.89
Males	61.48	66.45	67.37

Sources: Anuarul Statistic, various issues; 1974 Anuarul Demografic; UN Statistical Yearbook, various issues.

TABLE 3.8: Zonal Variation in Agricultural Investment*

Lowland Zones	1951-55	1961-65	1971-75
I. Lower Danube	1.63	6.43	16.83
II. Southern Plains	1.34	3.25	8.43
III. Western Plains	0.49	4.47	5.76
Mid-Altitude Zones			
IV. Eastern Transylvania	0.40	3.38	6.53
V. Western Transylvania	0.12	2.35	4.10
Upland Zones			
VI. Southern Carpathians	0.15	1.61	3.58
VII. Moldavia	0.37	1.91	3.85
VIII. Maramures	0.24	1.73	2.57

* Five year investment per rural person, in millions of lei. 1951-55 calculated at 1959 prices; 1961-65 and 1971-75 calculated at 1969 prices.

Zone I. consists of Braila, Constanta, Galati, Ialomita and Tulcea;
Zone II. Dolj, Ilfov, Mehedinti, Olt and Teleorman;
Zone III. Arad, Bihor, Satu Mare and Timis;
Zone IV. Brasov, Covasna, Sibiu and Mures;
Zone V. Alba, Cluj, Harghita and Hunedoara;
Zone VI. Arges, Buzau, Caras-Severin, Dimbovita, Gorj, Prahova, Vilcea & Vrancea;
Zone VII. Bacau, Botosani, Iasi, Neamt, Suceava, and Vaslui;
Zone VIII. Bistrita-Nasaud, Maramures and Salaj.

Calculated from Anuarul Statistic, various issues.

TABLE 3.9: Net Migration per 1000 of Population by County, 1966-1977

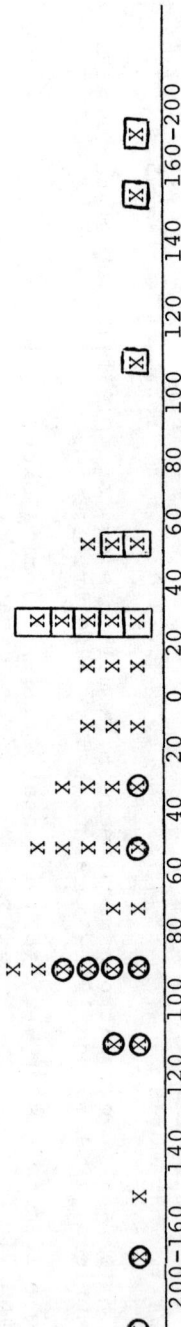

Calculated from data in Measnico and Trebici (Note 33).

☐ - Indicates ten most urbanized counties.
◯ - Indicates ten most rural counties.

TABLE 3.10: Urban and Rural Birth Rates, Death Rates and Rates of Natural Increase (1977)

	Birth Rate	Death Rate	Natural Increase
National average	19.6	9.6	10.0
Total urban	18.7	7.8	10.9
Counties over 50% urban	16.4	8.5	7.9
All rural	20.4	11.3	9.1
Counties over 75% rural	21.9	10.1	11.8

Source: calculated from 1978 Anuarul Statistic.

TABLE 3.11: Dependency Ratios, by County (1973)*

```
             X
             X
             X
  X  X       X              X  X
  X  X    X  X  X  X        X  X
⊠ ⊠ ⊠  X  X ⊠  X  X ⊠ ⊗ ⊗ X ⊗     ⊗           ⊗        X
⊠ ⊠ ⊠  ⊠  ⊗ ⊠  ⊠  X ⊗ ⊗ ⊗ X ⊗     ⊗           ⊗        X
└──┴──┴──┴──┴──┴──┴──┴──┴──┴──┴──┴──┴──┴──┴──┴──┴──┴──┴──┴──┴──┴──┴──┴──┴──┘
44 45 46 47 48 49 50 51 52 53 54 55 56 57 58 59 60 61 62 63 64 65 66 67 68 69
```

* The Dependency Ratio has been obtained by adding the number of individuals under 15 years of age to the number of individuals 65 and over, dividing by the number of individuals between 15 and 65 years of age and multiplying by 100. The Dependency Ratio for Romania as a whole is 54.3. The squared numbers are the most urbanized counties; the circled numbers are the most rural.

The twelve counties with dependency rations of 58 and above includes all of those in Zones VII and VIII and three from Zone VI (Gorj, Vrancea and Vilcea) (Table 3.8).

Source: Calculated from data in the 1974 Anuarul Demografic.

TABLE 3.12: Personal Agricultural Production. Expressed as a Percentage of Total National Production

	1965	1970	1975	1977
Surface area cultivated	8.2	8.5	8.1	7.9
Corn (maise)	13.8	15.2	16.0	16.0
Beans	22.6	18.0	18.5	20.3
Potatoes	35.1	34.5	35.7	34.2
Legumes	27.7	26.5	36.1	34.4
Onions	39.6	37.1	35.2	39.1
Cabbage	27.3	26.6	37.4	39.6
Cattle	32.1	29.3		26.7
Pigs	43.8	28.4		23.9
Sheep	12.8	12.7		14.1
Fowl	19.5	18.7		13.8

Source: calculated from *Anuarul Statistic*, various issues.

NOTES

1. I.T. Berend and G. Ranki, *Economic Development in East-Central Europe in the 19th and 20th Centuries* (New York: Columbia University Press, 1974); Daniel Chirot, *Social Change in a Peripheral Society: The Creation of a Balkan Colony* (New York: Academic Press, 1976); John W. Cole, "Ethnicity and the Rise of Nationalism," in Sam Beck and John W. Cole, editors, *Ethnicity and Nationalism in Southeastern Europe* (Amsterdam: University of Amsterdam, forthcoming). Henri Stahl, *Traditional Romanian Village Communities* (Cambridge, Cambridge University Press, 1980 [1969]).

2. Henry Roberts, *Romania: Political Problems of an Agrarian State* (New Haven: Yale University Press, 1951).

3. Eugen Weber, "Romania," in *The European Right*, Hans Logger and Eugen Webb, editors (Berkeley and Los Angeles: University of California Press, 1965); Kenneth Jowitt, editor, *Social Change in Romania 1860-1940: A Debate on the Development of a European State* (Berkeley: Institute of International Studies, Research Series No. 36, 1978).

4. Phillip Eidelberg, *The Great Rumanian Peasant Revolt of 1907: Origins of a Modern Jacquerie* (Leiden: E.J. Brill, 1974).

5. Eugen Weber, "The Men of the Archangel," *Journal of Contemporary History*, vol. 1, no. 1, pp. 101-127, 1966.

6. E.J. Hobsbawm, *Primitive Rebels* (New York: Norton, 1959); Eric R. Wolf, *Peasant Wars of the Twentieth Century* (New York: Harper & Row, 1969); Henry A. Landsberger, editor, *Rural Protest: Peasant Movements and Social Change* (New York: Barnes & Noble, 1973).

7. I.T. Berend and G. Ranki, op. cit., 268-284, 319-341; passim; Hugh Seton-Watson, *Eastern-Europe Between the Wars, 1818-1941* (New York: Harper & Row, 1967).

8. Lenin's ideas were presented in *Imperialism, the Highest Stage of Capitalism*, first published in 1916. Ideas on the nature of the world capitalist order were also developed by Rosa Luxemburg in *The Accumulation of Capital*, published on the eve of World War I. Many individuals have contributed to the development of modern world systems theory, including I. Wallerstein in *The Capitalist World-Economy* (Cambridge: Cambridge University Press, 1979) and Samir Amin in *Unequal Exchange* (New York & London: Monthly Review Press, 1976).

9. Kenneth Jowitt, *The Leninist Response to National Dependency* (Berkeley: Institute of International Studies, Research Series no. 37, 1978), page 75.

10. John M. Montias, "Background and origins of the Romanian dispute with COMECON," *Soviet Studies*, vol. 16, pp. 125-152, 1964.

11. Political independence is always a matter of degree since the decisions of any national leadership are always constrained by the nature of their relationship to other states. Some time ago Richard Adams explained the options open to small nations in a world dominated by large Powers ("Power and Power Domains," America Latina, vol. 9, no. 2, pp. 3-20, 1966). Ronald Linden has explored the limits to independence in modern Romania in this volume.

12. Unless otherwise noted, all statistics in this paper are either taken directly from, or are calculated from, data in various issues of the Anuarul Statistic and the Anuarul Demografic, both published by the Directia Centrala de Statistica in Bucharest.

13. David Mitrany, Marx Against the Peasant: A Study in Social Dogmatism (New York: Collier Books, 1961 [1951]).

14. Steven L. Sampson, "Urbanization--Planned and Unplanned: the case of Brasov City, Romania." In The Socialist City, T. French and F.E.I. Hamilton, editors (London: John Wiley & Sons, 1979), pages 507-524; Andreas C. Tsantis and Roy Pepper, coordinating editors, Romania, The Industrialization of an Agrarian Economy Under Socialist Planning (Washington, D.C.: The World Bank, 1979), page 137.

15. From a speech at the Plenum of the Communist Party of Romania, March 17-19, 1980.

16. Henry Roberts' Romania: Political Problems of an Agrarian State (op. cit.) includes a useful discussion of the post-World War II reforms. Mihail Cernea, Sociologia Cooperativei Agricole (Bucharest: Editura Academiei Republicii Socialiste Romania, 1974) is an outstanding analysis of the development of socialist agriculture in Romania and David A. Kideckel has both put Romanian agrarian development under socialism into a world perspective and provided a detailed case study of socialist agriculture on a cooperative farm in Brasov County (Agricultural Cooperativism and Social Process in a Romanian Commune, Ph.D. dissertation, University of Massachusetts, Amherst, 1979).

17. An extended analysis of the integration of uncooperativized upland peasant production into the socialist system is included in Sam Beck, Transylvania: The Political Economy of a Frontier (Ph.D. dissertation, University of Massachusetts, Amherst, 1979).

18. The Leninist Response to National Dependency (op. cit.).

19. John W. Cole, "Familial Dynamics in a Romanian Worker Village," Dialectical Anthropology vol. 1, no. 3, pp. 277-285, 1976; David Kideckel, "The dialectics of rural development: cooperative farm goals and family strategies in Romanian commune," Journal of Rural Cooperation, vol. 5, no. 1, pp. 43-61, 1977; Sam Beck,

Transylvania: The Political Economy of a Frontier (op. cit.); Steven Sampson, National Integration Through Socialist Planning: An Anthropological Study of a Romanian New Town (Ph.D. dissertation, University of Massachusetts, Amherst, 1980).
    20. Trond Gilberg, Modernization in Romania Since World War II (New York: Praeger, 1975); Tsantis and Pepper (op. cit.), pp. 172-188.
    21. Modernization in Romania Since World War II (op. cit.), p. 199.
    22. In addition to the Anuarul Demografic and Anuarul Statistic, data for this table comes from various issues of the U.N. Statistical Yearbook.
    23. In spite of the significance of consumerism in Eastern Europe, I am not aware of any attempts by Marxist scholars to develop a theory of consumption under socialism. Western economists tend to assume a natural human propensity to accumulate--Homo economicus--but studies of pre-state societies call such assumptions into question (c.f. Marshal Sahlins, "The Original Affluent Society," in Stone Age Economics [Chicago: Aldine, 1972] pp. 1-40). It also appears that China, being more insulated from the capitalist world system than Eastern Europe, has more successfully resisted the development of consumerism. Whether this will continue under the present leadership is problematic.
    24. Kenneth Jowitt's The Leninist Response to National Dependency (op. cit.) is an excellent theoretical treatment of bureaucratisation in Romania.
    25. I have pirated the concept of "sloppy systems" from Robert Rotenberg's "Networks in Vienna or sloppy systems and social relations," Anthropology, vol. 1, no. 2, pp. 89-98, 1977.
    26. J.C. Scott, "The analysis of corruption in developing nations," Comparative Studies; Society and History, vol. 11, pp. 315-341, 1969; Jane Schneider and Peter Schneider, "The Civile Class and the Persistence of Broker Capitalism," Chapter 8 in their Culture and Political Economy in Western Sicily (New York & London: Academic Press, 1976, pp. 149-172); Jeremey Boissevain, Friends of Friends: Networks, Manipulators and Coalitions (Oxford: Blackwell, 1974).
    27. John W. Cole, "In A Pig's Eye: Political Economy and Daily Life in Southeastern Europe," IREX Occational Papers, vol. 1, no. 3, pp. 3-24, 1980; Steven Sampson, National Integration Through Socialist Planning: An Anthropological Study of a Romanian New Town (op. cit.).
    28. Sampson (loc. cit.); Kideckel, "Agricultural Cooperativism and Social Process in a Romanian Commune" (op. cit.).
    29. Sampson (op. cit.), pp. 377-378.
    30. More than fifty percent urban: Arad, Brasov,

Braila, Caras-Severin, Cluj, Constanta, Galati, Hunedoara, Sibiu and Times; more than seventy percent rural: Bistrita-Nasaud, Botosani, Buzau, Ilfov, Olt, Salaj, Teleorman, Vaslui, Vilcea and Vrancea.

31. David Turnock, An Economic Geography of Romania (London: G. Bell & Sons, 1974) has a discussion of the distribution of different forms of agricultural production in the country, in Chapter 5, "The Agricultural Sector," pp. 203-241.

32. Thomas L. Evascu, "Seagea: Economic and social change in a mountain village. Anuarul Muzelului Etnografic al Transilvaniei, vol. 10. Cluj-Napoca, 1978, pp. 67-84.

33. Ioan Measnicov and Vladimir Trebici, "Aspecte ale Migratiei interne si urbanizarea in lumina rezultatelor preliminare ale recentamintuli din 5 Ianuarie 1977," Revista de Statistica. vol. 27, no. 4 (April 1978), pp. 30-39.

34. Steven Sampson, "Urbanization--Planned and Unplanned" (op. cit.).

35. Mitchell Ratner, Educational and Occupational Selection in Contemporary Romania: An Anthropological Account, Ph.D. dissertation, American University, 1980.

36. For more detailed discussions of the variety of contemporary Romanian domestic groups, see the articles by Sam Beck, John W.Cole, David Kideckel, Steven Randall, Marilyn McArthur and Steven Sampson in Dialectical Anthropology (vol. 1, no. 3, pp. 239-286; vol. 1, no. 4, pp. 321-375, 1974); as well as the other articles and doctoral dissertations by these same individuals cited above. Also see Katherin Verdery, Ethnic Stratification in the European Periphery: The Historical Sociology of a Transylvanian Village, Ph.D. dissertation Stanford University, 1976.

37. John W. Cole, "Familial Dynamics in a Romanian Worker Village" (op. cit.) and references in note 36.

38. Katherin Verdery, Ethnic Stratification in the European Periphery (op. cit.).

39. Evascu (op. cit.).

40. See, for example, Mihail Cernea, "Large Scale formal organization and the family primary group," Journal of Marriage and the Family, vol. 37, no. 4, pp. 927-936, 1975. Kenneth Jowitt agrees with Cernea that the development of formal organization based on impersonal norms undermines the extended family household and sees its days as numbered: he notes that the extended family has not yet "been completely eliminated" and that it "still functions" in certain places. However, he also makes the important observation that the presence of absence of the extended family is less important than the institutional context in which they exist (The Leninist Strategy of Development) (op. cit.), pp. 63-69.

41. Sam Beck, "Uncooperativized but articulated: the myth of 'private' peasants in Romania." Paper read at the AAA annual meeting, Washington, D.C., December 4-7, 1980.

42. However, it should be noted that the separation between socialist and familial production is not total. For example, cooperative farms authorize tractors to plow the personal plots of its members and hay grown on cooperative land can be cut by its members on a share cropping basis.

43. Virgil Constantinescu, "The Cultural behavior of persons with double occupational status," <u>Viitorul Social</u>. Special Issue for the 9th Congress of Sociology in Uppsala, Sweden, August 14-19, 1978, pp. 81-90. Also see Steven Sampson, "Urbanization--Planned and Unplanned" (<u>op. cit.</u>).

44. Andreas C. Tsantis and Roy Pepper, <u>Romania: The Industrialization of an Agrarian Economy Under Socialist Planning</u> (<u>op. cit.</u>), pp. 375-396.

45. C.f. Ioan V. Totu, editor, <u>Progresul Economic in Romania 1877-1977</u>, Part II, section IV. Edificarea societatii socialiste multilateral desvoltarea Romaniei spre comunism (Bucharest: Editura Politica, 1977), pp. 501-672.

46. See Steven Sampson, <u>National Integration Through Socialist Planning: An Anthropological Study of a Romanian New Town</u> (<u>op. cit.</u>) for an explanation of the concept of systematization and a discussion of the Romanian literature on the concept.

47. Constantin Ionescu, editor, <u>Omogenizarea Sociala in Republica Socialista Romania. Process si Factori</u> (Bucharest: Editura Academiei R.S.R., 1977).

4
Idol or Leader?
The Origins and Future of the Ceausescu Cult

Mary Ellen Fischer

Romania is best known outside the Soviet bloc for frequent deviations from Soviet norms in foreign policy. Just as distinctive a feature of the Romanian political system in the 1970's has been the prominence of President Nicolae Ceausescu, who has become the omnipotent and omniscient leader of Party and state. By the end of the 1980's Ceausescu will be only seventy-one; hence his personal priorities and choices could continue to direct Romanian policies throughout the decade. A close study of both the style and the substance of Ceausescu's leadership, as well as his relations with those he leads --the Party and the population at large--should indicate the major political, social and economic trends likely to appear in Romania in the next ten years. Ceausescu's leadership style evokes comparison with other prominent communist leaders such as Lenin, Stalin, and Mao: all four men have been the objects of personality cults. There is no question that Lenin, Stalin and Mao imposed their own priorities onto their respective bodies politic, creating features that have been difficult, sometimes impossible, for their successors to alter. Ceausescu has done the same. Even were he to leave office tomorrow, for whatever reason, accompanied by adulation or rejection, the Romanian political system would still bear his imprint for some time to come.

An unprepossessing and almost unknown figure during the rule of his predecessor, Ceausescu assumed office as head of the Party in 1965 when Gheorghe Gheorghiu-Dej died. At the time, he was the youngest Party leader in East Europe (47) and for almost two years he shared political power in a "collective leadership" with a number of long-time comrades of Gheorghiu-Dej. In December 1967, however, Ceausescu was elected Chairman of the Council of

---

Mary Ellen Fischer holds a Ph.D. from Harvard and is an Associate Professor of Political Science at Skidmore College.

State (titular head of state) in addition to retaining his top Party position. Over the next few years his honors and offices proliferated until, in March 1974, the office "President of the Republic" was created especially for him. By that time he was also Chairman of the National Defense Council, Supreme Commander of the Armed Forces, and chairman or honorary chairman of a plethora of Party and state commissions and committees. References to his personal contributions in formulating policy gradually increased until, by the mid-1970's, no Romanian official could deliver a report or write an article without referring to President Ceausescu's political insight and leadership as the major source of inspiration and guidance.

The extreme adulation accorded Ceausescu has frequently been termed a "cult of personality." Indeed, it is a real cult with an iconography, a Bible,[1] and an infallible leader. Icons, or portraits of Ceausescu, are found in most public places and private offices (not as yet, however, in most homes). The sixteenth volume of his collected speeches, the "Bible" of Romanian communism, was published in Bucharest in 1979, and a series of subject "concordances"of these works has also appeared.[2] The Romanian President is infallible in his own country: successes are attributed to him, failures to organizations or individuals that have not correctly carried out his suggestions.

These characteristics of the Ceausescu cult--icons, scriptures, and infallibility--are reminiscent of the Lenin and Stalin cults in the Soviet Union. Ceausescu, like the Soviet leaders, is portrayed as a great revolutionary who, despite lowly origins, rose to become a national hero through hard work, courage, and intellectual ability--a socialist Horatio Alger. But, in addition to such admirable personal qualities, these three men had a special source of guidance in their achievement of worldly success. Unlike religious leaders, charismatic in the original sense of the world, these socialist heroes derive their infallibility not from divine guidance, but rather from a "scientific" belief, Marx's philosophy of history. If the term "charismatic" is extended to include a "call" based on such a "science," then these men might be deemed "charismatic" leaders.[3] However, charisma also implies a close personal relationship between leaders and followers which enables the leader to inspire the followers. Here the charismatic nature certainly of Stalin's leadership could be questioned. Stalin's relationship with the masses was never direct and personal; in fact, he created an image of himself that was so idealized, so far from reality, that he shrank from direct and spontaneous contact with large groups. He became an idol, and "idolized leaders" cannot be "authentic leaders," if we accept James MacGregor

Burns' definition of leadership, since there is no "true
relationship...characterized by deeply held motives,
shared goals" between idol and followers. Rather, the
followers become mere "spectators."[4] Indeed, neither of
the cults--Lenin's or Stalin's--could be termed charismatic if charisma is an "authentic form of leadership
involving a "true relationship" between leader and
followers. The followers of the Lenin and Stalin cults
may have been inspired by the cult, but they were inspired by a false image rather than by the actual personality of the leader. This is not to say that Lenin
himself was not a charismatic figure; he did in fact
achieve a charismatic relationship (if the "scientific"
definition of charisma is accepted) with his followers in
the Bolshevik party. But that authentic leadership of
the Party was not a cult aimed at the masses. Lenin,
while still alive, was not a cult object. Lenin's
colleagues in the Politburo created the cult after Lenin's
death, and they used the worship of Lenin for their own
purposes.[5]

The creation of a cult does not necessarily preclude
authentic leadership. Mao Tse-tung, for example, was
both a cult figure and an authentic leader. Such a
leader must, however, resolve two major difficulties in
order to maintain a "true relationship" with his followers.
First, he must be certain that his own motives and goals
continue to be shared by his followers and, if he senses
a difference--that his own perception of needed change
differs from that which is taking place--he must be able
to instill in his followers beliefs similar to his own.
He must be able to mobilize them, persuade them, and woo
them by the force of his own personality, and not merely
by projecting a false image of himself or by claiming
special anointment by his predecessor. He must lead the
masses, but not fool them. Second, the leader must
retain an accurate picture of his own strengths and weak-
nesses. This permits an accurate estimate of the limits
(as well as the possibilities) of his leadership.

An authentic leader must also have a dual sense of
confidence: in himself, and in the intelligence of the
individuals he is leading to understand his goals and be
persuaded by his arguments. Stalin absorbed Lenin's
elitism--his distrust of mass spontaneity--rather than
Mao's confidence in the capacity of the masses to effect
needed change. Hence the cults which Stalin and his
colleagues established (that of Lenin and later his own)
were intended to fool the masses by setting up an idol
to be obeyed. Mao's cult as well as the Cultural Revolution itself, kicked off by his famous swim in the river,
appealed to the best instincts of the population by setting up an example to be imitated.[6] But Stalin lacked
both confidence in the masses and faith in his own abili-

ties. He did not have available to him one essential source of self-confidence possessed by leaders such as Mao, Tito, and Castro: Stalin had not led a successful revolution. Stalin's road to leadership had never necessitated the establishment of an authentic relationship between himself and the masses, and therefore he had no confidence in his ability to do so. He found the position of an idol demanding obedience more comfortable than that of a role-model eliciting imitation. A distinction can be made among leaders of revolutionary parties between the first and second generations, between those who have achieved supreme power by actually leading their own revolution, and those who gain that top position through post-revolutionary political competition. These two types of individuals would be expected to have contrasting qualities, both personal and professional. But the second generation of leaders would also be less likely to have that dual sense of confidence which can be produced by the crucible of revolution and which, in turn, can promote authentic leadership.

Where, then, does Nicolae Ceausescu fit into this picture? Does he have that dual sense of confidence less likely in post-revolutionary leaders? He is clearly the object of a cult, but is he, like Mao, an "authentic leader," or, like Stalin, an "idolized leader"? Is he an example to be imitated or an idol to be obeyed? To answer these questions, we will need to examine the evolution of image and ritual since 1965, how the adulation is shown, and for what qualities Ceausescu is revered. A precise understanding of the Ceausescu cult should help us to evaluate the role that the cult plays in Romania--the political needs it fulfills, and the effect it has upon the Romanian political system. Finally, we will make some tentative predictions about the future of the cult and Ceausescu's leadership. It could be argued, for example, that Mao's cult started out as an authentic relationship between himself and his followers, a relationship which deteriorated in the last years of his life as his intellect weakened and his understanding of their motives and goals declined. By the end of his life, the argument goes, he had become an idol rather than a leader. We hope to determine whether Ceausescu ever managed to establish such an authentic leadership in Romania and, if so, whether its authenticity continues or may be re-established.

CONSOLIDATION OF POWER: 1965-1969

When Gheorghiu-Dej died on March 19, 1965, the succession took place in an atmosphere of extreme formality. Public precedence among the leaders depended completely on an individual's post, and no one took over the privileges of an office until he had been duly elected.[7] There was no obvious heir to the position of First Secretary of the Romanian Communist Party (RCP). Gheorghiu-Dej was only 63 at his death, and a number of his comrades in the Politburo seemed possible choices for the top position.[8] Certainly Nicolae Ceausescu's public role in 1964 and 1965 was not prominent. He had been in the Central Committee Secretariat as Secretary for Party Organizations and Cadres, but this was not apparent from the press. The post had, however, given Ceausescu extensive control over Party appointments since the late 1950's,[9] so his election as First Secretary in the new "collective leadership" was no great surprise. A triumvirate was set up with Ceausescu as head of the Party, Chivu Stoica as Chairman of the Council of State, and Ion Gheorghe Maurer as Chairman of the Council of Ministers. Maurer was continuing in the same position, while Ceausescu and Chivu Stoica were splitting Gheorghiu-Dej's functions between them.

The major themes of the new leaders were continuity of policy and collectivity of decision-making. Indeed, there were no startling shifts in policy, although the stress on "exchange of opinions" and "the open confrontation of viewpoints" in scientific sessions and in specialized publications[10] raised hopes that some changes might be accomplished in the future. The leadership took particular pains to reassure the Romanian population that the independent foreign policy symbolized by Gheorghiu-Dej would not be altered. In addition, the Politburo seemed to be operating as a collective body. There were, for example, no major differences visible in the public speeches of the members. However, even during this early period Ceausescu played the most prominent role. By far the most visible of the new leaders, Ceausescu spoke for the collective in a number of major appearances before such professional groups as scientists, artists and writers, the Ministry of the Interior, and Party activists in the armed forces and Bucharest city and region.[11]

This role of Ceausescu as first among equals continued at the Ninth Party Congress held in July. Although as head of the Party he opened and closed the Congress, and his "Report of the Central Committee" was by far the longest single speech, other individuals such as Maurer, Chivu Stoica, and Apostol also played prominent roles in the proceedings.[12] Collective leadership was the concept used to justify any organizational changes. The Politburo, for example, was divided into a smaller Presidium and a larger Executive Committee so that, according to Ceausescu, the Presidium could solve "daily problems" as a "group";[13] a new Party statute (Article 13b) forbade an individual to hold full-time positions simultaneously in both the Party and state hierarchies;[14] finally, the title "First Secretary" was changed to "General Secretary" since, as Apostol explained, Ceausescu was not to be the "first," or most important secretary, but the one with "general" responsibilities.[15] Most speakers at the Congress did mention Ceausescu's name, but such references were actually made to "the report of the Central Committee, delivered by Comrade Nicolae Ceausescu,"[16] rather than directly to the person of the General Secretary. Symbolic of the constant emphasis on collective decision-making was the main photograph of the leadership group which appeared July 21 on the front page of <u>Scinteia:</u> in the middle was an old Party member, a striking figure in a white suit, who held no position of political significance; Ceausescu was on his right, and Maurer on his left, neither the center of attention.

The two years following the Ninth Party Congress saw a gradual increase in Ceausescu's prestige and press coverage compared to the rest of the leaders. He began making heavily publicized trips to the provinces, and delivered the main reports at the Central Committee Plenums in November and December 1965, and June 1966. In October 1966 he began to deliver the closing speech at each Plenum. During 1966, however, it was still not habitual for other speakers to refer to Ceaușescu in a speech. For example, in the first days of an agricultural congress held in February, only nine of thirty-eight speakers mentioned him, usually only once. Four months later, in the discussions at the Grand National Assembly sessions of June/July 1966, twenty-three of fifty-two participants named Ceausescu. By mid-1967 it was still not obligatory to mention Ceausescu in a Grand National Assembly speech. Specialists giving technical reports sometimes did not, but almost every Party and government official did so. On the first day of the July 1967 Grand National Assembly session, for example, twelve of the thirteen speakers referred to Ceausescu, seven naming him three times, and four naming him twice.[17]

Despite this rise in Ceaușescu's status, the triumvirate of Ceausescu, Chivu Stoica, and Maurer continued to function officially until the end of 1967. At that time, a Party Conference brought major changes. First, Ceausescu replaced Chivu Stoica as Chairman of the Council of State, and thus held both top political positions himself. This meant that Article 13b, introduced in 1965 to prevent just such a combination, had to be revoked. But it was not revoked only for Ceausescu; henceforth each Party official in charge at county and local levels would also directly administer the state organs. The same individual would be both Party first secretary and chairman of the People's Council. Thus the parallel hierarchies of Party and state were to be

linked together at key points from top to bottom. A
number of other reforms were introduced at the same time
--most notably an economic reform and an administrative-
territorial reorganization--both of which would allow
extensive personnel change over the next few years.
Ceausescu's two colleagues in the triumvirate publicly
supported all of the shifts with great enthusiasm.
Maurer stressed Ceausescu's "personal role" in initiating
and finalizing the reforms, and seconded the Party
Secretary's interpretation of almost every change.[18]
Chivu Stoica himself proposed that Ceausescu replace him
as Chairman of the Council of State.[19] Not only were
Ceausescu's power and prestige increased at the Conference, but the position of almost every other important
figure from the Gheorghiu-Dej group was weakened.

   The year 1968 was a crucial period in the evolution
of the Ceausescu leadership: in April he eliminated a
major rival, Alexandru Draghici, from the Party leadership, and in August he reached one of the high points in
his domestic popularity by denouncing the Warsaw Pact
invasion of Czechoslovakia. The crucial Central Committee
Plenum in April discussed a number of important issues
from education to foreign policy. But certainly the
most dramatic session, described in the agenda as "the
rehabilitation of some Party activists,"[20] involved the
denunciation of Gheorghiu-Dej for "transgressions of
legality" which included the arrest and execution of
Lucretiu Patrascanu.[21] Patrascanu, a founding member of
the Romanian Communist Party (RCP), was dismissed as
Minister of Justice in March 1948, "abusively arrested"
the next month, and finally executed in April 1954.[22]

   The parallels between Ceausescu's denunciation of
Gheorghiu-Dej and Khrushchev's anti-Stalin speech of
February 1956 are striking.[23] Ceausescu, like Khrushchev, admitted that his predecessor had "indisputable
merits," but judged that "no merits...can excuse his
abuses."[24] Ceausescu, again like Khrushchev, insisted
that the blame was to be placed on individuals, not on
the system or the Party, that such "abuses" were not
the "inevitable companion of socialism," but stemmed
from the "personal character" of those involved:
Gheorghiu-Dej and Alexandru Draghici.[25] Draghici's
involvement points to a third parallel with the Khrushchev case: the advantage derived by the new Party
leader over his colleagues in the Party leadership.
Ceausescu had joined the Politburo and Secretariat just
two days after the Patrascanu execution and so could
claim innocence, unlike the other major figures in the
1968 Presidium and especially Alexandru Draghici.
Draghici, as Minister of Internal Affairs in 1954, had
been personally responsible for the death, the "organizer
and executor" of the crime, as Ceausescu put it. Due

to his "particular and direct responsibility," Draghici was removed in 1968 from all of his high positions in the Party and state.[26]

Even Ceausescu's solutions were parallel to Khrushchev's: he called for a strengthening of the role of the Party, broader participation in the Party decision-making process (Khrushchev spoke of a return to "Leninist norms"), and a strengthening of "socialist legality."[27] By denouncing his predecessor Ceausescu, like Khrushchev, not only removed or weakened major rivals while trying to preserve the Party's infallibility, but also implied a new age without abuses which would be characterized by a new style of "participatory" and democratic leadership. By dissociating themselves from the past, Ceausescu and Khrushchev attempted to initiate an authentic type of personal leadership, based on their own policy preferences and their perceptions of popular desires.

The one issue on which Ceausescu's goals coincided with those of every Romanian was the need to prevent another Soviet occupation. Less than four months after the denunciation of Gheorghiu-Dej, Ceausescu was able to establish himself as an authentic national leader based on this single issue: at least temporarily, Ceausescu became the defender of the fatherland (patria). When Warsaw Pact troops "penetrated" Czechoslovakia in August 1968,[28] Ceausescu's reaction was public and vehement: a rally was held in the Palace Square in Bucharest, and the Romanian leader described the invasion as "a great mistake and a grave danger to peace,...a shameful moment in the history of the revolutionary movement." He went on:

> There is no justification whatsoever...for... military intervention in the affairs of a fraternal socialist state... The entire Romanian people will not allow anybody to violate the territory of our Homeland... We are communists and anti-fascists who faced prisons and death, but we have never betrayed the interests of the working class, of our people. Be sure...citizens of Romania, that we shall never betray our Homeland...

The rally in Bucharest was followed by rallies throughout the country and visits by the various RCP leaders to many localities.[29] At the time, there were rumors throughout Romania that a Soviet invasion was imminent, and that shots had actually been exchanged across the USSR-Romanian border. Whether the Soviet leaders ever considered using military force against Romania in 1968 is questionable. The incident at the border may have been mere rumor, or the result of mistake or confusion. On the other hand, Ceausescu's strong stand may actually have helped to deter the CPSU leaders from a move which, according to all evidence, would have met with resistance and ended in bloodshed. Romanian resistance could hardly have been effective for long against combined action by members of the Warsaw Pact, but military occupation would have demanded a great many troops. Whatever the truth about Soviet intentions, the Romanian population perceived danger, and Ceausescu received the credit for averting invasion. Ten years later, both opponents and supporters of the Romanian President agreed on that issue: Ceausescu had kept the Soviets out in 1968.

The most important result of August 1968 for Romania, then, was the immediate (and long-term) increase in Ceausescu's popularity. His defiant stand gained him the personal stature which no amount of economic achievement or diplomatic success could have given him. In some ways, Ceausescu's emotional speech in Bucharest on August 21 can be regarded as a gamble; provocative and dangerous it left no alternative but to fight and be defeated if the Soviets should choose to enter his country. But, at the same time, such a public statement leaving no room for retreat established the credibility of Ceausescu's resolve vis-à-vis the Soviets. And Ceausescu really had nothing to lose; even without the public defiance, an invasion by Soviet troops in 1968 would have meant an end to Ceausescu's personal power as it had to Dubcek's.

As soon as the immediate shock of the move into Czechoslovakia was over, the Romanian leader returned to his more usual tactics of maneuver and compromise rather than confrontation. He even began to hint at increased cooperation in Comecon.[30] Yet Ceausescu's public anti-Soviet stand had consolidated and legitimized his own rule and that of his Party. For the next decade, Romanians disillusioned with other aspects of Party policy would point to August 1968 as the major reason for supporting the RCP.[31] In 1974, for example, many Romanians could not understand the Watergate crisis. "Why," they asked repeatedly, "should Nixon resign? His foreign policy is good. Look what we put up with in order to maintain an effective foreign policy!"

If the December 1967 Party Conference had witnessed the beginning of the end of collective leadership in Romania, the Tenth Party Congress brought its final demise. After August 1969, only three of the nine Presidium members remained from the Politburo of Gheorghiu-Dej--Ceausescu himself, Maurer, and Emil Bodnaras[32]--and only Ceausescu had been on the Secretariat before 1965. Thus the composition of the highest Party organs had almost totally changed during Ceausescu's first four years as General Secretary. In addition, the supremacy of Ceausescu within this new leadership was quite clear at the 1969 Congress. Every speaker felt compelled to begin and end his remarks by praising the Party leader; many, especially Party workers, referred to him in almost every paragraph, crediting him personally with the great economic achievements made since 1965.[33] The era before 1965 was scarcely mentioned. It was as though socialist development in Romania had begun with the Ninth Party Congress. In just over four years, Nicolae Ceausescu had achieved a radical turnover in personnel in the top organs of the Romanian Communist Party, had become the undisputed leader of the Party and state, and had established himself as the fount of all knowledge in Romania.

THE NEED FOR AN IDOL

Since 1969 Ceausescu has dominated the Romanian political system. By that year he had eliminated any opposition within the top leadership. But he had also achieved a measure of popular support based upon his anti-Soviet stand during the Czechoslovak crisis and his denunciation of Gheorghiu-Dej. During the 1965-1969 period, Ceausescu had been portrayed as the brilliant initiator and author of a number of basic political policies: national independence, increased discussion and "participation," socialist legality, and rapid economic development. To the extent that these policies expressed the needs and desires of a large proportion of Romanian society, Ceausescu had the chance to become an authentic leader, worthy of imitation, with whom the citizen felt a close bond. Indeed, by late 1968 his positions on the first three issues had gained for him a genuine popularity based on citizens' views of his policy priorities. In the 1970s Romanians looked back on the late sixties as their country's "Golden Age."[34]

Yet the decade following 1969 saw the creation of a leadership cult around Ceausescu rivaling those of Stalin and Mao. Unfortunately, Ceausescu's popularity in 1968 was based as much on expectations as on reality: he was perceived as willing to bring about a much greater departure from past practice on all four issues than was ever achieved. After the Tenth Party Congress, Ceausescu's priorities began to differ more and more sharply from the personal goals of many Romanians. The crucial area of disagreement was the economy. At the Congress in 1969, Ceausescu announced that the high rate of investment would continue (twenty-eight percent of national income), and he justified this at length in terms of future consumption funds; he must, therefore, have been aware of the discontent his statement would elicit. The figures were later revised <u>upward</u> when he began his campaign to fulfill the Five Year Plan in Four-and-a-half Years. The disappointment was intensified in 1974, when the Eleventh Party Congress brought an even higher investment rate (thirty-three percent). Again, this was justified in terms of future consumption, acceptable to Ceausescu, but not to the majority of Romanians.

Starting in 1969, therefore, Ceausescu needed to shape and direct public opinion, to increase his authority so as to persuade the masses, to "woo them by the force of his own personality" into changing their expectations. Here he began to run into difficulties. Ceausescu's skills are not those of a Trotsky, or a Mao, or a Castro; he has evidently been able to gain the respect of those with whom he deals on an individual basis, but he does not move crowds by his oratorical abilities. He appears impressive on television during a crisis, issuing directives to local officials as they deal with floods or earthquakes. But in such a situation, he is handling individuals and making quick decisions. When Ceausescu faces a large crowd, he becomes awkward and retreats into formality, reading speeches in a monotone, and underlining crucial phrases by unrhythmic first-pounding with the stress all too often falling on the wrong word. He may have total faith in his own abilities, and his own decisions, but he does not have the ease and confidence in his relationship with the masses that is a prerequisite for authentic mass leadership.

Once the gap between his own priorities and the expectations of the masses became clear to him -- and a variety of indicators such as absenteeism or low productivity would have revealed the lack of support--the cult began. Ceausescu and his colleagues had to create an idol to be obeyed, an image which would mobilize the popular support which regime goals and Ceausescu's personality could not produce. Ceausescu could not lead the masses, and so had to fool them. He did, however, have more faith in their potential than Stalin, or even Lenin--hence his attempts to reform and re-educate ordinary Romanians, attempts which began during the "mini-Cultural Revolution" of 1971.[35]

THE IMAGE

The Ceausescu idol created after 1969 has been given a number of faces. First, it is omniscient, the Party oracle, the interpreter of Marxism-Leninism, initiating, planning, and announcing all major policies. Ceausescu's speeches have become the Romanian Bible, to which academics as well as political officials look for guidance on any subject. "Ceausescuism," as Trond Gilberg refers to such a phenomenon in this volume, specifies an entire set of postulates about social, economic and political goals. As proof of his intellectual capabilities, Ceausescu has received honorary doctorates from a number of universities beginning with the University of Bucharest on his fifty-fifth birthday in January 1973. A total of eleven doctorates "honoris causa" have been granted to him from universities in Latin America, Lebanon, France, the Philippines, and Iran. Then on his sixtieth birthday, he was given a doctorate in political science by the Stefan Gheorghiu Academy (the Party academy) and one in economics by the Academy of Economic Studies, both in Bucharest. Messages to the Romanian President on this occasion praised his "theoretical and practical contribution to the development and enrichment of political science," and credited him with the "decisive role" in developing the Romanian economy "at a rate that has aroused admiration in the whole world." He was also given credit for Romania's foreign and defense policies, the broadened "participation of numerous groups in the political process," and "strengthening socialist legality in all fields of activity."[36] He remains, therefore, the brilliant initiator and administrator of the same policies laid out a decade ago as the RCP follows its scientifically determined path to developed socialism.

A second face of the image, one which appeared in the early 1970's, is that of the poor peasant who overcame diversity through bravery, devotion, and hard work. Biographies of the leader[37] stress the hardships of his childhood as the third of ten children in a peasant home, so poor that at age eleven he was forced to go to Bucharest to find work. Ceausescu himself frequently reinforces this image of poverty and suffering; on his sixtieth birthday, for example, he began his biographical resume: "As the son of a peasant, I have experienced the landlords' oppression and, since the age of eleven, capitalist exploitation."[38] Even his parents were included in the image. When Ceausescu's mother died in the summer of 1977, her picture appeared on the first page of <u>Scinteia</u> in traditional peasant dress and kerchief. Her obituary described her own birth into a family of poor peasants, her early experience with privation and suffering, her difficult life of hard labor beside her husband in raising the ten children. The "entire nation" then recognized her great contribution in giving life to "the great statesman...who today leads the destiny of the people with such competence, devotion, and unselfishness."[39]

Here, then, is still another aspect of the image: Ceausescu's personal qualities, his unselfishness, stamina, and courage. One of his sisters remembers him as the child who endured the hardships with the best humor, and became indignant when confronted with "injustice."[40] According to the image, it was his concern for others and his hatred for injustice which led him into the worker protest movement in Bucharest and then into revolutionary activity. He was arrested several times (first at age fifteen), and eventually earned his "old-school" credentials by imprisonment in both the Eton and the Harrow of the Romanian Communist Party - the prison at Doftana and the internment camp at Tirgu Jiu.[41]

These personal characteristics are projected into his present life as well. Even those Romanians who actively dislike the President admit that he is industrious. It is widely believed in Bucharest that Ceausescu's arrival at his office just before 8 a.m. occurs so regularly that anyone can set a watch by it. His schedule of public activities is formidable, and well publicized in books, newspapers, and on television. The evening news usually carries ten minutes of videotape relating only to Ceausescu's activities. Omagiu, an enormous volume published in honor of his fifty-fifth birthday in 1973 (the book measures about ten by fourteen inches, is over 500 pages in length, and comes complete with color photographs especially attached by hand after binding), contains a list of Ceausescu visits to various places inside Romania.[42] The list implies that Ceausescu visited over a thousand different economic units between July 1965 and January 1973, and took part in a hundred major working meetings, most of them on a country-wide scale. These would not include his trips abroad or meetings with individuals or small groups. But he is not only hard working; he is also courageous. That courage which stood him in good stead during confrontations with the police during the 1930's the media implies, now supports him in disagreements with the Soviet leaders. The courage and the devotion to duty which are part of his public image combine to indicate his unselfishness; he was unselfish in the 1930's when he received a longer sentence for speaking out in defense of a fellow prisoner,[43] and he remains so today as "defender of the right of each and every nation to decide its destiny by itself..."[44]

Courage, stamina, and unselfishness are not the only personal qualities of Ceausescu held up for admiration and emulation. There is, in addition, an almost puritannical aspect to his image, in both a professional and personal sense. Ceausescu frequently demands adherence to socialist ethics and makes public examples of those who violate them. In 1972, for example, two members of the Central Committee were excluded for abuses of function and breaches of communist ethics.[45] Other expulsions occurred in 1976, 1977, and 1978 for "grave violations" of "socialist ethics" and "moral behavior."[46] Newspaper accounts of Ceausescu's appearances report tirades against hiding mistakes or taking one's job for granted.[47] Ceausescu also has the reputation for strict morality in personal life. The measures introduced by the Party in 1966 to increase population size (regulations making both divorces and abortions very difficult to obtain[48]), contribute to this image. But the image is also consciously created, as it was in Omagiu[49]:

> We gaze with esteem, with respect, at the harmony of his family life. We find a special ethical significance in the fact that his life, together with that of his life comrade, former textile worker and young communist militant, member of the Party when it was still illegal, today Hero of Socialist Labor, scientist, Central Committee member, comrade Elena Ceausescu , offers an image of exemplary significance of two communists. We observe that they have taught their own children with parental and responsible concern... Valentin is a researcher at the Institute of Atomic Physics, Zoe a mathematician... and the youngest, Nicu, studies physics at the University of Bucharest. And it is proper that we know that the three children of the President of the country work, just like any of us, following the example of the parents, for the socialist fulfillment of the country. This attests...that work and personal example are moral attributes obligatory in the Ceausescu family.

The extremes to which the media go in enhancing the total image create skepticism as to its validity even among otherwise sympathetic observers. No one could be quite so brilliant, courageous, hard-working, unselfish, and honest as Ceausescu is supposed to be. He has indeed become so perfect that he cannot be emulated; rather than an example to be imitated, Ceausescu has indeed become an idol to be obeyed.

THE FUNCTION OF THE CULT

As an idol, however, he does play an important role. He is, after all, a symbol of Romania, a symbol of Romanian unity and independence, and a symbol of Romanian prestige and acceptability throughout the world. This seems to be the major function of the cult: Ceauşescu plays the role of a royal personage and, as such, satisfies the instinctive needs of the Romanian "masses" for a strong monarch. At least this is the explanation of the cult usually given by sophisticated Romanian citizens or Romanian officials--the "low political level" of most Romanians, and their need for an individual to symbolize political authority in his own person. For many

Romanians, the epitome of Ceausescu's international success was the literal rolling out of the red carpet in London and his ride through the streets of that city in a carriage with Elizabeth II. Ceausescu had been received several times by US Presidents, who have also visited Romania amid great enthusiasm. But Presidents of the United States are, after all, mere commoners. For the Queen of England to receive Ceausescu was an even clearer indication that the socialist government had achieved equality and respectability in the international system.[50]

In domestic terms, the height of Ceausescu's symbolic prestige probably occurred in March 1974 when he was elected President of the Republic. As *Scinteia* described the occasion:

> March 28, 1974, will remain engraved in the history of the homeland, in the consciousness of our people. On this memorable day, fulfilling the will of the entire nation, the Grand National Assembly...proclaimed Comrade Nicolae Ceausescu President... This most brilliant son of the Romanian nation, the leader who crowns a succession of great statesmen of our lineage, is the first President...

Ceausescu was then presented with "the symbols of worth and prestige, of state power," as a sash in the national colors was placed across his chest and he was handed the mace symbolic of the new office. He took the oath of office, and those assembled sang the national anthem.

> The solemn session...was transmitted directly by Romanian radio and television; thus the entire country witnessed this historic act.

Ceausescu was thus invested into his new office with all the pomp and circumstance of any monarch.[51] His daily routine reinforces this symbolic royalty. He travels in a fleet of Mercedes, for which all traffic is stopped, or by helicopter, an innovation of the mid-1970's. His suburban Bucharest residence, already cut off from ordinary sightseers by traffic blockades, is no longer sufficient: several palaces, including the fairy-tale Peles Castle at Sinaia, are being renovated for his personal use and so are no longer open to visitors.[52]

There are, of course, major problems for the RCP in this regalia. The symbolic royalty contradicts other vital parts of the Ceausescu image, particularly the image of the puritannical, hard-working revolutionary, devoted to the egalitarian goals of Marxism-Leninism which, after all, is the scientific justification for Party rule. Ironically enough, while certain aspects of the Ceausescu image may indeed appeal to various segments of the society, other groups may be embarrassed or alienated. Perhaps the symbolic royalty does attract support among the masses, but it embarrasses loyal Party members. While Ceausescu's claims to academic brilliance and infallibility in policy innovation may impress Party members, such pretensions alienate the intellectual elites.[53]

In November 1974, at the Eleventh Party Congress, there was a move to elect Ceausescu General Secretary of the RCP for life (as Tito was honored in Yugoslavia). The election of Ceausescu for life would have contributed to his royal image, but would have disillusioned many of his most loyal followers at lower levels of the political elite. Such an election would have contradicted Ceausescu's constant assertions that individuals must earn and retain any position only through merit--part of his image of socialist morality. The origins of the move are still uncertain. The suggestion was first made publicly shortly before the Congress at a meeting of the Bucharest Party organization. When the head of the Bucharest delegation then made the proposal to the Party Congress, Ceausescu refused the honor by requesting the delegates not to pass the proposal. However, he also stated that he had served and would continue to serve the Party all of his life, and in this sense the Congress should support the suggestion.[54]

There was never any formal action on the floor regarding the matter. Perhaps Ceausescu himself had secretly initiated the proposal as a trial balloon to see whether or not there was support. Or perhaps it was initiated without his knowledge by enthusiastic supporters whose ardor he was forced to quench (the officially accepted interpretation). It may even have been suggested by enemies who wished to create a Caesar to be destroyed (the view popular among foreign reporters during the Congress). Finally, the entire incident--both the proposal and the refusal--might have been orchestrated by Ceausescu as an example to officials throughout the political system that no political position can be held for life. This last interpretation was supported later at the Congress by the remarks of a county first secretary who praised Ceausescu's moral example in refusing the honor.[55] Whatever the origins of the move, Ceausescu did refuse election for life and so, on that occasion, Ceausescu the moral example won out over Ceausescu the King and President.

On most occasions, however, Ceausescu has been trying to be both an idol and an example, a cult figure and an authentic leader, and in neither attempt has he been completely successful. In fact, unlike the Chinese case, the combination of cult figure and authentic leader seems impossible in Romania. Ceausescu's goals

are not for the most part those of the "masses," and he
has not been able to persuade and move the "masses" by
the force of his own personality (except briefly after
the Soviet invasion of Czechoslovakia). Since he has
not been able to "lead" the Romanians, he has tried to
fool them. In addition, Ceausescu has lacked that dual
sense of confidence in himself and in his followers. He
did not have the self-confidence that the leader of a
mass movement would have gained, and he had absorbed
enough of Lenin's elitism to distrust mass spontaneity
which would, after all, lead only to demands for higher
living standards (exactly what has happened in Romania).
He has found it somehow easier to be an idol demanding
obedience than to be a leader mobilizing support. The
cult, therefore, has been a way of pursuing his own
goals and those of his close colleagues, despite his inability to make those goals popular with the vast majority of Romanians.

THE FUTURE OF THE CULT

The decade following the Soviet invasion of Czechoslovakia was a period of increasing frustration for many
Romanians as their hopes for major changes in RCP priorities under Ceausescu were not realized. Floods in
1971 and 1975 and the tragic earthquake of 1977 provided
the regime with excuses for a continued low level of
consumer satisfaction. By mid-1978, however, it was
clear to the RCP leadership that still more sacrifices
would be necessary to maintain the planned level of
economic growth. Ceausescu's speeches had become more
strident in demanding dedication, efficiency, and hard
work from the population. Then, in late November, came
a crisis within the Warsaw Treaty Organization, a crisis
evidently publicized first by the Romanians themselves
as they rejected the Soviet demand for an increase in
military spending.[56] Western reporters immediately
pounced on the story, stressing the strains apparent in
Soviet-Romanian relations since the visit of Hua Kuo-
feng, Chairman of the Chinese Communist Party, to
Bucharest in August.[57] The Soviets by mid-December were
sufficiently annoyed with Romanian policy on both issues
--military spending and relations with China--to have
Pravda choose just those points on which to castigate
the Romanian speaker at a conference of communist parties
in Sofia.[58] But even more significant than the disagreements themselves, which after all were not new, was
the use made of the quarrel within Romania.

Ceausescu had implied the existence of strain in
Soviet-Romanian relations before Hua's trip to Romania.
Before leaving for his annual August visit to Brezhnev
in the Crimea, Ceausescu had departed from tradition by

returning to Bucharest from his own Black Sea villa and making a nationally televised speech on August 4 to explain Romanian foreign policy goals. He thus created the appearance of a need to demonstrate popular support in Romania for his goals on the eve of the talks with Brezhnev, usually a sign of impending, Romanian recalcitrance on some issue. Nothing dramatic appeared to happen in the Crimea, although the subsequent visit by Hua to the Balkans was not exactly welcomed by the Soviets. Hence, no public Soviet-Romanian confrontation occurred until the end of November, when Ceausescu left the Warsaw Pact meetings early and publicly voiced his refusal to comply with Soviet demands. Then, on his return to Bucharest, he immediately took steps to create the image of a crisis situation. The Political Executive Committee of the RCP met the next day and issued a communique supporting Ceausescu's position, "even his refusal to agree to certain measures which had not already been approved by all members."[59] He then held mass meetings, one with workers, and another with peasants, intellectuals, and youth.[60] On the following day he met with representatives from the armed forces and the Ministry of the Interior.[61] Then a special Central Committee Plenum took place, followed by a jubilee Joint Plenum of the Central Committee, the National Council of the Socialist Unity Front, and the Grand National Assembly.[62] Throughout this period Scinteia printed dozens of letters from citizens and groups expressing their full support for Ceausescu and his decisions. Even United States' support for the Romanian position was evidenced by a visit from Secretary of the Treasury Michael Blumenthal.[63] And in such a crisis situation, the population of course had to make its contribution: there were reports of bread lines and gasoline rationing in Bucharest.[64] Once more Romanians were expected to rally around the RCP, and Ceausescu personally, as defender of the fatherland.

Ultimately, the future of the personality cult and Ceausescu's leadership will depend upon the response of the Romanian population to this perennial appeal. If the majority of Romanians are indeed moved by this anti-Soviet posture, Ceausescu may again, although temporarily, establish himself as an authentic leader, creating that bond between himself and the population which makes him an example to be imitated rather than an idol to be obeyed. Ceausescu has already proven himself formidable at intra-Party maneuvering, eliminating or shifting potential rivals seemingly at will since 1969. He has surrounded himself with colleagues who contribute unashamedly to the cult, and whose major abilities seem to involve (aside from technical specialization) keeping the confidence of the President of Romania. His stature within the Party itself therefore appears unchallengeable, at least so long as he maintains a relationship between the Party and population that is minimally acceptable to most Party members (measured in large part by annual economic growth). In so doing, he maintains the bond between himself and the Party members which has made him an authentic leader of the RCP--at least, of that portion of the membership who are true believers.

Preserving a proper relationship with the entire population is not an easy task. Disaffection has been growing in recent years at all levels of society. Violence broke out among miners in the Jiu Valley during August 1977, for example, and earlier that year a number of intellectuals had been arrested, some for signing protest petitions. Individuals of varying backgrounds have evidently become disenchanted with the sacrifice of concrete economic support from the Soviet Union in favor of a national independence that does not pay off in ways which immediately benefit the citizens. In addition, Ceausescu has been pushing several reforms which backfired on Khrushchev in the USSR--the closer linking of education and production, for example and regular infusion of new personnel into Party and state offices. Ceausescu has, though, backed off on the latter since the Eleventh Party Congress in November 1974. Before the Congress, new Party guidelines were published which would have required that at least one-third of the members of any Party organ not have served during the previous terms;[65] they were not passed by the Congress. At the Congress itself, Ceausescu stressed that a balance had to be achieved between new and experienced Party officials, but he then rejected any mandatory guidelines in favor of enunciating general principles in the Party Statutes.[66] Ceausescu is a prudent politician; he does not have confidence in his relations with the masses, and carries that caution into his leadership of the Party as well. Opposition within the Party causes him to retreat. His sense of the politically possible is keener than that of Khrushchev.

Ceausescu would like to be an authentic leader. He would like to establish a close bond between himself and his followers. He appears to have done so within the Romanian Communist Party, or at least he has managed to maintain a proximity between his goals and the goals of most Party members. But he has not been so successful with the majority of Romanians, as Gilberg notes when he assesses socialization programs, except briefly in 1968 and perhaps again in 1978. The nature of the Romanian political system is such that he actually needs authenticity as a leader only within the Party. RCP control of the country is absolute; unless Ceausescu's policy priorities threaten that control by producing continued violent reactions against Party rule, his personal hold on the Party should be unchallengeable. If the split continues, as appears to be the case, between the goals of the Party--tight political control and rapid economic development--and the goals of the population--more and more centering on a higher living standard--then the rather strange image of Ceausescu within Romania should also remain a part of political life. He must be both king and revolutionary, both idol to be obeyed and example to be followed. And the existence of the double image prevents either from being accurate--artistically blurred, perhaps, but not clearly defined. Such an image, however, is that created by other Presidents as well who must be political animals as well as television stars.

In any case, as long as the split between Party and popular priorities remains irreconcilable, Ceausescu will not achieve that authentic leadership that he desires. Only when a threat to Romanian sovereignty produces a bond between Romanians and their President does he become the defiant "example" to be imitated. Ironically enough for Ceausescu and those who do support him, in the absence of a Soviet threat he must remain primarily an idol to be obeyed, maintaining his power through coercion. If the domestic political and economic priorities of the regime in the 1980's remain those of the 1970's (and Ceausescu has given no indication that they will change), then only a crisis, real or perceived, in relations with the USSR will gain him popular support. In other words, given his priorities and personality, Ceausescu can become an authentic national leader only when there is a perceived danger to the Romanian state; for Ceausescu, Romanian strength and security precludes authentic leadership.

NOTES

1. The terms "iconography" and "Bible," as well as "Gospel" and "shrine," were applied to the Lenin cult by Nina Tumarkin-Fosburg in "The Image of a Leader: Lenin 1922-23," a paper presented at the Annual Meeting of the New England Slavic Association, Harvard University, April 15-16, 1977.
2. The first three volumes of the collected speeches were published as Nicolae Ceaușescu, Romania pe drumul desavirșirii constructiei socialiste (București: Editura politica, vol. I, 1968; vol. II, 1968; vol III, 1969). The remaining volumes are from the same publisher, and are all titled: Romania pe drumul construirii societății socialiste multilateral dezvoltate. They appeared as follows: vol. IV, 1970; V, 1971; VI, 1972; VII, 1973; VIII, 1973; IX, 1974; X, 1974; XI, 1975; XII,

1976; XIII, 1977; XIV, 1977; XV, 1978; XVI, 1979. The English edition, now up to 13 volumes, already totals 10651 pages. The series of what are essentially concordances to these works is entitled: "Documente ale Partidului Comunist Roman." Each volume is merely a series of long quotations from Ceausescu's speeches on a particular topic such as socialist democracy, national defense, literature and art, development of the technical-material base, or the role of science in building socialism.

3. Under this condition, even Carl Friedrich reluctantly grants charismatic status to Lenin; see his "The Theory of Political Leadership and the Issue of Totalitarianism," in R. Barry Farrell (ed.), Political Leadership in Eastern Europe and the Soviet Union (Chicago: Aldine, 1970), p. 22.

4. James MacGregor Burns, Leadership (New York: Harper and Row, 1978), p. 248.

5. See, for example, the paper by Tumarkin-Fosburg cited in note 1.

6. Burns implies this contrast in his discussion; see esp. pp. 248-54.

7. Scinteia, 20 March 1965, and the day following.

8. Men such as Emil Bodnaras, Chivu Stoica, and Ion Gheorghe Maurer were senior to Ceausescu. Two others, Gheorghe Apostol and Alexandru Draghici, were certainly in positions to challenge him for Party leadership.

9. For details on his control at the county level, see my "Political Leadership and Personnel Policy in Romania, 1965-1976," in Steven Rosefielde (ed.), World Communism at the Crossroads (Boston: Martinus Nijhoff, 1980), pp. 210-33.

10. See, for example, Scinteia, 9 May 1965. For a more detailed discussion of this period, see my dissertation "Ceausescu and the Romanian Political Leadership" (Harvard 1974), pp. 96-118.

11. He addressed these groups as follows: scientists, May 9; men of culture and art, May 19; Ministry of the Interior, June 22; Party activists in the armed forces, June 15; Bucharest city conference, June 12; Bucharest regional conference, June 26. The speeches were printed in Scinteia the next day in each case.

12. Maurer reported on the 1966-1970 economic plan, Chivu Stoica on the long range plan for power and electrification, and Apostol on the Party Statutes; see Congresul al IX-lea al Partidul Comunist Roman, 19-24 iulie 1965 (București: Editura politica, 1966).

13. Congresul al IX-lea..., p. 732. The new Presidium, however, contained seven of the nine Politburo members; the only two eliminated were reported sick and died within a few years.

14. Ceausescu described this change also as an expression of collective leadership and internal Party democracy (see Congresul al IX-lea..., p. 79), although its main effect was the weakening of two Ceausescu rivals, Chivu Stoica and Alexandru Draghici.
15. Congresul al IX-lea..., p. 345.
16. Ibid. See, for example, pp. 126, 134, 142.
17. Data on the speeches in 1966-1967 were compiled from Scinteia.
18. Scinteia, 8 December 1967, pp. 1-2.
19. Ibid., p. 7.
20. Scinteia, 23 April 1968, p. 1.
21. As described in the Decision of the Central Committee Plenum, printed in Scinteia, 26 April 1968, pp. 1, 3.
22. Ibid.
23. For the text of the Khrushchev speech, see, for example, Bertram D. Wolfe, Khrushchev and Stalin's Ghost (New York: Praeger, 1957), pp. 88-252.
24. The proceedings of the Central Committee Plenum were not published. Ceausescu gave an extensive explanation of the decision in his speech to the Bucharest Party organization; this appeared in Scinteia, 28 April 1968, pp. 1, 3, esp. p. 3; for an English translation, see Nicolea Ceausescu, Romania On the Way of Completing Socialist Construction, III (Bucharest: Meridiane, 1969), pp. 163-90, esp. 172-73, 177-78.
25. Ibid., esp. pp. 181-82.
26. For Ceausescu's statement, see Ibid., p. 173. For Draghici's expulsion, see Scinteia, 26 April 1968, p. 3; he was removed from the Presidium, the Executive Committee, and the Central Committee by the Plenum, which also recommended his dismissal as deputy chairman of the Council of Ministers: that body acted the next day, Scinteia, 27 April 1968, p. 5.
27. Scinteia, 28 April 1968, p. 3, or Ceausescu, III, pp. 181-84; on Khrushchev, see Wolfe, pp. 92-96, 106-10, 118-22, and passim.
28. The term "penetration" was Ceausescu's; the quotations which follow are from his speech at the public rally, Scinteia, 23 August 1968, p. 1, or Ceausescu, III, pp. 382-85.
29. For example, Ceausescu himself spoke in Brasov, the two Hungarian counties, and Cluj; Maurer went to Tirnaveni and Tirgu Mures, and Chivu Stoica to Craiova and Turnu Severin. Apostol spoke in Braila, Bodnaras in Iasi, Niculescu-Mizil in Timis, Arad, and Bihor, Trofin in Suceava and Botoşani, and Verdet in Hunedoara. See Scinteia, 27 August - 2 September 1968; all speeches were printed.
30. Scinteia, 27 August 1968, pp. 1-2, or Ceausescu, III, pp. 392-95.

31. This occurred on numerous occasions in 1973, 1974, 1975, and 1978 in this author's conversations with individual Romanians of different political orientations.

32. Maurer resigned from the top leadership in March 1974 "for reasons of health," and Bodnaras remained a top official until his death in January 1976.

33. Congresul al X-lea al Partidului Comunist Roman, 6-12 august 1969 (București: Editura politica, 1969), passim.

34. The term "Golden Age" was used by several Romanians in talking with this author to indicate the positive nature of political and cultural policy during the late 1960s. Hopes were high, they suggested, that Ceausescu personally would bring about a fundamental change in the system.

35. For Ceausescu's explanations of the high investment at the Tenth and Eleventh Party Congresses, see Congresul al X-lea..., pp. 37-38, and Congresul al XI-lea al Partidului Comunist Roman (București: Editura politica, 1975), pp. 52-53. For his push to raise the figures of the Five Year Plan, see his speech to the Central Committee Plenum, Scinteia, 3 June 1972, p. 1. On the "mini-Cultural Revolution" see especially Ceausescu's speech to the Central Committee, Scinteia, 4 November 1971, pp. 1-5, entitled: "On improving ideological activity, raising the general level of socialist consciousness and education of the masses, and basing social relations in our society on socialist and communist ethics and equity."

36. For the list of doctorates, see Agerpres, Romania, Documents--Events (Special Issue, January, 1978), p. 18. See Scinteia, 25 January 1978, pp. 1-3, for the awards, and 26 January 1978, pp. 1-2, for the joint message of the Central Committee, Council of State, and Government. The latter was translated in Agerpres, Romania, Documents--Events (Special Issue 4, January 1978), pp. 28-43; see esp. pp. 32, 34-35, 41.

37. See, for example, Omagiu Tovarașului Nicolae Ceaușescu (București: Editura politica, 1973), esp. pp. 10-24; Michel P. Hamelet, Nicolae Ceaușescu (Paris: Seghers, 1971); and Donald Catchlove, Romania's Ceaușescu (London: Abacus, 1972).

38. Scinteia, 26 January 1978, p. 1.

39. Scinteia, 6 July 1977, p. 1.

40. Hamelet, p. 10.

41. Catchlove used this "old school" comparison, p. 63.

42. Omagiu..., p. 20.

43. Omagiu..., p. 23. A contemporary description of the trial can be found in Cuvint liber, 6 June 1939.

44. From the joint message to Ceausescu on his sixtieth birthday; Scinteia, 26 January 1978, p. 2, or

Agerpres, Romania, Documents--Events (Special Issue 4, January 1978), p. 40.

45. Vasile Ruş and Ilie Fasui; Scinteia, 19 April 1972, p. 1.

46. Gheorghe Crişovan, Scinteia, 15 April 1976, p. 1; Ion Jescu, Scinteia, 30 March 1977, p. 1; and Ştefan Boboş, Scinteia, 2 November 1978, p. 3.

47. See, for example, his warnings to county Party secretaries and university professors, Scinteia, 24 September 1977, pp. 1-3.

48. For more details, see my "The Romanian Communist Party and its Central Committee: Patterns of Growth and Change," Southeastern Europe, 6 (1979), pt.1, 1-28, esp. pp. 11-13, and the sources cited there.

49. Omagiu..., p. 24.

50. For coverage of the trip to Britain, see Scinteia, 14-17 June 1978. Both Nixon and Ford went to Bucharest; Ceausescu's most recent visit to the US was in April 1978.

51. Scinteia, 29 March 1974, pp. 1, 3.

52. As this visitor was informed.

53. On the other hand, the cult does broaden and diversify his support, particularly among non-Party and non-intellectual groups in the society. Groups do, after all, influence the policy-making process in socialist states, even though they may not be "interest groups" as defined in the West. The seminal discussion of this process may be found in H. Gordon Skilling and Franklyn Griffiths, Interest Groups in Soviet Politics (Princeton: Princeton University Press, 1971). Probably the strongest case for group influence in Soviet politics has been made by Jerry F. Hough; see his The Soviet Union and Social Science Theory (Cambridge: Harvard University Press, 1977), and How the Soviet Union is Governed (Cambridge: Harvard University Press, 1979).

54. Scinteia printed the original suggestion on 17 November 1974, p. 1. For the proposal to the Congress, and Ceauşescu's refusal, see Congresul al XI-lea..., pp. 302, and 291-292.

55. The Party official was Miu Dobrescu; see Congresul al XI-lea..., pp. 439-40.

56. According to a Reuters dispatch from Vienna which appeared in the Baltimore Sun, 27 November 1978, p. A4.

57. See, for example, reports in the New York Times of 29 and 30 November 1978.

58. According to the New York Times, 17 December 1978; the Pravda article appeared on 16 December.

59. Scinteia, 25 November 1978, p. 1.

60. Scinteia, 26 November 1978, pp. 1-4.

61. Scinteia, 28 November 1978, pp. 1-4.

62. *Scinteia*, 30 November - 2 December 1978.
63. See the *New York Times*, 9-10 December 1978, and *Scinteia*, 10 December 1978.
64. *New York Times*, 15 December 1978.
65. *Scinteia*, 30 July 1974, p. 5.
66. This was in response to a proposal made during the Congress for a mandatory retirement age for Party officials. The proposal was evidently a surprise to most delegates, since there was a loud murmur and ripple of excitement when the one delegate rose from the back to walk up and present his suggestion. Ceausescu read his response, and so did not appear surprised. The incident allowed him to play the role of mediator. The text of the motion and Ceausescu's response are in *Congresul al XI-lea...*, pp. 580-82; the description is my own.

5
Political Socialization in Romania: Prospects and Performance

Trond Gilberg

INTRODUCTION

    Political scientists have long maintained that the process of "political socialization" is indispensable for the establishment and maintenance of a societal system and its institutions. Defined as a learning and acculturation process, whereby the populace (especially children) is introduced to societal procedures, institutions, symbols and slogans as well as to positive feelings ("affect") about that system, political socialization presumably <u>bonds</u> disparate individuals into a cohesive citizenry positively disposed towards existing institutions and procedures.[1]
    This definition of "political socialization" is sweeping indeed, and has been criticized in recent years. The concept is so broad that it defies operationalization and, some charge, fits the category of "rubberband concepts," which can be stretched to meet any situation thus being useless in generating testable hypotheses. Out of this concern has come renewed emphasis on other, older concepts which presumably discuss the same process (or parts thereof) such as "civic education," "nation-building," and "the creation of a common consciousness." Social scientists and historians alike therefore continue to utilize different concepts for their description and analysis of this crucial but elusive process of human interaction.[2]
    No matter what the term used, the primary concerns of scholars studying phenomena listed above seem to be focused on several key questions. First, one wants to know the origin and extent of the "we feeling" among

---

Trond Gilberg received his Ph.D. from the University of Wisconsin, Madison, and is now a Professor of Political Science at Pennsylvania State University.

inhabitants of a geographical unit, e.g. a country. How did the individuals located on this territory come to think of themselves as a unit rather than just the sum total of individual human beings? How deeply felt is this sense of unity, and what would it take to destroy it? Does it include all the individuals occupying the territorial space of the country, or only part of this sum? If the latter, what establishes inclusion and exclusion?

Second, scholars would like to know how a feeling of "oneness" is maintained. Is it maintained through material payoffs, which equate income and property with continued membership in the collectivity? If so, is there anything other than material self-interest that keeps each individual inside the collectivity? If not, how will this collectivity weather the vaugaries of economic cycles and still remain intact? Other, related concerns in this general category have to do with the maintenance of the collectivity through procedures, charisma, deism, or heredity; put briefly, the collectivity may maintain itself because it establishes elaborate procedures of political and social behavior which act as the cement of society. Alternatively, a forceful, charismatic personality could maintain some element of unity during his or her lifetime. If unity is dependent upon an individual, that individual may wish to perpetuate his influence and power beyond his biological span by claiming continued authority from God or, conversely, pass it on to his children by means of heredity.

Third, all scholars (and rulers as well) face the perplexing problem of the necessity for change which appears immediately after some element of unity has been established. Societal changes composed of complex interactions among human beings, most of which are non-political, will nevertheless require political change in short order. How do elites maintain some political and societal cohesion and stability in the face of this ceaseless change?

Fourth, scholars examining the development of "we-feeling" in a society have also, inevitably, come to examine the attitudes of those who are included in the collective "we" towards those who are on the outside, "they." What is the attitude of citizens in a society towards non-citizens? How do these attitudes change over time? What happens if the territorial "we," as defined by borders, does not correspond to the psychological "we" as defined by values and attitudes? Will there be discrimination, separation, or integration?[3]

These broad questions continue to occupy the time and attention of rulers and scholars alike, since the process of creating the "we" and the "they" appears to be a continuous one, so that no one can postulate a time when the process of "nation-building" is completed. The decade of the 1970's was a particularly good example of this unsettling fact. After two hundred years or more of "nationalism" in Western Europe and North America, questions of identity and political consciousness came to the fore with considerable impact, and regionalism and separation threatened to pull apart some of the oldest states in the world.

In Eastern Europe, the process of creating a common identity has been even more difficult than was the case further west, and strong centrifugal forces continue to threaten the fabric of togetherness so painfully constructed. National consciousness came late to this area. In the Russian Empire, the existence of an autocratic system of arbitrary rule, unbounded by legal or constitutional rules of behavior, produced a situation in which political and economic power became synonymous and there was no sense of attachment to abstractions such as "the state." In most of the areas which now are controlled by the states of Eastern Europe, political authority was associated with the cruel and exploitative rule of foreigners. There was no need for the exploited Romanian peasant of Transylvania to feel any attachment to, or sympathy for, the Magyar rulers of the area, and the Bulgarian peasant had little reason for developing roots in a political system run by the Turks (the latter, through the millet system, in fact discouraged any development of national political values, except those that directly served Constantinople's rule).[4]

When a sense of common destiny and togetherness did develop in Eastern Europe, it tended to focus on opposition to establish rule. The bonding of the disparate individuals became a solidarity directed against something; positive solidarity, on the other hand, was primarily directed towards one's peers in the local community and in the extended family. Hence, the national solidarity of the East European peoples appeared much less solid than the local solidarity of the village, which always distrusted outsiders, whether they be co-nationals or foreigners. This two-layered system of bonding has remained to this day, and it has created a great deal of difficulty for ruling communist elites, whose chief preoccupation is to break down such parochialism and instead create a national, perhaps international, sense of togetherness.

When the great empires, which had dominated Eastern Europe for centuries, were dismantled after World War I, the political and socio-economic elites of the area came to power in independent states. The old chasm between political leaders and the general population was not eliminated, however; the political leaders, taking their cue from the only model they knew, established autocratic systems which continued to exploit the rank and file of the population, even though this kind of rule was somewhat tempered by limited social mobility and some economic progress. The "man in the street" and "in the village", on the other hand, continued to see the autocratic regimes as yet another manifestation of the old rule that political power was exploitative, no matter who controlled the seat of power. There was, therefore, inadequate political bonding, even after the establishment of national independence and a national political machinery. This rule holds also for those states which had achieved independence prior to World War I (e.g., Romania and Bulgaria). In Czechoslovakia, where democratic procedures and an efficient machinery of the state and bureaucracy were promoted, bonding foundered on the animosities between Czechs and Slovaks and the occasionally heavyhanded rule by the former over the latter.[5]

There were certain sources of commonality between political elites and the masses of the population, however. Having come to power against foreign authority, the national leaderships of the East European countries continued to look for enemies beyond the border, in an effort to solidify their domestic sources of public support. Eastern Europe during the interwar period was a hotbed of foreign policy conflicts which stirred the flames of nationalism and helped legitimize the regimes of the area in their local populations. By the same token, some bonding of the masses could be undertaken by means of ethnic separation and animosity between ethnic groups. Here age-old prejudices were utilized by the political regimes of the area to increase their popularity in parts of the population by alienating other, smaller parts. Thus, the minority policy of most of the regimes in this area leaves a great deal to be desired during this period from the point of view of civil rights and equality before the law.[6]

THE CASE OF ROMANIA

Romania fits well into the pattern discussed above. For centuries, the Romanian peasant had been held in political and socio-economic bondage by a variety of foreign rulers, ranging from Turks via Russians to Hungarians. In many cases, these foreign rulers utilized other nationals as their agents of tax collection and law enforcement in the Romanian population; this was especially the case with the Phanariot Greeks, the trusted handmaidens of Constantinople in Moldavia and Wallachia. In addition to this, certain crucial functions such as trade, commerce, and banking, were in the hands of non-Romanians, especially Armenians and Jews. Germans also appeared to have a privileged position in Romania, especially in the bureaucracy. All of this produced a situation in which foreignness, exploitation, and official power came together as a common aspect of an undesirable situation for the Romanian peasant. Understandably, an average individual in these provinces became thoroughly alienated from most aspects of political authority. Instead of bonding as a form of national political consciousness, the Romanian peasantry developed a sense of negative solidarity among themselves, against national power and all of its manifestations. The gulf between political elite and the masses of the population became an unbridgeable abyss.

The process of national liberation, which culminated in the 1850's, could be expected to enhance the process of bonding, insofar as the new political elites were at least Romanian rather than foreign. Two tendencies nevertheless continued to disturb the development of a genuine national political consciousness in Romania. First, the establishment of a Romanian political elite was not greeted with enthusiasm among the ethnic minorities; in fact, those groups among them whose position had hitherto been privileged had good reason to expect that the new regime would pose a threat to their status in society. These fears were partially fulfilled during the years of Romanian independence up to the end of World War II.

Second, the new elites, made up of the boyars of the Romanian nation, did little to enhance the status of political authority in the general population. In fact, the Romanian leaders turned out to be every bit as rapacious, incapable, and corrupt as the former, alien masters had been, and this kind of behavior dispelled the notion that exploitation had something to do with ethnicity and nationality. Average citizens, Romanian or otherwise, had their suspicious confirmed, in that exploitation became synonymous with political power and authority per se. It was only much later, during the 1920's and part of the 1930's, that the development of a fairly vigorous political pluralism in Romania helped reintegrate certain segments of the population by means of interest groups and political parties.[7] Even so, many of the groups that developed did so in contradistinction to political pluralism and advocated, in fact, a new system of "national salvation," in which the forces of religion and corporatism, coupled with nationalism and ethnic chauvinism, would save the "soul" of Romania. Thus, even the development of participant structures tended to undermine civility, thereby helping to refocus political consciousness away from precedural and competitive democracy to a movement orientation dedicated to the organic society, in which you were either totally "in" or fundamentally "out." In addition to this, the establishment of a royal dictatorship and subsequently a fascist regime helped alienate significant portions of the population once more.[8]

The establishment of a communist-dominated regime in Romania in the fall of 1944 and the achievement of political monopoly by the Romanian Communist Party (RCP) in 1947 brought the problem of political attitudes in the population to a head once more. For the new regime, it was vitally important that it be able to consolidate its position in a population which had hitherto been either indifferent or hostile to the cause of communism, and political socialization and indoctrination therefore became functions directly related to political survival for the new rulers. At the same time, the new leaders were Marxists, and they had a vision of the new society to be constructed and the way to get there. In order to launch Romania on the road to socialism and communism, it was necessary to destroy the old bonds, ties, and solidary relationships and to forge new ones, especially a new dedication to the "socialist culture" and the "new socialist man and woman." This herculean task could only be undertaken with maximum commitment and fervor. The hectic pace of the indoctrination efforts has continued since and has in fact been intensified during certain periods, especially since the summer of 1971.

Because of the thorough-going change which was ushered in by the new political elite in Romania, and the speed with which major changes in virtually all fields of human life were executed, the RCP also managed to alienate large segments of the population, and this fact produced the need for an even more frenzied effort at political socialization and indoctrination. The regime could not wait for societal change to permeate men's minds and thus create a new set of values; these values must be hammered home in the most forceful manner to willing subjects and recalcitrants alike.

This massive effort of socialization and resocialization was further hampered by each new policy which disestablished existing socio-economic classes and helped produce new ones. Members of the former could rightly be expected to harbor hostility against the new elite, which had disenfranchised them, and they had to be "re-educated" (except for the most recalcitrant, who were physically liquidated). By the same token, the new industrial working class, which developed rapidly as a result of the massive modernization program launched by the regime in 1947-48 and maintained ever since, was made up of raw recruits from the countryside, whose life experiences, cultural background, and educational and political level made them totally unfit for their role as the "vanguard class." Massive political education was necessary for this new army of untutored.[9]

The Romanian experience was not unique, although the low level of industrialization and urbanization plus traditions of anti-communism and anti-Russian feelings were more formidable obstacles in Romania than elsewhere among the Soviet satrapies. All of the satellite regimes were confronted with the need to retrain the older generations and create a new sense of "we feeling" among the children. In many countries, the early attempts of "storming" the problem of low political consciousness soon gave way to activities designed to maintain the essential features of the regime rather than to change the people in it. It is likely that Romania, too, would have entered this ideological "middle age" if it had not been for the advent to power of Nicolae Ceausescu upon the death of Gheorghe Gheorghiu-Dej in 1965. Ceausescu, who was considered a true apparatchik (and therefore a safe compromise candidate) by the dead leader's peers, turned out to be a real ideologue with his own personal brand of Marxism, mixed with populism and Romanian nationalism. Because of the peculiarities of Ceausescu's notion of Romanian society and the direction in which it should be heading, the Romanian Communist Party (hereafter RCP) during the last fifteen years has emphasized political education, indoctrination, and the creation of a new "bonding" of Romanian citizens at a qualitatively higher level to an extent unprecedented in Eastern Europe in scope, intensity, and the period of time over which it has been sustained. This quest for a new level of consciousness, of "societal bonding," can only be examined with reference to the blend of Marxism and personalized philosophy which we can call "Ceausescuism."

CEAUSESCUISM — THE BLUEPRINT FOR POLITICAL SOCIALIZATION IN ROMANIA

The blend of Marxist-Leninist orthodoxy and personalized views which characterize "Ceausescuism" has produced a regime effort of political indoctrination and socialization at present unknown elsewhere in Eastern Europe. "Ceausescuism" proceeds from a set of fundamental postulates about necessary and desired conditions in society "on the road to socialism," which currently is described as "the multilaterally developed society." From the basis of these postulates the General Secretary of the RCP proceeds to establish a series of practical goals in the field of political education and socialization. The party leader also often includes detailed prescriptions for how the goals are to be reached, as well as the allowable time frame for their achievement.

Among the fundamental bases of the General Secretary's philosophy is the conviction that individual needs and acts and the needs of society are integrally related. According to this outlook, no citizen can claim to be outside of the societal collectivity; "dropping out" of the process of nation-building is simply impermissible.

Thus, there can be no fully private sector, and no field of specific activity can be excluded from the total societal experience. The unwillingness to distinguish between the private and the public realm means that "everything is related to everything else." Since the needs of the collectivity in the quest of socialism and communism are paramount, "everything" is either <u>political</u> or <u>partially political</u>. This vision, which resembles the notions of totalitarianism described by Hannah Arendt, is also consistent with Marx's quest for the "whole man" who lives in harmony with his society, his peers, and nature. The Ceausescu view is also in line with the concepts of "organic societies," in which individuals coexist with others, and with political authority, in a symbiotic relationship in which Man is truly outside the pale if he refuses to contribute to that society and in turn accepts its decisions as well as its material benefits. In the final analysis, the Ceausescu vision resembles that of the classical Athenian thinkers and statesmen, who considered citizenship and political activity as one, while those who refused to participate were outside the polis and thus barbarians. But the similarities with Athens stop here; while the Athenians viewed politics as <u>participation</u>, the Ceausescu vision emphasizes <u>mobilization</u>. There is, of course, a world of difference between the two concepts.[10]

The Leninist practice of Marxism eschews politics as participation. Participation implies that those who engage in political activities do so with a view towards choice between alternatives and elites; such a view invariably leads to competition and pluralism. Lenin, as well as his disciple Ceausescu, emphasizes participation in one of its subforms only, namely that of mobilization. According to this view, the question of political elites and political programs has been settled in the most decisive manner, and there is no need for alternatives in either category. The political program is the practical manifestation of the unfolding of history in line with Marxist analysis. The force that will help supervise and expedite this development is the communist party, "the handmaiden of history," the "vanguard" force in society. Political participation therefore means the greatest possible degree of mobilization of all human and material resources for the quickest and most thorough way of implementing historical necessity. There can be little doubt that those who are thoroughly politicized, i.e., familiar with the programs of the Party and dedicated to its fulfillment, are also best suited to the historic task of achieving socialism and communism. Politicization, in this context, thus means political socialization. Once again, the individual citizen presumably does not have the option of refusing induction into this organic society, and political socialization and indoctrination therefore become universal, hence the enormous scope of this effort in contemporary Romania.[11]

The concepts of the inseparability of private and public realms and the universal politicization of the citizenry represent the most basic building blocks in the present-day socialization effort in Romania. From these basic concepts, Nicolae Ceausescu and the ideologues of the RCP build a second-level set of propositions which have great practical ramifications in society. The most important of these are the following:

a. Given the nature of society in pursuit of socialism and communism, it is clear that a new bond, a new <u>socialist culture</u>, must be created. This culture will then also produce new socialist individuals, whose thought processes and consequent behavior are fundamentally different from, and superior to, individuals in non-socialist cultures. The new socialist culture will contain elements of pre-socialist society, yet it will be qualitatively different from it, and not just the sum total of its constituent parts. This conceptualization is of the greatest importance in a multiethnic society. Romania's socialist culture will have elements of Romanian, Hungarian, German, and other cultures in it. Yet it will <u>not be</u> Romanian, Hungarian, or German. The unique blend of these elements will be brought about by jettisoning the negative aspects of "bourgeois" national cultures, while the positive elements of these pre-communist value systems will remain. To this residue will then be added the "scientific" elements of Marxism-Leninism, by means of political socialization and indoctrination.[12]

Specifically, the old values and behavior patterns associated with national chauvinism, localism, egotism, greed, and the concern for the needs of the nuclear family rather than society as a whole must be eliminated for the new socialist culture to take hold. Nepotism, corruption, loose morals, and, above all, the exploitation of man by man are manifestations of pre-socialist culture, but should have no place in the qualitatively higher form being established through political indoctrination and education.[13]

By the same token, important, positive elements of the old should remain in the new culture, to be fused with the values and behavior patterns of Marxism-Leninism.

The most important of these traditional values include patriotism and love of the fatherland, dedication to hard work, a sense of collectivism, (which was an important element in Romanian village life), and a capacity for sacrifice for some cause that is beyond the immediate needs of the individual. While Mary Ellen

Fischer details the moral attributes Ceaușescu claims, the most important of qualities promoted by the General Secretary is patriotism, which includes total loyalty to the Romanian state, the nation, and the guardians of the national patrimony and its physical borders - the RCP.[14]

   b. Together with these older values, the new values and outlooks of the socialist man and woman will produce a higher culture. Specifically, socialist values include complete dedication to the leadership of the country, as manifested by the programs of the RCP. Furthermore, each individual should possess the basic knowledge required of a citizen in a socialist country, namely a thorough reading of the classics of Marxism-Leninism, Romanian history and the history of the RCP, and also a fair amount of "socialist ethics," which can help him or her live a life "befitting a citizen of socialist Romania." Above all, the new socialist individual must be mobilizable at all times and thus be ready to fulfill the tasks alotted to him by the bonding force in society, the RCP, even if such duties involve personal sacrifice. Such tasks and duties can best be fulfilled by the socialized individual, who has internalized the values and outlooks of the regime of Romanian-style Marxism-Leninism.[15]

   While the political and moral-ethical aspects of the Ceausescu program are important, it should not be forgotten that the RCP is a modernizing elite which is fundamentally concerned with economic development. An important part of the socialization effort revolves around the need for "modern" individuals, i.e., citizens who have the requisite skills for a rapidly expanding economy whose relationships, tasks and duties are becoming more sophisticated every day. Nicolae Ceausescu has headed a vigorous educational campaign which has produced thousands of experts in all fields, especially in the technical areas and in the hard sciences.

   But more important than the mere transmission of knowledge to even wider sectors of the population is the need to instill a new attitude towards work. In old Romania, labor productivity was low, waste was appalling, and pilfering of raw materials and finished products was rampant. Corruption was an everyday fact of life, as venal officials augmented their meager salaries in various ingenious ways developed over centuries of exploitation, Balkan-style. The peasantry, long-suffering subjects of this kind of system, retaliated by producing for itself, while withholding as much as possible from "the authorities." Above all, the peasant mentality approached work in a fashion developed over the ages as a result of the interrelationships between planting and harvesting and seasonal change. This approach involved frantic economic activity during the spring, summer, and early fall, and almost total withdrawal from such activity during the winter months. What is needed in a modern economy is the day-to-day fulfillment of routine tasks, regardless of seasons and weather. For this reason, the transmission of values such as punctuality, honesty, integrity, frugality, and incorruptibility became a major task for the regime in its quest for economic performance. Economic performance was also seen more broadly: Socialism and communism cannot be reached without a sufficient material base. Once again, Ceausescu and his colleagues stress the inseparability of realms, in this context the economic and the political.[16]

Problems in economic and political performance may be related to the stubborn remnants of "old" values in the population, but they may also stem from "contradictions under socialism." Socialism, it will be recalled, is a stage in which each individual contributes according to his or her ability, and is remunerated according to his or her contribution. While classes have been eliminated, social strata nevertheless remain, and this implies social differentiation. Contradictions, which are defined as "non-antagonistic," may arise between these social strata, or between the city and the countryside, or between elements in functionally different occupations. Political socialization and education must eliminate such contradictions by instilling a mindset in which all individuals, regardless of their status or function, cooperate for the most expeditious fulfillment of the RCP programs, whether it is in the cultural, socio-economic, or political realm.

Another contradiction under socialism is the misuse of political and economic power by elites in society. The RCP is an elite invested with the lofty mission of leading Romania towards the achievement of socialism and communism. This exalted task requires, however, a great deal of personal power for many individuals, raising the possibility that unscrupulous individuals will take advantage of their crucial position in society. It is vital that these elites be properly socialized and educated, so that they will act as a model for the citizenry. The sense of "oneness" between the elite and the mass must be fostered in leadership cadres at all times. For this reason, Nicolae Ceausescu carries out a ceaseless campaign against misuse of personal power, and for this reason, the political and socio-economic elite of Romania is subjected to ceaseless ideological campaigns and frequent recycling. It is for this reason, too, that the General Secretary adopts a populist style of leadership (explained in more depth in this volume by Mary Ellen Fischer) and frequently takes his cause to the masses by means of "flying visits" to economic units and territorial and regional towns and cities, even the countryside; it helps foster the image of a leader concerned with the well-being of the masses, while the "bureaucrats" are kept on their toes.[17]

THE PRACTICAL MANIFESTATIONS OF POLITICAL SOCIALIZATION, CEAUSESCU-STYLE

From the first and second-level propositions about society and the relationship between the individual and the collectivity come specific manifestations of socialization and indoctrination behavior. This third set of manifestations should be separated in terms of <u>acts</u> and <u>values</u>, and also in terms of requirements of the <u>elite</u>, <u>the activists</u>, and the general citizenry. Taken together, these manifestations represent the current practical program of socialization and indoctrination in Romania.

For the top political elite, as well as the elite in the regional and district headquarters, the main emphases in political socialization and indoctrination are as follows:

    a. Transmission of values designed to merge political/ideological and other functions of RCP activity on a daily basis. Nicolae Ceausescu has charged repeatedly that there is a tendency for ideological activities to be relegated to formalism and sloganeering, and that only individuals specializing in political agitation and propaganda actually use these resources in their daily jobs; other cadres are absorbed by the technical and managerial functions which are demanded of them. Thus, the General Secretary charges, leaders who are supposed to supervise the fusion of political rule with all other functions have been the first to abandon this principle. To combat this tendency, Ceausescu produces frequent ideological campaigns, routinely (and sometimes abruptly) recycles party cadres to prevent bureaucratic ossification, and promotes the need for constant political education campaigns and meetings. These campaigns frequently remove cadres from their primary functions for considerable periods of time. The General Secretary has also emphasized the need to streamline the administrative apparatus, which in practice has meant that RCP cadres now increasingly carry out functions assigned to the governmental appratus. A frequent practice is also the shuffling of cadres between administrative jobs and posts in the RCP apparatus. All of these moves are designed to enhance the ideological level of party activists and leaders at the center as well as in the provinces.[18]

In conjunction with the ideological campaign and its message of the merger of functions under the "political" umbrella, the General Secretary also constantly emphasizes the need for a better knowledge of the Party's decisions, so that application and implementation can be improved. Once again, such implementation is presumed to be enhanced greatly by the achievement of a higher level of political consciousness.

b. Instilling a better sense of socialist ethics and morality is viewed as an integral part of the political education of leading party cadres. For Ceausescu, "socialist ethics and morality" is a complex concept which incorporates behavior patterns and mind sets as disparate as political commitment, personal honesty, and a dedication to hard work. The General Secretary also emphasizes the need for officials to lead personal lives which are models of propriety, thus enhancing the image of the communist order as lean, dedicated, and frugal, constantly concerned with the well-being of its citizenry. Only by behaving in such an exemplary way can the elite expect to obtain the moral leadership required for societal bonding and the creation of a new and superior culture.[19]

c. Political leaders must be fierce patriots. One of the most important messages of the political education drive supervised by Nicolae Ceausescu is the heavy emphasis on nationalism and patriotism. On practically every occasion, the General Secretary hammers home the message that the present leadership is heir to the national patrimony and, as such, the true descendants of Romanian heroes from earlier centuries. It is the duty of political cadres everywhere to conduct themselves and their subordinates in such a way that their national patriotism becomes a major part of their work. Such conduct will ensure greater legitimacy for the current regime and will help propel Romania on the path chosen by history, so that the country can assume its rightful place among nations and thus achieve sovereignty and socio-economic and political progress.[20]

The emphasis on creating political leaders with the requisite mind set, as described above, also carries with it a set of required <u>behavior patterns</u> for RCP leaders. Specifically, such a leader is expected to show the following behavior characteristics:

1. He should be an activist dedicated to the smooth implementation of RCP decrees and decisions. The political socialization messages of the Ceausescu era depict a super-active <u>apparatchik</u> who is eclectic in his concern for the area he is supervising. Furthermore, he is presumed to be active ceaselessly, organizing a study group here, supervising a building site there, all the while ensuring the optimal functioning of party machinery under his jurisdiction. Such an official is also scrupulously honest, accessible to the rank and file and the non-party masses, and constantly vigilant

to any sign of aberrations in the rank and file as well as the party cadres in his jurisdiction.[21]

2. He should be a source of inspiration for others. All too often the General Secretary charges, officials become "fatcats," more concerned with their own well-being than the good of the collectivity. Furthermore, there is a tendency towards formalism and sloganeering-practices which fail to connect party work with real life. A true activist, on the other hand, escapes these debilitating temptations and relates to the masses in such a way that "the man in street" or "in the village" will be inspired to carry out tasks with elan and gusto. In order to facilitate this task, the party leader must also have superior organizational abilities, so that he can establish the necessary structures and set in motion needed processes for the full mobilization of the citizenry.

3. He should be the central authorities' watchful eye in the area under his jurisdiction. All of the desired activities discussed above are meant to fulfill programs established at the political and administrative center. Successful implementation of such programs depends on the transmission of necessary information by cadres from lower levels to the real decision-makers, and carrying decisions down the hierarchy overseeing their implementation. Leaders of Romania, where an unprecedented amount of decision-making power is centralized in the hands of one person, are essentially middlemen between the leader and the general population. The central and regional leaders of the RCP must, above all, perform this middleman function to the satisfaction of the General Secretary, thereby helping to ensure the penetration of the periphery (geographical and political) by the center.[22]

The numerous requirements of attitudes and behavior, outlined above, are transmitted to RCP cadres at the central and local levels by means of a complicated system of political socialization and indoctrination mechanisms, which will be discussed below. Local cadres are expected to perform in ways similar to those outlined for their supervisors, and similar socialization messages are transmitted to them. Local cadres are also charged with the function of relating constantly to the non-party masses. This requirement puts even greater burdens on their image as honest, efficient, and reliable enthusiasts of the new order, and the socialization effort directed towards these cadres is most intensive.

While the regime issues stern socialization messages to RCP cadres at all levels, it does not neglect other societal elites, who are connected with the Party through overlapping memberships and interlocking directorates, but whose primary functions are separated from party work. The RCP socialization program envisions, in essence, harnessing all societal elites for further indoctrination of the general population as well as of more specialized audiences.

The General Secretary is paying special attention to the technical intelligentsia and the leaders in the fields of the arts, literature, cinema, theatre, and the emerging social sciences and humanities. Such an emphasis in certainly understandable; one of the most persistent features of the modernization process has been the heavy emphasis on technical education for economic needs, and the utilization of the artistic and literacy intelligentsia to spread "the good word" to the population in general is therefore indispensable. Both of these sets of societal elites, then, are crucial for the successful implementation of the socio-economic and political programs of the RCP and Nicolae Ceausescu.

Specifically, these societal elites are expected to act as socialization agents for the regime. Thus, writers are utilized for the glorification of the political and socio-economic programs of the Party, and they are also expected to be major sources of inspiration for the masses of the population to engage in even greater efforts in the future. The writer is also a chief source of ideas and description concerning "the new socialist man and woman" and their actions in different societal situations, which cannot be specified in minute detail by RCP programs and exhortations. By writing "correct" literature, the artistic intelligentsia thus helps bring the socialization messages to the masses in forms and ways which are relevant for each individual in terms of his or her own social situation.[23]

Other members of the artistic intelligentsia, such as theatre producers, playwrights, and film-makers are also enjoined to participate in the spreading of the correct and inspirational message of the RCP and its General Secretary.[24]

For the social sciences and humanities, the tasks are essentially the same; only the methods and emphasis vary from those expected of the artistic intelligentsia. In the humanities, the regime consistently has emphasized the need to integrate the study of history in the political socialization process, by stressing the "organic link" between the Romanian past and the present in teaching, research, and publications. Social scientists, especially sociologists and "political scientists,"* are

---

*Who in Romania hitherto have concentrated in the study of Party documents and implementation of decisions, rather than political science in the Western sense.

required to study the relationships between Party and people in the quest for the "multilaterally developed society," thus finding better ways to implement the RCP program in the present situation. Economists must struggle with the requirements of transmitting knowledge in such a way that efficiency and labor productivity can be increased.25

While the intelligentsia in the social sciences and humanities thus work directly in the field of value transmission and value change, the technical intelligentsia is required to perform a difficult dual task — to transmit the necessary technical information in an increasingly complex and sophisticated society, and at the same time help in value formation. One example of this dual function would be the teaching of, for example, mathematics at the university level. In that position, the professors would be expected to devote a considerable amount of time to ideology in addition to their field of specialization (even though some of the political indoctrination classes are taught by specialists in that field). The regime's reason for involving the technical intelligentsia in value formation and transmission is clear. The RCP does not want the student body to distinguish between political education and the "real stuff" by separating personnel who teach these subjects. Consequently, the requirement that technical personnel also teach ideology presumably ensures the proper understanding by the students of the "organic link" between these two sets of criteria for performance. At the same time, technical specialists are expected to transmit the very best and latest of knowledge in their fields, since this will help fulfill the important function of training individuals who are prepared for modern Romania and her requirements in terms of necessary skills.26

While the regime's expectations of both attitudes and behavior on the part of political and socio-economic elites in the socialization process are many and extensive, they are not unique in Eastern Europe. All communist political systems expect both correct attitudes and enthusiastic activity on the part of their elites in this field. It is in the area of mass attitudes and behavior that Romania occupies a special place among the East European systems at the present time. Briefly put, the Romanian regime requires both conforming (and enthusiastic) behavior and correct attitudes, hence the emphasis on the creation of "the new socialist man and woman" who thinks correctly and therefore acts correctly. Many years ago, Janos Kadar defined the Hungarian Workers' Party's attitude in this field by saying: "Whosoever is not against us is with us". If individuals refrained from sabotaging the socialist order, but otherwise went about their economic and social activities in an orderly fashion, a considerable area of privacy was thus accorded them. For Nicolae Ceausescu, such an attitude is foreign. The political socialization process is seen as a failure if people conform in actions without also having internalized the values of socialist society, Romanian style. This emphasis on full-scale value transformation even for the masses of the population sets Romania apart from the rest of the East European systems in the 1970s.[27]

THE MECHANICS OF POLITICAL SOCIALIZATION: STRUCTURES AND PROCEDURES

The political socialization effort, described above, is only feasible by constructing and utilizing a vast organizational network of socialization agents. One of the foremost aspects of communist systems everywhere is the heavy regime emphasis on building up its own network of groups and structures and also of subverting other, pre-revolutionary organizations so that they can be utilized for political education and indoctrination. Romania is no exception to this rule. During the generation of RCP dominance, the country has experienced an unprecedented expansion in organizational activity, and it is fair to say that even the most remote mountain village now is exposed to the regime by way of social organizations and informal structures, all presumably engaged in the task of political socialization and control.

This vast network of regime "agents" for socialization includes the following primary structures:

a. The RCP apparat. The Communist Party in Romania has experienced a tremendous numerical and organizational growth since August 1944, when the RCP first came to power as the senior member of a coalition. In August 1944, the Party had roughly 1,000 members; by the fall of 1955, this had increased to 595,398. By 1977, this figure had skyrocketed to 2,700.000. This figure represents one of the highest proportional levels of membership in any East European Communist Party.[28]

The RCP is not only a vast organization with a massive membership; it also has achieved good coverage of the entire country in territorial terms. In 1977 there were 59,000 primary party units. Furthermore, there has been a concerted effort to "balance the ticket", so that there is adequate representation for the most important socio-economic, - ethnic - and age groups in the party, while at the same time maintaining its character as a "proletarian" party. The RCP has done reasonably well in maintaining the workers' ratio of membership at the grass roots. In 1977, 51 per cent of the membership came from the industrial working-class. Of the new members admitted in 1977, 60 per cent were workers, - a figure which indicates the current RCP drive to enhance the proletarian elements in the Party base. By the same token, peasants are underrepresented relative to their strength in the general population, while the intelligentsia is somewhat overrepresented.[29]

There is also an underrepresentation of women relative to their share of the general population, and this continued discrepancy has prompted a drive to recruit more women. There is rough equivalence of age groups, and the main ethnic minorities are represented roughly in the same proportion as their strength in the general population.[30]

This vast organizational network operates on the basis of "interlocking directorates," "overlapping memberships," and "democratic centralism". A hierarchical organizational system incorporates the grass-roots party locals into a network of territorial units which include the county (judeţ) party organizations, finally connected in the central RCP apparatus in Bucharest. The RCP Central Committee and its Secretariat supervise numerous committees at the central levels which are officially charged with "cadre control." Through this integrated network, then, political socialization messages flow, personnel are assigned to carry these messages to the rank and file of RCP members and indeed beyond to "activists" in the general population, and supervision and control with implementation are provided. The crucial functions of information gathering and transfer within the hierarchy presumably are also carried out in this vast apparat. This, then, is a formidable structure even though many mistakes and malfunctions can be found (as discussed below).[31]

In addition to the RCP apparat itself, the principles of "overlapping membership" assure the political leadership of control over other indispensible agents of political socialization. The huge governmental apparatus, roughly paralleling the party structure discussed above, can be harnessed for direct and indirect political socialization — in the latter case through this apparat's implementation of its primary functions. This formidable army of "socializers" has been used extensively in Nicolae Ceausescu's ideological campaigns, and the General Secretary's penchant for "rotation of cadres," whereby prominent leaders are shunted back and forth between party and government posts, has further helped to "politicize" the administrative bureaucracy, thereby enhancing its value as a political socialization mechanism.[32]

As stated above, one of the most fundamental principles of communist rule is the synchronization between the ruling communist party and the many mass organizations in society. The Party, through the principles of multiple memberships (whereby the role of each party member as a member takes precedence over any other role he or she may perform in other organizations) ensures full control over the many organizations established for the purpose of societal mobilization. Romania is no exception to this rule. Literally dozens of such organizations exist in the country. For the purpose of analyzing vehicles of political socialization, the emphasis will be on the RCP Youth Organization (Uniunea Tineretului Comunist — UTC), the councils for workers of Hungarian and German origin, the student organizations, and the women's groups inside and outside the Party structure. The mass organizations of Romanian society are further tied together in the Socialist Unity Front (Frontul Unitatii Socialiste--FUS), an umbrella organization incorporating other organizations and structures. Finally, the centralized nature of Romanian economic life ensures full RCP domination of the trade unions, which incorporate virtually all employed personnel in the country. During the Ceausescu era, it has become increasingly the practice that party leaders also head the regional and local "People's Councils," thus supervising the presumed representative and executive structures in their respective localities in a direct fashion.[33]

The UTC has expanded greatly during the Ceausescu era. In 1973 the youth organization had some 2.4 million members; by 1978, the figure was up to 2.8 mill. The UTC network parallels that of the Party, and thus has considerable "coverage" throughout the country, although its network is generally weaker in the countryside than in the cities and towns. The UTC is particularly active in certain categories of young people, such as enlisted soldiers, and a great deal of energy is also expended in socialization tasks among young workers.[34]

Compared to the UTC, the Union of Students' Associations of Romania, the umbrella organization for student groups in Romania, is by its very nature focused on a particular audience, the key group of highly trained personnel coming out of the country's universities and other institutions of higher learning. These individuals, the future leaders of Romania's modernization, must be trustworthy, hard working, and honest — three key aspects of the socialization program discussed above. Heading the students' organization therefore has been a traditional path to more important positions in the RCP leadership for several individuals but, due to the problems associated with this particular group (see "Results" section below) the job has also frequently led to the political wilderness for some of its incumbents.[35]

During the 1970's there has been increasing emphasis on the recruitment of women to political and socio-economic positions "of responsibility" in Romania, and the General Secretary has carried out a systematic policy of increasing the proportion of women in the RCP and in the administrative apparat of the state. This trend has been accelerated with the recent elevation of Elena Ceausescu, the General Secretary's wife, to the apparent function of supervision of RCP cadres at the central level. This recruitment effort has been coupled with a continuing drive to increase the membership of several women's organizations throughout Romanian society (although the emphasis during this decade has definitly been on RCP membership recruitment from this category). With women representing 51 per cent of the total population and with a tradition of little political activity on the part of this group, substantial mobilization reserves exist here. The present RCP leadership is "going after" these reserves with a vengeance.

While the organizations discussed above focus on large social categories and age cohorts, the councils for workers of Hungarian and German origin deal with one of the most difficult aspects of political socialization, namely the transmission of values derived primarily from the Romanian cultural tradition and formulated by the predominantly ethnic Romanian political elite, to national minorities whose cultural background, collective memories, and behavior patterns differ considerably from the norms of the ethnic majority. These agents of political socialization have a dual task, which is of particular significance; not only must they attempt to convince the minorities of the basic rectitude of the system and its goals, which is indeed the same task as faced by all other socialization agents, but they must also convince ethnic groups of the elite's right to define the basic aspects of the system, its goals, and the ways of goal achievement and implementation; the elite is of course predominantly Romanian in terms of ethnic origin and culture. These councils become particularly important during periods of external pressure, as was the case in the summer of 1968, and again in 1971 and 1978. In addition, periods of rising internal dissention, which has characterized political life and mass attitudes during the latter part of the 1970s, tend to bring forth an added effort of such agents. At the present time, the nationality councils are particularly active trying to combat the drive for emigration exhibited by many in the German population group, while at the same time renewed Hungarian concern for their conationals in Romanian Transylvania has been combated by increased efforts on the part of these agencies. A flood of literature on the work of these councils and the status of ethnic minorities in contemporary Romania is also sweeping Western countries in an effort to combat negative press and public opinion here.[36]

Of the greatest importance for the mobilization of labor, especially the industrial working class, is the trade union umbrella organization UGS (Uniunea Generala al Sindicatelor). This organization, which functions in the classical "Stalinist" manner as a transmission belt of commands from the political and economic leadership to the rank and file, has been securely under RCP control since the early years of communist participation in the coalition governments of 1944-1947; since the establishment of political monopoly by the Party the UGS has been one of the most significant organizations of the country. This agent is of particular importance in the regime's quest for "modern" attitudes with economic overtones such as punctuality, honesty, reliability, frugality, and the requisite technical knowledge necessary for the fulfillment of increasingly complex tasks. At the same time, the RCP maintains that the industrial proletariat is the "vanguard class," and this necessitates hammering home principal elements of political and moral/ethical values, discussed above.[37] (The degree to which such efforts have succeeded is evaluated in the Nelson contribution to this volume.)

Political socialization in Romania, which depends heavily on organizational penetration of the general population as well as certain social categories and age groups, is further enhanced by the fact that the RCP maintains strict control with the flow of information and communication throughout the country, and between Romania and the world beyond its borders. There are joint party — and state agencies controlling radio and television; censorship for political material persists, despite Nicolae Ceausescu's "abolition" of "formal" censorship in 1978. Other agencies oversee the production of films and theatre plays, and the so-called "plastic arts" (sculpture and various other art forms is this genre) are closely supervised by a variety of structures, such as local RCP bodies, artists' unions, and state committees, as well as "vigilante" units of the "working population." Of particular importance in this context is the trend towards direct participation by political militants, representing the "working people," on all sorts of bodies supervising and commissioning artistic and literary production. Such watchdog bodies, augmented by the presumed voice of the people, are now exercising closer control over the printed word and various art forms then at any time during the Ceauşescu era.[38]

Finally, the very operational style of the General Secretary is in itself a powerful vehicle for political socialization. Through his frequent "flying visits" to industrial and agricultural enterprises and regional centers the RCP leader engages in a great deal of direct communication to the masses of the population as well as to cadres. Because of the increasing personality cult surrounding the General Secretary, this vehicle of political socialization has become the most important weapon in the struggle for the "multilaterally developed society" and subsequently socialism and communism.

THE RESULTS OF THE SOCIALIZATION PROGRAM: A BALANCE SHEET

While the major manifestations of the contemporary political socialization program in Romania are clear, and the analyst also has a relatively detailed picture of the agents and mechanism for the implementation of such programs, the effects are much more difficult to ascertain. Taking the main goals of the socialization program in descending order of ambition and scope, the following conclusions seem warranted:

a. The creation of "new socialist men and women" has not been achieved. The extremely ambitious conception of value transformation – and creation, which is espoused by Nicolae Ceausescu, precludes rapid achievement of this goal, and the regime leaders appear to be aware of this problem. The General Secretary is nevertheless an impatient man, and he habitually voices his concern over the lack of progess in this field. Specifically, he points out that there is insufficient political participation in Romania; many of those who do participate engage in "the chanting of empty slogans" and in "formalism," i.e., they voice the required slogans, but their actions are not infused with the kind of enthusiastic commitment that the leadership prefers. As for formalism, it is clear that many activists and citizens alike take few measures to ensure the link between theory and practice, between the necessary ritual of learning the RCP program and its requirements, on the one hand, and actually implementing them in daily life, on the other hand. This lack of willingness to relate party doctrine to life pertains to RCP cadres as well as the general population, according to the many and frequent criticism by Ceausescu.[39]

While there is a serious deficiency in political and socio-economic actions in accordance with the socialization program, considerable evidence exists that even the internalization of values and attitudes is lacking in many cases. Ceausescu consistently criticizes the persistence of "retrograde" attitudes which tend to emphasize the individual and his or her needs at the expense of societal, collective needs. Furthermore, there is a tendency for "bourgeois – landowner mentality" to reassert itself in economic matters, once again emphasizing personal gain at the expense of the gains for

all, and practical manifestations of corruption and
pilfering of materials, foods, and other scarce commodities indicate the persistence of "old" values and traditions in a society where such practices were commonplace
prior to communist rule. To make matters worse, the
rapid socio-economic transformation of Romania and the
concentration of power in the hands of party and government bureaucrats have produced certain "contradictions
in socialist society," which are said to be non-antagonistic but nevertheless serious. The most important of
these contradictions has been the misuse of power and
prestige by "unhealthy" elements in the RCP and administrative hierarchies. During the Ceaușescu era, frequent
purges have been carried out to limit such excesses, but
they stubbornly remain, showing the inadequate internalization of major regime goals and values on the part
of some of those designated as leaders in the ambitious
Romanian nation-building program.[40]

Since the General Secretary is extremely outspoken
in his criticism of the failures and aberrations of
program internalization and implementation in Romania,
we have a great deal of material about other problems of
political socialization as well. Nicolae Ceausescu
habitually castigates both RCP cadres, other societal
elites, and "elements" in the general population for
"kowtowing to the West," — the latter exhibited by uncritical acceptance of Western music, dress, literature,
and other aspects of Western mass culture (which the
Party leader often considers unculture). The Americanization of the Romanian youth scene is profoundly disturbing to Ceausescu — the self-styled populist, Marxist,
and nationalist. The fervent nationalistic campaign,
exemplified in the "Hymn to Romania" movement of 1976
and 1977, is designed to offset this dangerous incursion
of Western ideas among the most important age cohort in
the population, the youth, who have grown up under
communist rule but nevertheless fell victim to such
nefarious Western influences.[41]

Incorrect attitudes and behavior are not only
displayed by elements in the general population and the
youth, however; some members of the technical and
artistic intelligentsia and RCP cadres also display an
unhealthy admiration for Western achievements. A
frequently cited aberration is the tendency among
scientists in Romania to depend excessively upon foreign
patents and innovations, thereby reducing the creative
spirit of Romania and making the country dependent upon
foreign sources of technology. The General Secretary
has repeatedly denounced such attitudes and has forced
through a partial realignment of technological research,
which has led to the utilization of inadequate domestic
sources rather than more sophisticated imports. This

kind of policy is bound to increase costs and decrease efficiency, at least in the short run, but the RCP leader appears willing to accept such temporary economic problems in exchange for more independence in this field. At the same time, the Romanian leadership continues its quest for Western technology through carefully implemented schemes of economic cooperation, which ensures regime control over programs and results and also produces the training of domestic cadres, — a sort of piggy-back infusion of technology on the regime's terms.[42]

Other Western ideas are also competing with the Ceausescu vision of life under socialism. The so-called "Basket Three" of the Helsinki Accords, and the early aggressive emphasis on human rights in the Carter Administration, produced an atmosphere in Romania which was conducive to the elaboration of a view emphasizing the needs and rights of the individual rather than the collectivity, thus standing in sharp contact to the Ceausescu concept of the "organic society" under RCP leadership. While the so-called dissident movement, emphasizing "Western" ideas of human rights, was small in Romania as compared to East Germany, Poland, and Czechoslovakia, the ambitious socialization program of the Ceausescu regime made the RCP leaders extremely wary of such manifestations, and the General Secretary devoted a great deal of his time to this subject during 1977. When some of the ideas concerning human rights were coupled with complaints from the German and Hungarian minorities concerning the alleged policy of "Romanianization" of the young generation, the RCP leader responded with a series of virulent attacks on "retrograde views" and "bourgeois nationalism." He denounced especially the tendency among many ethnic Germans to demand the right of emigration to West Germany, which they claimed to be their ethnic homeland. Ceausescu vehemently denied this allegation, stating that ethnic Germans, whose ancestors settle in Romanian territory eight hundred years ago, cannot possibly talk about another homeland. Instead, the RCP leader sharply intimated that the urge to emigrate was closely tied to the perceived needs of the individuals for an easy increase in the standard of living in the Western "fleshpot," a comment sharply colored as well by a sense of betrayal — those wanting to emigrate had set themselves outside of the organic society presumably in the making, thereby demonstrating the failure of an important socialization platform. To make matters even worse, Budapest resurrected old claims and concerns pertaining to the treatment of ethnic Hungarians in Romania, and an erstwhile prominent Hungarian in the RCP at the central and regional levels, Karol Kiraly, openly denounced "assimilationist" policies of the regime in nationality policies. The implication was that the RCP, under the guise of creating a socialist culture, was in fact attempting to reduce or even eliminate the cultural manifestations of Hungarian ethnicity in Romania altogether. Kiraly was subsequently moved from the county of Covasna, with its heavy concentration of Hungarians, to Caransebeş, an area almost exclusively inhabited by Romanians.[43]

b. Another area of desired behavior is economic in nature; this is the area of labor productivity and reduction in the use of raw materials and fuels for each unit of finished production. The RCP leader is constantly pointing out that labor productivity in Romania is low compared with the other socialist states of Eastern Europe (let alone in comparison with the U.S. or Western Europe). By the same token, the use of raw materials and fuels is high, indicating a wasteful production process and inadequate public concern. Successful implementation of the labor productivity plans will help propel Romania into the "multilaterally developed stage," and a more economical use of resources will become indispensable in an era of skyrocketing costs and depletion of raw materials and fuels; by the same token, failure to solve these problems will spell the postponement, if not the abandonment, of the Romanian modernization program, which is such an indispensable part of the regime itself. The continued concern on the part of the General Secretary shows the extent to which attitude formation has failed to meet regime plans.[44]

The many and varied problems of system performance in the political socialization field are real enough, but their magnitude is at least partly a function of regime goals in the first place. If the regime were content with a citizenry which basically had accepted the reality of communist rule, without seeing the need to change individuals' minds and attitudes, the Romanian regimes could claim considerable success in political socialization. There is little evidence that masses of Romanian citizens are ready to overturn the present system; on the contrary, there is evidence to show that many are reasonably satisfied with certain aspects of the Ceausescu regime's performance, especially in foreign policy and in the field of cultural nationalism. The main point, however, is that the regime is not satisfied by such passive acceptance, but sets its sights much higher. Given that kind of goal, the perception of failure and the magnitude of that failure will also be enhanced.

By the same token, the high goals for economic performance also tend to exaggerate problems with implementation. The Romanian economy has been growing very rapidly indeed; the growth rate is in fact among the highest in Europe. Romania is changing from an agrarian society. The level of technology is steadily increasing in the economy, and the educational level of the population has improved dramatically under communist rule. All of these achievements should give cause for considerable satisfaction. That Nicolae Ceausescu and his close associates are men in a hurry, however. aiming to catch up with the most advanced industrial states by the turn of the century, does not alow for any rest on present laurels. Given this perspective, the failure to root out "old" values quickly, and the failure to instill in the population new attitudes and efforts of performance in the short perspective of thirty years loom as a larger deficiency than is actually the case. Success or failure is partly a function of the beholder. Nicolae Ceausescu is adverse to partial successes, unless they are way stations to complete achievement. Our assessment of the results of political socialization in Romania under communist rule must be seen in this perspective.

FUTURE PROSPECTS: TOWARDS A "MULTILATERALLY DEVELOPED SOCIETY"?

Any attempt to assess the future of the Romanian political system, and especially the function of political socialization, must discuss three related aspects, which together determine the concept and function of "political socialization." First, will the attitudes and goals of the political leadership remain the same, or will there be a change in their perceptions in the 1980s? Second, will the methods of transmitting values, attitudes, and goals remain the same, or will these agents change? Third, will the impact of socialization remain the same, such that the results among societal elites and the masses can be expected to remain similar to the present level of achievement, or will there be changes here as well? One may assume that changes in regime goals and in the methods and agents will also produce different results. By the same token, persistence in goals and methods may produce similar results; conversely, the very fact of persistence may produce "payoffs" which were premature in the 'sixties and seventies'.

Several scenarios may be constructed. Since Nicolae Ceausescu is only a little over sixty years of age, it is likely that he will coninue as RCP state leader for the entire decade of the 1980s. This assumption is further strengthened by the fact that Ceausescu is, as Mary Ellen Fischer has described in this volume, firmly in power and clearly intends to stay in control by means of policies which have been discussed above. If Ceausescu remains in power, it is likely that the basic regime goals, which have also been discussed in some detail above, will be maintained. It also seems likely that the operational style of political socialization, developed since 1965, will remain in its basic features, and that many of the methods and agents will be maintained. The politicization of Romanian society, in this first scenario, will continue; the ideological campaign will be maintained without basic modification, and the frantic pace of forced economic development will continue to be the basic feature of economic policy.

A second, and most extreme scenerio suggests that the level of disaffection among citizens and elites with the personalized rule of Ceausescu and his economic policies will become so severe that the General Secretary is forced to step down. Finally, one must consider a third scenerio wherein Ceausescu's charismatic style is toned down while the political-ideological campaign is slowed without abandoning its basic features. The latter would have beneficial effects; it would lower the goals, and the pressure on the population would decrease, both of which allow for regime conclusions that success has indeed been achieved in this field. Should such a development indeed occur, the RCP leadership would be able to "declare victory" in its quest for the multilaterally developed society and the new socialist man and woman. Such a development would further influence the function and processes of political socialization, insofar as the regime goals in this field would change, presumably towards value maintenance rather than value transformation. But the pace and scope of the ideological campaign under way in Romania in the 1970s continue at the beginning of the 1980s and indeed, appear to be intensified. At the same time, there is growing evidence of popular dissatisfaction with the policies of the regime in general and cynicism concerning the breathless socialization campaign in particular.[45] At some point in the 1980s, both the intelligentsia and the general population are likely to begin a serious reassessment of the discrepancy between theory and fact, between rhetoric and performance, in the Romanian political and socio-economic system. The making of a new socialist man or woman is seriously hampered by the continuation of economic problems, malfeasance, and corruption. The fusion of nationalism and the Ceauşescu personality cult has alienated even many staunch Romanian nationalists, and the minorities are chafing under the policies of the elite, which is predominantly Romanian in origin. In this ethnic controversy, old memories and animosities, old privileges and slights, and difference in life-styles and cultural traditions are brought to the fore once again in time-honored Balkan fashion. Political socialization as ideological indoctrination and personality cults is unlikely to solve these massive problems.

While the general population and the ethnic minorities in Romania are beginning to emit signals of resentment against the continued ideological campaign, the growing numbers of the technical, managerial, and cultural intelligentsia are experiencing "cognitive dissonance" between their professional values of rationality, technical expertise, and efficiency when contrasted with the political values of ideological conformity, quasi-religious veneration of an individual, and the continued emphasis on "red" rather than "expert" criteria of the Ceausescu regime. This is the classical confrontation between elements of the "professionals" and "apparatchiki" which can be observed elsewhere in communist systems. The confrontation is certainly more complex than illustrated above, and there are remedial policies which can be undertaken by the present regime to alleviate the problem. But, on the other hand, the nature of the Ceausescu leadership is such that the political elites in Romania are more "apparatchik" than almost any other elite in Eastern Europe, and this fact is likely to exacerbate the confrontation in this decade.

There exist in Romania in the 1980s, then, multiple paths of political and socio-economic socialization, and the regime version is but one of them. As Romanian society becomes increasingly complex due to the modernization policies of the regime, the pluralization of socialization paths is likely to continue, even to accelerate. As stated above, the regime, as long as it is firmly in the hands of Nicolae Ceausescu, is unlikely to accept such a development, and will most likely respond by intensification of the socialization program. Thus, the second major scenario discussed above is in fact being played out. In a few years, the discrepancy between regime goals and popular expectations in this field will have widened to such an extent that the observer and analyst may well find a real political crisis in Romania. That would become the acid test of both political power and political socialization as they have been practiced in Romania during the last generation.

NOTES

1. E.g. Fred I. Greenstein, Children and Politics (New Haven, Conn.: Yale University Press, 1965); Kenneth Jennings and Richard Niemi, The Political Character of Adolescence (Princeton, N.J.: Princeton University Press, 1974).

2. A good overview is found in Gabriel A. Almond and G. Bingham Powell, Jr., Comparative Politics: System, Process, and Policy (Boston, Mass.: Little, Brown, and Company, 1978, second ed.), esp. Ch. IV.

3. For a broad overview of this problem, see Cynthia Enloe, Ethnic Conflict and Political Development (Boston, Mass.: Little, Brown, and Company, 1972).
4. A thorough analysis of political and socio-economic life in the Balkans is found in L.S. Stavrianos, The Balkans since 1453 (New York, N.Y.: Holt, Rinehart, and Winston, 1958), esp. Part II.
5. E.g. Vaclav L. Benes, "Czechoslovak Democracy and Its Problems, 1918-1920", and Victor S. Mamatey, "The Development of Czechoslovak Democracy, 1920-1938", both in Victor S. Mamatey and Radomir Luza (eds.), A History of the Czechoslovak Republic 1918-1948 (Princeton, N.J.: Princeton University Press, 1973), pp. 39-98, and 99-167, respectively.
6. See, for example, Hugh Seton-Watson, The East European Revolution, (New York, N.Y.: Frederick A. Praeger, 1968), esp. Part I.
7. Examples of such groups and parties are: All for the Fatherland, Ploughmen's Front, League of National Christian Defense, Iron Guard, Front of National Rebirth, Legion of the Archangel Michael, Liberal Party, Romanian National Party of Transylvania, Party of Labor, Peasant Party, People's League, People's Party, Young Liberals. Many of these organizations were "movements" rather than parties and interest groups in the Western sense. See my article on the Romanian party system in Vincent McHale (ed.), Political Parties of Europe, a volume in the series Encyclopedia of Political Parties of the World (Westpoint, Conn.: Greenwood Press, forthcoming).
8. R.W. Seton-Watson, A History of the Roumanians (Cambridge: Cambridge University Press, 1934) is still the best overall history of Romania in English.
9. Ghita Ionescu, Communism in Rumania 1944-1962 (London: Oxford University Press, 1964), esp. Part II. See also Andrei Otetea (ed.), Istoria Poporului Roman (Bucharest: Biblioteca de Istorie, 1972), esp. Part IV, Part V.
10. Ceausescu's views have been set forth in innumerable books, articles, and speeches; one of these collections is Documente ale Partidului Comunist Roman: Activitatea Ideologica si Politica-Educativa (Bucharest: Editura Politica, 1972).
11. E.g. Elena Zamfir, "Participare si Competenţa in Procesul Afirmari Democratiei Socialiste," Era Socialista, August 5, 1978.
12. For a discussion of this point, see "The Integration of Ethnic Minorities" in my Modernization in Romania since World War II (New York, N.Y.: Praeger Publishers, 1975), ch. 8.
13. Ibid.
14. The continuity of these values in Romanian life is discussed in Gh. Cosma, "Independenta- Simbol al Ideii de Libertate si Demnitate Nationala-Oglindita in

Artele Plastice," Era Socialista, Sept. 1977.

15. Patriotism is incessantly hammered home in political literature as well as fiction; for an example of the regime's views on the writer's role in society, see Aurelia Batali (ed.), Misiunea Scriitorului Contemporan: Idei si Atitudini Literare (Bucharest: Editura Eminescu, 1974).

16. E.g. V. Enache, "Perfectionarea Sistemului de Retributie si Cresterea Cointeresarii Materiale", Era Socialista, June 1978.

17. Sometimes the RCP leader must do so as a real troubleshooter, e.g. in the miners' stike in the Jiu Valley in August 1977, when striking miners held lesser officials hostage until the General Secretary arrived on the scene.

18. I have discussed this style in "Ceausescu's Romania", Problems of Communism, July-August 1974, pp. 29-44.

19. This was the principal theme during the national conference of cadres in the RCP regional branches, the social sciences, and youth organizations, October 1976. (for Ceausescu's speech on this occasion, see Scinteia, October 8, 1976).

20. E.g. the plans for cultural programs for the centennial celebrations in 1976 and 1977, discussed by Ion Mitran in Contemporanul, December, 1975.

21. "Stilul Comunist de Conducere", Era Socialista, Sept. 1977 (lead article).

22. Ceausescu has ensured continued control over the regional RCP apparat by means of frequent personnel changes. For an analysis of this, see my "Political Leadership at the Regional Level in Romania: The Case of the Judet Party, 1968-1973", East European Quarterly, January, 1975, pp. 99-111.

23. Batali, Misiunea Scriitorului Contemporan.

24. E.g. Dan Grigorescu, "Implicarea Artelor Plastice in Viata Socialia", Era Socialista, July 1978.

25. Stefan Costea, "Cresterea Rolului Stiintelor Sociale in Procesul de Educare si Formare a Omului Nou" ibid. June 20, 1978.

26. As early as 1971 the General Secretary castigated many scientists for their tendency to downplay ideology in their teaching; see, for example, his speech to the RCP Central Committee, early November 1971, in Scinteia, November 4, 1971.

27. There has been no reduction in this emphasis, as witnessed by recent statements from Nicolae Ceausescu, e.g. in ibid, June 23, 1978 (speech at the national conference of the Romanian Fine Arts Union).

28. Figures for 1955 in Gilberg, Modernization in Romania since World War II, p. 35; for 1977, in Scinteia Sept. 24, 1977.

29. <u>Scinteia</u>, Sept. 24, 1977. The classification of social class in membership figures always presents problems of analysis. When the statistics state that a certain percentage "comes from" or "originates from" a certain class, the reference is to <u>social origin</u>, not necessarily occupation at the time of entry. Thus, the figures for working class membership already in the RCP are overstated. On the other hand, Romanian figures also specify <u>new members</u> enrolled in 1978. These individuals presumably come from the industrial proletariat in terms of function, and thus are workers <u>by occupation</u>.

30. <u>Ibid</u> (the percentage of women was 26).

31. See, for example, sharp Ceauşescu criticism of party performance in <u>Scinteia</u>, September 10, 1977.

32. I have discussed this in <u>Modernization in Romania since World War II</u>, esp. ch. 2.

33. For an interesting study of the U.T.C. in Romanian history, see C. Barbulescu (ed.) <u>File din Istoria U.T.C.</u> (Bucharest: Editura Politica, 1971).

34. This effort is only moderately successful; see Ceausescu's criticism of party performance in this and other fields (<u>Scinteia</u>, September 10, 1977.

35. The story of Traian Stefanescu is illustrative. After heading the students' union, he was promoted to an important position in the RCP Central Committee apparat. He was subsequently dropped from that position after continued problems in the field of political indoctrination among students.

36. E.g. <u>Hungarians and Germans in Romania Today</u> (report from a meeting of the Councils of Working People of Magyar and German Nationality in the Socialist Republic of Romania, March 13-14, 1978) (Bucharest: Meridiane Publishing House, 1978).

37. <u>Programme of the Romanian Communist Party for the Building of the Multilaterally Developed Society and Romania's Advance Toward Communism</u> (Bucharest: Agerpres, 1975), esp. Part III.

38. The new system was discussed in <u>Scinteia</u>, June 30, 1977.

39. E.g. <u>ibid</u>. September 10, 1977.

40. One of the largest personnel changes in RCP history took place in January 1977, see <u>ibid</u>., Jan 26 and 27, 1977.

41. One element of this campaign is the veneration of traditional Romanian heroes, such as Vlad Tepes (the Impaler). See <u>Luceafarul</u>, Dec. 1, 1976.

42. For a sophisticated analysis of the relationship between technology and society, see Valter Roman in <u>Cronica</u> (Iasi), July 29, 1977.

43. Ceausescu's concern with the potential for political trouble among the minorities prompted a long speaking tour in Transylvania during the summer of 1978; see <u>Scinteia</u>, June 21, 22, 23, 1978.

44. E.g. the General Secretary in *ibid*. September 10, 1977.

45. An example of the dissatisfaction and growing assertiveness of part of the intelligentsia was the publication of the Writers' Union literary awards for 1979; these awards had been made on artistic grounds in the face of the RCP's campaign for "responsible" literature. The "party" writers immediately launched a concerted attack against the awards. The awards were announced in *Luceafarul* and *Romania Literara*, June 27, 1979; the attacks on them can be found throughout the summer, e.g. in *Luceafarul*, June 30, and July 14, 1979.

6
Workers in a Workers' State

Daniel N. Nelson

ISSUES

Karl Marx's argument for collective control of the means of production[1] is inherent to the rhetoric by which communist parties seek legitimacy. Particularly where communist parties rule in nation-states with a significant stratum of industrial labor, as in Eastern Europe, the Marxist call for redistributing economic power (by which he meant political power) is a core tenet for rationalizing Party dictatorship. Simply put, communist parties take and hold the reins of government asserting that political power will pass, through the Party, into the hands of the working masses, usually seen to include not only industrial labor but all wage earners. As interpreted by Lenin, the development of socialism should bring workers into the "functions of control and accounting".[2] In developed socialism, therefore, the integration of the masses in the organization and management of production and "... the direct participation of all who work in taking decisions regarding economic and social development" are regarded as de facto.[3] In short, workers are to fill "participant roles"[4] in developed socialism; they are, collectively, to exercise decision-making authority in the economy and, implicit to a Marxist, the polity as well.

This essay has both descriptive and analytical purposes related to the foregoing observations. At the outset, I will seek to describe quantitative and qualitative dimensions of participatory behavior among workers (for the most part, industrial labor) in Romania--a

---

Daniel N. Nelson teaches in the Department of Political Science at the University of Kentucky. He holds a Ph.D. from the Johns Hopkins University. This article previously appeared in <u>Soviet Studies</u> (October 1980).

communist party state which has, since 1965, referred to itself as "socialist".[5] In this initial section, my concern will be objective political activity by private citizens vis-à-vis subjective attitudes about their role in the political system (e.g., feelings of efficacy). Following earlier studies of participation, I exclude those whose <u>career</u> it is to be engaged in mass organizations, the <u>Party</u> or the State in communist countries.[6] Descriptive statistics will enable us to portray, as a first step, workers' involvement at the micro-level of factories and other economic units. Aggregating such data can give us a view, albeit a fragmentary one (lacking a national sample), of the <u>extent</u> to which workers exhibit participatory behavior <u>and how</u> they participate.

A second section, also descriptive, will examine the evaluation by workers of their participation, that is the subjective attitudes excluded from the essay's first portion, including sense of efficacy, levels of satisfaction and sources of dissatisfaction, and the degree of identity with or confidence in Party-provided participatory channels.

The third and fourth parts of my discussion are devoted to analytical issues by which I mean, first, the impact of workers' participatory behavior and attitudes on communist governments, their stability and political change and, second, the significance of findings regarding such behavior and attitudes for comparative hypotheses about political participation. The first of these issues brings us beyond the microcosm of factories and other places of employment since, in socialist states, workplace behavior is not only relevant to politics but <u>is</u> a locus of political life. That the Party in Romania and other socialist systems recognizes such an equation is evident by the great amount of cadres' time and party funds devoted to both creating channels for workers' participatory behavior and to assuring that there is a semblance of enthusiasm for such activities. The success or failure of structures and processes for worker involvement is, therefore, a political "stake" invested by the Party--an investment it <u>must</u> make not simply because of its Marxist heritage but <u>also</u> because the economic plan it pursues requires higher worker productivity. Where a key basis of Party legitimacy rests on its identity with interests of workers, where the achievement of the Party's policies depends on workers' performance and their willing obedience and where, in light of such conditions, the Party strongly emphasizes, via rhetoric and statutes, outlets for workers' involvement, the political nature of participation by working people becomes clear. Ultimately, the issue at hand for communist systems is one of power. Do workers fill participant as opposed to subject roles, thereby sharing political power

in developed socialism? Do workers have influence in
making public policy as opposed to performing roles in
symbolic involvement?[7] And, if workers do influence
public policy thus acting in participant roles to some
degree, what proportion of such influence falls within
the bounds of their officially sanctioned authority?
Such questions, for the moment left unanswered, are foci
for this essay's third section.

    Finally, I will turn to the relationship between
workers' participation in a communist party state and
broader, comparative hypotheses. A widespread expectation, so prevalent that it is stated as a given rather
than in hypothesis form, is that "citizenship roles" in
authoritarian political systems are "confined to the
political output processes".[8] In other words, only <u>after</u>
policy is made and its implementation begun do citizens
in authoritarian systems, "(take) advantage of opportunities to contact bureaucrats, or informal 'fixers' in
order to have governmental action as it affects their
lives".[9] This paper suggests reasons to doubt such an
expectation, and I will offer some alternative hypotheses
about citizenship roles in authoritarian polities maintained by communist parties. Hypotheses regarding the
relationships between and among development, political
participation and socio-economic equality will also be
considered. The pursuit of socio-economic development
and the ideological commitment to equality are twin tasks
of communist governments which cannot be divorced from
citizen involvement, particularly the participatory behavior of workers upon whom the developmental goals depend and for whom communist parties ostensibly strive to
attain equality. Within that stratum of the population,
then, relationships among these variables should be more
strongly evident, if, indeed, they are to be found at
all.

THE QUANTITY OF WORKERS' PARTICIPATION

    There is little purpose to operationalizing "parti-
cipation" in a communist state through statistics regarding trade union membership; such membership is inherent to being employed and the number of benefits, in
any case, contingent upon being nominally associated with
the trade union make membership mandatory. It is not
much more beneficial to use Party or Young Communist
League membership as an indicator of participation since
the category of "workers" as reported for both the PCR
and UTC (Partidul Comunist Roman and Uniunea Tineretului
Comunist) cannot be assumed accurate. Local organs, in
reporting the backgrounds of their membership, are not
necessarily uniform in defining the term "worker", nor
are individuals uniform in emphasizing certain aspects

of their life for Party membership purposes. To know, therefore, that trade unions in Romania encompass the vast majority of the workforce says little about workers' participatory behavior. It is, moreover, difficult to judge whether or not the Party's claim of 52% workers in its membership is at all close to an accurate reflection of industrial labor in political activity.[10]

Since 1971, the Romanian Communist Party has promoted workers councils (Consiliilor Oamenilor Municii or C.O.M.) as the key mechanism through which the participation of industrial labor in the making and implementing of decisions was to be effected.[11] Party leader Ceausescu had raised, as early as December 1967, the need for some form of collective management to resolve the multiple problems of economic life, to eliminate arbitrary decision-making and to bring the experience of specialists, cadres and working masses into management.[12] By 1971, the intra-Party debates had run their course, and the Political Executive Committee's (i.e., Politburo equivalent) decision, soon announced at a Central Committee plenum, was then enacted by the Grand National Assembly.

Workers' Councils, however, received little attention until 1977. In these first six years of their existence, the operation of workers' councils was given only occasional propaganda emphasis. In early 1978, a strong push for workers' councils was reinstituted, making them the cornerstone of a campaign denoted by the word "autoconducerea"--self-management.

It is a reasonable presumption that such renewed concern for the C.O.M. system had some relationship to 1977 labor strife among miners in the Jiu Valley, and strong sociological evidence building over the early-mid 1970s that dissatisfaction at the work place was correlated with high rates of job turnover (instability of the workforce) and had a negative impact on productivity. Although I will return to discuss attitudinal indicators below, it is worth noting at this point that data exist regarding workers' evaluation of their lives and jobs, as well as the degree to which they identify with or rely upon workers' councils and other channels of participation established by the Party. Often the product of research conducted for the Party or a Ministry under contract, empirical data make their way into some published articles, books, and monographs. (Unfortunately, the highest proportion of such data remains "pentru uz intern"--for internal use only.)

Varying from 9 to 25 members according to an enterprise's number of employees, workers councils in Romania involved over 153,000 workers and management cadres only two years after their inception.[13] As originally conceived, however, the majority of each council was composed of non-elected members, primarily those occupying the highest management, technical and political positions in a factory or enterprise. Those "elected" by workers at a general assembly of the enterprise to be their "representatives" in the workers' council constituted but a minority of the council. Only eight of a nineteen-member C.O.M. at the Bucharest central post office were "elected", for example, in the 1976-77 period, of whom three were foremen (production department chiefs), one was an engineer, one a national post office official, and only three could be labeled as manual workers--two technicians and one postman.[14] Eight of the nineteen were de jure members from the highest Party and managerial positions--director, assistant directors, chief accountant, Party secretary, chief of quality and technical control, president of the trade union and Young Communist League Secretary. Three "nominated" members (nominated by the Party leadership of the enterprise) filled out the workers' council. All three were chiefs of administrative departments.

With such a minor presence in the principal mechanism for their self-management, it is not surprising that workers play a small role in most of C.O.M. discussions and debates. Sessions are, indeed, dominated by de jure (mebrii de drept) members or the several individuals present as nominated members. In the example cited above, an analysis for fifteen meetings (once per month) suggested that elected members spoke for only 18% of the time.[15] The three people one might label as "manual labor" spoke for a combined total of 2.1% of the council's sessions over the same fifteen months, an aggregate less than any single de jure or nominated member except for the UTC secretary. An earlier research effort reinforced the above finding. For all of 1972 and the first half of 1973, C.O.M. members in the "elected" category were asked how often they spoke at workers' council meetings. Ninety-five of the 215 respondents said that, over 18 months, they had spoken fewer than 5 times. Since a median C.O.M. had 18 members in 1972-73, speaking fewer than 5 times over a year and a half in a small group suggests a reluctance or inability to speak out--i.e., every third meeting one elected C.O.M. member might speak. A more interesting question that was not asked might have inquired who spoke at every meeting and for what proportion at the time.[16]

One such example does not allow us to make nationwide generalizations. Corroboration can, however, be inferred from other fragmentary evidence. Of his experience in a workers' council in Bucharest electronics factory, the chief quality control engineer (a de jure member of the council) told me:

>...I am often unsure why we meet at all. Surely the few workers' representatives present know what will transpire, and I am quite aware of the messages that will be conveyed. They are, in fact, symbolic gatherings at which we say what is required of us, and listen to the factory director repeat our enterprise's planned production targets, the need for economies in material, etc. If these meetings serve a purpose, I think it is to see one another face to face... I haven't participated in decisions of significance for the factory <u>at the workers' council</u>... (emphasis added)[17]

Manual labor seems to be cognizant that workers' councils have little power and offer little opportunity to them. Notwithstanding constant reminders via signs in factories, newsletters, and verbal communication by Party cadres, few workers devote their attention to the councils or their activities. Although I will return to evaluative measures below, it is interesting that one-fourth to one-third of 215 workers sampled from machine construction and chemical refining industries were unable to identify by name <u>any</u> of their "elected" representatives on their respective councils, and about two-thirds knew either none or only a few.[18] Moreover, almost half of workers on C.O.M. said fewer than ten workers from the enterprise during a six month period had sought their help in their capacity as council member.[19]

General Assemblies (adunarile generale) in each enterprise, of which the workers' councils are de facto executive committees, have "a special role in affirming workers' self-management..." through which the working masses participate directly in the socio-economic management activities, in debating and resolving problems related to filling the production plan, and exercising control as leading organs.[20] Meeting twice a year, general assemblies of the enterprise bring together all employees--over 5,000,000 at such assemblies held at the beginning of 1977, for example. As reported by Romanian government sources, past 360,000 expressions of opinion (no definition is offered of such a term) were made at those early 1977 sessions, while about 180,000 proposals were formulated to better the work program... the construction, the planning and research of socialist production units. Presumably, the proposals are those made in written form or presented as floor motions.[21] These statistics imply rather significant quantities of participatory behavior.

A 1975 survey, however, suggested that participation at general assemblies of the enterprise varied with political identity, i.e., if a worker was a Party or

Young Communist League member beyond the mandatory trade union affiliation. Since only 15% of factory workers might be Party members and an additional 15% in the UTC[22], it is instructive to see the disproportionate share of certain kinds of behavior performed by Party-UTC members. (See Table 1)

Only "preparing for the session" necessarily implies an action with some initiative, insofar as that phrase suggests assigning roles and tasks to others while determining the session's agenda. Almost one-fifth of the Party members stated that they had performed such behavior, while somewhat more than a twentieth of workers with only trade union background gave such a response. These data, then, put a different light on undifferentiated statistics about worker participation at general assemblies. It may be true that millions attend the assemblies, hundreds of thousands speak and tens of thousands of proposals are made. Party members, however, dominate these forms of participatory behavior, while others perform functions assigned by cadres.

Sections of an enterprise (which can be a particular shop, assembly unit, or office) hold "production meetings" before general assemblies. In these smaller gatherings, workers are to air proposals, grievances and complaints relevant to their immediate work place. Management attends, usually in the person of the plant director or assistant director. Whereas the general assembly of the enterprise appears to have many pro forma aspects to it, the production meetings evoke more generalized participatory behavior; topics more germane to daily conditions and tasks are raised. A national sample in the early of 1970s of 6,236 workers from three sectors of Romanian industry (see Table 2) found that a third to two-fifths of industrial labor 30 years or younger "made proposals" at production meetings--a category which lacks specificity in the report of this research but which, one can presume, involves a workers' assessment as to whether or not he "speaks up" at such sessions.

Quantitatively, then, there is considerable participatory behavior among Romanian workers in the sense of trade union membership, attendance at general assemblies, and at the lowest level of production meetings. But Party cadres dominate general assemblies of the enterprise and discussion in workers' councils, constituting a majority of the council membership in any case.

QUALITATIVE ASPECTS OF WORKER PARTICIPATION

Romanian workers' are not without opinions about channels for their participation as well as assessments of their own efficacy. From a mid-1970s survey of workers in two major Bucharest industrial plants (the chemical factory "Grivita Rosie" and the Intreprinderea de Utilaj Chimic), for example, only 38% of employees thought their participation was a regular part of decision-making processes.[23] Moreover, between 23.3% and 38.9% of those samples declared that they were neither informed about the main problems of the enterprise before decisions by their representatives in workers' councils or in general assemblies nor after such decisions.[24] Approximately 18.5-20% of the workers thought their opinions were considered, while foremen more frequently said their opinions were considered.

It is difficult to compare such findings with Western or American experiences. To be sure, assemblyline workers at General Motors might not see themselves as part of decision processes either. Yet, there is no effort to promote the rhetoric of self-management nor is the party system explicitly tied to interests of the proletariat. Also, while participation at any single American union local may not be high, the strength of the union vis-a-vis management may be seen nationally or can be witnessed during strikes. In communist systems, however, there is no national voice for workers except one sanctioned by the Party; workers must, in fact, rely upon their local interaction for the resolution of workplace grievances. Were even a large minority to sense a lack of efficacy at the local level, the nation-wide result could seriously impair the legitimacy of Party-provided channels for participation. Indeed, other data suggest that even among those who do participate, there is widespread acknowledgement that workers have little effect on policy. Asked about their participation in production meetings, only one third of surveyed workers replied that they had made proposals at these sessions. But, of that one-third who do make proposals at production meetings, a mean (across different industries) of about 40% thought their proposals would be ineffectual. In other words, a sizeable part of the minority of workers' who do more than attend production meetings are dubious about the value of their participation. (See Table 3)

This sense of minimal efficacy may also be responsible for the small proportion of foremen who would bring matters of "excessive bureaucracy" to the attention of supervisors (only 6-7%). Over half of women in such posts (53.5%) and a fourth (23.4%) of men with such factory jobs offered no response to this kind of questionnaire item, which may have some significance as well as in terms of the liberty with which employees think they can respond. Even among that stratum above workers, then, the responsiveness of managerial elites and Party cadres to complaints of inefficiency and unfairness is doubted.

Concern or cynicism about their efficacy exacerbates the dissatisfaction among Romanian workers regarding material rewards. A smaller proportion of workers than any other category of employment (only 5.12% of a national sample) are motivated at their job by creating something of "social value". Other categories such as engineers, administrators, etc. scored higher.[25] Material rewards dominate workers' motivation and are first among the points leading to their dissatisfaction. Female workers, for whom family identity and the role of wife remain vital, nevertheless rank material rewards most often (46.15% in one survey[26]) as a motivation in their on-the-job performance. It (pay and related incentives) and personal requests such as transfers and promotions are most often the topics brought up at C.O.M. sessions.[27] Dissatisfaction with salaries seems to vary with age, being most acute in the 40-60 year old categories, reaching 60.7% among 40-44 year olds.[28] Across three principal industries, young workers nevertheless place pay as the chief factor likely to create dissatisfaction more than difficulty of promotion, working conditions, lack of free time and other circumstances.[29]

More generally, workers rank their primary life duties or obligations as familial or interpersonal, not in terms of their professional or citizen roles.[30] The organization of work, implicitly the Party's organization, is not regarded as satisfactory either since tasks are distributed in a "bureaucratic" way such that there is "too much or too little demand on one's capabilities, thereby not permitting an optimal development of one's capacities".[31]

Young workers (under 30), although less concerned about pay, have the poorest self-image of any age category, regarding themselves as inferior to others.[32] Other research, ironically conducted in the Jiu Valley, has found young people without advanced education to be those least likely to intervene when witnessing "hooliganism". Such a category, of course, is largely coextensive with industrial labor in that part of Romania. Thus far, some findings can be summarized:

1. Romanian workers are almost always trade union members, and about fourth to a third are Party or Young Communist League members, depending on the enterprise.
2. Workers attend regularly production meetings in their section or shop plus general assemblies of the enterprise and vote, in uncontested elections, for a few of the workers' council members, the exact number varying with the council size which depends upon the

       number of employees.
    3. Workers' participation at such sessions
       tends to be perfunctory, with the agenda,
       tasks and roles assigned by Party cadres.
    4. Workers Councils are not primarily composed
       of workers nor do workers who are "elected"
       members contribute to debates or discussions.
    5. Elected members of workers' councils (C.O.M.)
       are not widely known or consulted by enter-
       prise laborers.
    6. Appeals to superiors are not frequently made
       to correct inefficiencies or arbitrary deci-
       sions.
    7. Material rewards motivate workers and per-
       sonal, not societal, concerns hold their
       attention.
    8. Young workers exhibit the most alienated
       attitudes.

COMMUNIST GOVERNMENTS AND WORKERS' PARTICIPATION

   Most of the foregoing conclusions will startle no student of communist politics. But we need to consider an issue of sizeable importance which is not widely pursued--namely, what is the systemic impact of such quantitative and qualitative assessments of workers' participatory behavior on communist governments?
   Put succinctly, the impact has been enormous. Because dissatisfaction coexisted with an alienation from Party-approved participatory roles, Romania's government has been required to mount an immense propaganda campaign of "self-management" after the December, 1977 National Party Conference. My use of "required" is purposeful, since the sudden decision to place more emphasis on workers' councils cannot be viewed as part of a previous long-term plan. Between that 1977 conference and March 1978, media, scholars and mass organizations prepared Romania for the coming campaign by pointing to the need for new measures to better manage and plan the economy. The March 1978 plenum of the Central Committee announced that <u>autoconducerea</u> and <u>autogestiunii</u> (self-management and self-accounting) would be, henceforth, key principles guiding the country's path toward a multilaterally developed society. The economic and financial autonomy of industrial units were to be effected through the leadership of each enterprise's C.O.M. Each C.O.M. was, moreover, "democratized" by expanding the number of elected members. Simultaneously, the President of each C.O.M. was united with the office of Party Secretary of the enterprise; previously, the enterprise director had functioned as president of the workers' council.

In other words, the Party's leadership seems to have responded to not only the immediate threat of renewed miners' violence but also to widespread disaffection among workers readily discernible to Party leaders through sociological research (as cited earlier) and/or productivity data.[33] The measures taken appear to be aimed at diminishing the rationale for further anti-regime sentiment and re-inforcing Party oversight of participatory channels.

Linking the self-management campaign of 1978-79 with the rejection of Party-approved participatory channels must be intuitive for we have no decisive leadership statements to that effect or attitudinal data for central elites. An interview with a member of Romania's Political Executive Committee in the summer of 1978 suggested that top leaders did not reject linking these events, although he emphasized that workers' councils had existed for a number of years. A judet Party first secretary and Political Executive Committee member, was asked if the hypothesis linking autoconducerea to a direct Party response to worker dissatisfaction had validity:

> Such an interpretation would not be accurate since workers' councils and the structures of self-management are not new. But we are concerned, of course, that workers have the means by which to effect democracy at the enterprises, to involve themselves in the decision-making at that level. We hope that productivity will continue to rise, or rise more rapidly, as workers sense their interests are served. Some people will always be unhappy--nothing will satisfy them. But for most, workers' councils and general assemblies in enterprises are important, and their effect will be continued improvement in efficiency and economy of materials.
> (emphases added)[34]

This national leader appears to be saying that the negative economic impact (low productivity, waste) of workers' alienation from Party-approved channels for their participation were recognized and had to be counteracted. The newly reformed C.O.M., as a structural embodiment of self-management was, then, linked by the leadership to the resolution of urgent political difficulties--namely, negative attitudes towards Party-approved participatory mechanisms in the midst of general workplace dissatisfaction. The Party tried, quite consciously, to identify itself with workers' autonomy and the material interest which motivate the class. The rubric of self-management, the expansion of each C.O.M. to include more elected members, and the self-accounting (autogestiunii) of each enterprise were all part of a broad effort to counteract alarming signals from opinion surveys, productivity figures, rumor and 1977 violence from Lupeni, Petrosani and the mines of the Jiu Valley.

If such an interpretation is accurate, then the Party has demonstrated the limits of its flexibility and has implied dilemmas for Romania's future. Moreover, we might be able to anticipate some of the problems faced by ruling communist parties in states elsewhere in which development and modernization play such a pre-eminent policy role. Having failed to maintain its alleged identity with interests of working people, and faced with the apathy or antipathy of industrial labor toward Party-approved means of workplace governance, the Romanian regime has been forced to take a risk by adopting the rhetoric of self-management. No Leninist party can, however, submit itself to a diminution of democratic centralism, i.e., the absolute subordination of lower units to higher authorities, because it would then admit to a diversity of interests and needs allegedly diminishing under Party rule. The limits Ceausescu must defend are those of any Leninist organization; how to speak the language of self-management and create the institutions for its nominal operation without decentralizing authority is his dilemma.

Ceausescu's problem is exacerbated by relationships among developmental policies, workers' participatory expectations and "democratic centralism"--relationships crucial not only in Romania but in any centrally-planned economy ruled by one Leninist party. To pursue development and modernization is the sine qua non of legitimacy for many political systems and for that reason, as well as to establish the societal bases of a Marxist polity, communist parties also push for these socio-economic advances. Particularly in Marxist states, modernization and development cannot be separated from an emphasis on the interests of that stratum which must bear the greatest burden. To expect a greater voice in workplace affairs and increasing material rewards are logical correlates of developmental policies in the eyes of the working class. In order to assure worker cooperation and productivity for the achievement of Party-decreed plans, industrial labor cannot be as dissatisfied with their material rewards or as indifferent to participatory mechanisms provided by the Party as data reveal had become the case in Romania. But to relinquish decisions within the factory to non-cadres or to provide enterprises with autonomy in budgetary matters suggests that the ultimate subordination of lower levels to higher authority (democratic centralism) is being weakened.

Over time, it may well be that Leninist parties can resist the extension of rhetoric to actuality--that self-management and workers' councils will remain symbolic activities with no impact on public policy or conditions in factories. Nevertheless, ruling communist parties will have to manage their relationship with the working class, never being confident in the willing obedience or productivity of industrial labor. Whether in the Jiu Valley, Ponzan and Radom or Shanghai, evidence is quite clear that communist regimes cannot be sanguine about workers in a workers' state. If national leaders must speak the language of self-management to pacify industrial labor, the question will not long remain moot as to whether or not participatory expectations have been heightened or blunted by such rhetoric. Long before the Jiu Valley or autoconducerea, it was evident that workers and Party had different expectations for workers' councils. Workers in the C.O.M. structure were indicating that the degree to which information is shared by management is the key to the participation of workers while people in cadre posts argued that a "collective spirit" was the key to encouraging worker participation.[35] While recent Romanian history does not exhibit a strong tradition of worker unrest, unlike Poland by contrast, it is clear to miners and other key sectors of industrial labor that their collective action in a strike or protest can rapidly bring the attention of the country's leaders to grievances.

In conversations during the summer of 1978 in the Jiu Valley, i.e., the year after strikes there brought Ceausescu and the Romanian Army to the area, I recorded some of the responses to questions I asked of workers in chance encounters at numerous snack bars (the Romanian word for these small restaurants, where liquor is served, is bufet). Although I was unable to talk with many miners, my effort was to discuss their work in general and, when possible, to bring up the topic of strikes. Of those who were willing to discuss this sensitive and sometimes bitter issue, sixteen said that they would be willing to strike again, while only two said they would not and two others being unsure. A dozen others were not willing to talk about this matter--at least with a foreigner. Of those who indicated a willingness to use the weapon of a strike again, almost all of them (fourteen) qualified their answers with phrases such as, "If the Party leaders don't respond..." or "If we are treated unfairly again..."

These personal encounters serve not as data but as one kind of impression to be gained from conversations; it would seem that there is sentiment favoring strikes as a potential weapon were the need to arise. Having "drawn blood" in 1977, the miners are cognizant of their strength. Do they now expect that their opinions will be sought, their needs will be conveyed, and their grievances resolved with regularity? In the same series of conversations cited above, I sought to ask whether or not the Party would do more for miners now (i.e., after the strikes). I categorized their responses as follows:

Will the Party do More for Miners Now?

	Yes	No	Don't Know
miners N=20	10	7	3
*others N=27	16	4	7

*All non-mining occupations.

Since these answers are not the product of a sample, the numbers might well not reflect the Jiu Valley population's opinions; there were only two women among those with whom I spoke, for example, and I have excluded people from both occupational categories who would not talk about such issues. Yet, most visitors would not miss the lack of rapport between government and miners. If all miners are not, in fact, of the opinion that strikes will lead to more beneficial attention from the Party it could be because they doubt the efficacy of a strike and/or the Party's responsiveness. At the least, it appears that those who struck (the miners) are less sure about the benevolent response of the Party. These are, however, the same people who seem to be willing to strike again. That one cannot generalize from such conversations should not prevent us from noting that a sizeable number of people in an area where violent strikes have taken place do not reject the possibility of additional work stoppages even when they are not certain of such action's efficacy.

Although the Romanian Communist Party is confronted by no Committee for the Defense of Workers as in Poland (and the abortive attempt to form an independent workers' union in Romania has faded under government pressure), there is nevertheless unmistakeable tension between the Party and industrial labor. The stratum for whom the Party is to rule are (1) generally dissatisfied with pay and work-place conditions, (2) have little enthusiasm for or confidence in the mechanics for their involvement established by the Party and (3) in some industries such as mining may be increasingly cognizant that their interests will be served only by confronting the Party. We can be confident in such findings roughly in that order, with the latter point most subject to doubt. So severe have these indications become that the Romanian Communist Party acted in late 1977 and early 1978 to effect the massive self-management campaign cited earlier.

All of this does not suggest a new-found responsiveness or liberalization in Romania. More accurately, the past few years have witnessed the continued efforts to offer rhetoric in lieu of decentralization. Only within the confines of democratic centralism will workers' self-management be allowed. While the Party program mentions the principle of democratic centralism in the same breath as "autonomy and initiative of ... economic enterprises and other social units", it does so only by emphasizing that such autonomy falls within the scope of "unitary leadership of socio-economic life."[36]

Having trumpeted autoconducerea, the Party is now (1979-1980) busy limiting its application being careful to draw the lines beyond which no workers' council or enterprise assembly can step. In the unlikely event that some workers would hope to turn such sessions into tests of the Party's strength at local levels, none will be able to claim ignorance of the primacy of unitary leadership and the central plan. Whether through its theoretical organ, daily press, factory sessions or Ceausescu's visits to enterprises, the limits of autonomy were being stressed by early 1979--if, indeed, anyone had forgotten. Ceausescu's warnings at the "23 August" enterprise in Bucharest on February 15, 1979 are a case in point. Criticizing the outmoded techniques and slow implementation of new designs for motors, compressors, etc., the Party leader noted that he had the impression that there was too much satisfaction with results from current production technology and that there was insufficient innovation to transforming the production line. Turning to the political organization in the enterprise, Ceausescu twice referred to the trade unions and youth organization as under the Party's leadership, which "together with workers' councils" must deal with problems more efficiently. Ceausescu also took care to mention the need for better political-educational efforts in the enterprise to encourage participation in the general assembly of the factory.[37] Meanwhile, articles on "Democratic Centralism and Workers' Self-Management" began to appear emphasizing the hierarchies beneath which workers councils must operate in "harmony"[38], most notably in Era Socialista, the Party's theoretical monthly.

Thus, the R.C.P. is confronted by a thorny problem with the class for whom it allegedly rules. Other communist states are not likely to avoid completely the same difficulty. Developmental plans required great sacrifice by workers while dramatically raising expectations, both material and political. Seeing the clear signs of discontent, a program of self-management was re-invigorated, the limits of which must now be explained to avoid another cycle of antagonism. There is, however, no guarantee that a largely rhetorical policy of self-management will placate workers in Romania or in other systems ruled by Leninist parties (e.g., Poland).

COMPARATIVE ISSUES

Two issues were raised in the introduction regarding relationships between workers' participation in a communist state and broader, comparative hypotheses. First, citizenship roles--in this case, that portion of the citizenry within industrial labor--are expected to be confined to "output" processes in communist states. Second, I also raised the issue of hypotheses linking development, political participation and socio-economic equality.

There is strong evidence to doubt the first of these hypotheses in Romania and, quite likely, other communist states as well. It is true, of course, that the policy-formulation ("input") phase offers fewer opportunities for the articulation of interests, and that a national organization by which workers' might aggregate their grievances is lacking (official trade unions playing no independent role). Moreover, the case of industrial labor (vis-à-vis other occupational categories) in communist systems has unique aspects, given that Marxist parties are to rule in the interests of working people thereby creating an onus from which communist leaders cannot easily escape. But there are clear indications that this stratum of people within communist states does not silently wait for public policies, only then to react with efforts to find intermediaries, i.e., ways to "beat the system". By contrast, the experience of the East European states suggests that workers are cognizant that their interests are not well served by the Party and that an alternative of confrontation cannot be ruled out.

Western observers will be led to doubt the "input" role of industrial labor since each trade union offers no outlet for grievances and visible organizations to counter the Party-provided channels are not always present. But we need not wait for the establishment of an underground newsletter, hear rumors of Party crackdowns, or read appeals for dissident labor leaders to know of policy influence during the formulation phase. Such influence is, in fact, omnipresent. In Poland, the Gierek regime came to an end in 1980 primarily because of its inability to respond to the economic disaster which looms--and fear of worker violence played a major role in that immobilisme. In this paper, I have sought to explain the influence workers have had in bringing the Romanian Communist Party to the point of taking a necessary risk by inaugurating a campaign of self-management at the enterprise level.

Ironically, communist parties have themselves created a situation in which industrial labor has an omnipresent role in policy formulation. In part because of their Marxist heritage, and in part due to goals of modernization and development, the Party has stressed with persistance "the political importance of increased production as an indication of individual political activism and as a contribution toward supremely important national goals".[39] Such a description, written by James Townsend referring to China, is no less true of Romania. Whether in Asia or Europe, the performance of daily work, workplace participation and the attitudes which motivate both work and participation, are incessantly political in the eyes of communist parties. In such circumstances, workplace behavior constitutes an ongoing plebiscite, with a permanent place in the formulation phase of public policy. This is surely not the participant role Lenin foresaw for workers in developed socialism, but neither should we dismiss industrial labor as insignificant in defining policy alternatives, advocating those closest to their material interests and personal concerns.

Finally, we must consider relationships among development, political participation and socio-economic equality. I think it fair to say that a consensus exists among comparativists regarding the link between socioeconomic changes vaguely labeled development and modernization and demands for participation and distributive equality. Taking liberally from many works[40], this consensus suggests that when a government pursues policies designed to increase the capacity and complexity of society and economy, a correlate will be an increase in the volume and intensity of demands made upon it by individual citizens and groups. This increase of demands for participation in policy-making or specific policies to distribute wealth can endanger a political system's stability. In other words, the very "development" of a political system--its stability and institutionalization--can be threatened in the wake of policies designed to bring socio-economic change.

The kinds of data and historical experience available by which we can test such an hypothesis offer convincing evidence to Western scholars.[41] For a political party with origins in a doctrine calling for the entry of the common man into politics, and which has rationalized its seizure of power and dictatorship by an alleged goal to build a classless society devoid of economically-based inequalities, the scenerio posed above is doubtless unnerving. Post-revolutionary, stable and institutionalized socialism under a communist Party can, it would seem, be achieved only by denying the fundamental tenets of such a system's legitimacy--mass participation and equality. Were participatory momentum and material demands from a key stratum such as workers to be translated into true self-management and distributive equality, the Party's hold on workplace governance would be compromised seriously, its ability to centrally plan would be constrained, and investments in such arenas as heavy industry would have to be curtailed. Sensing these dangers, communist parties offer the rhetoric and structures for autoconducerea or autogestiunii while limiting the application of such principles within the narrow confines of democratic centralism.

But workers see the limits on their participation and understand differences between their material interests and Party goals. Therefore, the Party's "solutions" to the destabilizing impact of socio-economic change may exacerbate the instability. Developed socialism as found in European communist states thus embodies a dialectic of its own making--where socio-economic policies foster increased demands which cannot be met but which, when not ameliorated, encourage further demands. Developed socialism in communist Europe, in effect, endangers its own stability and institutionalization by trying to become more "developed".

Although this characterization is broad, and cannot account for the many country-specific variations, there seems little question that ruling communist parties must engage in ongoing conflict-management. Of the ironies to be found in such a statement, perhaps the most poignant is that the occupational category for which Marx originally spoke has often been among the most vehement in confrontations with communist parties. Developed socialism in communist Europe has meant the rise of conflict between the proletariat and its erstwhile vanguard.

TABLE 6.1

PARTICIPATION AT GENERAL ASSEMBLIES OF THE ENTERPRISE BY POLITICAL IDENTITY
N=610
Political ID

Activity	Party	Young Communist	Trade Union Only
I prepared for the assembly session	18.9%	9.2%	4.4%
I filled a role at the session	28.1%	31.8%	21.4%
I accomplished a task for the session	46.4%	30.8%	26.6%
I was only present	6.6%	28.2%	47.6%

SOURCE: Mariana Sirbu, "Integrarea in Munca si Participarea Politica in Procesul Dezvoltarii Constiinte Socialiste" in Constantin Potinga and Vasile Popescu, eds., Constiinta Socialista si Participare Sociala (Bucuresti: Editura Academiei, 1977), p. 42.

TABLE 6.2

PARTICIPATION IN PRODUCTION MEETINGS BY YOUNG WORKERS

Behavior	Machine	Industry Chemical	Textile
made proposals	1233 (39%)	510 (32.7%)	534 (35.2%)
do not make proposals	1927 (61%)	1051 (67.3%)	981 (64.8%)
Totals	3160	1561	1515

SOURCE: Ovidiu Badina, "Participarea Tinerilor la Procesul de Realizare a Unor Inventii, Inovatii si Rationalizari" in Ovidiu Badina and Catalin Mamali, eds., Tineret Industrial (Bucuresti: Editura Academiei, 1973), p. 123.

TABLE 6.3

SENSE OF EFFICACY AMONG WORKERS WHO MAKE PROPOSALS AT PRODUCTION MEETINGS

Evaluation	Machine	Industry Chemical	Textile
Proposals have an Effect	699 (59.8%)	307 (60.3%)	353 (66.1%)
Proposals have no Effect	533 (43.2%)	202 (39.7%)	181 (33.9%)
Totals	1232	509	534

SOURCE: Ovidiu Badina, "Participarea Tinerilor la Procesul de Realizare a Unor Inventii, Inovatii si Rationazari" in Ovidiu Badina and Catalin Mamali, eds., <u>Tineret Industrial</u> (Bucuresti: Editura Academiei, 1973), p. 124.

NOTES

1. Karl Marx, Critique of Political Economy (Bazele Criticii Economiei Politice), 1 (Bucuresti: Editura Politica, 1972), p. 94.
2. V.I. Lenin, Selected Works, 7 (New York: International Publishers, 1943), p. 48.
3. Vasile Nichita and Marin Neagu, "Participarea Oamenilor Muncii la Conducerea Unitatilor Socialiste" in Academia de Stiinte Sociale si Politice, Perfectionarea Statului-Dezvoltarea Democratiei Socialiste (Bucuresti: Editura Politica, 1977), p. 235; see also Ioan Ceterchi, Democratia Socialista (Bucuresti: Editura Politica, 1974).
4. For a distinction between participant and subject roles, see Gabriel Almond and G. Bingham Powell, Comparative Politics: System, Process and Policy (Boston: Little, Brown and Company, 1978), p. 112.
5. Romania's 1965 constitution promulgated that change, thereby making the country the Socialist Republic of Romania not the People's Republic of Romania, while the Party became the Romanian Communist Party vis-a-vis the Romanian Workers' Party.
6. Samuel P. Huntington and Joan M. Nelson, No Easy Choice: Political Participation in Developing Countries (Cambridge: Harvard University Press, 1976), pp. 4-7.
7. Almomd and Powell use the phrase "roles of symbolic involvement" with implicit reference to communist states, although they do not employ the word communist, referring instead to "penetrative, mobilizational, one-party states"--of which communist states constitute, one must assume, the primary component. Their mention of symbolic roles is coupled with examples such as casting a vote for the single party's candidates, participating in parades and other political events, and vast youth recreation programs; see Almond and Powell, Comparative Politics, pp. 122-123.
8. Almond and Powell, Comparative Politics, p. 37.
9. Ibid.
10. Era Socialista LIX, 7 (5 Aprilie 1979), p. 1.
11. The formal establishment of, and powers for, workers' councils are detailed in "Legea Nr. 11/1971 cu privire la organizarea si conducerea unitatilor socialiste de stat".
12. Nicolae Ceausescu, "Cuvintare la Conferinta Nationala a Partidului, Decembrie, 1967" in Nicolae Ceausescu, Romania pe Drumul Desavirsirii Constructiei Socialiste 2 (Bucuresti: Editura Politica, 1968), pp. 540-541.
13. Maria Popescu, Conducere. Participare. Constiinta (Bucuresti: Editura Academiei R.S. Romania, 1973).

14. Florian Popa-Micsan "Informatie-Participare'si 'Responsabilitate-Decizie' in Activitatea Consiliilor Oamenilor Muncii", Viitorul Social 6, 3, 1977, p. 45.
15. Ibid.
16. Ion Petrescu, Psihosociologia Conducerii Colective a Intreprinderii Industriale (Craiova: Scrisul Romanesc, 1977), p. 98.
17. Oral Communication, February 1979.
18. Petrescu, p. 56.
19. Petrescu, p. 79.
20. Vasile Nichita, and Marin Neagu, "Participarea Oamenilor Muncii la Conducerea Unitatilor Socialiste" in Academia de Stiinte Sociale si Politice, Perfectionarea Statului--Dezvoltarea Democratiei Socialiste (Bucuresti: Editura Politica, 1977), p. 241.
21. Ibid.
22. There are some exceptions. The giant "23 August" Electrotechnical Enterprise in Bucharest has 17,000 workers, of whom 5,000 are in the Party--or about 29%. It is, however, a showplace, where Party leader Ceausescu often delivers lengthy addresses to workers.
23. Viorel I. Cornescu, Productivitatea Muncii si Factorul Uman (Bucuresti: Editura Politica, 1977), p. 214.
24. Ibid.
25. Georgeta Dan-Spinoiu, Factori Objectivi si Subjectivi in Integrarea Profesionala a Femeii (Bucuresti: Editura Academiei, 1974), pp. 94-95.
26. Dan-Spinoiu, p. 176.
27. Popa-Micsan, p. 451.
28. Mariana Sirbu, "Integrarea in Munca si Participarea Politica in Procescul Dezvoltarii Constiinte Socialiste" in Constantin Potinga and Vasile Popescu, eds., Constiinta Socialista si Participare Sociala (Bucuresti: Editura Academiei, 1977), p. 37.
29. Zissu Weintraub, "Indicatori Motivationali ai Integrarii Professionale" in Ovidiu Badina and Catalin Mamali, eds., Tineret Industrial: Dinamica Integrarii Socioprofesionale (Bucuresti: Editura Academiei, 1973), p. 104.
30. Dan-Spinoiu, p. 107.
31. Ibid., p. 124.
32. Ibid., p. 167.
33. See Elisabeta Traistaru, "Factorii Economici si Psihosociali ai Stabilitatii Fortei de Munca Intreprinderile Industriale," Viitorul Social 4, 2 (1974) and Roman Cresin, "Aspecte Privind Mobilitatea si Fluctuatia Profesionala a Tinerilor," in Ovidiu Badina and Catalin Mamali, eds., Tineret Industrial: Dinamica Integrarii Socioprofesionale (Bucuresti: Editura Academiei, 1973).
34. Oral Communication, July 1978.
35. Petrescu, p. 96.

36. Romanian Communist Party, Programul P.C.R. de Faurire a Societatii Socialiste Multilateral Dezvoltate si Inaintare a Romaniei Spre Comunism (Bucuresti: Editura Politica, 1975), p. 119.
37. Scinteia, 15 Februarie 1979.
38. Ion Mitran, "Centralismul Democratic si Autoconducerea Muncitoreasca, Era Socialista LIX, 7 (5 Aprilie 1979), pp. 8-12.
39. James Townsend, Political Participation in Communist China (Berkeley: University of California Press, 1969), p. 7.
40. Such a consensus is evident in innumerable works. Two of the most notable are Karl Deutsch, "Social Mobilization and Political Development," American Political Science Review 55 (September 1961), Samuel P. Huntington, Political Order in Changing Societies (New Haven: Yale University Press, 1968).
41. Hungtington and Nelson in their work No Easy Choice, op. cit., discuss much of the available evidence. See in particular, Chapter 1 and 2. They point out, however, that the relationship is not linear insofar as development does not always promote participation because of political and organizational factors independent of socioeconomic change, and other variables. See their Chapter 3.

Part 3
Foreign and Economic Policies

Romanian foreign and economic policies have both contributed to the unique quality of that country as seen from the West during the 1960s and 1970s. As earlier chapters have implied, and the three contributions in Part Three make explicit, we can expect that the communist government of Romania will continue to stress foreign policies which do not mirror those of the USSR, and economic plans that continue to emphasize investments in industry and consumer sacrifices to achieve "multilateral development". Both of these broad policy directions are integral to the regime's legitimacy and the personal political fortunes of Nicolae Ceausescu. In both realms, however, Romanian policies and their degree of success will be affected by a large number of variables outside the control of Bucharest.

As one aspect of Romanian independence from Soviet international leadership of communist Europe, the Ceausescu government has evolved a military policy which deviates significantly from integration in the Warsaw Treaty Organization. A "people's war" doctrine, involving as it does a reliance on partisan and guerilla-type operations in the face of a technologically superior opponent (i.e., the USSR), has been adopted by the Romanians since it was one of the few military options available for national defense. As Walter Bacon's chapter details, political and military needs dictate such a policy as do economic limitations imposed by Romanian developmental plans. Romanian military policy is, then, "locked in" to the current focus on a low-technology national defense strategy, given other demands on its resources and political constraints of its international position.

Constraints are the theme of Ronald Linden's analysis as well as he exemplifies the complex and interwoven factors which influence Romanian foreign policy. Certainly, the assertiveness of Romania in foreign affairs during the Ceausescu years is linked, as Linden argues, to domestic economic performance and citizen tolerance of material sacrifice while "multilateral development" is underway. That linkage cuts both ways, since the nationalism of Romanian foreign policy "buys" some of the legitimacy needed for domestic economic sacrifices (which is, of course, a point made implicitly in several earlier chapters). Again, Romania seems "locked in" with few options--and Linden suggests that factors quite beyond the control of Bucharest may render the current "trade-off" (between the nationalism of foreign policy or its accompanying prestige and deferred material gratification) no longer workable. Principal among these external variables, concludes Linden, are the lessons of increasing interdependence.

The potential breakdown of a balance between

internal socio-economic and political demands on the one hand and a nationalistic foreign policy is, then, something Romanian policy-makers may not be able to prevent. For over a decade and a half, economic performance and military and foreign policies divergent from Warsaw Pact norms have reinforced each other. With high rates of growth and little reliance on outside sources of energy, the Romanian economy supported an assertive foreign policy and lessened WTO military integration, which in turn portrayed Ceausescu's regime in the positive light of Romanian nationalism allowing it to demand continued material sacrifice. But, recalling Fischer-Galati's arguments, this formula is not one which will operate in perpetuity. The postponement of material gratification and expectations of equality as the Ceausescu-brand of patriotism wears thin may, as Linden suggests, point to a "tunnel at the end of the light". At the very least, Romania's options are few with regard to military and foreign policies. Nicolae Ceausescu's ability to influence the international environment and his country's place in it will be limited to that of a small, poor state facing growing interdependence.

Marvin Jackson's concerns are those conditions internal to Romania which will affect economic development. He specifically excludes consideration of political and organizational change. Nevertheless, Jackson's analysis offers the reader a detailed look at challenges to Romanian economic plans to 1990 and beyond. These challenges are neither apolitical nor unconnected to the foreign and military policies discussed by Linden and Bacon. As suggested above, the ties between developmental goals and foreign policy are direct, both crucial to and dependent on the regime's legitimacy. Jackson deals extensively, for example, with the role of foreign trade for Romanian economic growth, and internal uncertainties in labor availability, agricultural productivity and management decentralization. These latter items, of course, refer the reader back to earlier chapters by Cole and Nelson regarding Romanian labor, its organization and life-style.

Taken together, Bacon, Linden and Jackson portray a country and government set on certain courses with relatively little room to maneuver. Romania's military, international and economic policies are those of a ruling communist party, in the historical, social and political milieu discussed in Parts One and Two, struggling to maintain its legitimacy in an environment it can do little to control. Ceausescu's government embarked long ago on ambitious developmental schemes requiring dislocation and sacrifice of the country's population. In the short-term, now concluded, rapid development both assisted and was explained in terms of

Romanian independence. But in the 1980s and after, these chapters seem to tell us, economic and political requirements will bind Romanian military policy, Romanian foreign policy will find outlets for independence only if domestic and external factors permit (and, in any case, nationalism will not suffice for deferred gratification), and Romanian economic policy will confront challenges of an international marketplace, domestic labor shortages, difficulties in agricultural production and the diffusion of decision-making authority in the more complex economy planned for the next decade.

7
Romanian Military Policy in the 1980s

Walter M. Bacon, Jr.

Like its foreign policy, Romania's military policy has attracted the attention of Western analysts because it so obviously deviates from the policies of the Soviet Union and the other East European member-states of the Warsaw Treaty Organization (WTO).[1] These analyses suffer from the inaccessibility of crucial data and the limited holdings of published materials in Western research institutions. The nature of the Romanian political system also inhibits distinguishing military policy from other domestic and foreign policies.

Romanian military policy has evolved from a faithful imitation of Soviet doctrine and direction to a Romanian version of "people's war." Military policy deviation from the Soviet norm followed initial foreign policy deviation by roughly five years and is an integral part of Romania's pursuit of national independence and sovereignty.

> In the period which followed the Ninth Congress (1965) our party (the Romanian Communist Party - RCP) has firmly sustained and applied the thesis according to which the right of decision over the problems of defending the country, over the organization and direction of the armed forces, constitute an inalienable <u>sovereign attribute</u> of each socialist state (and) <u>of each communist</u> party in the respective states. (emphasis in the original)[2]

The adoption of "the struggle of the entire people" ("Lupta intregului popor") as Romania's military doctrine was the result of the RCP leadership's analysis of Romania's military capabilities weighed against those

---

Walter M. Bacon, Jr., who received a Ph.D. from the University of Denver, is an Assistant Professor of Political Science at the University of Nebraska, Omaha.

of potential adversaries after the Ninth Party Congress, and especially after August 1968.[3]

The RCP had supported the Czechoslovak Communist Party's right to deviate from Soviet policy norms in 1968. When that deviation elicited the intervention of the European Warsaw Pact armies (with the exception of Romania's), the RCP correctly concluded that one reason for Czechoslovakia's vulnerability was its lack of a credible defense against "fraternal assistance." The relative ease with which the invasion was accomplished was due to a combination of Soviet political and military preparations which all but eliminated the possibility of effective resistance. Romania decided to avoid similar vulnerability.

Complementing orthodox domestic policies which neutralized one set of possible Soviet excuses for intervention, Romania took steps to create a credible defense against a Soviet-led invasion. In Czechoslovakia, the four key military factors of the invasion's success were the Soviet-inspired ambivalence and indecisiveness of the Czechoslovak armed forces, the surprise of the operation, the speed with which it was accomplished and the maintenance of high morale among the invading troops. Romanian military policy is designed to deny these important advantages to the aggressor.[4]

Since the end of World War II, collegial and material lines of dependence had developed between the Romanian armed forces and those of the Soviet Union. Romania's multilateral escape from Soviet dominance necessitated a decrease of Soviet influence in the Romanian armed forces. In 1969, the armed forces were thoroughly subordinated to the national leadership's control through the creation of the Defense Council of the Socialist Republic of Romania (RSR), the body responsible for military policy. The Defense Council's membership is dominated by the civilian RCP leadership and is chaired by General Secretary Nicolae Ceausescu who is thus Supreme Commander of the RSR's armed forces. The Council is directly responsible <u>first</u> to the RCP Central Committee and <u>second</u> to the Grand National Assembly.[5] The RCP also exerts its control at the base of the military organization through military and local party units and by careful selection of politically reliable officers for command positions.[6]

Few, if any, officers go to the Soviet Union for advanced training, and joint exercises with Romania's Warsaw Pact allies are kept to a minimum.[7] In 1965, only 27% of the arms delivered to the Romanian armed forces were of domestic manufacture whereas in 1975, 66% of the deliveries were of Romanian origin.[8] Although the greatest part of foreign arms used by the Romanian armed forces remain of Soviet origin, Romania has diversified its sources of supply, obtaining heavy equipment from China, France, and Great Britain.[9] With Yugoslavia, Romania is developing the "Orao" twin-jet multi-purpose aircraft.[10] While there was some evidence to suggest residual military loyalty to the Soviet Union in the early 1970s, the officer corps now appears to support Ceausescu's national military policy.[11] Unlike the Czechoslovak armed forces in 1968, the continued weakening of Romanian-Soviet military ties should make the Romanian armed forces of the 1980s virtually immune from Soviet subversion.

Romanian military strategy is designed to tie down large numbers of invading troops. The success of the North Vietnamese and Viet Cong proved that small, lightly armed, independently operating guerilla units could deny technologically superior forces speed and mobility, prolonging the conflict and undermining the morale of the invaders.[12]

"The struggle of the entire people" involves the participation of both the regular armed forces and the irregular forces of the RSR. The latter are composed of approximately 750,000 "Patriotic Guards," a paramilitary organization hurriedly reestablished and reemphasized immediately after the WTO invasion of Czechoslovakia.[13] Units are composed of ordinary citizens drawn from economic units and residential areas and are commanded primarily by reserve officers under the direction of local party organs.[14]

All Romanian teenagers receive preinduction military training. "Units of youth receiving military training" participate with the armed forces and the Patriotic Guards in national defense.[15] These paramilitary units have the task of harassing enemy communications and defending important economic units.[16] The enemy, whose speed and superiority in weapons are thus compromised, is forced to use a huge army of occupation. Romanian estimates of the force required to occupy the country range as high as one million men,[17] an expenditure of manpower and material even the Soviets and other "fraternal armies" could not long sustain given their Central European priorities. A prolonged occupation and a guerilla war of attrition would undermine the morale of WTO forces just as similar conditions adversely affected American forces in Vietnam. The strategy is clearly one of deterrence. Romania must convince potential invaders that the costs of the operation would outweigh its benefits. Such a conviction can be effected only by creating a credible defensive capability.

Romania institutionalized "the struggle of the entire people" in the opening paragraphs of the basic law on national defense of December 1972.

> The Romanian people, weapons in hand, have
> always defended (their) right to liberty
> and independent existence and development
> with dignity and courage.. Continuing this
> glorious tradition, in today's conditions
> when victory in an anti-imperialist war of
> defense can only be achieved by the general
> struggle of the entire people, all of the
> country's citizens must be ready to fight,
> even at the cost of their lives, for the
> preservation of the (fruits) of the people's
> peaceful labor and (for) the country's sov-
> ereignty and integrity.
>
> . . . .
>
> The country's defense, the cause and work of
> the entire people, is the sacred duty of
> every citizen... Romanian citizens, both
> men and women, regardless of their nationality,
> religion or occupation, have the right and
> obligation to participate in one of the forms
> of military preparation stipulated by law...[18]

Article 22 of the same law specifies the aforementioned forms as the forces of the Ministries of National Defense and of the Interior, the Patriotic Guard, civil defense units, "units of youth receiving military training," and other organizations created by law.[19]

The credibility, and thus the deterrent value, of a mixed professional and paramilitary defense depends on the demonstrable efficacy of such a strategy. Rigorous regular training of the Patriotic Guard is emphasized in the Romanian literature.[20] Coordination of the paramilitary formations with the regular military units is a repeated theme in large-scale military maneuvers. In the widely publicized September 1978 maneuvers, for example, Patriotic Guard and youth formations participated alongside regular army and air force units in a mass bridging of the Danube under "enemy" fire in the Braila-Galati region.[21] The composition of the participating units, the coordination of which won praise from General Secretary Ceausescu,[22] and the location of the exercises left little doubt about the content of the message delivered and for whom it was intended. Aurel Braun correctly contends that, with their excellent intelligence network, the Soviets would recognize a "bluff."[23] The deterrent posed by an institutionalized "people's war" is apparently effective when combined with Romania's passive, primarily political, defenses against Soviet intervention.[24]

Romania's defense against surprise is a function of the regime's constant reminders to the population that there are differences with the Soviet Union which might

trigger a Czechoslovakia-style intervention. The
Romanian leadership speaks out vigorously and often
against threats of the use of force and maneuvers close
to national borders, both of which the Soviets used in
1968.[25] Romania's relatively large diplomatic missions
and intelligence network keep the government attuned to
the most subtle changes in the international environment.
Western intelligence agencies have begun, in the aftermath of Lt. General Ion Pacepa's defection (Pacepa had
been Romania's leading intelligence officer), to learn
the far reaching extent of Romanian intelligence
activities. Other defectors, such as Vigil Tipanut from
Romania's embassy staff in Norway, have identified
Romanian agents in many Western capitals.

Aside from their preeminent role in national
defense, the armed forces play other important educational, economic, and political roles in contemporary
Romania. The diversification of the armed forces'
traditional mission complements the diffusion of responsibility for national defense. As paramilitary units
share in the responsibility for national defense, the
armed forces participate in the RCP's grand design of
rapid socio-economic development.

The armed forces, in which all Romanians of both
sexes are required to serve,[26] play an essential part in
the political socialization of youth. Nicolae Ceausescu
often stresses that the armed forces are "...an advanced
school of political and patriotic education (dedicated
to) the formation of the new man, the builder of a multilaterally developed social society."[27] In keeping with
the emphasis on ideological indoctrination which has
characterized the 1970s, the Higher Political Council of
the Armed Forces and individual RCP "activ" within the
military carry on political indoctrination among all
ranks of soldiers with the aim of creating the "new man".
In mandatory political education classes, soldiers study
the RCP program and policies and the works of General
Secretary Ceausescu.[28] Modern pedagogical techniques,
such as directed discussion and debate, have replaced
the heavy-handed harrangue of earlier years. In
addition, thousands of soldiers participate in the "Hymn
to Romania" national arts festival which is designed to
instill socialist patriotism in all citizens.[29] Many of
the characteristics of the "new man," (e.g., patriotism,
discipline, dedication, duty, and self-sacrifice), are
identical with traditional elements of the military
ethos. The RCP hopes that former conscripts will carry
back these qualities into their productive civilian
lives.[30] One would expect that the armed forces'
important role in the political socialization of
Romanian youth will continue in step with the RCP's
efforts in the intensive ideological indoctrination of

the entire population.

Even the casual visitor to Romania is struck by the number of uniformed workers on construction sites. The army has been asssigned significant tasks in the national economy. For example, the Sixth Five Year Plan (1976-1980) called for the army to complete the irrigation of 350,000 hectares of farmland and to play an important part in the renewed construction of the Danube-Black Sea Canal.[31] Given projected worker shortages in the 1980s[32] and soldiers' status as conscript labor, the army will continue to be an active participant in the RSR's program of rapid economic development, especially in construction projects where its engineering "expertise" and equipment can be put to best use.

In addition to its purely economic role, the army occasionally is used as an instrument of social and political control. After the coal miners of the Jiu Valley protested substandard living conditions and the inadequacies of a pension "reform" in August 1977, a reported 2,000 troops were brought in to restore order and to work the mines.[33] Romania also maintains a large militarized security police force which has both domestic and foreign intelligence responsibilities.[34] Security forces have not performed well in recent years. The July 1978 defection of Lieutenant General Ion Pacepa significantly compromised Romanian intelligence operations in the West and resulted in a large-scale purge of senior security officers.[35] Despite repeated incidents of foreign penetration, incompetence, and corruption, Ceausescu's authoritarian regime must continue to depend on these Ministry of Interior forces to maintain social and political control and to provide vital intelligence gathered both in the West and in socialist countries.

Like other RCP and state officials, commanders fulfill roles outside ordinary military duties. The Twelfth RCP Congress (1979) "elected" eight high ranking military officers to full membership in the Central Committee and an additional four to alternate membership.[36] Three generals serve as full or alternate members of the Political Executive Committee and two generals ran the Bucharest RCP organization for a time during the 1970s. Military officers have also been used as diplomats, implementing Romania's independent foreign policy.[37]

Romanian military policy has provided the country with a credible defense, an essential factor in the leadership's ability to pursue national policies which deviate from the bloc norm without eliciting intervention. Emphasizing the national element in policy deviation, in turn, legitimizes the regime and makes its demands for citizen sacrifices for the sake of national independence all the more acceptable to an overburdened populace. The armed forces also play important political, economic, and educational roles and are, at the same time, thoroughly integrated into Romanian society. Social integration and role diffusion decrease the autonomy of the military, making it less of a potential challenger of regime authority and less vulnerable to Soviet subversion.

These accomplishments have had their costs. There is evidence to suggest residual resistance to the deprofessionalization of the army's traditional role and to its use in the economy.[38] In response, the leadership employs various material and emotional incentives to win the acquiescence of both professional and conscript troops.[39] General Secretary Ceausescu has also called attention to the deterioration of discipline in armed forces, hinting that their socio-economic tasks may be the cause.

> We must understand that <u>the army must be the army</u>. (In) the development of socialist democracy, the participation of soldiers in political life is a very important aspect of our socialist order, but participation in political life, in the solution of the problems of socio-economic development, in the implementation of the domestic and foreign policies of our state must in no way lead to a weakening of military discipline and order...
>
> It is clear that military order and discipline must be the basis of the political consciousness of <u>both cadres and conscripts</u>... (emphasis added).[40]

The deterioration of discipline may be due, in part, to the waning intensity of political indoctrination which is characteristic of advanced socialist systems.[41] Ceausescu, however, insists on "more combative" indoctrination which goes beyond the mere explanation of policy.[42] Lax discipline and lack of conviction in the Romanian military undermines the credibility of national defense and must, therefore, be eradicated.

Despite Romanian adherence to the principle of the primary importance of the individual in any future war,[43] the realities of modern warfare and the desires of command personnel trained in technology-intensive Soviet institutions necessitate the modernization of the armed forces. Ground forces are entirely motorized and will soon be mechanized.[44] The proportion of engineers and technicians is steadily increasing within the officer corps and computers are being utilized in command decisions.[45] The technological education of the troops, however, has failed to keep pace with the modernization process. General Secretary Ceausescu has warned that drastic steps are needed to bring the level of training up to the level of technology, a gap which, if unattended, will grow with the continued modernization process.[46] Like many other countries, Romania is faced with a disparity between the technological complexity of its weaponry and the capacity of its educational system to produce graduates capable of utilizing advanced weapons systems. Such a disparity weakens the credibility of national defense and must, therefore, be mitigated.

As a developing country, Romania's economy places constraints on its military policy. Lightly armed territorial defensive units are inherently less expensive than technology-intensive units which characterize the military systems of most industrialized states. Integration of paramilitary forces into the defensive design of a state reduces the per effective cost of defense since expenses are, in part, defrayed by the individuals (subsistence) and by the economic and residential units from which they are drawn (pay and training).[47] Inferiority in weaponry and technology is conceded but is offset, in theory, by the survivability and prolonged operational efficiency of the partisan units whose ability to harrass and demoralize the invader makes the potential costs of invasion and occupation greater than the potential benefits. Such a strategy is only appropriate for a state, such as Romania, whose military capabilities are strictly defensive and intramural. The people's war concept is attrative to developing states because it requires minimal diversion of scarce resources from economic development and social modernization investment priorities.

Romanian and Western data show that, while absolute budgetary expenditures for Romania's armed forces have steadily increased, military expenditures as a proportion of total governmental expenditures and of GNP have recently remained stable and have actually decreased in the decade of the 1970s.

TABLE 7.1
Military Budget of the RSR in (1) Billions of Lei; (2) As a Percent of Total Government Expenditure; (3) As a Percent of GNP.[48]

	1970	1971	1972	1973	1974	1975	1976	1977	1978	1979	1980
1)	7.1	7.4	7.7	7.8	8.7	9.7	10.6	11.0	12.0	12.0	12.5
2)	5.4	5.5	5.3	4.7	4.2	4.1	4.2	3.9	3.8	3.5	4.0
3)	2.1	2.0	1.9	1.7	1.7	1.7	1.7	1.7	1.7	n.a.	n.a.

Comparative Western data (raw and extrapolated) reveal that Romanian military expenditures are at, or near, the bottom of European Warsaw Pact expenditures in a number of categories. (See Table 7.2)

TABLE 7.2

Relative Rank (of 7) for Romania on Nine Measures of
Military Expenditures for European Warsaw Pact States.[49]

(1) Total military expenditures (1978): 5th (Hungary 6th, Bulgaria 7th)

(2) Military expenditures as a percent of GNP (1977): 7th

(3) Military expenditures as a percent of government spending (1978): 6th (Hungary 7th)

(4) Military expenditures per capita (1978): 7th

(5) Active Armed Forces per thousand inhabitants (1977): 7th

(6) Value of arms imports (in current dollars, 1977): 7th

(7) Arms imports as a percent of total imports (in current dollars, 1977): 5th (Hungary 6th, U.S.S.R. 7th)

(8) Military expenditure per effective (1978): 6th (Bulgaria 7th)

Romania's developmental goal is to achieve "industrialized nation" status by 1990. Its strategy is essentially Stalinist: large investments in heavy industry, extensive labor mobilization, and severe restrictions on consumption. Economic independence is both the cause and the effect of Romania's deviationist policies. The precarious legitimacy the regime enjoys rests on its ability to resist Soviet integrationist demands. Self-reliant multilateral development is essential for continued successful resistance which is more and more difficult because of international commodity inflation. Thus far the results have been impressive: the Soviet bloc's highest growth rate and two to threefold increases in fixed capital, labor productivity and capital productivity for the period 1965-1975. But the price has been a stagnant standard of living, frequent shortages in consumables, and the inevitable popular discontent - discontent considered by the Nelson chapter in this volume, for example.[50] Diversion of scarce capital to unproductive military programs would frustrate an investment program already in serious jeopardy. It is thus in Romania's interest to maintain the least capital-intensive and most cost-efficient military policy possible. Current policy does just that.

The Romanian reluctance to divert larger sums to military programs was best illustrated by General Secretary Ceausescu's resistance to the Soviets' November 1978 demand that the Warsaw Pact member-states increase their national military budgets.

> It would be a big mistake if we chose the path of allocating great sums for arms since this would reduce the possibility of fulfilling the program of economic and social development for the country, would impede the program of raising the people's welfare, and consequently, would not strengthen, but rather would weaken (our) defensive capacity. This is why we believe that we must act in full responsibility to the fate of socialism and of the people and spend only as much as is strictly necessary to be prepared at any time to defend (our) independence and revolutionary achievements.[51]

As if to underscore the links between economic and foreign policy considerations, Ceausescu went on to reiterate Romania's opposition to further integration of the Pact's decision-making machinery.

> Nevertheless, we want this collaboration (with the WTO member-states) to be based on the socialist principles of relations between states, thus between armies; on the principles of equality and respect for the independence of each (state)-- based on the fact that each national army can only be under the command of the respective party and state organs. (The army) can only act on the order and because of the decision of those organs, the only (entities) legally entitled to commit the army to any kind of action. No one else can do this! We will never allow anyone else the possibility of committing the Romanian army to any military actions (!) (O)nly we ourselves, our people (can do this)![52]

The November 1978 crisis in Romanian-Soviet relations was only the most recent evidence of Ceausescu's determination to pursue a national military policy, a decision for "factories over guns."

If Nicolae Ceausescu continues to determine the direction of Romanian policy, significant changes in its military component are unlikely. There are two sets of related reasons which lead to this conclusion.

The aggregate policy of the Socialist Republic of

Romania under Ceausescu is to achieve multilateral development based on a national definition of needs and resources. The attainment of this goal by these methods excludes "dependency" of all sorts on the Soviet Union or a Soviet-controlled East European bloc. Both the achievement of Romania's developmental goals and the maintenance of a modicum of regime legitimacy depend on the continuation of assertive policy independence.53 Successful escapes from or realignments in dependency relationships have invariably included the escape from or realignment of military dependency: Egypt (1954-1957 and 1972-1978), Guinea (1958-1963), and Cuba (1959-1961). Unsuccessful attempts often failed because of a dissonance between a regime seeking independence or realignment and a military elite still dependent on and penetrated by the superordinate power: Chile (1973) and Brazil (1964).54 In developing countries, escape from one military dependency relationship usually entails the acceptance of another because they do not possess the industrial base for weapons development and production or a specialized educational system capable of training military cadres. Such a "renversement d'alliances" is clearly beyond the parameters of acceptable policy deviation in the Soviet bloc. Romania has, therefore, chosen the only alternative which meets both its political and military needs. It has renounced military modernization beyond the capacity of its national economy. By opting for a "people's war" doctrine which deemphasizes the advantages of technology, Romania has implicitly foresworn offensive capabilities--the price of escape but one which is consistent with its foreign policy objectives. The regime has thus far successfully mollified the professional military's natural resistance to the circumscription of its capabilities and its decreased access to advanced technology through material and emotional inducements. These incentives for acquiescence should be deemphasized in the 1980s as the "struggle of the entire people" becomes more legitimate among the military elite, a process aided by time and the regime's careful officer selection and promotion policies.

Second, Romanian military policy in the 1980s will probably remain unchanged because Romania simply cannot afford the alternative--a technology-intensive military capability. With capital accumulation projected at 30-32% for the Seventh and Eighth Plans (1981-1990)55 and the increasingly strident demands for substantial increases in the standard of living, Romania cannot spare much more than the approximately 4% of total government expenditures (1.7% of GNP) now spent on "defense of the state" without adversely affecting developmental priorities. General Secretary Ceaușescu has often stated his belief that economic development and social modernization

are the only sure defense for the socialist state in
particular and the European socialist state system in
general.56 This curious logic has a strong foundation in
fact since only a developed socialist state has the capability of delivering the promised fruits of socialism to
its population which, consequently, would be more inclined to defend the political system as well as the political community.

One may conclude, therefore, that Romanian military
policy in the 1980s will remain essentially that pursued
in the 1970s, barring internal upheaval or external intervention. The former might occur if Ceausescu, who is
sixty-two years old in 1980, dies or is incapacitated or
if the regime is unable to deal with Romania's serious
economic problems and is thus forced to give in to Soviet
hegemonism. The latter might come about if the post-
Brezhnev Soviet leadership is more insistent on bloc
integration and conformity. Present military policy is
an integral and essential element in the complex of contemporary Romanian political and economic policies and
cannot be significantly modified without endangering
national independence and the legitimacy of the regime.

NOTES

1. Most recently, Alexander Alexiev, "Party-Military Relations in Romania" (Santa Monica: Rand, 1978), P-6059; Aurel Braun, "The Yugoslav/Romanian Concept of People's War" Canadian Defense Quarterly, VII No. 1 (Summer 1977): 39-43; Arie Chaplin, "Security of Weak States: The 'Popular War' Doctrine in Romanian Defense Policy" (Ph.D. diss., New School for Social Research, 1977); Dionise Ghermani, "Die Rumanische Volksarmee" in Peter Gosztony (ed.), Zur Geschichte der europaischen Volksarmeen (Bonn-Bad Godesberg: Hohwacht Verlag, 1976), pp. 189-226; and, Walter M. Bacon, Jr., "The Military and the Party in Romania" in Dale R. Herspring and Ivan Volgyes (eds.), Civil-Military Relations in Communist Systems (Boulder, Colo.: Westview, 1978), pp. 165-180, and "Romania: Value Transformations in the Military," Studies in Comparative Communism, XI, No. 3 (Autumn 1978): 237-249.
2. Col. Aurel Petri, "In slujba apararii patriei socialiste" in Col. C. Soare et. al., Istoria gindirii militare romanesti (Bucharest: Editura militara, 1974), p. 372.
3. The first specific reference to the phrase "lupta intregului popor" in a recently published collection of documents on Romanian defense policy dates from RCP General Secretary Nicolae Ceausescu's speech to basic cadres in the armed forces, February 5, 1970. Apararea nationala a Romaniei socialiste. Documente 1965-1977 (Bucharest: Editura militara, 1978), p. 137.
4. Aurel Braun, Romanian Foreign Policy Since 1965: The Political and Military Limits of Autonomy (New York: Praeger, 1978), pp. 126, 144-189.
5. "Legea 5/1969 privind infiitarea, organizarea si functionarea Consiliului Apararii Republicii Socialiste Romania," in Documente pp. 500-503. These stipulations are reiterated in the basic legal document on national defense, "Legea 14/1972 privind organizarea apararii nationale a Republicii Socialiste Romania," Article 8, in ibid., pp. 517-518.
6. Bacon, "The Military and the Party," pp. 173-174 and "Value Transformation," p. 244.
7. Alex Alexiev, "Romania and the Warsaw Pact: The Defense Policy of a Reluctant Ally" (Santa Monica: Rand, 1979), P 6270, pp. 16-17.
8. Col. Gen. Vasile Ionel, "Politica Partidului Comunist Roman de dezvoltare a productiei proprii de technica militara" in A. G. Savu (ed.), Armata Republicii Socialiste Romania: traditii si contemporaneitate (Bucharest: Editura militara, 1975), p. 147. It should be noted however that the value of annual arms imports rose by almost 200% from 1968 to 1977. At the same time arms imports represented only 2% of total imports in 1977, down

from 4% in 1973. United States Arms Control and Disarmament Agency, World Military Expenditures and Arms Transfers 1968-1977 (Washington: U.S. Government Printing Office, 1979), p. 144.

9. Gregory R. Copley (ed.), Defense and Foreign Affairs Handbook 1976-1977 (Washington: Copley and Associates, 1976), pp. 382-383; World Military Expenditures and Arms Transfers 1967-1976, p. 156; and, Chaplin, "Romania Defense Policy," p. 11.

10. Bacon, "The Military and the Party," p. 169.

11. For details of the "Serb case" and other rumored Sovietophilism in the army and security forces, see ibid. p. 170. For a concurring conclusion see Braun, Romanian Foreign Policy, pp. 161-166.

12. A point not lost on Nicolae Ceausescu, e.g., "Cuvintare la consfatiurea cadrelor de baza din Ministerul Fortelor Armate," February 5, 1970, in Documente, p. 137.

13. The Military Balance 1979-1980 (London: International Institute for Strategic Studies, 1979), p. 96; Ceausescu's speech to citizens of Bucharest, August 21, 1968 in Documente, p. 85; "Decretul 765/1968" of September 5, 1968, as cited in Cols. Leonida Loghin and Alexandru Petricean, Garzile patriotice din Romania (Bucharest: Editura militara, 1974), p. 128.

14. "Legea 14/1972," Articles 104-114, in Documente, pp. 548-551.

15. Ibid, Articles 118-119, pp. 551-552.

16. Loghin and Petricean, Garzile patriotice, pp. 135-136.

17. Braun, "Yugoslav/Romanian Concept," p. 41; Romanian Foreign Policy, p. 173

18. "Legea 14/1972", preamble, in Documente, pp. 513-514.

19. Ibid, p. 528.

20. E.g., Loghin and Petricean, Garzile patriotice, p. 139; Viața militara, 1977-1979, passim, [E.g., XXXII, No. 3 (1979): 24-25; No. 6 (1979): 8-9; No. 4 (1979): 13].

21. Scinteia, September 9, 1978, p. 1.

22. Scinteia, September 17, 1978, p. 1.

23. Braun, Romanian Foreign Policy, pp. 151 and 184.

24. Ceausescu's affirmation of this conclusion is absolute (Scinteia, September 17, 1978, p. 1) but Braun cautiously couches the point, maintaining that while Romania appears to have proven its "will to resist," its material capacity to carry out a protracted war is in doubt ("Yugoslav/Romanian Concept," p. 43).

25. Since the Czechoslovakian intervention Romania has regularly added the renunciation of the use force or the threat of force, such as maneuvers close to national frontiers, to its litany of foreign relations principles. E.g., Legea 14/1972, preamble, in Documente, p. 514, or

more recently in "Hotarirea plenarei Comitetului Central al Partidului Comunist Roman cu privire la politica internationala a partidului si statului nostru" in Scinteia, March 30, 1979, p. 3.

26. "Legea 14/1972," Article 118 (in Documente, p. 529) stipulates that all boys and girls from Grade IX (14 year-olds) participate in military training until they have finished school. 16-20 year-olds not in school are also required to undergo similar training. However a 1978 State Council decree, Article 5, apparently lowers the minimum age to fifth graders (10 year-olds!). Amended Law No. 33/1968 on Training of Youth for National Defense," (Buletinul oficial al Republicii Socialiste Romania Part 1, No. 59, July 13, 1978) JPRS #71874, p. 39.

27. "Cuvintare la adunarea activului de comanda si de partid de baza din armata," October 1, 1976, in Documente p. 372.

28. Cols. Mihai Inoan and Tudor Tamaş, Armata-parte componenta a statului. Functiile ei in etapa actuala (Bucharest: Editura militara, 1975), pp. 125-142; Col. Mihai Inoan et. al., Armata romana in primii ani ai revolutiei si constructiei socialiste (Bucharest: Editura militara, 1975), pp. 303-327.

29. Col. Gen Ion Coman, "Activitatea Partidului Comunist Roman, a tovarasului Nicolae Ceausescu pentru intarirea capacitatii de aparare a cuceririlor revolutionare, a independentei si suveranitatii nationale," Anale de istorie, XXIV, No. 1 (1978), pp. 77-78. Viata militara also regularly features the armed forces' participation in the "Hymn to Romania" festival.

30. For the ideal type see "Armata, inalta scoala politica - 3 tineri, 3 intrebari, 3 raspunsuri," Viata militara, XXVII, No. 3 (1973), p. 14."

31. "Cuvintare la adunarea activului de comanda şi de partid de baza din armata" in Documente, pp. 368-369. For a more complete list of army projects in the national economy see Cols. Mihai Inoan and Tudor Tamaş Armata-parte componenta a statului, pp. 115-125. The Higher Political Council of the Armed Forces' monthly magazine, Viaţa militara, usually carries a featured report on military participation in the economy.

32. Marvin R. Jackson, "Industrialization, Trade, and Mobilization in Romania's Drive for Economic Independence" in East European Economies Post-Helsinki. A Compendium of Papers Submitted to the Joint Economic Committee, Congress of the United States (Washington: United States Government Printing Office, 1977), pp. 932-938.

33. New York Times, November 22, 1977, pp. 1, 3.

34. Col. Mihai Arsintescu et. al., Apararea nationala a Romaniei socialiste, cauza şi opera a intregului nostru popor (Bucharest: Editura militara, 1974), pp. 170-173.

35. New York Times (Supplementary Material), Septem-

ber 7, 1978, pp. 39-40; The Times (London), September 4, 1978, p. 4.

36. George Cioranescu, "The New Romanian Communist Party Central Committee," Radio Free Europe Research, RAD Background Report/24 (Romania), 5 February 1980, pp. 17-18.

37. Bacon, "The Military and the Party," pp. 168-169.

38. Ibid., pp. 171-172; "Value Transformation," pp. 243-246; New York Times, November 22, 1977, p. 3.

39. Braun, Romanian Foreign Policy, pp. 158-159; Alexiev, "Party-Military Relations," pp. 18-26; and Bacon, "The Military and the Party," p. 172. Personnel costs, both pay and subsistence, have increased steadily over the last decade. Among the European member-states of the WTO, only Bulgaria spends a greater proportion of its military budget on personnel costs. Thad P. Alton et. al., "Defense Expenditures in Eastern Europe, 1965-1976" in East European Economies Post-Helsinki, pp. 275-276, 281-282.

40. Ceausescu's speech to the basic activ of the army, Scinteia, September 17, 1978, p. 1.

41. Dale R. Herspring and Ivan Volgyes, "The Military as an Agent of Political Socialization in Eastern Europe," Armed Forces and Society, III, No. 2 (February 1977), pp. 251-252.

42. Scinteia, September 17, 1978, p. 3.

43. Petri, "In slujba apararii patriei socialiste," p. 383; "Cuvintarea Tovarasului Ion Coman...(to the Twelfth Party Congress)," Scinteia, November 22, 1979, p. 5.

44. Georges Marey, "The Army of the Socialist Republic of Romania" Est et Ouest, January, 1979, pp. 15-21, in JPRS #72881, pp. 166-167.

45. Col. Gen. Ion Coman, "Activitatea Partidului Comunist Roman," p. 75.

46. Scinteia, September 17, 1978, p. 1.

47. See "Legea 14/1972," Article 110, in Documente, p. 550; and, "Amended 'Law 33/1968'," Articles 11, 15, 18-20, 22-25, JPRS #71874, pp. 42-45.

48. (1 and 2) Anuarul statistic al Republicii Socialiste Romania 1978 (Bucharest: Directia centrala de statistica, 1978) pp. 473-475; 1978 - projected 1980 figures extrapolated from state budgets found in Romania: Documents - Events, VII, No. 54 (November 1977), pp. 19-20; VIII, No. 38 (November 1978), pp. 27-29; and IX, No. 73 (December 1979), pp. 19-20. Military pay raises, according to the latter, account for all of the 1980 increase, (3) Thad P. Alton, et. al., "Defense Expenditures," p. 270; and, The Military Balance 1979-80, p. 94. It should be remembered that some paramilitary costs are hidden elsewhere in the official statistics.

49. The Military Balance 1979-1980, pp. 94-96; World

Military Expenditures and Arms Transfers 1968-1977, pp. 78-104, 121-147. It is interesting to note that among major European countries only Luxembourg, Erie, and Hungary devote a smaller proportion of their national budgets to defense expenditures (measure 3). Albania and Yugoslavia, both of which follow a people's war doctrine, have lower per effective (measure 8) and per capita (measure 4) expenditures.

50. See Jackson, "Economic Independence," pp. 886-940; Thad P. Alton, "Comparative Structure and Growth of Economic Activity in Eastern Europe," in East European Economies Post-Helsinki, pp. 244-246; and, Dionise Ghermani, "Der Lebensstandard in Rumanien," Wissenschaftlicher Dienst Sudosteuropa, XXVI, No. 12 (1977), pp. 310-316.

51. Ceausescu's speech to representatives of the armed forces and the Ministry of the Interior after his return from the meeting of the WTO's Political Consulative Committee in Moscow, Scinteia, November 28, 1978, p. 3.

52. Ibid.

53. Francois Fejto, "Socialisme et nationalisme dans les democraties populaires (1971-1978)," Defense Nationale, XXXIV, No. 8 (August-September 1978): 31; Teresa Rakowska-Harmstone, "East European Communism in the Seventies," in Morton A. Kaplan (ed.), The Many Faces of Communism (New York: Free Press, 1978), p. 208.

54. Romania is well aware of the implications of the overthrow of the Allende regime by the Chilean military. Lt. Vasile Secares, "Armata ca grup social" in Studii social-politice asupra fenomenului militar contemporan, Vol. IV (Bucharest: Editura militara, 1975), pp. 109, 113, and 115.

55. Jackson, "Economic Independence," p. 903.

56. E.g., Scinteia, November 18, 1978, p. 3.

8
Romanian Foreign Policy in the 1980s

Ronald H. Linden

INTRODUCTION

Since the mid-1960s, the Romanian Socialist Republic has pursued a foreign policy strikingly at variance with the policies of its socialist allies, including the Soviet Union. In terms of both international interactions such as trade, visits, agreements, and positions on key international issues, the Romanian government has executed a foreign policy characterized variously by analysts as "dissident"[1] "partially aligned"[2] "independent"[3] and "deviant".[4] To assess the course of this policy during the 1980s is both a fascinating and challenging task, one which presents the investigator with an intriguing mixture of internal and external factors acting to stimulate, allow or circumscribe the course of Romanian foreign policy.

Although the purpose of the present work is an assessment of the future, it is appropriate to begin such an analysis with a glance toward the past, in order to better comprehend the causes and course of Romania's unique policy during the past two decades.

A LOOK BACKWARDS

Almost two decades ago, Romanian foreign policy emerged from a dutiful, if laconic, imitation and approval of Soviet international policies into a period of murmuring dispute with the Soviet Union over the question of national economic planning and development. After some zig-zagging on the issue, Moscow had come in 1962 to oppose the autarchic development of the East European states. It proposed instead the strengthening of the Council for Mutual Economic Assistance (CMEA) to

---

Ronald H. Linden received his doctorate from Princeton University and is now an Assistant Professor of Political Science at the University of Pittsburgh.

the level of a supranational planning body in order to improve the "international division of labor" among the socialist states. As envisaged, each state would have specialized in the production of those commodities it could produce most efficiently, and import from its fellow CMEA members those it did not produce. For Romania this would have meant the continuation of a rural-based economy producing essentially agricultural goods and raw materials (chiefly petroleum products).[5] The Romanian five-year plan and fifteen year projection, however, foresaw a broad and rapid industrialization of the country (12% per year) and the country's movement as fast as possible from the status of "breadbasket and gas station of Europe."[6] After several interparty visits failed to resolve the dispute, it emerged into the open with the publication in April, 1964, of the "Statement on the Stand of the Romanian Worker's Party Concerning the Problems of the International Communist and Working Class Movement."[7]

This Statement, while addressed overtly to the escalating "public controversy" between the Chinese and Soviet parties, in addition took the liberty of pointing out what the correct form of "new type" relations between socialist states should be, and made clear that, as far as economic development is concerned,

> The planned management of the national economy is one of the fundamental, essential, and inalienable attributes of the sovereignty of the socialist state--the state plan being the chief means through which the socialist state achieves its political and socioeconomic objectives, establishes the directions and rates of development of the national economy, its fundamental proportions, the accumulations, the measure for raising the people's living standard and cultural level. The sovereignty of the socialist state requires that it effectively and fully avail itself of the means for the practical implementation of these functions, holding in its hands all the levers of managing economic and social life. Transmitting such levers to the competence of superstate or extrastate bodies would turn sovereignty into a meaningless notion.[8]

The Romanians, quoting chapter and verse from Lenin himself on national distinctiveness, explained that superstate planning bodies were "not in keeping with the principles that underlie the relations among the socialist countries."[9]

After the death of Gheorghe Gheorghiu-Dej in 1965

and the ascension to party and, soon after, state
leadership of Nicolae Ceausescu, Romanian opposition to
Soviet policy and initiatives on party and state relations was expanded. The following familiar list recalls
the Romanian course:

- the RCP's refusal until the end of the decade to agree upon, help prepare or attend a conference of communist parties except on its terms;
- its studied neutrality in the Sino-Soviet dispute;
- its consistent cultivation and improvement of ties with the Yugoslav party;
- and its vigorous defense of the Czech party's right to construct socialism according to its own dictates.

On the state level, unlike any of its allies, Romania:

- refused to break relations with Israel after the 6-day war of 1967;
- established diplomatic relations with the FRG the same year;
- questioned both the structure and continued existence of the Warsaw pact and declined to take part in military maneuvers or allow them on its territory;
- condemned the WTO discussions of the Czech developments and the invasion designed to end them;
- pursued the same neutrality in the Sino-Soviet border dispute that it had in the dispute between the CPSU and CCP;
- and staked out positions differing from its allies on other issues such as nuclear non-proliferation, mutual force reductions in Europe and the proposed conference on security and cooperation in Europe.[10]

During the decade, Romania reoriented its foreign trade until the Soviet--East European share fell from roughly two thirds in 1960 to less than half by 1970. At the same time, the Western share of that trade grew from roughly a fifth in 1960 to more than a third by 1970.[11] Finally, its overall patterns of international interactions (treaties, visits, exchanges) revealed a country paying more attention than its allies to non-WTO or non-communist nations and less attention than the others to its East European allies and to the Soviet Union.[12]

During the 1970s, eyebrow-raising foreign policy actions were missing. Since 1968, and especially since

1971, Romanian foreign policy attitudes and actions became more moderate in tone. This led some observers to conclude that Romania was becoming more bloc-oriented, more conformist in its international policy.[13] However, with few exceptions the Romanians seem as fervent as ever in their delineation and affirmation of the conceptual bases of their foreign policy. These are that:

1) The Romanian national state, as part of the full exercise of its sovereignty, is the sole determiner of the nature, pace and direction of Romanian economic development. Economic sovereignty cannot be separated from national sovereignty, which itself cannot be "limited" in theory or practice.[14] In addition, the modern nation is a fundamental, enduring force in the contemporary world and will continue to have paramount significance in world politics for the foreseeable future.[15]
2) Each communist party--the Czech, the Chinese or the Romanian, has the right and obligation to determine the most appropriate manner of building socialism in accordance with its specific national conditions. There can be no "leading center" or superior and subordinate parties, and no parties can be "expelled" for pursuing distinctive policies.[16]
3) States, in pursuing their development plans need to take full advantage of the "scientific and technological revolution" and therefore must be free to have relations with all states "regardless of social system" without discrimination. "The socialist international division of labor cannot be mean isolation."[17]
4) The existing military situation, both conventional and nuclear, is detrimental to the security of all states, especially the small and medium-sized states. Hence genuine nuclear disarmament and conventional arms reduction are crucial. In addition, the bifurcation of the European continent into military blocs should be abolished.[18]
5) The international political and, especially, economic order needs to be restructured in order to improve the situation of the developing countries. Since it is itself a developing socialist state, Romania needs to develop more broadly and more rapidly than the industrialized states; it needs to pursue multiple economic contacts with all states; and it is deserving of special treatment and assistance from other states, including its socialist allies.[19]

The persistence and strength of these principles in Romanian foreign policy has meant a continuation of ardent, if often less spectacular, deviance in foreign policy. One implication, for example, of the shift in Romania's self-definition from a socialist country to that of a socialist developing country is that Romania supports more strongly than any of its allies the movement for a New International Economic--and the Romanians add, Political--Order, i.e., one in which the needs of the less developed and small and medium-sized states would be more adequately served. This "democratization of international relations" can only take place, of course, at the expense of the superpowers.[20] In 1976, Romania secured "guest" status (along with Switzerland, the Philippines and Portugal) at the Conference of the Nonaligned States; joined the Group of 77; and participated in the U.N. Conference on Trade and Development "side by side with other developing countries."[21] The Romanians have also been at the forefront of the movement at the United Nations to restructure the organization in a manner which would give the smaller states more power vis-a-vis the great powers.[22]

In terms of economic interactions the Romanians have engaged in similarly distinctive behavior. During the first five years of the 1970s, Romanian exports to developed capitalist states more than doubled while imports almost tripled. In 1974, trade with the developed capitalist countries surpassed for the first time trade with Comecon states, though it has levelled off since then.[23] In 1973, Romania became the first Comecon country to receive generalized preferences from the European Economic Community and in 1976 became the first to sign a trade agreement with that organization.[24] Romania was until 1978 the only East European country to have accepted MFN status from the United States under the stipulations of the Jackson amendment (Hungary received MFN in March, 1978; Poland has had this status since 1960). Politically, Bucharest has maintained discordant positions on Mutual Force Reduction talks, on the Conference on Security and Cooperation in Europe[25] and on several significant international political issues, such as the Middle East and war in Southeast Asia.[26]

On the party level, the RCP has not only supported the independence of communist parties in general, but in particular has given ostentatious support to Eurocommunists such as Santiago Carillo.[27]

In some areas, Bucharest seems to have recognized that discretion is the better part of valour. Ceausescu's visit to Soviet Moldavia in August 1976, brought to a formal close the recurring Romanian--Soviet dispute over Bessarabia.[28] While the issue may yet emerge again[29] and in any case is a low priority item for both parties, this conciliatory act by Ceausescu, the first visit by a Romanian leader to the Moldavian SSR, showed a clear recognition of and respect for limits to Romanian assertiveness.

Similar recognition was demonstrated earlier in the decade when Romanian-Chinese relations cooled considerably after Ceausescu's visit to China (1971) elicited significant opprobrium from Romania's allies.[30] However, Romania has continued to praise the course of China's development and high-level contacts have even increased.[31] In May of 1978, Ceausescu again visited the People's Republic[32] and in August hosted a highly publicized visit by CCP Chairman Hua Guofeng.[33] Hua's travels (he also visited Iran and Yugoslavia) and their implications ("danger") were blasted by the Soviet Union, and the Romanians subsequently felt constrained to respond in clarification and defense of their party and state prerogatives.[34]

Most recently, the Romanians reacted in a restrained if distinctive manner to the Soviet invasion of Afghanistan. Instead of the emotional rhetoric which followed the invasion of Czechoslovakia, or the explicit condemnation which followed the Vietnamese invasion of Cambodia, Bucharest reaffirmed its standard condemnation of policies of force or "dictat," of interference in the internal affairs of other states and of dividing the world into spheres of influence or hegemony.[35] Ceausescu called for "unflinching respect for the right of each nation to develop itself freely, independently, to choose independently its path of social and economic development, without any kind of interference from outside."[36] When the United Nations General Assembly passed a resolution (by a vote of 104-18-18) "deploring" the intervention and calling for "the immediate, unconditional and total withdrawal of the foreign troops from Afghanistan," the Romanians did not participate in the vote.[37] They did, however, state the need for "respect by all states for the independence and sovereignty of Afghanistan and for the Afghan people's right to choose their development path themselves, without any outside interference."[38] Thus in this case the Romanians were conspicuous by their lack of support for the invasion, and by their forceful, if indirect, criticism.[39]

THE 1980s: INTERNAL AND EXTERNAL FACTORS IN ROMANIAN FOREIGN POLICY

Will the Romanians be able to sustain their deviant foreign policy for a third decade? The answer to this will depend upon a mixture of complex factors, operating both inside and outside Romania. For analytic purposes

we can assess the factors crucial to the persistance of
the present course of Romanian foreign policy in terms
of their internal and external dimension while remaining
aware that such analytical boundaries frequently blur
more than analysts would like.

Internal Political Factors

The position of Ceausescu has grown consistently
stronger. He has replaced virtually all significant
political actors from the previous regime with people of
his own choosing, whose primary political loyalties are
to <u>Conducatorul</u> (the leader) himself.[40] In addition he
has also replaced even some of those long associated
with Romania's autonomous foreign policy, e.g., Alexandru Birladeanu, and has kept potential political rivals
insecure with a policy of "rotating" key positions in
the party and government.[41] At the same time, Ceausescu
himself has assumed leadership of virtually every significant party and state institution in the country:
Secretary-General of the Party: President of the Republic--a new position created for him in 1974; Commander-in-Chief of the Armed Forces. Some of the organs were
themselves reorganized to facilititate his personal control; for example, the establishment of the party Executive Committee in 1965, and especially a Permanent
Bureau of this committee in 1974 to replace and circumvent the party Presidium and Central Committee.[42]
Finally, as Mary Ellen Fischer discusses in her chapter
in this volume, the late 70s saw an exploding campaign
of glorification of Ceausescu personally and of his contributions to the social, economic, political and ideological life of the country.[43]

Both the constant outpouring of adulation for
Ceausescu and the steady replacement of officials by him
may conceal, or indeed be a symptom of, a fundamentally
insecure leadership. But firm evidence of any significant opposition at the elite level, i.e., a group or
faction willing and capable of replacing Ceausescu and
abandoning his policies, is slim.[44]

Although especially difficult to assess on regional
and local levels, cadre support related to foreign
policy seems high for reasons similar to those which
make Romania's foreign policy popular to the public at
large: its anti-Soviet, nationalistic nature. However,
there are indications that the party's overall vitality
and the present regime's support is becoming increasingly dependent upon its ability to provide material
goods and privileges to members and their families. The
party is becoming "familialized"[45] as party officials
seek and pass on privileges and favors to their friends
and family.

Local leaders are in any case concerned much more with local "economic" issues, e.g., the provisions of public goods and services, and these concerns vary depending on their region's needs and on their own perception of their role.[46] This should not prevent effective support upward and transmission downward of Romanian foreign policy goals and activities. However, future threats to party coherence could arise from either a) the continued growth of a familial and/or personal reward-oriented party; or b) an increasing recognition by party cadre of the need to de-control and de-centralize in order to meet the country's ambitious development goals. Frustrating of the desires of the first group or satisfying of the goals of the second group could undermine the control and support of the national party leadership.

Public support for Ceausescu's foreign policy is high, though in the absence of a galvanizing issue as the invasion of Czechoslovakia, it is perhaps not at the demonstrative levels reached in 1968. General support for, or at least accommodation with, the Ceausescu regime seems to be the norm, though there exists a small dissident movement in Romania. The level of public support for this movement is virtually impossible to assess, but the regime has moved quickly against it using both the carrot (emigration) and the stick (suppression).[47]

The active foreign policy is designed to secure for the RCP a degree of national legitimacy by establishing its autonomy vis-à-vis the Soviet Union, by presenting the state as a highly visible, respected and effective international actor, and by characterizing its actions as being squarely within the finest traditions of Romanian diplomatic history, from the time of the Roman empire to the Second World War. It is the party's attempt to move close enough to the stove of nationalism to be warmed by it, while avoiding the dangers of being scorched. It has been, for the most part, generally successful. The greatest internal threat to the regime's continued pursuit of this foreign policy stems from: 1) economic sources, i.e., a dissatisfied and increasingly militant proletariat; and 2) cultural/ethnic factors, i.e., the large Hungarian minority. These are discussed further below. Future dangers specifically in the political realm lie in the party's obsessive fear and suppression of democratizing reforms, especially on the interface between itself and the population. To the degree that party legitimacy pursued through a nationalistic foreign policy needs to be supplemented with the permitting of greater popular input into the domestic political process, the regime will run the risk of allowing faction-building, ever greater pressure for reform, or possibly, public turbulence.[48]

The danger therein would stem from the opportunity such a situation would provide for external manipulation and pressure, and/or from the Soviet Union's demonstrated concern over preserving "the leading role of the party" in the states of Eastern Europe. At present, the leading role of the RCP is threatened only by the <u>more</u> leading role of its General Secretary.

Internal Economic Factors

Romanian foreign policy is designed to serve the goal of developing the country "multilaterally." The RCP is committed to achieving industrial development and an urban-based economy by 1990. Since the mid-1960s, Romania has sought from the West most of the technology and "know-how" to make rapid development possible.[49] To import such goods, the Romanian economy must be able to consistently earn hard currency through its exports. Despite a general overhaul of foreign trade operations in the last decade,[50] an improvement in trade opportunities--including the granting of MFN by the United States--and substantial western credits,[51] and realitively high--albeit fluctuating--domestic growth rates,[52] the Romanian ability to export to the West remains limited in both amount and diversity. Expanding the export of foodstuffs and industrial consumer goods is still crucial to the country's ability to continue to run deficits in its importing of machines and, increasingly, raw materials.[53] This need is likely to increase as a growing western debt has made both creditor and debtor nervous and further financing of trade deficits uncertain.[54] Production will have to continue growing at a time when most indicators suggest that high growth rates of the past decade will be difficult to sustain.[55]

As the current (seventh) five-year plan comes to an end, the party, in addition to trumpeting its achievement (in 4 to 4½ years), has been pressing for ever greater productivity, efficiency and attention to quality and the needs of customers in the manufacture of goods. Both before and during the Twelfth Congress, Ceausescu engaged in pointed criticism of various enterprises, and of party cadres involved with them, for delays, waste and other "shortcomings."[56] Taking their cues, virtually all of the leading speakers at the Congress engaged in both criticism and self-criticism, railing against a variety of "bureaucratic manifestations."[57]

The five-year plan for 1981-1985 forecasts ambitious economic targets, including an average annual growth rate of 6.7-7.4 percent, a growth in net industrial production of nine to ten percent, in agricultural production of 4.5-5.0 percent, and in foreign trade of

8.5-9.5 percent. Investments are scheduled to increase 5.4-6.2 percent. This is all to be accomplished, moreover, while achieving a forty percent <u>reduction</u> in energy consumption by 1990. The driving force in the growth is to be labor productivity, which is projected to increase at 7.0-7.5 percent annually and to account for eighty percent of overall production increases.[58]

For the Romanians, as for the other East European states, the effects of the worldwide energy squeeze, though somewhat delayed and somewhat less dramatic, have nevertheless spurred the government to push for greater conservation and efficiency, bigger cuts in consumer use of energy, and more intensive searches for both domestic sources of energy and international sources of petroleum. The Romanians currently depend on coal and hydrocarbons for approximately forty percent each of their energy needs (deriving the rest primarily from hydroelectric power). The new five-year plan projects a sharp cut in the latter, to twenty percent by 1985, and an increase in use of the former, to fifty-five percent, with small increases elsewhere, including nuclear power.[59] Domestically this will require not only conservation, improved exploitation of existing reserves and discovery of new ones,[60] but the willingness and ability of Romania's new proletariat to: 1) improve its productivity and efficiency dramatically, and even more important, 2) to continue to pay for the country's economic growth with sacrifices in their standard of living. If the dissatisfaction of the Jiu Valley miners, evident demonstrably in 1977,[61] is an indication of the future, and if the regime should have to redirect substantial resources to meet new domestic demands, some serious questions relating to Romania's foreign policy would be raised. First, such a reallocation would likely further reduce the country's ability to produce quality exportables in sufficient quantity. Second, and perhaps of greater long-term consequence, the government's capacity to satisfy the demands of the workers, e.g., for better housing and other consumer goods, higher wages, lower prices, etc. is likely to be limited, even with significant budgetary and investment shifting. Failure to do so hurts the credibility of the regime and, as Ceausescu clearly recognizes, economic issues can very quickly become political. In recognition of this, the party relentlessly points to the improvement of the living standards of the workers and peasants, and toward even greater improvements in the next five years.[62] In addition, in particularly critical sectors, such as mining, the regime responds relatively quickly and substantively to the demands of the workers.[63] For the most part, though, the RCP has thus far been able to rely to a remarkable degree on nonmaterial incentives and payoffs; but the histories of the other socialist states and signs within

Romania itself indicate that the limits of this ability may be nearing.[64]

Internal Cultural Factors

Romanian leaders have successfully capitalized upon the non-Slavic identity of the population. Both Gheorghiu-Dej and Ceausescu have sought to negotiate the narrow ground between constructive, supportive Romanian nationalism, e.g., pride in Romanian culture, history, accomplishments and international role, and destructive, dangerous anti-Russian expressions. The RCP executed a broad de-Slavification campaign in the early 60s and Ceausescu himself was able to capitalize on post-1968 anti-Soviet sentiment, while avoiding dangerous excesses of nationalism.[65] The 1970s provided no similar crises but the regime still profits by a strong identification with the past and present Romanian nation.

There are two groups whose response to efforts at Romanianization of the country can be considered skeptical at best, hostile at worst. The Hungarian minority, almost eight percent according to the last census,[66] presumably regards the independent aspects of Romanian foreign policy as positively as do the majority Romanians. However, the other edge of this nationalistic sword has been de-Magyarization. Hungarians have found themselves alternatively banned and blessed by the regime and are not above casting public appeals for support to attentive ears in Budapest and elsewhere.[67] If anti-regime political factions based on opposition to international actions or domestic policy are not available for Soviet manipulation, a large resentful ethnic minority does represent a major potential source of opposition and a useful potential lever for external pressure.[68]

The German minority, smaller (1.6 percent) and evidently more interested in leaving Romania than in improving their lot within it, represents a potential problem in another way. To the degree that their desire to emigrate to West Germany is satisfied by the government, the capacity of the country's economy to perform and grow could be hurt, due to the significant role the German minority plays in Romanian industry.[69] Aware of this and as yet relatively free from substantial public pressure from West Germany to allow greater emigration, the regime has been unwilling to tolerate the departure of its German minority in the way that it has allowed emigration of its Jews. Should such pressure be forthcoming, or should the volatile mix of cultural and economic factors significantly raise the level of either Hungarian or German opposition to the regime, the RCP's choices and freedom of action could be significantly constrained.[70]

External Political Factors

In the last two decades, sources of external political support for Bucharest have varied. Relations with the People's Republic of China, for example, have fluctuated considerably. During the 1960s, Chinese support for the Romanian view of autonomy, development, inter-party and interstate relations was helpful but limited.[71] Romanian support for similar Chinese views was as instrumental as that which it received; it served to legitimize each party's own way to socialism. But with the recognition of the clear limits of mutual support, the substantial increase of Soviet concern over Sino-Romanian interactions evidenced in the early 70s, and Moscow's explicit imprimatur being placed on separate roads to socialism at Berlin in 1976, Romanian-Chinese relations, while remaining cordial, seemed to reach a plateau.[72]

The August 1978 visit of CCP Chairman Hua Guofeng to Romania was significant mostly for what it indicated about Chinese foreign policy: a return to active attempts to counter Soviet influence; an evident desire not to lose influence in the Balkans despite Albania's rejection of the policies of the new CCP leadership; a more pragmatic non-ideological approach to politics. From the Romanian perspective the visit was similar to visits from Chinese officials in the past. The Romanians were evidently able to temper Chinese condemnations of the USSR and seemed inclined to let Hua's presence speak for itself as an assertion of national and party sovereignty--that is, until vocal Soviet opposition to the visit provoked explicit restatements of these positions by Bucharest.[73] Provocative as this assertion of autonomy was, Romania is unlikely to veer far from its course of studied neutrality between Moscow and Peking, as a movement in either direction could foreclose on the very freedom of action that the Sino-Soviet split has provided the Romanian leadership.[74]

United States' support for Romanian deviance is similarly limited and, more importantly, of less value to Washington than to Peking. As U.S. priorities shifted toward insuring the prospering of direct US-Soviet detente, it became clear to the Romanians that American support for Romanian autonomy did, at the very least, take second place to the assuring of a low level of tension between the United States and the Soviet Union.[75] Still it is precisely such a low level of tension which allows the Romanians greater room for independent foreign policy choice. Thus when the Afghanistan invasion produced a serious deterioration in US-Soviet relations, the Romanians were eager to try to mitigate the effect on U.S.-Romanian relations[76] and overall European detente.[77] In terms of external support, however, the

West European states have been quite cautious about incurring Soviet wrath, and are unlikely to provide significant support for Romanian challenges to Soviet hegemony.

A full Romanian embrace of either the United States or China is likely to be deterred by Bucharest's recognition of two other factors. First, each of these powers has had important, though differing, reasons to be critical of Romania's domestic situation: The US, due to erratic but occasionally quite public human rights concerns; and China, due to equally erratic but equally public concerns over the purity of the revolution. Although both Washington and Peking now evidence less enthusiasm for their respective causes, these could emerge again and create significant sticking points in their relations with Romania. Second, greatly improving or increasing ties with either of Moscow's major adversaries--but especially China--would likely be a net loss for Romania as such actions would stir active attention and concern in the Kremlin.

As for other communist states, the Romanians do exchange expressions of political support with Yugoslavia and, to a lesser extent, North Korea.[78] But looking to the 1980s, neither the uncertain leadership situation in the former nor the extremely limited nature of support available from the latter can be very reassuring.

On the other hand, the RCP, as noted, has not retreated from--indeed they have reiterated--their support for Eurocommunism. Future support from this source would be derived in two ways. First, outspoken national communist leaders such as Enrico Berlinguer or Santiago Carillo will presumably continue to remind the CPSU of its proper international role, should it seem to be forgetting its pledge in East Berlin.[79] Second, if any of these parties should in fact come to power, diplomatic and economic benefits presumably would accrue to steadfast friends such as Ceausescu. Yet this European sword--more of a dagger actually--is two-sided. The prominence of a parliamentary alternative, a communist ruled state with open borders, relatively greater democracy and economic freedom, etc., might be too dangerous for Romania to embrace very warmly. On the other hand, the potential "demonstration" effect of such a state should be recognized but not overstated. The Romanian government was quite able in 1968 to both support the Czech party's "rennovation" of social and economic life and insulate itself from the infection such reforms might have carried.

Romania has also played a "Balkan card" from time to time; i.e., emphasizing the country's Balkan identity, history and the possibilities of Balkan cooperation and unity.[80] But given traditional Soviet antipathy to

Balkan unity, not to mention the enormous difficulties of achieving cooperation in that region, this course is unlikely to provide a solid platform on which to build a distinctive Romanian foreign policy.[81]

It is toward the developing countries of the Third World that Romania has cast its net in search of support. As noted earlier, Bucharest has engaged in a persistent campaign to modify its self-definition from that of a socialist country to that of a socialist <u>developing</u> country. In the RCP view, this sets it apart not only from the developed capitalist states but also from most of its East European allies who are developed socialist states. Bucharest has sought to buttress this position institutionally--by joining the Group of 77 for example--and politically through ardent support of the movement for a New International Economic Order.

The political returns Romania could derive from such a policy is uncertain. It could not in any event be termed decisive, or even vital to the continued pursuit of an independent foreign policy. But the revised self-definition and the activities that flow from it do give Romania a high degree of visibility in Third World fora, and having a populous, supportive "attentive public" such as the less developed countries might to some degree insulate Bucharest from at least overt Soviet pressure. This will be true, of course, only if the regime's international and domestic policy remain within certain parameters which are set, but not precisely defined, in the Kremlin. In the former category, for example, the Romanians have presumably reached the lower limits of permissable minimal contribution to the Warsaw Pact.[82] Domestically Moscow has made it clear that any serious challenge to the leading role of the party must be eliminated, a goal and policy which the RCP and Ceausescu ardently support.

External Economic Factors

Of all sources of external support, the economic is the most crucial. There are several dimensions to this factor. First, the contacts with the West are directed primarily at securing for Romania the technology and goods necessary to enable the Romanian economy to develop broadly and rapidly. To the degree that a deviant foreign policy is matched by trade gains, it is supported; it pays off. While Romania's trade with the capitalist states is second only to that of Poland, in recent years this trade appears to have reached its limits. This has occurred despite the granting by the United States in 1975 of MFN status and its annual extension since then. A chronic negative balance of payments situation, rather inelastic parameters in western markets for Romanian exports, increasing concern over mounting hard currency debt, and worries in Romania about tying the economy to the boom-and-bust cycles of the capitalist countries, are all conditions underlying this leveling off.[83] In an attempt perhaps to make up for its sagging ability to continue purchases in the West, the Romanians have increasingly turned to the use of joint production agreements. As of 1976, there were fifty-four such agreements with the United States, comprising a total second only to that of Poland.[84]

Romania has been able to greatly expand its export trade with the developing countries, a process which complements their shift in self-identification. This trade has more than tripled since 1960,[85] and according to the five-year plan, is expected to account for twenty-five percent of Romanian foreign trade by 1985.[86] Not only does this spur Romanian economic growth, especially in the vital machine and semi-manufactured goods sectors, but the diversification reduces Romanian vulnerability to pressures that might be exerted by its largest customer, the Soviet Union.

A factor of increasing significance will be the ability of the Romanians to continue to secure diversified and dependable energy supplies. Though, as noted above, they foresee a long-term drop in dependence on oil, their immediate need for imports--especially in light of economic growth targets--will continue to be significant (roughly half of the country's crude oil needs).[87] Romania has, until recently, not been buying Soviet oil and thus has a head start on its allies who are now searching for other suppliers as Moscow reduces the flow and raises the price for what does flow.[88] While this preference for OPEC suppliers does insulate them to some degree from possible Soviet pressure using this particular lever (Romania remains dependent on the USSR for a number of other important raw materials such as coking coal and iron ore), it does render them vulnerable to other kinds of often quite unexpected disruptions. The loss of an estimated five million tons of Iranian crude oil after the fall of the Shah, for example, sent Romanian diplomats and traders off in search of new supplies.[89]

In the Romanian case, almost as crucial as long term planning has been short term emergency assistance after natural disasters. The widespread flooding of 1970 and 1975 and the devastating earthquake of 1977 were all body blows to the industrial development of the country. If the Romanians were not able to recover quickly or if they were forced to severely curtail production in major sectors of the economy, the capacity of the country to support the foreign policy economically-- either through production of exportables or by producing sufficient domestic material payoffs--would be greatly reduced.[90]

Viewed from the opposite perspective, Romania is also a giver of aid. Since the period 1966-1970 when Romanian foreign aid averaged but forty million per year, aid commitments jumped to an average of $350 million per year for 1971-1975, by far the largest in Eastern Europe.[91] Large donors of foreign aid have found that such aid has not often purchased influence, or even good will, but Romanian aid does stimulate the sale of its exports and may benefit the Romanians politically as a supplement to its own "developing country" orientation.

External Military Support

The Romanian regime has learned two important and similar lessons about external military support. First, the lesson of 1968: the West will not risk war or even a worsening of relations with the USSR by opposing, with any more than token protest, Moscow's use of force in Eastern Europe. Second, the lesson of geography: China is simply too far away, too weak militarily, too unpredictable internally, and too preoccupied with its own Soviet border to offer any significant military support. Thus Romanian defense against a hypothetical Soviet attack, probably teamed with invasions from the west by Hungary and the south by Bulgaria, would depend almost entirely upon Romania's own capacities, with some assistance possibly from Yugoslavia. This does not mean, however, that Romania's non-Soviet contacts cannot serve concrete military purposes, as the acquisition of several Chinese gunboats and attack craft has indicated.[92] In the end, though, the continuation of Romanian foreign policy deviance depends on the leadership's ability to secure economic and political support where it can and avoid or prevent Soviet military intervention, rather than try to defeat such an intervention once begun.[93]

Level of Soviet Tolerance

While the unique course of Romanian foreign policy stems from indigenous causes, e.g., economic mobilization, desire for party legitimacy, and depends on political and economic support both at home and abroad, it also requires a degree of Soviet tolerance. No one could seriously doubt Soviet ability to curtail or stop altogether Romania's independent actions should Moscow become concerned or alarmed at the directions of such actions or their implications. Thus, to assess the factors underlying the future course of Romanian foreign policy one must discuss to some extent those factors underlying Soviet tolerance.[94]

Romania's military/geographic position, one of extreme vulnerability, is ironically a strength of sorts. A low level of Soviet threat perception due to the country's relative isolation, enables the Romanian leadership to engage in foreign policy actions which, if taken in Prague, might provoke a quite different response from the Soviet Union. Peter Bender, discussing the Romanian geographic position puts it as follows:

> NATO cannot break into the Eastern alliance there, either militarily or politically, and Bucharest cannot break out to the West. Even a neutral status like that of neighboring Yugoslavia hardly seems thinkable in this geographical position. On the other hand, this situation also has advantages for the Romanians. Because they are less important to their great ally, because it is 'sure' of them, they can allow themselves more independence of action. Moscow would probably not have permitted in any other party what it has allowed the Romanians to do since the mid-sixties.[95]

Since in the absence of a general European war this geopolitical situation is unlikely to change, Soviet perceptions of military threat from Romania are also likely to remain low. What could change this level of threat perception would be a serious Greek-Turkish conflict or, less likely, instability within the Bulgarian regime, either of which would present a Soviet rationale for increasing its pressure on Romania.

Less inconceivable, however, is another contingency which leaders in Bucharest can only envision with dread: a leadership crisis in Yugoslavia. The Soviet Union, among others, is vitally interested in the leadership personnel and policies of post-Tito Yugoslavia. Military demonstrations designed to support a pro-Soviet faction, or indeed even an "invited" introduction of troops, would substantially worsen the military situation for Romania, even without the actual stationing of Soviet troops on Romanian territory. On the other hand, a clear ascension to power of a group hostile to the Soviet Union, or one eager to press the Macedonian issue with Bulgaria, would be equally troubling to Romania as it too would be likely to stimulate increased Soviet attention--especially military attention--to the area. And in the nightmarish event of a complete fragmentation of the Yugoslav state, with the resulting regional and international tension, Ceausescu might well be expected to dust off his dramatic "call to arms" of August, 1968.[96] There is almost no future in Yugoslavia which the Romanians can contemplate with equanimity except one that virtually duplicates the present.

Most crucial to the Soviet view of its own security is its perception of the <u>political</u> threat, i.e., the threat of system-changing reforms which might fundamentally alter or undermine the socialist system in an East European state or, more seriously, spread to the Soviet Union itself. The lessons of Hungary, 1956, and of Czechoslovakia, 1968, and the Draconian reaction they produced are instructive. While Romania is not, as noted, in as sensitive a geographic position as Czechoslovakia, it does border on the Soviet Ukraine, where political stability and loyalty is a continuing Soviet concern, to say the least.[97] Any widespread or widely publicized internal political or economic reform in Romania which the Soviet Union could interpret as having broader ramifications would very likely call forth as forceful a reaction as those mentioned above. While it is a simplification to say that the Romanians have made an explicit deal with Moscow to keep a tight reign at home in return for tolerance of their deviance in foreign policy, the RCP's ardent desire to maintain stability and control of domestic politics does serve <u>inter alia</u> its foreign policy goals by not allowing actions that would arouse Soviet suspicion, alarm or ultimately intervention.

The breadth of Soviet tolerance is also affected by the status of Sino-Soviet relations. It should be recalled that the original Romanian deviance took place under extremely favorable conditions. Khrushchev was preoccupied with keeping peace in his backyard while dealing with Mao Zedong, and in particular with frustrating further Chinese enchroachment into Eastern Europe.[98] As Soviet concern with Chinese-Romanian relations increased in the early 70s, Soviet pressure seemed to exercise a significant limiting effect on those relations. To state future contingencies in their extremes, in the unlikely event of a substantial Soviet-Chinese rapprochement, the Romanians would be denied even the limited leverage they presently enjoy. Conversely, in the event of full scale hostilities in the Far East, Moscow would be increasingly ill-disposed towards continued Romanian "neutrality."

Soviet economic relations with the rest of the world also affect Romanian deviance indirectly. Reference has already been made to Moscow's weaning of its allies from the Soviet oil supply. Decisions such as this, derived both from Soviet domestic and from international factors, affect the trading policy and capabilities of the East European states, though the Romanians are in a somewhat better position in this regard. In addition there is the position of the Soviet Union as a partner to Western trade and credit, one with much greater attractiveness than Romania due, at the very least, to sheer size. As hard currency debt mounts and Western markets for Eastern goods reach their limits, it is likely to be the smaller Eastern countries who are shut out. This is especially true to the degree that trade is seen as an economic complement to detente. In addition, direct Soviet--East European economic relations need to be considered, as the Soviet Union can in a number of ways spur or retard both the trade and internal economic development of its allies.[99] In this respect, however, the Romanian economy, less developed, less dependent on the Soviet Union and having a more diversified import and export structure, seems to be in a better position.

Finally, internal political developments in the Soviet Union affect the limits of Soviet tolerance of all types of deviance, domestic and international. The weakness of the Khrushchev regime in its final days, and the uncertainty in the initial period of the Brezhnev-Kosygin regime, allowed greater latitude for the Romanian policies of the 60s. The present Soviet leadership, with Brezhnev more firmly in control, has nevertheless been willing to live with its maverick ally assuming its continued respect for certain limits; but should the internal dynamics of the Soviet regime bring to power a more conservative group, Romanian foreign policy would very likely come under close scrutiny.

Milieu--Opportunity Factors

In addition to the two sets of factors which directly stimulate or allow Romanian foreign policy deviance, there is a third dimension which should be recognized, that of milieu or opportunity. It should be recalled by observers of Romanian foreign policy--especially those interested in charting the country's independent course--that there needs to be opportunities for the assertion of that independence. Foreign policy actions take place in certain arenas which may or may not provide opportunities for the assertion of a distinctive position. More broadly, international events which occasion such assertions may be present or absent; and may or may not be uniquely appropriate to such assertions, e.g., Czechoslovakia, 1968, Afghanistan, 1980. One of the chief differences between the period 1965-1970 and 1970-1975, for example, was the relative lack of such opportunities in the latter period.

Moreover, many of the initiatives of Romanian party and state which were dramatic acts showing autonomy in 1967, such as the recognition of West Germany, have been ultimately imitated by the other East European states, diluting the present--though not the past--uniqueness of

the Romanian position. Similarly, Romanian defense of
the right of each communist party to set its own policies and follow its own national line may appear rather
superflous now given the formal acquiesence of the CPSU
to the legitimacy of this notion. However, to the
degree that Moscow acts as if, in <u>extremis</u>,it still knows
best, then Romanian adherence to its position would once
again appear distinctive.

One should not overemphasize the milieu aspect,
however. Certain "opportunities" do persist, for
example, in fora such as Comecon, the Warsaw Pact and the
United Nations. Others can be created by, for example,
ostentatiously entertaining the leader of one of Moscow's
<u>betes noires</u>. The point of deliniating this factor
separately in an analysis of the future directions of
Romanian foreign policy is to remind ourselves of the
need to take account of the <u>milieu</u> within which foreign
policy takes place. Romanian foreign policy needs to be
assessed contemporaneously. Assertions of foreign
autonomy by Bucharest serve certain important purposes
and thus can be expected to persist, within limits, as
long as they continue to serve such goals and as long as
the goals themselves persist. But such assertions will
also depend to a degree upon the appearance of appropriate opportunities. The Romanians have demonstrated
remarkable skill in both recognizing and exploiting,
albeit carefully, such opportunities. It is the task of
the analyst to be as keen in his assessment of the
<u>milieu</u> in arriving at a judgment of Romanian policy.

CONCLUSION

Romanian foreign policy, like the foreign policy of
any state, is a product, a mix of stimulating and enabling factors and of opportunity. It is appropriate in
concluding to move further out on the limb to underscore
the significance of those factors considered most crucial to the future directions of Romanian foreign policy.

Romanian policy is dependent upon: 1) the performance of its domestic economy; related to this, 2) the
continued willingness of the population to defer
material gratification while the country achieves
"multilateral development", and 3) the continued need of
the regime to pursue national authority--as opposed to
power--through its foreign policy. The RCP so far has
been able to provide "psychic payoffs" to the population in the currency of Romanian nationalism, international visibility and prestige, and, to a lesser
extent, general assertions of progress. In this connection, Ken Jowitt's phrase is apt, "domestically the
regime is in a race." [100] Such a description also
applies to the regime's ability to continue to purchase

legitimacy with a nationalized foreign policy and to hold off ethnic/cultural pressure and political demands which might threaten the position of the RCP. How long this trade-off will continue to work is difficult to predict, but present signs seem to point to a tunnel at the end of the light.

Internationally, Romanian economic growth and the independent foreign policy are tied to economic relations with the West, to a lesser extent with the developing countries, and to a considerable degree with its East European and Soviet trading partners. Thus the vitality of the domestic economy, which both supports and feeds upon the international policy, depends in great measure on economic and political conditions outside its control, in the developed East and West and in the developing world. Perhaps more quickly and to a greater degree than its socialist allies, the Romanians have had to learn the lessons, good and bad, of interdependence. The manner in which the RCP chooses to negotiate the dangerous shoals of this interdependence--of East European interdependence--in the 1980s will determine the overall directions of Romania's foreign policy for this decade.

NOTES

1. David Floyd, Rumania: Russian's Dissident Ally (New York: Praeger, 1965).
2. Robert L. Farlow, "Romanian Foreign Policy: A Case of Partial Alignment," Problems of Communism (November-December, 1971), pp. 54-63.
3. M. K. Dziewanowski, "The Pattern of Rumanian Independence," East Europe, vol. 18, no. 6 (June, 1969), pp. 8-12.
4. R. V. Burks, "The Rumanian National Deviation: An Accounting," in Kurt London (ed.) Eastern Europe in Transition (Baltimore: The Johns Hopkins University Press, 1966), pp. 93-113.
5. See the discussion in John M. Montias, "Background and Origins of the Rumanian Dispute with Comecon," Soviet Studies, vol. 16, no. 2 (October, 1964), pp. 125-152.
6. "Directivele Congresului al II-lea al PMR cu Privire la Planul de Dezvoltare a Economiei Nationale pe Anii 1960-1965 si al Schita Planului Economic de Prespectiva pe 15 Ani," in Congresul al III-Lea al Partidului Muncitoresc Romin (Bucharest: Editura Politica, 1961), pp. 645-697.
7. Text in English in William E. Griffith, Sino-Soviet Relations 1967-1968, (Cambridge: MIT Press, 1967), pp. 269-296.
8. Ibid., pp. 282-283.
9. Ibid., p. 282.
10. For a fuller discussion of these and other Romanian positions, see: Ronald H. Linden, Bear and Foxes: The International Relations of the East European States, (New York: Columbia University Press, 1979); Jeanne K. Laux, "Intra-Alliance Politics and European Detente: The Case of Poland and Romania," Studies in Comparative Communism VIII, 1 & 2 (Spring/Summer, 1975), pp. 98-122; Robert R. King, "Rumania: The Difficulty of Maintaining an Autonomous Foreign Policy," in Robert R. King and Robert W. Dean, East European Perspectives on European Security and Cooperation, (New York: Praeger, 1974), pp. 168-190.
11. Trade statistics in English can be found in Paul Marer, Soviet and East European Foreign Trade, 1946-1969, Statistical Compendium and Guide (Bloomington: Indiana University Press, 1972), pp. 30, 40; and John M. Montias, "Romania's Foreign Trade: An Overview" in Joint Economic Committee, East European Economies Post-Helsinki: A Compendium of Papers (Washington: U.S. Government Printing Office, 1977), pp. 865-885. The main Romanian source is Anuarul Statistic al Republicii Socialiste Romania 19--published by Directie Centrala de statistica, Bucharest. See also Comertul Exterior

al Republicii Socialiste Romania, 1973 (Bucharest: Directia Centrala de Statistica, N.D.).

12. See Linden, op. cit., pp. 10-52.

13. See King, op. cit.; Robert F. King, "Rumania and the Sino-Soviet Conflict," Studies in Comparative Communism, 5, 4 (Winter, 1972), pp. 373-393; Graeme J. Gill, "Rumania: Background to Autonomy," Survey, 21, 3 (Summer, 1975), pp. 94-113. One observer has even been moved to suggest that Bucharest's past policies were not in fact as independent as they appeared and thus the present path is simply more of the same. See Vladimir Socor, "The Limits of National Independence in the Soviet Bloc: Rumania's Foreign Policy Reconsidered," Orbis, 20, 3 (Fall 1976), pp. 701-732, and the letter by Robert R. King in response, Orbis, 21, 2 (Summer 1977), pp. 423-427.

14. See the discussion in Nicolai Ecobescu and Sergiu Celac, Politica externa a Romaniei Socialiste (Bucharest: Editura Politica, 1975). On limited sovereignty, see Ceausescu's "Expose made at the jubilee meeting of the Grand National Assembly Dedicated to the 50th anniversary of the Union of Transylvania with Romania," November 29, 1968, and his "Speech delivered at the All-Country Conference of the Teaching Staff," February 7, 1969, both in Romania on the Way of Completing Socialist Construction, 5, 3 (Bucharest: Meridiane Publishing House, 1969); see pp. 682-683 and 826. Cf. Gheorghe Moca, Socialislmul si suveranitatea de stat (Bucharest: Editura Politica, 1972).

15. El. Florea, "Cu Privire la evolutia conceptutuli marxist natiune," Analele Institutului de Studii Istorice si Social-Politice de pe linga CC al PCR, 12, 6 (1967), pp. 66-79; M. Marian, "Comunitatea de natiune," in Ibid., pp. 54-65; Ana Gavrila, "Natiunea socialista-etapa superiora in viata natiunilor," Analele Institutului de Studii Istorice si Social-Politice de pe linga CC al PCR, 14, 5 (1968), pp. 101-108. Cf. essays by Ervin Hutira and Constantin Vlad in Forta Creatoarea Ideilor Leniniste (Bucharest: Editura Politica, 1970) and speech by Ceausescu at the 1972 National Conference of the Romanian Communist Party in Romania on the Way of Building up the Multilaterally Developed Socialist Society, 5, 7 (Bucharest: Meridiane Publishing House, 1973); see pp. 501-506. I. Madosa, "Independence--A Sine Qua Non for Actual International Cooperation," Lumea no. 9, March 28, 1979.

16. See Ceausescu's Report to the Eleventh Congress of the RCP in Congresul al XI-lea al Partidului Comunist Roman (Bucharest: Editura Politica, 1975), pp. 41-42. Cf. Romulus Caplescu, "An Important Contribution to the Assertion of the New Principles of Relations in the International Communist Movement, to Strengthening

Solidarity in the Struggle for Security, Peace and Social Progress," <u>Lumea</u>, no. 20, July 14-20, 1978, pp. 25-26; Constantin Florea, "RCP's Stand on New Phenomena and Trends in the Communist and Workers' Movement," <u>Era Socialista</u>, no. 19 (1978), pp. 30-34.

17. "Statement on the stand of the Rumanian Workers' Party. . ." in Griffith, <u>op. cit.</u>, p. 284. Cf. Alexandru Puiu, <u>Comertul Exterior si Rolul Lui in Realizarea Programului de Dezvoltare Economica a Romaniei</u> (Bucharest: Editura Politica, 1974).

18. See, e.g., N. Ecobescu, "A Ban on Nuclear Weapons--the Imperative Demand of the Peoples," <u>Lumea</u>, no. 1, March 3, 1978, pp. 10-12; "Disarmament--Top-of-the-line Priority," <u>Lumea</u>, no. 16, April 20-26, 1979, p. 16; George Serafin, "European Security--Imperative of Continuity, of Constructive Efforts," <u>Idem.</u>, pp. 8-9. Corneliu Bogdan, "Europe in a Changing World," <u>Revue roumaine d'etudes internationales</u>, 11, no. 2 (36), 1977, pp. 1-12.

19. The impact of the shift in Romania's self-definition from a socialist country to a socialist <u>developing</u> country can be seen in a comparison of Ceausescu's reports to the Tenth and Eleventh Congresses of the RCP. At the Tenth Congress, held in 1969, section VI of Ceausescu's report, "Romania--Active Factor in the Struggle for the Triumph of Socialism and Peace in the World" was divided as follows:

1. Report on forces worldwide
2. In the center of our foreign policy--friendship and collaboration with the socialist countries
3. An extensive international activity in the spirit of peaceful coexistence
4. Strengthening internationalist solidarity with communist and workers parties, with all anti-imperialist forces

At the Eleventh Congress, in 1974, section II of Ceausescu's report entitled, "The Activity and International Policy of the Party and State between the Two Congresses, the Guiding Lines of the Future Policies of Romania in the World Arena," was divided as follows:

1. The great changes produced in the development of the contemporary world
2. The consistent development of friendship and collaboration of our country with all socialist countries
3. Multilateral collaboration with developing countries, with all the states of the world, in the interest of the cause of progress, detente and international peace

4. The necessity of eliminating underdevelopment, of establishing a new world political and economic order, of democratizing international relations, of creating a better and more just world
   5. Disarmament--an urgent requirement of detente and peace, a vital cause of all people
   6. The internationalist policy of the RCP, the strengthening of collaboration and solidarity with all communist parties, with socialist and democratic parties, with the progressive, revolutionary, anti-imperialist forces of the whole world.

See Congresul al X-lea al Partidului Comunist Roman (Bucharest: Editura Politica, 1969), pp. 74-89; Congresul al XI-lea al Partidului Comunist Roman (Bucharest: Editura Politica, 1975), pp. 21-44. For Ceausescu's designation of Romania as a developing country see his speech to a 1972 National Conference of the RCP in Romania, vol. 7, pp. 519-520. For a discussion of Romania's policies in this regard see Ion Barac, "Romania and the Developing Countries," Revue roumaine d'etudes internationales, 11, 1 (35), 1977, pp. 55-72.
   20. See, e.g., Silviu Brucan, Democratizarea relatiilor internationale: premise si realitati, (Bucharest: Editura Politica, 1975); Marin Voiculescu and Victor Dulculescu, "La democratisation des relations internationales dans le processus d'edification d'un nouvel ordre mondial," Revue roumaine d'etudes internationales, 11, 1 (35), 1977, pp. 17-32.
   21. Barac, op. cit., p. 72. Cf. Ion Mielcioiu, "The Colombo Conference of the heads of state or government of the non-aligned countries, Romania's participation," Revue roumaine d'etudes internationales, 11, 1 (35), 1977, pp. 73-88.
   22. The Romanians have proposed among other things, increasing the size of the Security Council--"taking account of such factors as the increased role played by small and medium-size States"--to include geographically rotated permanent members, i.e., those possessing a veto; and several measures designed to increase the power of the General Assembly vis-a-vis the Security Council. See Report to the Special Committee on the Charter of the United Nations and on the Strengthening of the Organization, United Nations, General Assembly, Official Records: Thirty-Second Session, Supplement No. 33 (A/32/33), pp. 176-181. Cf. "Demands for a Greater UN Role in the Settlement of our World Problems," Lumea, no. 28, September 7-15, 1978, pp. 6-7.
   23. Radio Free Europe Research (hereafter RFER), January 20, 1977; cf. Montias, op. cit., pp. 882-885.

24. RFER, November 15, 1976.
25. See RFER, March 9, 1978; Recent statements of Romanian views on European security are contained in Serafin, op. cit., and Bogdan, op. cit.
26. Unlike its allies, Romania supported the Camp David Middle East peace framework (Scinteia, September 22, 1978) and the peace treaty which eventually emerged between Egypt and Israel (Scinteia, March 15, 1979). Bucharest also condemned the invasion of Cambodia by Vietnam in terms reminiscent of its views of the Soviet invasion of Czechoslovakia in 1968: "No kind of motive or argument can justify intervention and interference into the affairs of another state--under whatever form this should appear--especially when the two countries in question are socialist!" (Scinteia, January 10, 1979). When China invaded Vietnam the next month, however, the Romanians confined themselves to a general call for peaceful settlement of international conflicts and the withdrawal of "all foreign troops within national frontiers." (Scinteia, February 20, 1979).
27. Carrillo was invited to Bucharest in August, 1977 at a time when he was the subject of harsh attacks from the CPSU. See RFER, August 4-10, 1977. Carrillo returned to Bucharest in August, 1978 (see Scinteia, August 29, 1978) and again in November, 1979 for the RCP Twelfth Congress (Bucharest Domestic Service, November 11, 1979).
28. See RFER, June 15, 1976, and August 12, 1976.
29. See RFER, January 30, 1978, and October 11, 1978; for a review of Romanian and Soviet historiography on the issue see, Jack Gold, "Bessarabia: The Thorny 'Non-Existent' Problem" East European Quarterly, 13, #1, Spring, 1979, pp. 47-74.
30. See King, "Rumania and the Sino-Soviet Conflict."
31. The following is a preliminary list of reported visits since the death of Mao Tse-tung (through December, 1978):

Romanian Delegations	to China
November, 1976	P. Niculescu*
December, 1976	Party/Govt.
March/April, 1977	Military
June, 1977	Party
July, 1977	Econ., Sci. & Tech.
September, 1977	Party/Govt.
December, 1977	Trade**
February, 1978	Government
March, 1978	Government
April, 1978	Military Press
May, 1978	Ceausescu
June, 1978	Transport; Cultural

June, 1978	Party
July, 1978	Government
September, 1978	M. Manescu (P.M.)
September, 1978	Military
December, 1978	P. Niculescu*

Chinese Delegations to Romania

December, 1976	Party
January, 1977	Trade
May, 1977	Party/Govt.
June, 1977	Military
Aug./Sept., 1977	Party/Govt.
September, 1977	Military
March, 1978	Tech., Econ.; Econ.
March, 1978	Party
April, 1978	Cultural
April, 1978	Government
April, 1978	Trade
May, 1978	Mining
June, 1978	Military
June, 1978	State planning
August, 1978	Hua Guofeng
September, 1978	Economic

*Member of RCP Executive Committee, Deputy Premier and one of Ceausescu's closest associates.
**In November, 1977, Ceausescu's son Nicolae visited China as head of a delegation from the Union of Communist Youth.

Source: RFER reports

 32. See Scinteia, May 16-20, 1978.
 33. Scinteia, August 16-22, 1978.
 34. See TASS of August 28, September 1 and September 4, 1978. Cf. Vladimir Goncharov, "'The European Cards' of the Peking Pharisees," Literaturnaya Gazeta, August 30, 1978. On September 3, Scinteia replied, saying, inter alia, "Unfortunately, it has to be shown that, in with the current commentaries in connection with this visit, at the same time are heard some dissonant voices, expressing malevolent interpretations, trying to misinform public opinion, to misrepresent the clear sense and constructive character of the visit, to present it in an unjust and tendentious light. Ignoring completely the facts, the content and aims of the visit, exposed openly, publicly, not only in the official declarations, but also in the documents adopted, these Western papers have published commentaries--few in number indeed-- which, appealing exclusively to fantasy, have tried to attribute to the visit completely different meanings

and significancies other than the real ones. Of course, in a way, the appearance of some such malevolent commentaries is not surprising, as it is well known that the same newspapers seek the sensational and sometimes do not even refrain from trying to provoke animosities and conditions of tension among states, to harm their relations of friendship and collaboration. It is, however, an incomprehensible fact that the press organs of some socialist countries have not taken objective realistic assessments of the visit, but have appealed precisely to the same tendentious unnatural interpretations, full or innuendoes in assessing the visit and in informing public opinion." Cf. Eugeniu Obrea, "Vigorous Assertion of National Independence Policies in the Service of Socialism and Peace," Lumea, no. 28, September 15-21, 1978, pp. 2-4.

35. See Ceausescu's New Year's Message (Excerpts), Scinteia, January 3, 1980, p. 1.

36. Ceausescu's New Year's Message (Text), Scinteia, January 4, 1980, p. 4; cf. his opening address to the Socialist Unity Front Congress, Scinteia, January 18, 1980 (FBIS, January 22, 1980, pp. H8, 11).

37. For a text of the resolution, see New York Times, January 15, 1980, p. A8.

38. The Romanians explained that they had wanted a resolution which would lead to "guarantees" that there would be no interference in the internal affairs of Afghanistan and "that no state will grant support to the antigovernment forces in that country." Bucharest Domestic Service, January 15, 1980.

39. And as he had after the Hua Guofeng visit, Soviet Foreign Minister Andrei Gromyko visited Bucharest, from January 31 to February 2. Agerpress, February 1 and 2, 1980.

40. These changes are outlined in Linden, op. cit., pp. 280-281, n 100.

41. See the discussions in Kenneth Jowitt, "Political Innovation in Rumania," Survey, 20, 4 (Autumn, 1974), pp. 132-151; and Mary Ellen Fischer, "Participatory Reforms and Political Development in Romania," in Jan F. Triska and Paul M. Cocks (eds.), Political Development in Eastern Europe (New York: Praeger, 1977), pp. 217-237.

42. Originally consisting of five members, this Bureau has grown steadily, and at the Twelfth Congress of the RCP was expanded to fifteen members. See RFER, November 28, 1979.

43. For two recent examples, see Scinteia, November 27, 1979, p. 3 and November 30, 1979, pp. 3-4. At the same time the entire Ceausescu family, but especially his wife Elena, have enjoyed wondrous success in their political careers. See RFER, February 5, 1980; New York Times, November 27, 1979, p. 2.

44. Mention of such an opposition can be found in Jowitt, op. cit., and in Trond Gilberg, "Romania: Problems of the Multilaterally Developed Society," in Charles Gati, ed., The Politics of Modernization in Eastern Europe (New York: Praeger, 1974), p. 148. One extraordinary event which may reflect the existence of an opposition of uncertain size was the speech at the Twelfth Congress of Constantin Privulescu, a veteran party stalwart of 84, who rose to accuse Ceausescu of placing his own interests above those of the country, and who declared--while others were exulting in the General Secretary's leadership--that he would not vote for his reelection. See RFER, November 28, 1979. For Bucharest's scant reportage, see Agerpress, November 23, 1979.

45. Much as I would like to claim this term for my own, it was part of Kenneth Jowitt's remarks at an Academic Roundtable on Romania, U.S. State Department, Washington, D.C., October 12, 1977.

46. See Daniel N. Nelson, "Sub-national Political Elites in a Communist System: Contrasts and Conflicts in Romania," East European Quarterly, 10, 4 (Winter 1976), pp. 459-494.

47. See, e.g., RFER, December 6, 1977, June 5, 1978, September 27, 1978 and May 4, 1979.

48. In December, 1979, the Political Executive Committee approved a proposal from the Socialist Unity Front for increasing the number of constituencies where two candidates would run for seats in the Grand National Assembly. Bucharest Domestic Service, December 12, 1979. For a discussion of these elections, see Fischer, op. cit.

49. See Montias, "Romania's Foreign Trade;" Marer, op. cit.

50. Josef C. Brada and Marvin R. Jackson, "Strategy and Structure in the Organization of Romanian Foreign Trade Activities, 1967-1975," in East European Economies Post-Helsinki, pp. 1260-1276.

51. Through 1979 Romania had utilized some $905 million in western, government-backed credits; $563 million in World Bank credits; and $385 million in IMF credits. See National Foreign Assessment Center, Estimating Soviet and East European Hard Currency Debt (Washington: Central Intelligency Agency, 1980), p. 11

52. See Thad P. Alton, "Comparative Structure and Growth of Economic Activity in Eastern Europe," in East European Economies Post-Helsinki, pp. 199-266.

53. Montias, "Romania's Foreign Trade."

54. Through 1979 Romania's net hard currency debt was an estimated $6.7 billion; see National Foreign Assessment Center, op. cit., p. 11.

55. See the discussion in Marvin R. Jackson, "Industrialization, Trade, and Mobilization in Romania's Drive

for Economic Independence," in East European Economies Post-Helsinki, pp. 886-970.

56. See his speech to the Bucharest party organization, Scinteia, November 9, 1979, pp. 1, 3; and his Report to the Twelfth Congress, reprinted (in English) in "Ceausescu: 19 November Report to Twelfth RCP Congress", FBIS Daily Report, Supplement, vol. 2, #238, supp. 038 (hereafter Ceausescu Report), esp. pp. 10, 11.

57. See speeches of Ilie Verdet (Prime Minister), Scinteia, November 21, 1979; Cornel Burtica (Minister of Foreign Trade), Scinteia, November 23, 1979; Paul Niculescu (Minister of Finance), Scinteia, November 22, 1979.

58. See Ceausescu Report, pp. 11-20.

59. See speech to Twelfth Congress of Virgil Trofin --who after the Congress replaced Vasilie Patilinet as Minister of Mines, Petroleum and Geology--Scinteia, November 21, 1979, pp. 11, 12.

60. At the Congress Ceausescu announced the discovery of new oil deposits beneath the Black Sea. See Ceausescu Report, p. 13.

61. RFER, August 12, 1977 and September 8, 1978.

62. See Ceausescu Report, pp. 6-9, 26-30.

63. RFER, August 12, 1977 and September 8, 1978.

64. For a comprehensive discussion of Romania's development strategy, see Trond Gilberg, "Comparative Developmental Strategies in the Communist Balkans: Romania," Paper prepared for the annual convention of the American Association for the Advancement of Slavic Studies, New Haven, October 10-13, 1979.

65. See the discussion in Linden, pp. 193-196; cf. George Schopflin, "Rumanian Nationalism," Survey, 20, 2/3 (Spring/Summer 1974), pp. 77-104.

66. RFER, June 22, 1977.

67. See the letter to the Central Committee by Karoly Kiraly, former alternate member of the RCP Presidium and member of the Central Committee, in The New York Times, February 1, 1978, p. 23; cf. Manuel Lucbert, "La minorite hongroise de Transylvanie est necontente de son sort," Le Monde, May 5, 1978, p. 4.

68. In an apparent attempt to satisfy cultural demands without weakening the country's political unity, the government has been willing to allow a degree of linguistic expression to remain, e.g., lower level education in Magyar, while circumscribing the regional autonomy of the Hungarian minority. See Mary Ellen Fischer, "Nation and Nationality in Romania," in George W. Simonds, ed., Nationalism in the USSR and Eastern Europe in the Era of Brezhnev and Kosygin (Detroit: University of Detroit Press, 1977), pp. 504-521. Cf. Francois Fejto, A History of the Peoples Democracies (New York: Praeger, 1971), pp. 200-201.

69. The three counties containing the largest German minorities (Brasov, Sibiu and Timis) together account for almost fourteen percent of Romania's industrial production, and these counties production figures represent, respectively, 2.75, 1.59 and 1.16 times their shares of the national population. See <u>Anuarul Statistic</u>, pp. 94-95; comparison based on <u>procedures used in</u> Fischer, <u>op. cit</u>., p. 517. As of 1966, 58.5 percent of the German population were classified as workers, compared with 45.9 percent of the Hungarian and 38.9 percent of the Romanian; in contrast, only 20.6 percent were engaged in farming compared with 45.2 percent of the Romanian and 36.2 percent of the Hungarian population. <u>Recensamintul Populatiei si Loucintelor din Martie 1966</u>, cited in Gilberg, <u>op. cit</u>., p. 140.

70. For a discussion along these lines, see Gilberg, "Romania: Problems."

71. See Jacques Levesque, <u>Le Conflit sino-sovietique et l'Europe de l'Est</u> (Montreal: Les Presses de l'Universite de Montreal, 1970), pp. 97-281.

72. See Robert R. King, "Rumania and the Sino-Soviet Conflict," <u>Studies in Comparative Communism</u>, 5, 4 (Winter 1972), pp. 373-412.

73. See Obrea, <u>op. cit</u>., pp. 2-4.

74. In October, 1978, for example, Ceausescu entertained a Soviet delegation led by Foreign Minister Andrei Gromyko (Agerpress, October 14-15, 1978).

75. While such a policy had in fact been evident in U.S. behavior toward East Europe, it was never explicitly enunciated as official policy until the views of State Department Counsellor Helmut Sonnenfeldt became public in March, 1976 (<u>Washington Post</u>, March 22, 1976, p. 19). At a briefing for U.S. European ambassadors in London the previous December, Sonnenfeldt had said, among other things; "It must be our (U.S.) policy to strive for an evolution that makes the relationship between the Eastern Europeans and the Soviet Union an organic one. Any excess of zeal on our part is bound to produce results that could reverse the desired process for a period of time, even though the process would remain inevitable within the next 100 years. But, of course, for us that is too long a time to wait... So our policy must be a policy of responding to the clearly visible aspirations of Eastern Europe for a more autonomous existence within the context of a strong Soviet geopolitical influence." See the State Department summary of Sonnenfeldt's remarks, <u>New York Times</u>, April 6, 1976, p. 14. Both President Ford and Secretary of State Kissinger were quick to try to modify both the wording and impact of this statement with statements of their own. See <u>New York Times</u>, April 6, 1976, pp. 1, 14 and April 7, 1976, p. 16. For Romanian reaction to

Sonnenfeldt's remarks, see Scinteia, April 13, 1976.

76. U.S. Undersecretary of State David Newsom visited Romania from January 26 to 28 and met with both Ceausescu and Foreign Minister Stefan Andrei. RFER, February 4, 1980.

77. In Ceausescu's speech to the Socialist Unity Front Congress he called the situation "tenser than at any time since World War II" and said, "We must prevent the current international tension from worsening relations in Europe." Scinteia, January 18, 1980 (FBIS, January 22, pp. H8, 11).

78. For a discussion of the latter see Jowitt, "Political Innovation," pp. 133-135.

79. For a discussion suggesting that the CPSU has indeed already done so, see Walter C. Clemens, Jr., The USSR and Global Interdependence (Washington, D.C.: American Enterprise Institute, 1978), pp. 57-58.

80. For a discussion see Linden, op. cit., p. 194, 277n81; cf. RFER, March 1, 1976 and March 4, 1977. During the period 1958-1972 Romanian exports to other Balkan countries (excluding Albania) grew at a faster rate than those of any other Balkan country. In addition, the percentage of Romania's total exports accounted for by sales to its neighbors was the highest for any of the Balkan states, though still modest at 5.76 percent; Romania's Balkan imports represented 4.56 percent of Romanian imports. See Eleftherios N. Botsas, "The Big Powers and Inter-Balkan Economic Relations," East European Quarterly, 12, 3 (Fall 1978), pp. 275-277. More recently, Bucharest refloated the idea of creating a "Zone of Peace" in the region. See Agerpress, March 13, 1979.

81. Obstacles to inter-Balkan cooperation would include: the differing status of the states' alliance commitments; their differences in political and economic structures; great differences in culture, religion and history; several contentious, even peace-threatening, issues between them, e.g., Cyprus; and some highly controversial issues of terra irridenta, such as Macedonia.

82. Indeed the most recent public dispute between Moscow and Bucharest erupted over the latter's refusal to increase its contributions to the WTO by increasing national defense spending. The Romanian rejection of this suggestion, put forth at a November, 1978 meeting of the WTO Political Consultative Committee in Moscow, was promptly publicized heavily in Romania as were supporting resolutions by all relevant organs. See Scinteia, November 25 and 26, 1978; and Ceausescu's speech to representatives of the Army and of the Ministry of Interior, November 27, 1978, (Agerpress, same date) and to the Plenary of the CC of RCP, November 29, 1978 (Agerpress, same date). The Soviet view of the Romanian position was expressed by Brezhnev in a speech

on December 5. "We are ready," he said, "for the most radical steps leading to disarmament, but at all stages of the struggle to achieve this end the principle of the equal security of the sides must be observed. We will not weaken our defense in the face of the growing military might of imperialism, whatever demogogic arguments are used to cover appeals for this," See Pravda, December 7, 1978.

83. See Montias, "Romania's Foreign Trade."

84. Data presented by Paul Marer at an Academic Roundtable on Romania, U.S. State Department, October 12, 1977.

85. See Montias, "Romania's Foreign Trade," pp. 883-885.

86. Ceausescu Report, p. 25.

87. RFER, November 2, 1979.

88. See John R. Haberstroh, "Eastern Europe: Growing Energy Problems," in East European Economies Post-Helsinki, pp. 379-395; cf. New York Times, November 21, 1977, pp. 53-55. RFER of November 23, 1979 quotes Reuters and UPI as reporting an undisclosed deal by which Romania was to have imported 350,000 tons of Soviet oil in 1979.

89. RFER, March 23, 1979; November 2, 1979. In October 1978 the government also successfully concluded long negotiations with Canada for the purchase of a nuclear reactor, the first such sale to an East European state. RFER, October 23, 1978.

90. Statistics on the relief assistance Romania received after the 1977 earthquake can be found in RFER, March 18, 1977 and April 1, 1977. At the Twelfth Congress Ceausescu stated that the earthquake had caused over two billion dollars in damages and affected over 760 economic units. He also indicated that evidently the old issue of economic self-determination was not dead:

> As is known, certain foreign circles--including some of our friends--were of the opinion that this huge catastrophe would set Romania back many years and that practically speaking, it would no longer be able to further implement the provisions of the current five-year plan. However, reality showed that, closely united around the party, our people, working day and night and sacrificing their days of rest, were able to overcome the difficulties; they quickly brought back to normal all socioeconomic activities and insured the integral fulfillment of the plan of development of the country, thus demonstrating the strength of a people who are masters of their destinies and consciously building their

own future, the force of socialism that we are building in Romania.

Ceausescu <u>Report</u>, p. 9.

91. <u>RFER</u>, April 29, 1977.

92. According to <u>The Military Balance</u>, 1979-1980 (London: International Institute for Strategic Studies, 1979), Romania has twenty-eight fast attack gun boats and twenty torpedo-equipped hydrofoils built in China (p. 16).

93. For a discussion of "Active Romanian military defenses of foreign policy autonomy," see Aurel Braun, <u>Romanian Foreign Policy Since 1965</u> (New York: Praeger, 1978), pp. 144-189.

94. It should be noted that there are those who suggest that, rather than being merely tolerated, Romanian foreign policy deviance is in fact a complex, Soviet-manipulated charade. According to this view, evident in Socor, <u>op. cit.</u>, the USSR allows the Romanians to pursue their apparently differing policies in order to maintain channels of communications with various Soviet <u>betes noires</u>, e.g., the PRC. While it is true that in the early sixties the Romanian party did attempt (unsuccessfully) to mediate the emerging Sino-Soviet dispute, such attempts occurred well before the vigorous public delineation by Bucharest of a divergent foreign policy. Clearly, communications channels do not require the enunciation of such a policy for their maintenance. To accept such a view--Socor labels Romanian policy an "impersonation of independence" (p. 728)--is to ignore or systematically discount the diverse behavioral and attitudinal aspects of Romania's foreign policy over the last two decades. Further, this view must also embrace an assessment of Soviet manipulative capacity well beyond any shown to have been held by the USSR, and to do so on the basis of virtually no supporting evidence

95. Peter Bender, <u>East Europe in Search of Security</u> (Baltimore: Johns-Hopkins University Press, 1972), p. 112.

96. Indeed after the Soviet invasion of Afghanistan, Ceausescu told the Socialist Unity Front Congress that "we have to make every possible effort to strengthen the unity and strength of our nation and our socialist state, to bolster the determination and will of all the people to defend their revolutionary achievements, their sacred right to be free and masters of their own country, and to build their new life in accordance with their wishes, without any foreign interference, to build their communist future on the ancient soil of their fatherland." <u>Scinteia</u>, January 18, 1980 (FBIS, January 22, 1980, p. H8).

97. For a discussion of the significance of the

Ukraine in the Soviet view of Czechoslovakia in 1968, the Grey Hodnett and Peter J. Potichnyj, The Ukraine and the Czechoslovak Crisis (Canberra: Australian National University Press, 1970).

98. See Levesque, op. cit., among others, on this point.

99. See Paul Marer, "Has Eastern Europe Become a Liability to the Soviet Union? The Economic Aspect," in Charles Gati, (ed.), The International Politics of Eastern Europe (New York: Praeger, 1976), pp. 59-81; Martin J. Kohn and Nicholas R. Lang, "The Intra-CEMA Foreign Trade System: Major Price Changes, Little Reform" in East European Economies Post-Helsinki, pp. 135-151; Arthur J. Smith, "The Council of Mutual Economic Assistance in 1977: New Economic Power, New Political Perspectives and Some Old and New Problems," Idem., pp. 152-173.

100. Jowitt, "Political Innovation," p. 145.

9
Perspectives on Romania's Economic Development in the 1980s

Marvin R. Jackson

An inquiry into prospects for Romania's economy in the 1980s could include many dimensions. Two chosen for this survey are needed to make sense of what may be coming in that country. One is the burden of sorting out important parts of a confusing statistical record. The other is the description of what already has happened since 1950 when the country's rapid industrialization was initiated under a communist government. After tending these tasks in Parts I and II of the paper, Romania's next economic decade will be discussed in Part III by exploring and evaluating official projections of economic development from 1980 to 1990.

The discussion throughout concentrates on quantitative dimensions. However, the analysis of Romania's past development processes in Part II is done without the benefit of empirically more powerful econometric techniques.[1] The assessment of Romania's official projections in Part III is done in a similarly heuristic fashion without the help of alternative projections based on a quantitative model of the economy's interdependences. Both exercises bear a high risk of error from the relatively limited associative abilities of the eye and the mind.

Of principal concern are the internal dimensions of the economy. The possibility of changes in Romania's internal political leadership and organization are ignored, as are possible changes in Romania's external political and economic environments. However, the discussion is concerned with identifying possible challenges for Romania's policymakers and planners by changes within the economy and with evaluating its prob-

---

Marvin R. Jackson is a Professor of Economics at Arizona State University. He received his Ph.D. from the University of California (Berkeley). Research for this paper was supported by NSF Grant No. INT-76-21084 and Arizona State University.

able capacity to respond to changed international economic relations. Romania's economic management in the past has been concentrated on macroeconomic magnitudes, essentially those concerning the generation of sufficient capital, the placement of capital among sectors of the economy, and the shifting of labor from agriculture to industry. It remains a major question when this process of extensive economic development will be replaced by the microeconomic concerns of generating greater productivity of resources already placed in given sectors. The ability of Romanian policymakers and planners to deal effectively with the new challenges of economic management goes beyond the formal organization of work processes. It will be influenced by how the quality of life, or more narrowly the standard of living of Romanians is changed, and how well money income incentives will be balanced with supplies of consumer goods and services. A shift to intensive economic development moves the burden of decisionmaking towards factory managers and workers. It will make the Romanian economy, for better or worse, a far more people-dominated affair than it has been.

THE PAST AND THE FUTURE - SOME STATISTICAL AMBIGUITIES

Romania's latest official projections for economic development in the 1980s were approved at the 12th Congress of the Romanian Communist Party in November, 1979. Their major dimensions (shown in more detail in Tables 9-4 and 9-6 below) provide for a population increase of about 12 percent from 1980 to 1990 and an increase in "national income produced", that is the Marxist concept of net material product, of about 105 percent, or 7.5 percent per year. Real per capita national product, that is without inflation of prices, will increase about 83 percent, or an average of 6.2 percent per year. Labor productivity or output per occupied person in the "productive" sectors (excluding services) will account for nearly all of the growth in national product, 81 percent of 6.1 percent per year. Real "final incomes" per capita, a quantity similar to the western measurement of disposable income and including both material goods and services, will increase 40-43 percent, or 3.4-3.7 percent a year. By 1990, the absolute level of national product per capita will reach 47,000-50,000 lei, compared to 22,670 in 1979, or translated officially $3,000-3,500 in today's prices.[2]

What these statistics imply for Romania's economic future is by no means clear. They need the perspectives of those used to describe Romania's past development at least since 1947. But in more than one sense, both

TABLE 9.1
Population and Labor Resources, 1950 to 1980 (mid-year estimation)

A. Number (1000 persons)

	1950	1960	1970	1978	1979	1980p[a]	1980E[b]
Population	16311	18403	20253	21855	22044	22270	22135
Urban Population	(3713)[c]	5912	2258	10626		11625	12454
Working age population[d]			11370	12375			12454
Occupied population	8345	9513	9880	10277	10305	10400	10333
Agriculture and forestry	6237	6361	4965	3467	3225	2886	3079
Industry and construction	1192	1814	2969	4313		4888	4578
Other "productive" sectors[e]	445	582	938	1264	7080	2626	1643
"Non-productive" sectors[f]	521	756	1008	1233			1033
Employees[g]	2123	3249	5109	6956	7183	7713	7435
Females	na	878	1544	2516	2658	na	2937
Non-employees[h]	6272	6264	4771	3321	3122	2687	2898
Non-agriculture	271	202	266	418	na	na	na

B. Shares (percent of total population)

	1950	1960	1970	1978	1979	1980p[a]	1980E[b]
Urban	(23.4)[c]	32.1	40.8	48.6		52.2	50.0
Working-age	na	na	56.1	56.6			55.9
Occupied	51.4	51.7	48.8	47.0	46.7	46.7	46.4
Of working-age population							
Agriculture and forestry	na	na	86.9	83.0		83.5	83.0
Of occupied population							
Agriculture and forestry	74.6	66.9	50.3	33.7	31.3	27.7	29.8

Industry and construction	14.2	19.1	30.1	42.0	47.0	44.3
Other productive	5.3	6.1	9.5	12.3	25.3	15.9
Non-productive	6.2	7.9	10.2	12.0		10.0
Employees	25.4	34.2	51.7	67.7	69.7	74.2	71.5
Of employees						
Females	na	27.0	30.2	36.2	37.0	39.5

Source: Era socialista, LV:12 (June 1975) p. 8; Revista economica, 1980:7 (March 7) p. 17; Revista economica, 1976:10 (March 12) p. 2; Anuarul statistic, various issues.

[a] As planned in 1976.
[b] As expected in 1979.
[c] 1948.
[d] Males 16-64; females 16-59.
[e] Essentially trade, transportation, and communications.
[f] Housing, education, culture, health and administration.
[g] Persons employed in state and cooperative enterprises and institutions, excepting agricultural cooperative members.
[h] Members of agricultural cooperatives and persons privately employed.

TABLE 9.1b
Growth of Production, Labor and Capital, 1950 to 1980
(average annual percent increase)[c]

	1951-60	1961-70	1971-78	1979	1980P	1971-80P
National Income[d] -A	10.4	8.4	10.5	6.2	8.8	9.9
-B	8.9					
Occupied Population-Productive[d]	1.1	0.0	0.2	0.3	0.9	0.5
-Total	1.3	0.3	0.5			
Fixed Capital Stock-Productive[d]	5.6	9.2	8.5			
-Total	4.7	7.6	9.6			
Investments in Fixed Capital-Productive[d]	15.4	12.5	11.9	5.1	4.9	10.3
-Total	15.9	11.8	11.7			
Capital per Unit of Labor-Productive[d]	4.5	9.2	8.3			
-Total	3.4	7.3	9.1			
National Income per Unit of Labor-A	9.2	8.4	10.3	5.9	7.8	9.6
-B	7.7					
National Income per Unit of Capital-A	4.5	-0.7	1.8			
-B	3.1					
National Income in Industry-A	14.0	13.3	11.8	(9.1)[e]	(11.5)[e]	11.5
-B	11.3					
Gross Industrial Output	13.0	12.8	12.2	8.0	11.4	11.7
Means of production	14.7	14.3	13.0			
Means of consumption	10.7	10.1	10.3			
Occupied in Industry	3.7	4.7	5.3			
Fixed Capital in Industry	8.4	11.4	12.2			

TABLE 9.1b (cont'd)

	1951-60	1961-70	1971-78	1979	1980P	1971-80P
Investments in Industry	15.7	12.0	12.8			
Means of production	15.5	12.0	13.1			
Means of consumption	16.7	12.7	11.0			
Output per Unit of Labor-A	9.9	8.2	6.2		(8.7)[e]	
-B	7.3					
Output per Unit of Capital-A	5.2	1.7	-0.4			
-B	2.7					
Capital per Unit of Labor	4.5	6.4	6.6			
National Income in Agriculture-A	5.4	-0.8	6.5			(5.2-7.5)[e]
-B	6.4					
Gross Agricultural Output	5.5	2.2	6.3			4.7-6.0
Occupied in Agriculture	0.0	-2.5	-4.5			
Fixed Capital in Agriculture	2.4	5.3	9.1			
Investments in Agriculture	22.8	10.5	8.9			
Output per Unit of Labor-A	5.4	1.7	11.5			
-B	6.4					
Output per Unit of Capital-A	2.9	-5.3	-2.4			
-B	3.9					
Capital per Unit of Labor	2.4	6.9	14.3			

NOTES: (A) 1950-59 in 1950 prices. (B) 1950-59 in 1955 prices. (C) Calculated as the average growth from the beginning year to the end year; figures do not represent trends. (D) Net material product; excluding services in the housing, education, cultural, health and administrative sectors. (E) Estimates from net output of sectors which differs from

TABLE 9.1b (cont'd) sector contribution to national income by turnover taxes, excluded from the former.

SOURCES: Except for production in 1950-59 in 1955 prices (see text): Anuarul statistic, various issues; Scinteia, 7 February 1980 and 15 December 1979.

sets of numbers need explanation and translation. They are official Romanian statistics which, for some readers, may imply that they mean very little. In any case, some readers may question if numbers describing economic growth can be given meaning for the human experience.

Special skepticism about the authenticity of Romanian official statistics arises because its record is among the most incomplete and poorly defined of the socialist countries of Eastern Europe. This record is far out of line with the country's official international policies and especially its membership in international organizations for whom it seems to remain a spoiled child. Faith in the official record is further undermined by the shoddy standards of reference followed by Romanian economists in their publications, a practice not just condoned but officially encouraged by state policy.[3] Obfuscation of the statistical record leads to the suspicion that published data could be distorted or falsified for the same motives - to hide the country's relative failures or problems and to exagerate its successes. However, the available evidence shows no instance where Romania has published fabricated statistics. Moreover, some cases of lacunae in the record may arise not because of a wish to hide the record, but because the available data are of a poor quality.[4] Still, the published record in some cases has been so poorly defined as to be misleading.

A case of poorly defined and, hence, misleading statistics are the only ones available on peasant incomes, recently published semi-officially in party documents and the party newspaper, <u>Scinteia</u> (they have not appeared in the official statistical yearbook). The figures in question are for peasant income from agricultural cooperatives, and personal and private farming, per active peasant.[5] The figures do not include all income from work because the average peasant also earns significant, but generally unidentified amounts of wage income. Moreover, they do not include other sources of peasant family income such as transfer payments (pensions, aid to children, etc.). Finally, the method of measuring an "active peasant" remains undefined; it could include peasants working any amount of time, only those working minimum amounts of time, or a calculated "full-time" equivalent number of peasants.

A second case, that of truth-bending, arises in the measurement of growth of Romania's national income produced. Here one encounters the so-called "index-number problem." This problem, which is not unique to Romania, is derived from two phenomena: (1) the much faster growth of industrial output than agricultural output, from 1950 to 1977 over 11 times more in the official figures; and (2) as a logical consequence of industrial products having become more abundant relative to agricultural products, a decrease of prices of industry relative to those of agriculture, from 1950 to 1977 possibly as much as five times. Consequently, if the growth of national product is estimated in sectoral weights using early year prices, say 1950, higher growth rates result than if estimates are carried out in later year price weights, say 1977. Romanian truth-bending has taken this form. In official data, prices of 1950 are used to measure real output growth (national income and its components) from 1950 to 1959, while prices of 1955 are used for the period, 1959 to 1965, and those of 1963 for the period, 1965 to 1975. Although alternative estimates in later-year prices have never been officially published, unofficial estimates of growth from 1950 to 1960 in prices of 1955 (shown as B items in Table 9.1b) give less growth than official figures (shown as A items in Table 9.1b). Probably the overstatement of growth in the official indices has been less in recent years. But how much remains among the too-numerous Romanian state economic secrets. Only since 1975, when the new official indices began to be calculated in 1977 prices, has the implicit "truth-bending" ceased.

No matter how faithfully the official indices of "national income" might reflect the realities of Romanian economic development, their use in comparisons of Romania with all cases but other communist countries lacks meaning. They intentionally do not measure the same phenomena as are measured by "gross national product" or "gross domestic product".

For comparative purposes, estimates of Romania's gross national product, both its growth and level, have been made and applied to analysis of the economy. One set of such estimates are those by the World Bank.[6] Its method is based on official Romanian national income (or net material product) in lei, to which are added estimates of depreciation and services. The resulting total grows slightly faster than official national income. Far more complex and sophisticated methods are used by Thad P. Alton and associates to estimate GNP for the European members of the Council of Mutual Economic Assistance (CMEA), Romania included.[7] They have estimated Romania's GNP in 1968 in lei in order to derive weights for the respective sectors of production. The derived weights, which differ significantly from the official sector shares of "national income", are then applied to independently calculated indices of sectoral growth in order to estimate the growth of total GNP. The Alton indices of GNP show less growth than the official indices of national income in all cases, Romania being no exception. In its case from 1965 to 1979, for example, the Alton GNP index grows only two-thirds as much as the official national income index, or at average rates of 6.1 percent per year compared to 9.2 percent per year.⁸ The slower growth of GNP results from a combination of differences. Generally, industry's growth rate is lower and the sector receives a smaller weight in the total, as compared to the official indices. Then, agriculture's weight is increased and a positive weight is given to the service sectors. Their slower growth pulls down the growth of the resulting total.

A general problem posed for the analysis of Romania's economy is which of these estimates provides the better indicator of significant changes in the growth and structure of the economy. At the least, one ought not confuse conclusions based on one set of data with those based on another set or indiscriminately mixed different sets. A problem is that movements in the alternative indicators do not always coincide. For example, Romania's average growth rate in terms of its official national income indicator in the period, 1976 to 1979, is lower than the average growth rate in the period, 1971 to 1975. But by the Alton GNP estimates, both periods show the same growth rates. Should one conclude that economic growth slowed down or remained the same? The answer turns out to depend on the relative importance given to industry and agriculture. In both the official index and the Alton index, industry's performance is worse in 1976-79 than in 1971-75, and, comparing the same periods, agriculture's performance is better. But the official index, so to speak, declares industry to be more important, gives it a higher weight, than in the Alton index. Conversely, the Alton index gives agriculture a higher weight than it receives in the official index.⁹

Were potential confusion about growth rates and growth patterns not enough, one must also face differences in the estimated levels of national production used to compare Romania with other countries. In this case, the common standard is an estimate of GNP per capita expressed in (US) dollars. The World Bank renders its estimate of Romania's per capita GNP by converting the figure in <u>lei</u> to dollars using one of three official Romanian exchange rates, the so-called "commercial rate."¹⁰ The Alton group also estimates Romanian GNP in dollars along with similar estimates for the other CMEA countries. Their estimates are derived from an earlier study of purchasing power parity and other exchange rates between West Germany and the countries of Eastern Europe. The dollar values are then moved forward to the present by the Alton estimates of GNP growth. What was the dollar value of Romania's per capita GNP in 1975? By the World Bank method it turns out to be only $1083; by the Alton method it turns out to be $2212 (with both figures expressed in dollars of 1975 purchasing power)! To compound confusion, Romania's own estimate of the dollar value of its national income (not GNP) per capita in 1975 was about $852.

In comparing the figures for Romania with those of other countries one must use estimates by comparable methods. In this case different methods are used by the World Bank and Alton for all countries. By World Bank comparisons, Romania's per capita GNP in 1970 was 66 percent of that of Yugoslavia and only 12 percent of West Germany's per capita GNP (as estimated by the Bank). Projecting Romania's per capita GNP to 1990 by the World Bank method results in a figure of $3817, or 86 percent of West Germany's 1970 level. By Alton's comparisons, Romania's 1975 figure was 88 percent of that for Greece and 32 percent of that for West Germany in the same year. Projecting this figure to 1990 at a rate of two-thirds the growth rate of Romania's officially projected growth of national income gives a figure of $5,321, or 78 percent of that for West Germany in 1975. Either way, if Romania grows as projected, it will arrive among the ranks of the developed countries.

Perhaps it has already occurred to the reader that even if economists' numbers always agreed, they lack the ability to render a more sensible notion of the meaning and impact of economic change. The author had similar thoughts recently while walking about Bucharest remembering that he had first visited Romania ten years earlier. The country's official statistics show that from 1970 to 1978 real final (or disposable) incomes per person increased an average of 69 percent.11 Did impressions of Bucharest in 1970 and 1980 reflect that magnitude of change? The answer was no; Bucharest seems to have changed little. New apartment blocks have appeared to replace those lost in the center of the city due to the 1977 earthquake and more new blocks have taken the place of colorful, but shabby commercial buildings and houses along most streets leading from the center to the city's suburbs. Several years ago, the reopening of numerous prewar hotels brought some better restaurants, but the common ones remain as crowded and their waiters as indifferent as before. One does not meet friends who have moved into better or more spacious apartments. Buses remain crowded even though a new "maxi-taxi" system operates. The one obvious change in the street scene is an enlarged swarm of private automobiles. But no accomodation for them has been made and soon there will be no room to walk on the sidewalks. It is hard to find a real counterpart to the official statistics showing that meat consumption per person has gone up since 1970 by over 76 percent. Chicken, even some imported from the United States, is the only item to be found without a considerable early morning queue. Cold weather and rain in the spring ruined the entire country's fruit supply and delayed vegetables even in the peasant market. People argue about the onset of poorer food supplies (the late or mid 70s) not if they have gotten better. Only non-food supplies and the number of outlets for them seem to have improved in quantity. Also, larger numbers of Romanains seem to be in the valuta (hard currency) shops. Ten years from now the official projection is that per capita real final incomes will be up by 40-43 percent. Will the Bucharest scene then seem to have changed as little compared to today as today seems to have changed from ten years ago?

Behind this question is the connection between statistics showing income growth and one's personal experience. Visits to both London and Munich in 1975 may not have allowed one to detect that West Germany's per capita GNP in dollars was 67 percent higher than in the United Kingdom. Nevertheless, their differences in Romania's estimated per capita GNP in 1980 and that projected for 1990. In Romania's case, personal experience, past or present, is likely to be a worse indicator of economic change. This is partly because large parts of its national product have been invested, spent for national defense or used to pay foreign debts. Experiences limited to Bucharest and a foreigner's acquaintances in the capital are probably even worse indicators because, as will be made clear, most economic change in Romania has been beyond that point.

PERSPECTIVES ON ECONOMIC DEVELOPMENT SINCE 1950

By 1980 Romania had passed through one century, in formal terms at least, as an independent state. Its course of political and economic development during this period was bent by both world wars. The msot profound effect of the first war was the rupture of Romania's economic ties with the rest of the world, seen clearly in the shift of its agricultural production from export markets to domestic consumption and of its domestic consumption of finished industrial products, especially consumer goods, from imports to domestic sources. While the interwar turning inward brought dramatic structural changes in production and markets, it did not see a rise in aggregate levels of per capita production, the usual test of successful economic development. After the Second World War, Romania's international economic ties were cut further not as a consequence of the war but rather due to political change. The new socialist government henceforth sustained increases in the rate of investment while, at the same time, it ensured an exagerated source of demand for products. Thirty years of dramatic structural change followed, now accompanied by rapidly increasing production per capita.[12]

During those thirty years Romania's industrialization seems to have passed through three cycles. One began in 1948 with the first socialist industrialization and lasted until about 1953-54. From then to 1957 national income growth rates and rates of investment were reduced during the "new course" following Stalin's death. A second period of rapid growth lasted until about 1965-66. It saw the completion of agricultural collectivization in 1962 and the beginning of the shift of Romania's foreign trade toward the West. The period ended with growing problems of managing swollen flows of investments and of a transition to the country's present political leadership under Nicolae Ceausescu.[13] The years from 1967 to the floods of 1970 were another period of slower development, characterized by increased international political tension and more relaxed internal politics, a rapid increase in Romania's imports from and debts to the West, and a generally poor performance of the recently collectivized agricultural sector. From 1970 to 1978 the country passed through another period of rapid growth and its greatest structural change. Since then, problems of investment management accompanied by massive trade deficits have again caused economic growth to slow.[14] The question remains whether the latter period is just another short cycle of slower growth to be followed by a fourth period of rapid growth, or is the first part of a permanent reduction in Romania's growth rate.

The Evolution of Extensive Industrialization Processes

The periods showing the quantification of Romania's economic development since 1950 in Table 9.1b are chosen to illustrate differences in growth processes rather than the growth cycles described above. One feature that stands out is that 1971-78 have been Romania's best years. A better agricultural performance makes the difference between the 1960s and the 1970s. The 1970s are remarkable years in that they came after 20 years of rapid growth. We must, then, raise the question of how growth could be even faster, while most other economies were waning in the face of energy crises and international inflation.

A second important feature of Romania's development pattern is the contrast in growth of labor and capital inputs before and after 1960. Both grew at moderate rates before 1960. Since then labor inputs have hardly increased, especially those in the "productive" sectors. But capital inputs have grown much more rapidly as a total and in both the industrial and agricultural sectors. Hence, since 1960 the main source of growth has been growth of capital inputs and some unmeasured "technical progress." In turn, capital inputs have grown from a combination of national income growth and a gradually rising share of national income allocated to investments. Over time the absolute quantity of annual production devoted to capital has become huge compared to all other magnitudes in the economy.

Third, growth of the industrial and agricultural sectors has been accomplished by significantly different processes. In Romania, industry, labor and capital have grown together at roughly the same proportionate rates since 1950. In Romanian agriculture capital has been substituted for labor. Before 1960 and the termination of agricultural collectivization, the process was less evident. During this period most capital in the sector was used to displace field labor in plowing, sowing and harvesting as a means to implement state control over the harvest. Most of the displaced labor remained in agriculture.

A fourth observation is that changes in industrial and agricultural employment have tended to accelerate. In each succeeding decade, the growth rate of industrial employment has increased. Similarly, the rate of decline of agricultural employment has increased. Behind the accelerating structural change of employment is found (1) the growing absolute size of increments to the capital stock compared to the number of persons occupied in the economy and (2) the growing absolute size of the industrial sector compared to the agricultural sector.

From these observations, one may abstract the essential processes of Romanian economic development since 1950. It has been based, first, on the relatively steady and rapid accumulation of capital. Disruptions have been few, usually the result of brief internal political considerations and rarely the result of changes in the availability of foreign capital. The share of imported equipment in total equipment investments, for example, has remained at a relatively low 20-25 percent since the early 1950s. Second, the larger share of capital formation has been devoted to industry. That rising share, plus the growth rate of industrial employment. During the period from 1950 to 1960 industrial employment grew relatively slowly because industrial capital did the same. Factors determining the growth of Romanian industrial capital during this period remain to be investigated more fully. One problem was that investments in petroleum, which took very large shares of total industrial investments, resulted in little growth of capital stock.[15] Another was that relatively large shares of investment, compared to Bulgaria, for example, went to transportation. Here, and with investments in construction, the aborted Danube-Black Sea canal project may have had a large negative influence.

The growth of industrial employment was also determined by the mix of industrial branches and technologies to which investments were committed. The average industrial capital:labor ratio grew about 4.5 percent per year in the 1950's and about 6.5 percent per year in the 1960's and 1970's. If Romania's policymakers and planners had been willing and able to reduce the growth rate of the ratio, then clearly more labor could have been absorbed into industry. For example, if the ratio had remained at its 1950 level and been combined with the actual growth rate of industrial capital, by 1970 employment in industry would have reached 7,930,000 persons, or 96 percent of the occupied population of the country. This example is an unrealistic extreme, but a more realistic alternative would have implied a different branch structure of industry, a different foreign trade orientation and possible different rates of urbanization, housing investment and agricultural development.

Romania's employment in agriculture has been, for the most part, a residual determined by overall labor force growth and job creation in industry. Before 1960 annual increments in total labor were large compared to the number of new jobs in industry. Investments in the sector were used to implement state control over crops in the collectivization process. While field labor was

TABLE 9.2
Labor Migration Tendencies in the Iasi District (1972)

	Total	Male	Female
A. Total occupied persons, age 16 to 60	100.0	48.9	51.1
Occupied in residence commune	81.4	70.1	92.2
Occupied outside residence commune	18.6	29.9	7.8
		100.0	100.0
B. Occupied outside residence commune	100.0	78.5	21.5
In industry	36.8	34.4	47.3
In construction	34.5	40.7	10.6
In other	28.7	24.9	42.1
		100.0	100.0
C. Destination outside residence commune	100.0	80.0	20.0
Urban place within district	68.8	67.9	72.5
Other commune within district	7.6	7.9	6.5
Urban place outside district	17.3	17.8	15.5
Other commune outside district	6.3	6.5	5.5
		100.0	100.0

Table 9.2 (cont'd)

	Total	Male	Female
D. Frequency of return to residence	100.0	80.0	20.0
Daily	57.2	57.3	57.0
Weekly	18.2	20.0	12.5
Monthly	9.0	9.0	9.0
Less than monthly	15.3	13.8	21.5
		100.0	100.0

Source: Alecu Floares, Mobilitatea populatiei (Iasi, 1977), pp. 62, 66, 67.

displaced in cereal production, it shifted elsewhere in the agricultural sector and in rural households. Labor in agriculture did not stop growing until a few years after 1960. It did so when the total labor force stopped growing and when the absolute size of the industrial sector had been increased. As industry continued to grow relative to agriculture, employment in the latter fell at an accelerating pace.

Romania's urbanization bears an uncertain relationship to the level of employment in industry. Early postwar urbanization may have been influenced by the growth of the administrative sector independently of the growth of industrial employment. Subsequent Romanian urbanization has lagged the growth of industrial employment as evidenced by migration patterns. In both 1966 and 1973 permanent urban male populations, aged 25-40 years, outnumbered females by 6-10 percent. Many of the excess urban males were married to rural females and were forced to live separately because of a lack of urban housing. In addition, large numbers of rural residents, mostly males, were temporary migrant workers to jobs in both industry and construction (see Table 9.2). A large portion of them probably would have moved if urban housing had been available. There is no evidence that the state directly forced migrants; rather, they were attracted by higher and more stable incomes. But part of their potential gains were lost in transportation (including time) and other costs. Thus, the state shifted part of the costs of industrialization to them.

The Role of Foreign Trade and Capital in Development

Romania began its turn away from the world economy during the period between the two wars when, by 1936-38, real per capita imports were only half of their level in the Old Kingdom in 1906-10 and the share of imports in domestic consumption of industrial products fell from about 82 percent in 1915 (in the Old Kingdom) to about 21 percent in 1938. Foreign ownership of all capital in Romania is estimated to have fallen from over half before the First World War to about 36 percent in 1929 and to 21 percent by 1938.[16] Since 1938 the record has remained murky, although one can be certain that once the joint Soviet-Romanian companies, set up after the war on the basis of Soviet confiscation of former German assets, were dissolved that foreign capital in Romania had been reduced to near zero.

No record whatsoever has been published by Romania's socialist government for foreign trade in constant prices. The lack of data easily leads to misunderstanding of Romania's foreign trade dependency since 1950. Romanian economists never hesitate to connect the growth of foreign trade in current prices to national income growth in constant prices as a way of showing the country's increasing participation in the "international division of labor". This linkage is not evident, of course, especially since 1973 and general world inflation. Other confusion arises from the considerable attention given to Romania's decision in 1950-60 to shift shares of its foreign trade from countries in the Council of Mutual Economic Assistance to the western developed capitalist countries. The shift did occur, but it did not necessarily imply increasing dependence on western trade or the western bank loans that financed part of it.

The author has estimated changes in Romanian foreign trade dependence since 1950 by using a combination of Bulgarian and other estimated foreign trade prices to deflate Romania's published foreign trade in current prices.[17] It appears that the real volume of foreign trade (exports plus imports) increased faster than the real volume of national production in only two periods, 1956 to 1960 and 1965 to 1970. From 1950 to 1955, foreign trade grew either more slowly or at the same rate as national income, depending on which prices are used to measure national income. From 1960 to 1965 the two grew at the same rate; from 1970 to 1978 foreign trade grew slightly more slowly than national income. By 1978 compared to 1950, foreign trade had increased only 15-30 percent more than national income, depending on which price base is used to measure national income from 1950 to 1959. If foreign trade growth is compared to Alton's estimated growth rates of Romania's gross national product, then a greater increase in foreign trade dependence has taken place.

The only published Romanian data suggesting its dependence on foreign trade are those showing the value of imported equipment (in internal prices) in total equipment invested. After importing 49.2 percent of invested equipment in 1950, Romania reduced the share to an average of only 20.6 percent in 1956-60. The imported share then rose in the 1960's from 30.6 percent in the first half to 33.2 percent in the second half. In the 1970's the share has averaged 30.6 percent again.

These data on imported equipment shares in investments can be combined with estimates of the shares of Romanian machinery and equipment imports from the western developed capitalist countries in order to approximate the latter's shares in total Romanian equipment investments. The western countries' share of Romania's equipment imports rose from about one-fourth in 1960 to a peak in 1967 of about 60 percent. During the 1970's, the western share was lower, in the range of 37-44 percent. As a share of total equipment invested, however, imports from western countries were much lower. They rose from about 7 percent in 1960 to 12 percent in 1965, remained at that level in 1970, then fell to only 10 percent by 1975.

These observations supplement the emphasis given to Romania's development pattern up to 1965 by J. Michael Montias.[18] The country exhibited unusual self-sufficiency, given its rapid growth, that remained evident after 1965 up to the present. No factor could account for such self-sufficiency other than the firm application of policy. Overall, one of the main tasks of Romanian industry has been to supply itself as much as possible.

The diminished role of foreign trade in Romania's development stands in great contrast to its role in the economic development of Bulgaria. Some differences are expected due to contrasting sizes and mineral resource bases. Beyond such distinctions, it is clear that the two countries have pursued quite different development policies. By 1960, Bulgaria's real foreign trade

TABLE 9.3
Comparative Romanian and Bulgarian Foreign Capital Dependence

A. Change in Hard Currency Net Debt Balance Compared to Imports from the West (percent)

	1956-59	1961-65	1966-70	1971-75
Bulgaria	28.9	20.0	24.4	22.9
Romania	--	15.9	22.8	20.4

Table 9.3 (cont'd)

B. Estimated Soviet Aid Deliveries Compared to Imports from the Soviet Union (percent)

	1955-60	1961-65	1966-70	1971-75
Bulgaria	9.9	16.8	na	na
Romania	7.2	6.6	na	na

C. Hard Currency Debt Per Capita (US dollars)

	1960	1965	1970	1975	1979
Bulgaria	12	31	75	259	436
Romania		12	50	175	305

D. Soviet Aid Deliveries Per Capita (US dollars)

	1955-60	1961-65
Bulgaria	14	51
Romania	5	7

Source: Marvin R. Jackson, "Romania's Economy at the End of the 1980's: Turning the Corner on Intensive Industrialization" in East European Country Studies, 1980, a compendium of papers submitted to the Joint Economic Committee, Congress of the United States. Washington, D.C.: USGPO, 1980.

increased 53 percent faster than its real national income and by 1975 nearly three times more. Its share of imported equipment in total equipment investments has rarely been less than 50 percent and during 1961-65 rose to an average 65 percent. Imports of equipment from western countries, as a share of total equipment investments, have usually been only slightly smaller than in Romania, and were actually slightly higher in 1965 and again in 1975.

Available evidence on Romanian and Bulgarian dependencies on foreign capital[19] indicate clearly the effect of policies to minimize borrowing by Bucharest from the West. There were funds readily available from western bankers in the early 1970s, but offered only on the condition that more information concerning the country's international finances be released. Romanian policymakers chose not to meet the conditions.

Summary of Romanian Development Patterns, 1950 to 1980

The key processes in Romanian economic development have been (1) the rate of investment and capital accumulation, (2) the proportions of investment allocated to industry and the growth of industrial capital, and (3) the industrial capital:labor ratio and the growth of labor in industry. Each is a focus of critical economic policy formation and execution which deserve more research. Regardless of how policies were formed and executed, the combination of values obtained for the three parameters above acquired the character of a self-generating growth process. With productivity initially higher in industry than agriculture, movements of labor to the former from the latter helped national income to increase rapidly. As national income increased, the share of it devoted to capital accumulation increased. At the same time, the share of investment and the mass of investment in industry increased, enabling even larger shifts of labor from agriculture to industry.

Romanian industrialization has been extensive in two senses. First, most investment in industry has taken the form of new facilities while few old ones have been scrapped. Thus, the industrial labor force was enlarged rather than modernizing capital facilities for existing industrial labor. Second, significant portions of industrial investments have been used for products not previously available in the country. The range of products was extended for more complete provisioning of the domestic economy rather than for export. Romania's less specialized industry must have initially been relatively expensive even though it probably gained the country independence. But once established, with rapid internal growth, many lines of production must have improved their efficiency. A few others found their economies of scale in export markets.

The limits of the effects of industrialization on structural change of the labor force and urbanization were derived from industrial capital:labor ratios which grew about 4.5 percent until 1960 and about 6.5 percent thereafter. If industrial capital:labor ratios had remained constant at 1950 levels, as noted above, Romania's labor force would have been shifted to industry at an extremely rapid pace. But at the same time, unless the resulting industry had been extremely decentralized (constructed in villages), much larger investments in urban housing and infrastructure would have been required. Investment in agriculture would have had to be reduced. Collectivization of agriculture would have been more difficult and output from the sector would have grown even more slowly.

The question remains if a concern for agriculture was a major factor in the rise of industrial capital:

labor ratios and the slower transfer of labor from agriculture to industry. It may be suggested that this was not the case. Rather industrial capital:labor ratios were determined by other factors. First, to have developed industry on the basis of 1950 levels of capital to output, if possible at all, would have required Romania to expand light industry production and exports. Its policymakers saw this alternative as one involving too much international dependence and limited possibilities for productivity growth. Instead, they chose to enlarge the number of products of Romanian industry and to reduce and then maintain a low level of import dependence. Industrial capital:labor ratios were then determined by the branches of industry chosen for development. Within branches of industry, they were determined both by the limited range of technologies available from the industrialized countries and by the desire of Romanian policymakers to acquire the most advanced technologies available. In any case, the available range of technologies was probably relatively limited.

DEVELOPMENT PERSPECTIVES AND PROBLEMS IN THE 1980'S

Romania's rapid growth in the 1970s resulted from the ability to absorb large numbers of persons from agriculture into its industrial labor force. Two major questions can be posed regarding its future economic development. First, when will Romania's pattern shift from extensive development to intensive development? Second, how effectively will its economic organization deal with the latter's different challenges? The shift to intensive development may arise from three sources: (1) the exhaustion of labor reserves in agriculture, (2) a need to reduce investment rates, and (3) a need for enlarged foreign trade dependence.

Sometime in the near future the withdrawal of labor in Romanian agriculture will have to diminish, unless, as seems unlikely, the country's policymakers should decide to depend on imports of human and animal food. The limits on labor withdrawal from agriculture will depend on (a) what levels of output from the sector are desired, and (b) the effectiveness of continued substitution of capital for labor. If today Romania would cease agricultural exports, present levels of production probably could satisfy domestic demand for food. Hence, barring any suprising change in agricultural technology that would make the sector capable of more production of non-food raw materials, future levels of output desired from the sector will depend on desired levels of agricultural exports. While Romanian policymakers have not evidenced a preference for agricultural exports since at least before the First World War, their outlook could be changing and, in the future, probably will be influenced by relative international price levels. The effectiveness of continued substitution of capital for labor in agriculture must be considered in light of the sectors dual organizational and technological structure. Romania's future demand for agricultural output will be greatest for meat, fruit, and fresh vegetables, where the socialist sector (state farms, cooperatives and machine tractor stations) has been least effective, not only in Romania, but in all socialist countries. Here, Romania must find a solution to the organizational problems where others have failed. Romania's private agricultural sector (private farms and personal gardens of cooperative farmers) has so far depended on labor which will soon move to better jobs in urban areas unless Romanian policymakers take measures to encourage capital investment in it. This seems unlikely at the present time.

A second reason that Romania may shift to intensive development arises from a policy of investing most of the growth of its national income. The rate of investment has risen to 35-40 percent, providing the economy with an ever growing mass of capital. At the present it faces two problems that will probably lower rates of investments. As in 1964-65, the country's planners have been unable during 1978-79 to effectively manage investment flows. At the same time, debt balances have risen very rapidly since 1975, culminating in massive trade deficits in 1978 and 1979. In the middle 1970's Romania's growth rate may have exceeded the management abilities of its organizational system. To avoid these problems, its future investment and growth rates may have to be kept at somewhat lower levels. An additional problem is that the policy of reinvesting most national income growth has restricted the growth of consumer supplies and real personal incomes. Moreover, reserves of consumer supplies have been insufficient to prevent periods of shortage such as those in the spring and summer of 1977 and again since 1979. Evidence also suggests that during the 1970's there has been a rapid increase in excess money supplies held by Romanian households. Lower investment rates in the future may be necessary both to prevent politically volatile market crises on the Polish model and to maintain the longrun incentive effects of the money wage and bonus systems.

Third, Romania has so far succeeded in a policy of limited overall dependence on foreign trade. In the future it could be forced to change this pattern if rising import dependence on energy and raw materials should be accompanied by continued declines in Romania's terms of trade (that is, the average price of imports rising faster than the average price of exports). In-

TABLE 9.4
Projected Growth of Production and Investments, 1975-1990 (annual average percent growth)[a]

Indicator	1976-80	1981-85	1986-90[b]	1981-90
National Income Produced	10.4	6.7-7.4	7.7-8.0	7.2-7.7
Labor productivity	9.6	4.3-5.0	7.3-7.8	5.8-6.4
Rate of Accumulation	(34.0)[c]	30.0		29.5-30.0
Investments[a]	11.7	5.4-6.2	8.0-8.2	6.7-7.2
Foreign Trade[a]	na	8.5-9.5	5.9	7.2-7.7
Exports		9.9-11.3		
Gross Industrial Output	11.0	8.0-9.0	8.1	8.1-8.5
Labor Productivity[f]	8.8	7.0-7.5	5.8-6.3	6.6
Gross Agricultural Output[a]	5.4-6.0	4.5-5.0	4.5-5.3	4.5-5.1
Share of Animal Output	(42.6)[e]	45-46		50

Source: Project-Directivele congresului al XII-lea al partidului comunist roman cu privire la dezvoltarea economico-sociala a romaniei in cincinalul 1981-1985 si Orientarile de perspectiva pina in 1990 (Bucharest, 1979); Nicolae Ceausescu, Raport la cel de-al XII-lea congres al partidului comunist roman (Bucharest, 1979); Project-Programul-directiva de crestere a nivelului de trai in perioada 1981-1985 si de ridicare continua a calitatii vietii (Bucharest, 1979); Directivele congresului al XI-lea al partidului comunist Roman cu privire la planul cincinal 1976-1980 si liniile directoare ale dezvoltarii economico-sociale a Romaniei pentru perioada 1981-1990 (Bucharest, 1974); Scinteia, 3 July 1976, 14 December 1977, 20 November 1979.

[a]Investments, foreign trade, and gross agricultural output growth are calculated in Romanian plans as the average of one five-year period to the preceding five-year period; in the case of these targets for 1981-90, the comparison is for 10 year periods.

bCalculated using 1981-90 and 1981-85 figures.
cPlanned.
dNot available in constant prices.
eAverage in 1976-78.
fFor "republican" industry, only.

dependent of the import side, greater export dependence
may be needed to acquire productivity growth. The
effects of exports on productivity are not restricted
to technological economies of scale, but include the
need to improve produce quality and marketing in order
to meet competition not found in the domestic Romanian
market.

Depending on the extent to which these three factors acquire influence in Romania's development, its
policy-makers and planners will have to face new challenges which emphasize productivity growth and microeconomic management rather than macroeconomic direction.
Their responses may be considered the final determinant
of the economy's prospects. It remains to consider the
economy's structure in more detail to understand when
the transition is likely to take place.

The Evolution of Present Official Projections to 1990

The present official projections of Romania's economy shown in Table 9.4 date from the 12th Party Congress
in November, 1979. Official projections dating from
1974, however, can be reviewed usefully to detect how
the outlooks of Romanian leaders and planners have been
revised in response to changes in the international
economy and to the economy's failures to meet 1976-80
growth targets.

The horizon to 1990 was first approved, along with
directives for the 1976-80 plan by the 11th Party Congress in 1974.[20] It provided a more optimistic view of
the 1980s, especially in terms of the high annual average rates of 10.8-11.0 percent growth for national income, about equal to the pace then being set by the
economy. In contrast, industrial growth was set at only
marginally higher rates of 8.6-9.7 percent and agriculture's projections set at wider margins, 3.7-5.9 percent.
Projections of total population were not different, but
labor force growth, for reasons unclear, was expected to
be less. The work-week targets, then established,
delayed reductions set in 1970 to have a 44 hour week by
1975 and a 40-42 hour week by 1980.[21] Instead, the 44
hour week was set for 1983. This was even two years
earlier than 1985, given in 1979 at the 12th Congress
(which also established a 46 hour week for 1980). The
expected shares of labor in agriculture by 1990 were
marginally lower, 12-15 percent instead of 15 percent,
and the expected share of urban population somewhat
higher, about 66.5 percent instead of 65 percent. Both
were probably products of the somewhat higher growth
rate of industry. Both the accumulation rate at 30-32
percent of national income and the growth rate of investments at 7.3 percent per year were slightly higher.

But real final (disposable) income growth was significantly higher, 5.2-6.7 percent per year instead of the 1979 projection of 4.6-4.8 percent per year.

A second view of the 1980s came in 1977 in the form of "guidelines" for the 1981-85 five-year plan and did not include a projection to 1990.[22] Now the growth rates of national income for the first half of the 1980s were set much below those first projected for the decade in 1974. Curiously, targets for growth of gross output in industry and agriculture remained about the same as in the earlier projection. The change suggests that either national income growth in other sectors (trade, transportation and communications) was revised drastically downward or that possibly the expected "material costs" of production had been increased, resulting in less national income per unit of gross output.

Nevertheless, figures for growth during 1981-85 in the 1977 "guidelines" were significantly higher than the 1979 "directives" in all but three indicators. One, for gross agricultural production, was lower in terms of average annual growth rates by about 94 percent. Two were the same, for retail sales and peasant real income from farming per active peasant. Average annual growth of national income was nearly 30 percent higher, figures for gross industrial output, foreign trade turnover, real final (disposable) income and real wages were all about 11-12 percent higher and those for investments and housing about 18 percent higher.

The first downward revision in growth expected for the 1980s from the 1974 to 1977 figures, might have been a response to the then more clear understanding of a greatly changing international economy, although one can not exclude the possibility that the first projections, with study, had merely been improved. The 1977 projections are noteworthy in that Romanian leaders and planners expected a slower growth of the economy in the 1980s than had been realized so far in the 1970s or planned to 1980. The change in versions of the 1981-85 plan from 1977 to 1979 must have been influenced by the economy's poorer performance in 1978 and 1979 and particularly by the very large and unplanned foreign trade deficits of those two years.

None of the projections for the 1980s contained growth rates of industrial output and investments and rates of accumulation as high as those experienced in the 1970s. In this light and in contrast with previous decades, the 1970s appear to have been a critical period in Romanian development strategy accompanied by significant pressure and mobilization. The next decade appears to project a significantly less "pressured" Romanian economy, although part of the reduced rate of accumulation and growth of investments must be based on plans to reduce Romania's recently swollen foreign debts. Still, it appears that, compared to the 1970s, consumption growth in the 1980s has been reduced less than investment growth. At the same time, projected industrial growth rates have been lowered, compared to the 1970s, more than those for agriculture. It is difficult to say how much this change should be attributed to increased emphasis on agriculture, perhaps resulting from the outlook for exports and how much it is merely the result of slower absorption of agricultural labor into industry.

Even though both downward revisions in the horizon for 1990, from 1974 to 1977 and from 1977 to 1979, clearly make that horizon more obtainable, it remains to explore in more detail several critical parts.

Sources of Labor Resources in the 1980's

The projected parameters of Romania's population and labor force in their several recent versions are given in Table 9.5. The sources of labor implied by them are more clearly summarized and compared with sources of labor in the 1970s in Table 9.6.

Projections of total population for a decade bear little consequence for labor force growth because the number of persons entering and exiting have already been determined by existing age cohorts and survival rates. However, two exceptions can be noted. One is the possibility of international migration which is subject to Romanian state policy. Emigration is likely to have only small influences on future labor resources. Second, female labor participation could be affected by any radical change in existing pro-natalist policies. Because population projections appear to have been made on the assumption of constant fertility rates, no change in state policy is expected.[23]

The important determinants of labor force are the growth of the working-age population and the change in labor participation rates. In the former, absolute growth in the next decade will suffer both small entry cohorts resulting from the small birth contingent before 1967 and large exit cohorts resulting from the baby-boom after the First World War. As a result, the working-age population will increase between 1980-90 by only 70-80 percent of the absolute increase experienced in the 1970s. The most critical factor in labor projections is the large increase in participation rates scheduled in the next five years. This change has been preceded by a significant decline from 1970 to 1974 and only a small increase up to 1980. The increase planned is from 83.5 percent of the working-age population in

TABLE 9.5
Projections of Population and Labor Resources, 1980-1990

	1980	1985	1990
Population			
11th Party Congress, 1974	22.3 mil	23.7 mil.	ca. 25 mil.
Party Conference, 1977		23.4-23.7 mil.	ca. 25 mil.
1979			
Urban population			
11th Party Congress, 1974	50.0%	54.5%	ca. 16.6 mil.
1979	52.2%		65.0%
1979	11.7 mil.	12.9 mil.	
Occupied population			
11th Party Congress, 1974		over 11.0 mil.	11.5 mil.
Party Conference, 1977		11,133 th.	
1979		11.5 mil.	11.8-12.0 mil.
1979	46.4%	48.1%	
1979	10.4 mil.	11.4 mil.	12.0 mil.
Employees			
Party Conference, 1977	7713 th.	8150-8450 th.	9.5-10.0 mil.
1979	7435 th.	8150-8350 th.	
1979	71.3%	73.2%	
Female employees	39.5%		45.7%
Occupied structure			
Agriculture			
11th Party Congress, 1974	29%	21%	12-15%
Party Conference, 1977			
1979			
1979	29.1%	21.6%	15%

TABLE 9.6
Sources of Labor, 1971-1980 and 1981-1990 (1000 persons)

	1971-78	1971-80	1981-85	1986-90	1981-90
Increase in occupied population	397	520P 453E	1100	400	1500
Increase in working-age population	1005	1084	405	391	796
Effect of change in activity rate	- 608	- 564	695	9	704
Change in occupations					
Agriculture and forestry	-1498	-2079P -1866E	- 603	- 675	-1278
Total non-agriculture	1895	2599P 2319E	1707	1075	2778
Industry and construction	1344	1919P 1609E	1327	254	1581
Other	551	680P 710E	376	821	1197
Total non-employees	-1450	-2084P -1873E	285	-1100	- 815
Total employees	1847	2604P 2326E	815	1500	2315
Females	972	1393E			1519
From peasant households					1200
From urban households					200
From new working age					119
Males	875	933E			796
From agriculture					500
From new working age					296

TABLE 9.6 (cont'd)

Source: Calculated from data in Tables 1 and 2; and from estimates in Era socialista, LIX:II (5 June 1979), pp. 7-9.

ªPersons occupied in the private sector and in agricultural cooperatives as members.
ᵇEmployees of state and cooperative enterprises and institutions (excluding members of agricultural cooperatives).

1980 to 88.8 percent in 1985, followed by a small rise to 89.8 percent to 1990. As seen in the lower part of Table 9.6, the main source of increased participation is intended to be females from agricultural households.

Two related shifts in occupation are projected. The absolute reduction of occupied persons in agriculture will be only two-thirds of the reduction now expected for the 1970s. The percentage reduction in the 1980s compared to numbers occupied at the beginning of the decade will be about 42 percent. In the first half of the 1980s nearly all of those from agriculture and of the increased labor force are scheduled for employment in industry and construction. But in the second half of the coming decade it appears that finally Romania's extensive industrialization will come to a completion. Then nearly all of the shift from agriculture and the growth of total labor will move to the service sectors of Romania's economy.

The second shift in Table 9.6 highlights what Marxists call the social composition of labor. The non-employee group, mostly peasants in agricultural cooperatives and fewer private farmers and artisans, appears to be scheduled for a small increase in the first half of the 1980s, but a large decrease in the second half. By 1990 this group will number about two million or 18 percent of the occupied population. Females will make up two-thirds of the new employees during the decade compared to 53 percent during 1971-78 and an expected 60 percent for the whole 1970s. Females from rural areas alone will provide over half of the increased employees.

An evaluation of Romania's labor projections may begin by discussing significant differences between labor force plans approved in 1976 for the five-year plan, 1976-78, the figures achieved by 1978 and those expected in 1979 for the end of 1980. There are relatively small differences in planned, expected and actually achieved increases in total occupied population which probably indicate that participation rates in labor of the working-age population had not increased as planned. More significant differences appear for shifts in labor. By 1978 only about 72 percent of the reduction of labor in agriculture and forestry originally planned for 1980 had been achieved and by 1979, Romanian planners appeared to be resigned to a smaller reduction of about 90 percent of the original figure. In a similar way, planned increases in industrial and construction employment were not being met, but other non-agricultural sectors appear to have expanded over the plan figures.

It is more difficult to explain why labor plans were not met. One explanation is that industrial growth and investment plans were also behind schedule. Scheduled new labor simply could not be put to work until new industrial facilities were completed. Possibly part of the intended employment increase has now been stretched out to 1981 and even 1982, thus accounting for the large figures for increased employment in 1981-85. A second possible explanation is that Romania was beginning to feel the pinch of a labor shortage in the last years of the 1970s.

Possibly the most important evidence of tightening labor supplies in Romania have been the continual delays in implementing a shorter work week. Even Bulgarians now enjoy a two day weekend while Romanians are receiving a 46 hour workweek with one extra day off scheduled each month. The difference between original promises and realizations in this regard may have added as much as 10 percent to total work time. Other evidence of labor shortages are numerous. Requirements for work by post high school students waiting for possible admission to higher education were recently tightened. Authorities in major industrial regions such as Brasov have complained of difficulties in recruiting new industrial workers.[24] Areas like Brasov and Bucharest already draw on very large numbers of commuting workers from surrounding rural areas.[25] In the next decade supplies available to Bucharest and the districts of the Banat will even be more restricted with the projected absolute decreases of their working-age population.[26] Harvest-time labor shortages in agriculture have been common for a number of years, especially around the more heavily industrialized cities. This is attested by the mobilization of students and even other working persons (although, it may be noted, the student mobilization also served as social disciplining).

Given the importance of females in the projections of increased labor and increased employees, it may be especially significant that the figure of their employment in 1978 (see Table 9.1) was still about 280,000 below levels expected in 1979 for 1980. A recent article in Era Socialista pointed out that, whereas the average increase in female employment in 1975-76 was 152,000 per year, it dropped to 100,000 per year in 1977-78. The situation has been described as a "serious problem", one made worse by the fact that female employees have higher absentee rates and are less often job-qualified than their male counterparts.[27] Could it be that Romania's labor plans have overlooked some special problems connected to increasing female employment?

Labor migration patterns reveal significant differences between females and males. The considerable permanent rural-to-urban migration since 1965 has been

predominantly male. The urban population contains a
6-10 percent excess of males from 25 to 40 years old.
The excess of rural females explains why women make up
over 60 percent of the occupied persons in agriculture
and why there are 1.2 rural births for each urban birth
as late as 1978. Rural fertility rates have not been
much higher; there are more fecund females and, of
course, not a small number of married males living in
urban areas without their families.

The relevance of female migration is, of course,
that rural females are and will be the major source of
increases in employees, total and industrial. Romania's
successful recruitment of rural females will probably
depend on factors differing from the recruitment of
rural males. More adequate urban housing, improved
commutor transportation, or the location of more industrial facilities employing females in towns that heretofore had industry dominated by male workers[28] are all
important steps. Finally, because a large percentage
of the rural female labor pool are already mothers, the
new industrial employment will have to cater to their
special needs - reduced hours, special time off, factory nurseries, etc. No quantitative assessment of
Romanian plans in these regards has been made. It
remains to be seen if both the plans and their execution
will be adequate for the new challenges in labor recruitment.

Structural Influences on Labor Productivity Growth in the 1980s

If Romanian labor grows and changes structurally
according to plans then the share of growth of national
income to be achieved by increases in the productivity
of labor (in the "productive" sectors) appears to be
relatively modest by standards of the 1970s. The annual
average growth rate of productivity planned for 1981-85
is less than half the rate expected for 1976-80; that
projected for 1986-90 is about 80 percent of that expected for 1976-80. Still, the more modest plans by
themselves are no security that they are more easily obtained because some typical sources of productivity have
also been planned or projected with more modest growth.

Investments, for example, have been an important
source of increasing labor productivity. Their growth
is planned in 1981-85 at remarkably low rates by past
Romanian standards. The projected growth rates increase
in 1986-90, but still remain relatively low. Planned
and projected capital stock growth figures are unavailable, but may be estimated at growth rates of about 75
percent of investments, the ratio of the two figures
from 1970-1978. Thus projected, capital stocks increase
in 1981-85 and 1986-90 at annual rates of 4.5 and 6.0

percent, respectively. In turn, capital:labor ratios for the same two periods will grow at 2.2 and 6.8 percent per year. In 1971-78 the ratio of labor productivity growth to capital:labor growth was about 113 percent. That is, labor productivity grew just slightly faster than would be accounted for by the increase in capital per worker. The projected ratios of labor productivity growth to capital:labor growth are about 212 percent for 1981-85 and 111 percent for 1986-90.[29] From these rough calculations, Romanian planners seem to expect the growth of capital per unit of labor to be a much smaller source of productivity growth in the next five years than has been the case in the 1970s. They may be hoping for some new capital from the unfinished investment stocks accumulated in the last few years (that is, for an unusually large ratio of growth of capital compared to growth of new investments released in the next five years). Their hope may also be for better organization and rationalization of production than has been possible during the rushed years of the 1970s. In the second half of the 1980s increased capital per worker seems to be projected for about the same role in increasing labor productivity as it had during the 1970s.

Another important source of increased overall labor productivity has been that acquired from shifting labor from low productivity employment in agriculture to much higher productivity in industry. For example, the total shift of labor out of agriculture from 1970 to 1980 is about 21 percent of total labor in the productive sectors in 1975 (the midpoint for estimating an average for the decade). At the same time, in 1975 one person in industry contributed to Romania's national income in current prices about 4.4 times the amount contributed by a person occupied in agriculture. Hence, the shift of labor alone during the decade will have accounted for an overall labor productivity increase of about 92 percent (4.4 times 21 percent), or about 61 percent of the actual 150 percent increase in labor productivity estimated for the decade. Similar calculations show that the shift out of agriculture between 1980-90 is projected to raise total labor productivity by about 33 percent, accounting for only about 41 percent of the total projected for the decade. Thus, the shift effect will be smaller and will account for a smaller share of total productivity increase than in the 1970s.

The two five-year periods of the next decade show markedly different relationships between labor productivity growth and structural changes. The next five-year plan, still subject to its final form in 1981, appears to call for an unusually low growth of capital per unit of labor. Relatively large increases in total labor are planned, mostly by increasing the rate of labor participation, combined with relatively low rates of investment growth. However, it is possible that capital may grow faster than indicated by new investments, if, in the first one or two years of the period, present inventories of unfinished investment projects are reduced. At the same time, a relatively large part of the lower planned increase in labor productivity will result from shifting labor from agricultural employment to employment in industry and construction. Industrial expansion plans contain a large component of branches capable of absorbing significant numbers of workers, especially females.[30] Recently, for example, President Ceausescu called for an expanded share of total industrial output to be in the small-scale and artisan sector, to increase from 7.7 percent in 1980 to 18-20 percent by the end of the decade.[31]

Almost no detail is available for the projected growth of separate branches of industry in the second half of the 1980s. Labor projections indicate a relatively large expansion of employment in the labor-absorbing service sectors will then take place. For the whole decade, it may be noted, services for households on a paid basis will grow 8.9-9.1 percent a year, faster than the growth of 5.6-6.0 percent projected for real retail sales from socialist outlets and appropriate for the probable income elasticities of demand of Romanian consumers. In the sectors of material productivity increases will be generated by a shift of labor out of agriculture. At the same time, the growth of capital per unit of labor will about equal the growth of labor productivity. One other relationship between the growth of labor productivity and structural change encompasses the domain of industrial sociology. In 1978, about 75 percent of the Romanian age cohort of 18 years, the age of those entering the labor force for the first time, had been born in rural areas. Many of these came to urban life through boarding schools or for the first time upon working. A large proportion of Romania's labor force, then, is first generation proletariat. Their early years of working life had undoubtedly met with great personal challenges. Under such circumstances, it would not be surprising if productivity on the job suffered. Urban population formation will be important in Romania for many years. Not until the turn of the century will more than half of the country's 18 year old cohort be born in urban areas. It is questionable whether Romania's economy will benefit from greater labor productivity until larger shares of its labor force enter the ranks of the second generation proletariat.

Labor Productivity and Economic Incentives

The less Romanian policymakers and planners can depend on shifting labor and the more labor stabilizes in technologically advanced sectors of the economy, the more economic growth will depend on the initiative and discipline among managers and workers. The determinants of the latter are not always clear as witnessed by the cases of Japan and West Germany. Romanians, however, do not seem to fit these unusual cases. They appear to be motivated by the link economists tend to apply generally, that between personal income and labor performance.

The link between personal income and labor performance is evident in several ways. One is the level of general consumption available in the country. Romania's level by European standards has been, and still is quite low. Indicators of Romanian consumption, when compared to Bulgaria (see Table 9.7), appear to suggest similar standards of living in the early 1950s. By 1965 Romania had fallen behind Bulgaria. In 1975, Romanians consumed only about 60-80 percent of the listed items of Bulgarian per capita consumption. Only since 1975 have the Romanian indicators risen generally compared to the Bulgarian ones. A question raised by comparison of Romanian and Bulgarian consumption levels is whether such levels may have given rise to relatively lower labor productivity in Romania and, in turn, tended to lower its level of national production. Nearly every visitor to Romania has encountered the joke, "They pretend to pay us while we pretend that we are working for them." But it is more difficult to demonstrate objectively that Romania's low consumption standards cause low productivity or that its comparative consumption standards would cause its labor productivity to be comparatively low. Association between low consumption and low productivity exists, but causation could be reversed; probably in Romania it has been.

A second link between personal incomes and labor productivity arises in planned economies in the balance between personal money incomes and goods (and services) available for purchase and consumption. At issue is a problem which remains a concern for socialist planners and which has been appropriately named "the Schweik shift".[31] It arises because in price controlled socialist economies a disequilibrium between the supply of money in the hands of household and the supply of goods for sale cannot be eliminated by a (legal) rise in prices. Rather, the reaction is likely to take the form of a decline in the amount of effort supplied by workers. Money bonuses become redundant and more time is consumed in leisure and in the search for goods. Statistics bearing on the problem in Romania's case are presented

TABLE 9.7
Level and Growth of Personal Consumption Indicators

Indicators	Level Percent of Bulgaria 1975	Annual Percent Growth Actual 1971-75	1976-78	Planned 1976-80	1981-85
A. Consumption per capita					
Meat and meat products		7.9	6.3	6.4	2.3
Milk and milk products		3.7	4.8	10.7	1.3
Total oils and fats		3.9	5.1	na	2.0
Total	71.0				
Eggs	146.6	8.6	6.0	4.8	0.5
Cereals and cereal products		- 0.6	- 1.7	- 0.6	- 3.0
Potatoes		8.9	- 6.0	0.9	na
Total Cereals and potatoes	153.8				
Sugar and sugar products	62.5	1.0	9.1	8.1	2.5
Vegetables and vegetable products	89.0	5.4	6.0	5.0	1.5
Fruit and fruit products	125.0	3.2	2.0	6.0	4.9
Footwear					0.0
Fabrics	74.0	4.6	3.8	3.8	4.3
B. Retail sales per capita					
Automobiles	29.5	11.5	16.0		
Motorcycles	15.9	10.1	8.4		
Bicycles	61.7	6.7	9.7		
Refrigerators	60.0	11.5	11.8		
Washing machines	43.2	5.3	8.3		
Sewing machines	70.4	2.0	2.7		
Vacuum cleaners	29.1	2.3	16.9		

Televisions	74.5	9.2	6.7	
Radios	160.8	6.2	3.5	
Cameras	33.4	8.9	na	
Watches and clocks	65.6	6.7	10.6	
C. Stocks per 1000 persons				
Automobiles	30.0	16.4	17.4	15.4	15.3
Radios		3.0	3.2	3.6	4.0
Televisions	74.0	12.1	9.7	7.0	3.8
Refrigerators	55.0	12.2	12.4	10.5	7.0
Washing machines	39.0	8.1	5.4	8.1	8.9
Housing (living space per					
capita)	(65.0)				
Urban areas	(77.0)				1.8
Rural areas	(53.0)				na
D. Other indicators					
Passenger transport per					
capita	57.0	8.6	1.7		
By rail	106.1	3.7	- 0.3		
By bus and automobile	39.9	18.1	4.0		
Telephones installed per					
capita	66.0	12.6	13.8		
Television sets registered					
per capita	73.4	11.6	7.2		
Radios registered per capita	68.6	- 0.2	0.3		
Students in higher education					
per capita	60.6	0.3	2.7		
Faculty in higher education					
per capita	59.8	0.0	- 0.6		
Hospital beds per capita	104.2	2.1	0.4		
Pharmacies per capita	75.8	0.0	- 0.2		
Doctors per capita	61.9	- 1.6	- 1.7		

Table 9.7 (cont'd)

Indicators	Level Percent of Bulgaria 1975	Annual Percent Growth Actual		Planned	
		1971-75	1976-78	1976-80	1981-85
Retail outlets per capita	58.1	2.1	1.3		
Share of labor in transportation, communication, trade and services	75.3	3.3	2.1		

Source: Country and CMEA yearbooks, various issues and sources cited in Table 9.5.

in Table 9.8. Since 1970 the money supply of households, considered the sum of savings deposits and currency in circulation, has grown significantly faster than any of the household expenditure indicators. The growth of the money supply has taken place in spite of recent increases in the prices of food, housing and energy. By 1978, it reached about two-thirds the annual volume of socialist retail sales in current prices.

It remains unclear how much of the money supply represents desired saving for intended purchases of apartments, automobiles and other durable goods and how much might be excess supply. It is also unclear how well Romanian planners will manage the money-goods (and price) balance in the future. One must assume that the same relative growth of money supplies and expenditures in the future will bring "the Schweik shift" into operation, even if it might not have yet occurred. Data in Table 9.7 suggest that Romanian planners will counter the Schweik shift with a relatively rapid growth of consumer services and durable goods, especially private automobiles. Part of the latter will be supplied by Romania's second factory, the Romcit under construction in Craiova as a joint venture with Citroen.

A more troublesome problem for the money-goods balance remains Romania's periodic food supply shortages and its inadequate retail network. Romanians seem to believe that the difficulty of finding beef and pork meat since 1979 results from exports. Yet President Ceausescu complained recently that the only way domestic supplies of animal products had been maintained was by reducing "year after year" exports below planned levels which, he noted, created serious balance of payments problems. Even when supplies are good the present retail network is inadequate for working persons without family members free to specialize in shopping. One often wonders why so many people are found shopping in the middle of the day. Could this be visual evidence of the Schweik shift?

A third connector between personal incomes and labor productivity is the use of differentiated incomes tied to individual work situation and performance. With peasant income from farm work less than half an employees wage in 1965, powerful economic incentives ensured permanent and temporary migration whenever jobs were available. Similar income differences among employee occupations have enhanced other motives for intergenerational occupational mobility, although little movement takes place after a person enters an occupation. Within occupations the operation of the Romanian incentive system remains unclear. From the 1960s to the 1970s differences in entry-level and top wage scales have been compressed to a 1:5.5 ratio and will remain there in the

TABLE 9.8
Growth of Consumer Expenditures and Saving

	1970	1970 = 100			1980 = 100 (Pl)	
	1970	1975	1978	1980c	1985	1990
Socialist retail sales	100	150	197	228	137	178
Food sales	100	151	194		127	
Public catering	100	151	192		136	
Non-food goods	100	149	201		142	
Socialist service sales	100	166	212	247	154	239
Total new housing expenditures a	100	184	234	na	na	na
Saving deposits	100	207	355	na	na	na
Currency in circulation	100	184	248	na	na	na
Total final income b	100	148	191		124	157

Source: Anuarul statistic, various issues, and data from Josef C. Brada and Marvin R. Jackson, The Arizona State University Data Book for Romania (unpublished).

a Estimated as the value of investments in housing in constant prices times the index of rents in the cost of living as a proxy for the price of new housing.
b In socialist countries, "final income" is similar to disposable income in capitalist countries, except that it is not of financial transactions with socialist organizations.
c Expected in 1979.

next decade. Besides the standard wages, persons working in industrial, agricultural and construction organizations have the possibility of earning bonuses (and sanctions) depending on plan fulfillment indicators which on paper appear quite large. Recent changes in the bonus indicators have emphasized, in place of gross output, net output and profits. In agriculture, construction and some branches of industry emphasis has been placed on a wage system called the "global accord", where wage payments are set as fixed percentages of the value of a unit of work contracted by a work team. Recently a similar system has been applied to small-scale service and artisan cooperatives where income payments will be based on a fixed percentage of their total receipts.[32] Yet, until the time when Romanian authorities should release hard evidence to the contrary, the bonus system may be considered as producing only minor incentives for higher labor productivity.

The area where economic incentives have seemed to bring results is in agriculture practiced on personal gardens by members of agricultural cooperative and private farmers, especially those located close to urban markets. Romanian policy has wisely provided higher price incentives and, recently, encouraged the turning over of unused land around the towns for small-scale private production. The problem for this sector is that it has lost labor to the non-agricultural sectors. Still physical production indices suggest that its output has kept up with the more land and capital intensive state and cooperative units.

Will Agricultural Production be Adequate in the 1980s?

Romania's population will grow, according to projections, about 1.14 percent a year from 1980 to 1990. Gross agricultural output is projected to average a growth of 4.5-5.1 percent a year over the levels achieved in the 1970s. The projections, then, provide about 3.3-3.9 percent growth per year to satisfy demands for increased consumption per capita, increased reserves in case of bad weather, and increased exports. The major source of increased domestic demand will originate with the population expected to shift residence from rural to urban areas, roughly 3.8 million persons, whose incomes will rise much faster than the average from the relatively low incomes in farming to the higher incomes earned by employees. Their incomes may be expected to increase about 20-25 percent, or 4.8-5.3 percent a year. Incomes for the remainder of the population will increase more slowly, about 2.8 percent a year. The income elasticity for all food products among all the Romanian population is now certainly less than one, but how much less is uncertain. If it should be as low as

0.5, then the average projected income growth of 3.4-3.7 percent will generate an increased demand for food of about 1.7-1.9 percent. If satisfied, it will leave a growth of 1.6-2.0 per year for reserves and export growth.

While projected growth appears adequate in general terms, the more critical aspects of domestic demand will be those of improving the composition of food, increased meat and fresh produce, and the reliability and marketing of supplies. In this light may be seen the projection calling for the share of animal output in gross agricultural output to rise to 50 percent by 1990 (compared to 44.3 percent achieved in 1978). Probable increased meat exports are also part of Romania's long term foreign trade plans, especially to the less developed countries and OPEC members in particular.

Whether Romania can achieve the projected growth and composition of agricultural output is another question. Its recent performance raises serious doubts. Agricultural output in the 1970s did rise considerably above the levels in the previous decade, but most of the increase came before 1977. Relatively large investments in land reclamation and irrigation, which recently fell behind plan targets, have not sufficiently, if at all, reduced the sensitivity of crop yields to bad weather. But the most evident failure in the plan period, 1976-80, has been in animal production. Cattle herds will end up a million below planned levels in 1980 with shortfalls of pig and sheep herds of about 1.5 and 2.0 million, respectively. Animal mortality rates in 1978 and 1979 were about double those for 1975. Problems appear to arise from inadequate fodder supplies, including feeding animals with spoiled silage, and inadequate care of young animals.[33]

Both the success and failure of Romania's agriculture must be seen as part of its dual (if not triple) organizational and technological character. One part of it, the state farms and cooperative farms with the machine-tractor stations serving them, receive most of the organizational effort, land and capital (in 1978 67.9 percent of agricultural fixed capital was in the three types of units and most of the rest in land improvements and other state units such as experiment stations). They produced most the the cereal, technical and fodder crops, about 55-60 percent of vegetables and grapes, but less than half of potatoes, fruit, meat, milk, and eggs.

Most of the capital investments in Romanian agriculture will continue to flow to these units. The total planned for 1981-85 was raised in November, 1979, by 16.5 percent over earlier versions of the plan. As a result, agriculture will continue to receive about the same share of total investments, 11.7 percent, as it was planned to receive in the last five-year plan. But, as in the case of total investments, the growth rate of agricultural investments will be significantly reduced, to about 5.3 percent. Most of the projected 2.5 percent a year decrease in agricultural labor from 1981 to 1985 will come from the cooperatives, especially females who, while they are counted as one occupied person, actually perform only part-time cooperative labor. Hence, the decrease in full-time equivalent units will be less. Still, the ratio of investment growth to labor decrease will be lower in 1981-85 than it was in 1971-78. This implies that capital per occupied person in agriculture will also grow more slowly and will provide less opportunity to increase labor productivity. In fact the projected growth of labor productivity in 1981-85 is higher compared to the growth of capital per unit of labor than in 1971-78. Thus, Romanian planners are hoping in agriculture, as in the economy as a whole, to get more productivity increases from sources other than capital in the next five years than has been the case in the past performance of the agricultural sector.

Romania's agricultural future, as now projected, will be a function of how well state and cooperative farm organizations serve as vehicles of capital for labor substitution and in the near future for capital intensification without reducing labor. Moreover, their tasks in the future will require that these processes are applied not only in the more simple technologies of field crops, but in irrigated farming in general and to livestock, fresh produce and fruit. As capital users, neither has proved very efficient; since 1962, output per unit of fixed capital on state and cooperative farms combined has fallen by about half. Only recently, the cooperatives had to have nearly 13 billion lei debts annulled, a sum representing about 60 percent of their long-term debts. Just how high producer prices would have to be raised to make them financially independent is unclear.

An important difference between Romanian agriculture and its neighbor, Bulgaria, remains a possibility for a better Romanian agricultural future. In 1976, private agriculture, not counting production from the personal gardens of cooperative farm members, provided nearly 10 percent of Romania's gross agricultural output compared to almost nothing in Bulgaria's case. Adding production from personal gardens to private farms, suggests that a third or more of Romania's gross production and even more of its net production came from its unorganized peasants and their labor intensive farming. In recent years Romania has not discouraged their efforts but even provided mild encouragements. As a result, the average income from farming of cooperative members (including that from their personal gardens) and of private farmers was about the same. For the future, the problem for this part of Romania's agriculture will not be official discouragement, but its manpower losses from migration to urban areas for better living conditions and more secure incomes. The migration is, no doubt, more intense from those areas without easy access to urban markets. The sector probably will not grow without additional encouragement that would be most effective if provided as more access to land close to urban markets and as sources of capital equipment, with financing, to improve productivity. Unfortunately, Romania's socialist government does not seem ready to provide the latter.

Foreign Trade and Economic Growth in the 1980s

If Romania's economy follows its present projections, 1990 will see the same overall level of foreign trade dependency as in 1980. The next five years will see foreign trade dependency rise about 7 percent more than national income, with exports planned to grow faster than imports. The deviation will allow real foreign trade to make up for part of the unfulfilled targets of 1976-80, a reduction in foreign debts, and time for planned reduced dependence on imported energy. In the second half of the decade, foreign trade is projected to grow more slowly than national income.

Romanian policymakers and planners appear to assume that foreign trade is necessary because industrialization requires imports of raw materials and industrial equipment or technology that cannot be produced domestically. They clearly have not arrived at the point where foreign competition in internal Romanian markets is considered important for improving the efficiency of Romanian firms. Thus, rarely will either Romanian consumers or producers have a choice between Romanian and foreign products.

The amount of Romania's future exports in real terms will be determined not only by how much it needs to import, but also by future export and import prices, or its terms of trade. Export and import prices will be influenced not only by the world economy but by Romanian development strategy and the sectors of growth chosen for growth. One reason Romania has imported so much crude petroleum is that it constructed refining capacity in excess of domestic needs in the later 1960s and 1970s. When petroleum prices started to rise in 1973, it was able to export petroleum products at advantageous terms of trade. The chemical industry, a major user of energy materials, was also built with export capacity; the same may be said for metalurgy. Generally, the main con-

straint on import and trade minimization has been
Romania's policy of pushing industrial exports before
agricultural exports. The latter have a much smaller
import content. If, for example, Romania had pushed
agricultural development with more investments and higher
incomes in the past, it now would have to import much
less. But, no doubt in the eyes of its policymakers, it
would be considered less developed and faced with less
promise for future development.

Romanian industry will supply the bulk of exports
in the next decade. Future physical imports, virtually
all industrial materials and producer goods, will be
defined by how fast industry grows, by the effectiveness
of programs for replacing imports with domestic materials
and for reducing the import content of industrial products, and by the success in substituting low import
(and high domestic labor) content exports for those with
high import content.

Romania's gross industrial output is projected at
8.1-8.5 percent a year, just about the growth of total
foreign trade of 7.2-7.7 percent and a marginally lower
growth of imports. The major program for saving imports
calls for the country to be self-sufficient in energy
sources in the narrow sense (that is, discounting imports
of energy for industrial raw materials in the chemical
and metallurgical industries). The focus is electric
power generation which alone consumed about 28 percent
of total energy consumed in the country including imports, in 1980.[34] Plans call for the share of power
generated from hydrocarbons to fall from about 40 percent
in 1980 to less than 4 percent in 1990. The major fuel
substitutes for hydrocarbons will be lignite coal and to
a lesser extent bituminous sands, sources which will
provide all additional power by 1985. At that time,
Romania's long-delayed nuclear capacity will be in com-
mission and will provide for the bulk of increased generating capacity through 1990. Hydroelectric stations
will provide marginal additions to output, with two, the
Iron Gates II project with Yugoslavia and the Turnu-
Magurele project with Bulgaria, alone counting 71 percent of the addition by 1985. Bu 1990, all of the available capacity from the Danube and 65 percent of the
country's total available hydropower will be exploited.

Romania has not backed off plans for further development of its other two major users of energy. Output
of the metallurgical industry, which consumed about 14
percent of all the country's energy in 1980, is planned
to grow at 7.0 percent a year. This is lower than its
actual or planned growth in 1976-80, but the industry
will see an expansion of output at the Galati complex
to 10 million tons of steel by 1985 and the commissioning of the new complex at Calarasi to produce 3 million

tons in its first phase, with more to come. The location of both on the Danube River is not accidental for all their increased needs for ore and coking coal will be met from imports. The chemical industry is planned for output increases of 10 percent a year from 1981 to 1985 and may by that year be the largest user of energy materials mainly to come from natural gas diverted from electric power generation. Plans call for domestic petroleum to be used to supply the refining industry and domestic fuels in transportation.

The other side of Romania's foreign trade may pose equal challenges. Export plans call for reducing items having a high energy to export value such as nitrogen fertilizer and standard rolled steel. Bulky and low value machinery is to be replaced by more complex products, including those in electronics. Hence, rather than a growth of Romania's export dependence, plans emphasize the need to shift the composition of exports to commodities having a low material and energy component and a high Romanian labor component.

Two problems will be encountered in the execution of Romania's export plans. One is that Romanian industrial and foreign trade organizations must meet the competition of more advanced countries. They face not only technological competition, but also competition in financing and marketing. In the latter, Romania has a clear advantage over its neighbor, Bulgaria, who may also have to turn to western or LDC markets. Romania's recent expansion of export efforts includes a growing number of jointly owned production and marketing companies.[35] What remains unclear about recent Romanian successes is how much subsidization and real cost to the economy has been required. A second problem is that there is no necessary reason why Romania's real comparative advantage in the next decade might exclude exports of commodities with high materials and energy components. For Romanian policymakers dogmatically to ignore them may increase the cost of foreign exchange and the burden of imports on consumption levels in the country.

CONCLUSION

Romania's economic development pattern since the advent of its socialist government has been dominated by extensive industrialization, a process that moved agricultural labor into new factories and increased the number of products supplied by domestic industry. The process moved relatively slowly in the 1950s compared to the pace in either neighboring Bulgaria or Romania in the following two decades. The acceleration of extensive industrialization was based on a relatively simple combination of reinvesting a major portion of national income growth in new industrial capital and of using that capital to extend the gamut of domestic products. Since the mid-1950s it has been remarkably steady with only minor disruptions in the mid-1960s and the late 1970s. Its stability may be attributed to Romania's low level of dependency on the international economy, the lack of internal political disruption and a reasonable order to the country's economic plans. The comparatively rapid growth of Romania in the 1970s was made possible by using most of its remaining reserves of labor in agriculture and represents a culmination to the extensive industrialization process.

If the economy develops as now projected in the 1980s the shift of labor from agriculture to industry will still account for a large proportion of increased labor productivity. But the extent of the shift compared to labor already in place will be greatly reduced. Investment rates will also be reduced in contrast to their steady rise since the mid-1950s. Altogether, the effort to be made in the first half of the decade appears to emphasize consolidation of gains made in the more hectic 1970s. It calls for putting order back into investments and the balance of payments, as well as adjusting the country's energy balances.

Intensive economic development will dominate in the second half of the 1980s. Total industrial labor will hardly increase. Most investment in industry will be used for modernization and for shifts of labot within industry, in partial response to whatever success Romania has in upgrading its industrial exports. Any growth of total labor plus any further shift of labor from the country side will find its place in Romania's heretofore relatively reduced service and trade sectors. Overall economic growth will be derived almost entirely from productivity increases of labor in place in each sector of the economy.

Realization of Romania's official projections faces at least three uncertainties. One is whether the expected growth of non-agricultural labor will be realized. Its principal source is to be females from agricultural households. At issue is whether Romania's urban development will accomodate their special needs as migrants and workers. Probable increasing evidence of labor scarcity will be found in the non-agricultural sectors of the economy. Competition among enterprises could give rise to unplanned wage and money supply increases. If labor proves more scarce than expected, Romanian planners will be forced into an earlier transition of investments to plant modernization.

A second uncertainty in the 1980s will be the performance of agriculture. Probably the private sector will decrease as persons respond to higher wages in industry. Insufficient rural development will continue to make it difficult to attract and keep qualified labor in the socialist sector, making its much needed improvement in efficiency all the more difficult to obtain. Probably Romanian crops will continue to be adversely affected by weather. How much the economy may be disrupted will depend on how taut are plans for the distribution of agricultural output. If Romanian planners continue to provide little or no margin for enlarging reserves of food and exportables, agricultural plan failure will disrupt balance of payment plans and possibly cause an internal market shortage severe enough to provoke another reaction among Romania's workers as happened in 1977.

A third major question is how well will Romanian policy makers and planners cope with the unavoidable downward shifts of decisionmaking to managers and workers that come with an increasingly complex and technologically sophisticated economy. That a downward shift will occur, whether or not it is wanted, is a fact derived from the limits on control by any central body. The only question is whether central controls will guide or misguide what managers and workers must do. A part of the control problem will be the technical management of incentives, including money-commodity balances and the appropriate differentiation of individual incomes according to work performances. The former will be increasingly difficult if labor proves more scarce than expected, while agriculture faces taut distribution plans.
In the case of the latter, other socialist countries have found that both managers and workers tend to resist augmentation of schemes to intensify the links between productivity and incomes and employment security. Romanians may be expected to exhibit at least equal resistance; they are hardly less demanding of job security or less suspicious of the motives and judgments of those controlling income distribution and jobs.

The recitation of uncertainties facing Romania in the next decade indicates that it will finally join the ranks of other socialist countries who have faced similar problems for a decade or more. The final question is whether Romania has any capacity or weakness for coping with the problems of a more mature socialist economy. This speculation will be left to the reader. Probably the best prognosis is that when Romania's structure and level of development resembles those of other socialist countries, so will its performance and problems.

NOTES

1. A project for such analysis is underway by the author, Josef C. Brada (Arizona State University) and Arthur E. King (Lehigh University) based on The Arizona State University Data Bank for Romania (unpublished).
2. In 1974 Romania's per capita national income in 1990 was projected to be $2,500-3,000. The later projections in 1979 actually reduced the expected growth rate in the 1980s, but were based on converting lei values to dollars at 15 lei per dollar rather than 20 lei per dollar.
3. A more detailed description of defects in Romania's published statistics can be found in Marvin R. Jackson, "Romania's Economy at the End of the 1980s: Turning the Corner on Intensive Development", in East European Country Studies, 1980, a compendium of papers submitted to the Joint Economic Committee, Congress of the United States. Washington, D.C.: USGPO, 1980. This paper hereafter is referred to as Jackson-1980.
4. An example of such data are said to be those resulting from survey analysis of Romanian family budgets. However, the expenditure side of the survey results was published for 1978 in the latest Romanian statistical yearbook.
5. The data refer to "veniturile ale taranimi provenite din munca prestata in agricultura, pe o persoana activa."
6. See, Andreas C. Tsantis and Roy Pepper, Romania: The Industrialization of an Agrarian Economy Under Socialist Planning, (World Bank: Washington, D.C., 1979), pp. xxiv-xxvii, 63, 414-419 and 560-561.
7. See the papers by Thad P. Alton in Joint Economic Committee Prints, East European Economies Post Helsinki (Washington, D.C., 1977), p. 224, and Reorientation and Commercial Relations of the Economies of Eastern Europe (Washington, D.C.), p. 270.
8. Calculations by the author based on data communicated by Thad P. Alton.
9. The difference is not a matter of caprice, but centers on the Romanian practice of charging all turnover taxes to the industrial sector which raises its share in national income above the value of factors of production used. Alton attempts to remedy this distortion which is admitted by Romanian economists.
10. Romania has used the "official" rate to convert foreign currencies into so-called "devisa" or "valuta" lei which are only accounting units. It also uses a separate "tourist" rate for actual exchanges by foreign tourists. Finally, it has used the "commercial rate" to convert the values of commodity imports and exports to internal lei. The latter was set at about

24 lei per (US) dollar in the early 1970s and has subsequently changed to 20 lei, 18 lei and, now, 15 lei. The commercial rate is said to equal the average value of all imports and exports expressed in internal lei and dollars. Beginning January 1, 1981, the devisa lei will be eliminated as an intermediate accounting unit and foreign trade will be expressed in internal lei and a single exchange rate based on the U.S. dollar used.

11. This statistic and others cited throughout the paper which come directly from the Romanian statistical yearbook are not cited by year and page number.

12. For far more detailed background on Romania compared to other Balkan countries, see John R. Lampe and Marvin R. Jackson, Balkan Economic Development, 1550-1950: From Imperial Borderlands to Southeastern European States (forthcoming, Indiana University Press: Bloomington, Ind., 1981).

13. For a detailed analysis up to 1965, see John Michael Montias, Economic Development in Communist Romania (The M.I.T. Press: Cambridge, Mass., 1967), especially, pp. 38-52 and 60.

14. Romania's economic development between 1965 and 1975 is discussed in Marvin R. Jackson, "Industrialization, Mobilization and Foreign Trade in Romania's Economy in the 1970s," in Joint Economic Committee Print, East European Economies Post Helsinki (Washington, D.C., 1977), pp. 886-940, henceforth referred to as Jackson-1977.

15. In 1950, the value of investments in the petroleum branch took 38.6 percent of all industrial investments.

16. Lampe and Jackson, op. cit., Tables 11.11, 12.7, 12.14, and 12.20.

17. See Jackson-1980, Table 19.

18. Montias, op. cit., pp. 14-16, 231-232 and 244-247.

19. Jackson-1980

20. Directivele congresului al XI-lea al partidului comunist Roman cu privere la planul cincinal 1976-1980 si linilile directorare ale dezvoltarii economico-sociale a Romaniei pentru perioada 1981-1990 (Bucharest, 1974).

21. The first targets for reduced working hours were announced at the 10th Party Congress in 1969. Also see Scinteia, 1 December 1970.

22. Scinteia, 14 December 1977.

23. Vasile Ghetau, Perspective demografice (Bucharest, 1979).

24. For evidences, see Jackson-1977.

25. Recent estimates of daily commuting as a percent of total employees are Iasi - 15 percent, Timisoara - 10.9 percent, Cluj - 10 percent, Brasov - 22.3 percent,

Ploiesti - 18 percent. See, Alecu Floares, Mobilitatea populatiei, (Iasi, 1977), p. 92.

26. Era socialista, LIX:11 (5 June 1979), p. 9.
27. Era socialista, LIV:11 (5 June 1979), p. 8.
28. (Project) Programul-Directiva de dezvoltare economico-sociala a Romaniei in profil teritorial in perioada 1981-85 (Bucharest, 1979), p. 20.
29. Ibid., pp. 14 and 58.
30. Romania libera, 25 June 1980.
31. See, Josef C. Brada, "Inflationary Pressures and the Optimal Tautness of Plans in a Centrally Planned Economy," forthcoming in the Journal of Comparative Economics, and Josef C. Brada and Arthur E. King, "A Structural Econometric Model of Czechoslovakia 1954-1975," in Empirical Economics, Vol. 4: 3, p. 315.
32. Romania libera, 3 July 1980.
33. Romania libera, 24 June 1980.
34. Data on energy are taken from Aural Iancu (ed.), Consumul energetic si structura productiei (Bucharest, 1979), annex; and (Proiect) Programul-directiva de cercetare si dezvoltare in domeniul energiei pe perioada 1981-1990 si orientarile principale pina in anul 2000 (Bucharest, 1979).
35. For background on Romania's foreign trade organization, see Josef C. Brada and Marvin R. Jackson, "Romania's Foreign Trade Organization," in Joint Economic Committee Print, East European Economies Post Helsinki (Washington, 1977), pp. 1260-1276, and "Foreign Trade Organization in Socialist and Capitalist Economies," in Journal of Comparative Economics, 1978: 4, pp. 293-320.

Conclusion: Development, Communism, and Balkan Tradition

Daniel N. Nelson

From their analyses of present trends and past conditions, each contributor to this volume has offered an assessment of Romania's prospects in the 1980s and beyond. Their views are, for the most part, short term in perspective, with a decade being the horizon for their estimates. As suggested in the Preface, authors have sought to identify and assess foreign and domestic policies, economic and political performance and societal transformations crucial to changes Romania is likely to experience in the near future.

Notwithstanding the short-term nature of authors' analyses, the limitations of social science to be "predictive" are apparent. First, despite care taken by contributors to examine all relevant internal and external variables, the international and domestic environment for Romania's government and its policies may change unexpectedly. The illness or death of major figures, a natural catastrophe (which Romania knows quite well) or international turmoil could alter severely the path of Romanian socio-economic or political change in the next decade or two. Case studies, even when done on a multi-disciplinary basis, have their own limitations as well. Certainly the reader is aware that some of the questions listed in the Preface, and their answers specific to Romania, are not generalizeable to all communist states or to all developing systems. Finally, contributors to this volume have not always agreed about traditions or trends evident in the Romanian system, or their relative impact on the country during this and future decades.

The latter constraint on a volume of this sort is evident in the differences between Fischer-Galati's interpretations, which emphasize the doubtful future of a Ceausescu-led Party and its similarity to the personalistic, autocratic traditions of Romania, vis-à-vis chapters by Shapiro and Cole which discuss a different set of traditions and the relatively flexible adaptations of the Romanian populace to changes brought about by industrialization and Fischer's view that Ceausescu faces no imminent challenge. Meanwhile, chapters such as Nelson and Cole appear to offer contrasting views of the degree to which material expectations and related disaffection from authorities will play a political role in years to come. Distinctions among interpretations made by other authors can be found as well. Suffice it to say that, even when analysts view one country in a comparable time period, frequently employing similar data, their conclusions may vary.

But the disagreements evident here do not obscure significant and generalizeable consensus. Most generally, contributors have concluded that the 1980s will see more internal and external constraints not fewer, on qualities which made Romania unique for a decade and a half, i.e., an assertive foreign policy and plan for "multilateral development" coupled with the Party's refusal to accept domestic liberalization. The latitude available for military and foreign policy deviation, already limited, will decline as will Romania's ability to pursue economic plans independent from world markets and energy supplies. Meanwhile, internal constraints will increase as the "second shift", declining efficacy of the Ceausescu "cult", widening gap between official and popular values and disaffection of workers from Party make it more difficult to achieve socio-economic targets.

None of the conclusions specific to Romania should be construed such that we are led to expect Polish-style unrest in the Balkans. The differences between such cases, for example, are many, and would require a full treatment to elaborate. None of the authors of this volume, however, suggest more than difficulties with economic performance, greater constraints on policy independence or leadership change at the top; there is no expectation of revolutionary change from within in Romania's short-term future. Evident in chapters by Fischer, Cole, and Jackson, for example, are the clear abilities of leaders and achievements of the population in developing the country's industry and transforming its society.

We should, however, expect Romania of 1990 and after to be a communist-party state with important differences from the way we have known that country since the mid 1960s. Regardless of the individual who may lead the Romanian Communist Party into the next decade, the analyses of this book suggest that the regime will have to live with fewer options. Romania's international position, already dependent on many factors, will be further linked to a trend towards interdependence. Romania's ability to "go it alone" will decline, as it must sell more abroad, and buy more energy abroad. Romania's domestic condition will require greater attention to conflict-management, as material and participatory demands of workers and other strata will no longer be placated by appeals to the image of an idol in lieu of genuine leadership, to nationalism or to rhetorical promises of self-management. Central economic planning will have to incorporate or resolve new issues such as a downward shift of management in a more complex economy, and the negative impact on socialist-sector productivity of a "second shift".

One's conclusions need not, however, be confined to the single case of Romania. Indeed, answers to questions listed in the Preface provided by the nine contributors suggest lessons about the wider arenas of inquiry such as studies of developing states, communist systems and the Balkan region. The case of Romania, moreover, is suggestive regarding the relationship among developmental processes, rule by a Leninist party and the traditions of a particular region.

Leninist parties brought to power in an agrarian state, with a population of which peasants composed the vast marjority, lacked the "natural" constituency Marx presumed for communist regimes, i.e., a sizeable proletariat. New governments, sans revolutionary legitimacy, had to rely upon a combination of 1) socialization techniques to build support and to convince the populace of the party's right to rule, 2) the personal charisma of an authentic leader or, lacking that, obedience to a leader whose image was that of an idol, 3) tangible economic progress and distributive equity, and 4) nationalism and its appeal to patriotic emotions. Fischer-Galati is certainly correct that political survival for Ceausescu has dictated the pursuit of some alternative to obedience through coercion which is an unacceptable and inefficient fifth "alternative". Each of the four plausible means by which to seek legitimacy is, of course, related to the others; socialization, for example, is not likely to have success if economic performance lags, inequity grows or national pride is dealt sharp reversals. Likewise, economic performance will never reach its maximum if productivity is harmed by antagonism within the workforce, impatient consumers, and a citizenry sensing a lack of its efficacy.

Thus, when new governmental systems take power without a firm or broad basis of support, socioeconomic development and nationalism came to play legitimizing roles. For Leninist regimes, of course, an added burden accrues because a Marxist heritage encompasses both the expectation of a proletarian-based revolution and the Party's intimacy with interests of working people. Simply put, communists must not only seek to develop their society and economy and pursue national independence to obtain popular legitimacy, but must also undertake such tasks looking over their shoulders (as it were) at an expectant citizenry.

These are not dilemmas confined to Romania, to the Balkans, or to communist rule. Almost every underdeveloped state has a government seeking its own legitimacy via a combination of development (usually synonymous with industrialization) and nationalism. Very often, the vague references to an ideology accompanying such legitimization efforts seek to link leaders to the masses, asserting an identity of interests. This is, most certainly, not a phenomenon of communist party states; one-party, authoritarian or revolutionary regimes from the Phillipines, Nicaragua, Burma or Mozambique reflect this struggle. But it is most pronounced in those cases, like Romania, where no revolutionary legitimacy existed, where coercion or foreign occupation inauguarated the current system of government and, perhaps most important, where expectations of distributive equality were raised by rhetoric and promises.

The relationship a Leninist regime has with developmental changes is not unique, then, but must be vexing nonetheless. Development, integral as it is to the legitimacy of regimes such as that in Bucharest, nevertheless undermines the bases for political control. Socioeconomic development and political decay are inextricably linked. There is a vast literature in the social sciences commenting upon and describing this relationship.[1] The rapidity of socioeconomic changes to which we refer using words such as "modernization" appear to exacerbate the association with political decay.

Nicolae Ceausescu is a "modernizing leader" because he must be; multilateral development is his label for the breakneck pace at which Romania is to be pushed into "developed" status by 1990. Such a goal provides a purpose and rationale for control, order and sacrifice as well as the power and guidance of Nicolae Ceausescu per se. For perhaps as long as a decade, the call for multilateral development featured a "moral equivalent of war" fervor. As a distinct side benefit, the process of industrialization brought Romania quickly closer to the societal composition and structure Marx expected.

The evidence suggests, however, that the relationship between development and political life is not benign, even in Romania where no one expects a Polish-style uprising. As chapters of this volume elaborated, a rural commuting laborforce "adapts" to changes in their environment with a "second shift" economy, producing food and crafts as part of the economic system but damaging socialist sector productivity. Values promoted by the regime are, meanwhile, less thoroughly "learned" by the educated and materially-conscious populace, and strong disaffection is evident in the working class. Having failed to become an authentic leader, Ceausescu must rule via a cult of personality unequaled in the communist world today. Autarkic economic policies appear likely to reach limits imposed by energy and commodity interdependence. Development itself exacerbates such limits by raising energy requirements through urbanization and industrialization, decreasing the rural laborforce for food production, and necessitating sales of products abroad in a technologically and managerially competitive market.

Romania's future will not be determined by the apparent dialectics between communism and development alone. Indeed, cultural attributes of a nation are interwoven deeply into any effort to predict a system's near-term future. Romania, while distinct from its Balkan neighbors in linguistic roots, shares many sociocultural and historical traits which one might label broadly as "Balkan tradition". If one were to compare Balkan states, including Romania, to the other parts of Eastern Europe, the Turkish occupation, a multi-national population, minimal pre-war industrial sector, and a large and poor peasantry are among distinguishing characteristics of that region vis-à-vis most of Europe. Socioeconomically, there is little doubt that southeastern Europe is distinguished from a "northern tier" of states.[2] But differences are more important and deeper than indicators of standard of living. These distinguishing features of the Balkans mean that attempting to develop a nation such as Romania under communist rule, while comparable in some respects to developing communist states elsewhere, nevertheless must incorporate adaptations to specific conditions of the region.

Several of the authors in this volume have dealt with Romanian political culture (Gilberg most directly); references to the survival of kinship and extended family links formed a major part of Cole's analysis as well, while Shapiro brought out the diverse political traditions of Romania, and Jackson underlined the rural, non-industrial past of Romanian economics. The system about which all contributors to this volume have been concerned, then, is recognized as one with distinct socio-cultural characteristics which affect efforts by any political leadership to bring about developmental change. Kin and family ties support a second shift economy that, in terms of socialist sector productivity, undermines central planning. The potpouri of Romania's political inheritance, including Turkish occupation, monarchy, competitive democracy in interwar years, and fascist dictatorship provides no single lineage to which the RCP can link its own legitimacy. A multi-national, urbanizing but still largely peasant populace (insofar as many urban residents are peasant by birth), presents a complex dilemma for a regime uncertain of its own linkage to the people. Relatii, pile and other forms of institutionalized corruption augment a poor distribution system or absence of consumer goods for public access. For all of this backdrop to a country's present and future, the term "Balkan", when used as an adjective, subsumes something of the broad connotations such characteristics bring to mind.

Where does a Leninist party fit into such a milieu? One answers, of course, as if one were considering other cases where the culture has been much more resilient than the polity which sought to alter it; one risks little by predicting that Balkan tradition will not only outlast Leninist parties, but will exist outside the influence of whatever political authority holds power. A communist party's strenuous attempts to find legitimacy through socialization techniques have produced little enthusiastic support, and personal values, family orientation, etc. continue to have more credence for Romanians in the manner of longstanding tradition. The authenticity of leadership has been elusive, pursued but not achieved by Nicolae Ceausescu. Through neither socialization nor political leadership has the Romanian Community Party become part of Romanian culture. The apparent failure of the system to achieve distributive equality as industrial development has consumed resources means that Romanians cannot rely on the political system either as a route for material rewards, thus perpetuating institutionalized corruption, and encouraging a reliance on kin-focused economic systems such as the "second shift".

Perhaps the "saving grace" for Romanian communist leaders has been, since the early 1960s, their identity with Romanian nationalism and appeals to patriotism. This was most evident, of course, in 1968 during the Czechoslovak crisis. Only via the confrontation with Soviet hegemony has the RCP touched the "cultural core" of Romania. But this avenue of legitimization appears to have less credibility as time goes on, particularly in light of constraints being imposed on Romanian foreign policy latitude.

A Leninist party has not, then, been integrated successfully into Romanian culture and the traditions of the Balkan region. The RCP remains apart from the nation it rules, with its values knows but not wholly accepted, its leadership obeyed but not broadly supported, with its policies implemented but not believed.

Contradictions between rapid developmental change and political stability, mentioned earlier, are not likely to be resolved when rulers, their beliefs and policies, are distant from the populace. Even after the wresting of land and property from owners, and an end to overt political terror, Leninist parties routinely demand continued sacrifice and delayed material gratification of citizens. Where revolutionary legitimacy, charismatic leadership, and/or thorough and ongoing redistribution of resources are present, great and long-term sacrifices are made by populations ruled by communist parties. The evidence of this volume, however, points to a time when conflict management will be necessary in Romania, where those qualities of legitimacy have failed to appear. In the 1980s and perhaps beyond, an undercurrent of tension is most likely in Romania, as legitimacy remains out of the RCP's grasp at a time when the negative political effects of rapid socioeconomic change are most evident. In an international environment fraught with uncertainty for the assertiveness of a small state, Romania will face a domestic political future characterized by obedience not support, and where the former is practiced by an increasingly dubious population.

NOTES

1. A review of some of this literature was included in Daniel N. Nelson, <u>Democratic Centralism in Romania</u> (Boulder, Colorado: East European Monographs, 1980), pp. 1-11.
2. See Daniel N. Nelson, "Socioeconomic and Political Change in Communist Europe", <u>International Studies Quarterly</u> 21, 2 (June 1977), p. 363-369.